T0335915

Online Communities as Agents of Change and Social Movements

Steven Gordon
Babson College, USA

A volume in the Advances in
Social Networking and Online
Communities (ASNOC) Book Series

www.igi-global.com

Published in the United States of America by
    IGI Global
    Information Science Reference (an imprint of IGI Global)
    701 E. Chocolate Avenue
    Hershey PA, USA 17033
    Tel: 717-533-8845
    Fax: 717-533-8661
    E-mail: cust@igi-global.com
    Web site: http://www.igi-global.com

Library of Congress Cataloging-in-Publication Data

Names: Gordon, Steven, 1948- author.
Title: Online communities as agents of change and social movements / Steven
    Gordon, editor.
Description: Hershey : Information Science Reference, [2017]
Identifiers: LCCN 2017003840| ISBN 9781522524953 (hardcover) | ISBN
    9781522524960 (ebook)
Subjects: LCSH: Social movements. | Online social networks. | Social media.
Classification: LCC HM881 .O64 2017 | DDC 303.48/4--dc23 LC record available at https://lccn.
loc.gov/2017003840

This book is published in the IGI Global book series Advances in Social Networking and Online Communities (ASNOC) (ISSN: 2328-1405; eISSN: 2328-1413)

British Cataloguing in Publication Data
A Cataloguing in Publication record for this book is available from the British Library.

All work contributed to this book is new, previously-unpublished material.
The views expressed in this book are those of the authors, but not necessarily of the publisher.

For electronic access to this publication, please contact: eresources@igi-global.com.

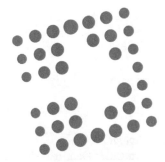

Advances in Social Networking and Online Communities (ASNOC) Book Series

ISSN:2328-1405
EISSN:2328-1413

Editor-in-Chief: Hakikur Rahman, BRAC University, Bangladesh

MISSION

The advancements of internet technologies and the creation of various social networks provide a new channel of knowledge development processes that's dependent on social networking and online communities. This emerging concept of social innovation is comprised of ideas and strategies designed to improve society.

The **Advances in Social Networking and Online Communities** book series serves as a forum for scholars and practitioners to present comprehensive research on the social, cultural, organizational, and human issues related to the use of virtual communities and social networking. This series will provide an analytical approach to the holistic and newly emerging concepts of online knowledge communities and social networks.

COVERAGE

- Knowledge Communication and Impact of Network Structures
- Knowledge Management Practices and Future Perspectives
- Knowledge as a Symbol/Model of Development
- Roles and Positional Models of Knowledge Communication Networks
- Local E-Government Interoperability and Security
- Information and Data Management
- Learning Utilities
- Methods, Measures and Instruments of Knowledge Management
- Communication and Agent Technology
- Communications and the Internet

IGI Global is currently accepting manuscripts for publication within this series. To submit a proposal for a volume in this series, please contact our Acquisition Editors at Acquisitions@igi-global.com or visit: http://www.igi-global.com/publish/.

Titles in this Series

For a list of additional titles in this series, please visit:
http://www.igi-global.com/book-series/advances-social-networking-online-communities

Social Media Performance Evaluation and Success Measurements
Michael A. Brown Sr. (Florida International University, USA)
Information Science Reference • ©2017 • 294pp • H/C (ISBN: 9781522519638) • US $185.00

Political Scandal, Corruption, and Legitimacy in the Age of Social Media
Kamil Demirhan (Bülent Ecevit University, Turkey) and Derya Çakır-Demirhan (Bülent
Ecevit University, Turkey)
Information Science Reference • ©2017 • 295pp • H/C (ISBN: 9781522520191) • US $190.00

Power, Surveillance, and Culture in YouTube™'s Digital Sphere
Matthew Crick (William Paterson University, USA)
Information Science Reference • ©2016 • 317pp • H/C (ISBN: 9781466698550) • US $185.00

Social Media and the Transformation of Interaction in Society
John P. Sahlin (The George Washington University, USA)
Information Science Reference • ©2015 • 300pp • H/C (ISBN: 9781466685567) • US $200.00

Cases on Strategic Social Media Utilization in the Nonprofit Sector
Hugo Asencio (California State University – Dominguez Hills, USA) and Rui Sun (California
State University – Dominguez Hills, USA)
Information Science Reference • ©2015 • 375pp • H/C (ISBN: 9781466681880) • US $195.00

***Handbook of Research on Interactive Information Quality in Expanding Social Network
Communications***
Francisco V. Cipolla-Ficarra (Latin Association of Human-Computer Interaction, Spain &
International Association of Interactive Communication, Italy)
Information Science Reference • ©2015 • 449pp • H/C (ISBN: 9781466673779) • US $255.00

Implications of Social Media Use in Personal and Professional Settings
Vladlena Benson (Kingston Business School, Kingston University, UK) and Stephanie
Morgan (Kingston Business School, Kingston University, UK)
Information Science Reference • ©2015 • 362pp • H/C (ISBN: 9781466674011) • US $195.00

For an enitre list of titles in this series, please visit:
http://www.igi-global.com/book-series/advances-social-networking-online-communities

www.igi-global.com

701 East Chocolate Avenue, Hershey, PA 17033, USA
Tel: 717-533-8845 x100 • Fax: 717-533-8661
E-Mail: cust@igi-global.com • www.igi-global.com

Editorial Advisory Board

Table of Contents

Detailed Table of Contents

Section 1
Online Communities, Protests, and Demonstrations

Chapter 1

    Marwa Maziad, University of Washington, USA
    Norah Abokhodair, University of Washington, USA
    Maria Garrido, University of Washington, USA

On January 25th 2011, Egyptians revolted, thereby making history. Before the date, roads to political activism were being incrementally built towards their eventual converging on Tahrir Square. This chapter argues that "nodes of convergence," defined as shared political and economic grievances, as well as shared virtual and physical spaces, had to be created first before mass mobilization for a collective action of millions on the street could ensue. Providing in-depth examination of events leading to January 25th, this chapter offers a case study for mobilization, from which generalized theory is extrapolated about online communities' convergence, networking, and coalition building. Two main Facebook pages were studied: April 6th Youth Movement and We Are All Khaled Said-- both in Arabic. The conceptualization is built on anthropological fieldwork trips in Egypt since March 2011. This covered ethnographic participant-observations and interviewing. For evidence triangulation purposes of the "convergence effect", the authors conducted qualitative content analysis of significant posts.

Chapter 2
Social Media Users Collectively Speak Up: Evidence From Central Asian
Kyrgyz Republic 44
Bahtiyar Kurambayev, Independent Researcher, Kyrgyzstan

An analysis of online community activities in the former Soviet Union Kyrgyz Republic shows that social media can facilitate an effective organization and expression of ideas in a constrained media system. Specifically, online users were able to collectively and successfully speak their minds when the country's lawmakers planned costly projects, ultimately causing these plans to be dropped. Also social media users facilitated spreading information about the abuses of power and government incompetence in the 2010 and in 2005 revolutions, causing presidents flee the country in both cases. These findings suggest that the internet can facilitate a broad and effective civic and political engagement. The implications of these findings in this media restricted context are discussed in relation to collective action theory.

Chapter 3
Social Media Support for the Occupation of Public Schools in São Paulo,
Brazil...67
Cynthia H. W. Corrêa, University of São Paulo, Brazil

Networked social movements have amplified the emancipation of protesters everywhere. In Brazil, a conflict arose after the São Paulo State Secretariat for Education announced the closing of 94 public schools, impacting 311,000 people. In response, about 30 students organized the occupation of the State School Fernão Dias Paes. Subsequently, the occupation spread to other schools. Based on a case study of the first school occupied in the city of São Paulo, this research aims to identify the role of information and communication technologies (ICTs) and social media tools in generating and sustaining the successful occupation protest of public schools in São Paulo. This chapter covers theories on demonstrations initiated online, on the social panorama in Latin America and educational issues in Brazil. It also addresses and analyzes the occupation process at this school, which reached visibility and support at national and international levels using ICTs and social media, confirming the steps of occupy movements around the world.

Chapter 4
Information and Communication Technologies as Drivers of Social Unrest 89
Martha Garcia-Murillo, Syracuse University, USA
Moinul Zaber, University of Dhaka, Bangladesh
Marcio Wohlers de Almeida, State University of Campinas – UNICAMP, Brazil

Information and communication technologies (ICTs) are alleviating frictions associated with the gathering and distribution of information, as well as reducing transaction costs related to the identifying, monitoring, and coordination of citizens dissatisfied with certain government policies. We conducted a random-effect logit tests based on a uniquely developed panel dataset of 138 countries from 2005 to 2014 to determine, ceteris paribus, whether or not ICTs play a role in facilitating changes to the status quo that gravitate against government policies. We found that ICTs although it can reduce hysteresis, the tendency to remain passive, inertia, is stronger. In addition, because ICTs are multi-purpose technologies they also support other beneficial economic and political activities which can explain why we don't see greater evidence of social unrest with these technologies. The literature on social unrest provide some clues about this phenomenon. People are willing to engage in these movements but it appears that only during a crisis.

Chapter 5

The objective of this chapter is to describe and analyze the use of ICTs by social movements in Mexico in their attempt to keep proposed legislation from concentrating, or at least failing to dilute, the already concentrated power of the Mexican media. These technologies not only have been a means of organization and synchronization for protests and mobilization, but also, before restrictions in Mexican law, served as alternative media for citizens to obtain more truthful information and make use of their right to communicate.

Section 2
Online Communities and Socio-Political Concerns

Chapter 6

We used survey data and collected data from the online social network Twitter between October 5, 2015 to November 9, 2015 to provide an overview related to political participation in Mexico. With the former we provided a qualitative assessment of participation by examining electoral participation, participation between regions, interest in politics and sources of political information. With Twitter data, we described the intensity of participation, we identified locations of high activity and identified movements including agencies behind them. We compare and contrast participation in Mexico to its counterpart in Twitter. We show that participation seems to be decreasing. However, participation through Twitter seems to be increasing. Our research points towards the emergence of Twitter as a significant platform in terms of political participation in Mexico. Our study analyses the impact of how different agencies related to social movements can enhance participation through Twitter. We show that emergent topics are important because they could help to explore how politics becomes of public interest.

Chapter 7

Ali Honari, Vrije Universiteit Amsterdam, The Netherlands

For several years now, the role that digitally mediated social movements and online communities play in challenging authoritarian regimes in the Middle East and North Africa has been extensively debated. The focus of attention on the political use of the Internet shapes conventional wisdom that political issues are widespread in online communities in these contexts and that the users are predominantly oppositional users with political democratic motivations. Using fresh methods and techniques to gather a variety of online data, this chapter argues and reveals that, at least in the case of Iran, this view selectively overlooks the diversity of users and the broad range of issues frequently and intensively discussed among users in online communities. The failure to examine a broader range of issues means that scholars have neglected how consensus forms and develops among online users in other issues. This study broadens our understanding of the current social issues and possible areas of change in Iran through investigating a more comprehensive frame of the Iranian web.

Section 3
Online Communities in Support of Personal Growth, Development, and Self-Actualization

Chapter 8

Helen Hasan, University of Wollongong, Australia
Henry Linger, Monash University, Australia

This chapter proposes that social use of digital technologies can play a useful role in meeting the social and economic challenges posed by the ageing populations in developed countries. Many citizens become increasingly isolated as they age and this has a detrimental impact on their wellbeing. The authors present research which shows how, with suitable devices and ongoing support, older people can develop the digital capability to remain connected to family and community. They can also engaged in activities that give meaning to their lives. The research shows the importance of taking an individualized approach to meeting the needs of each older person who is motivated to learn and of making this learning fun. It also demonstrates how mastering just one or two digital applications can not only enhance social wellbeing but also enable citizens to have more control of their lives and be less of a burden on others.

The primary objective of this chapter is to analyze the support of social media for social movements within the context of the anti-consumption movement. Social media have proved to be strategic for initiating, organizing and communicating social movements. The anti-consumption movement is a trend of the postmodernism era that has not yet reached a large following. A secondary aim of this chapter is to analyze the similarities and differences in the support of social media for the anti-consumption movement between one developed and one emerging market. To achieve this goal, a content analysis was employed to analyze Facebook accounts of anti-consumption online communities in the USA and Turkey. The findings show that social media can be the right medium to increase coverage of social movements in society. Additionally, the online institutionalization and decentralized organization of the online community as well as stable social media sharing help support non-radical social movements like anti-consumption.

Digital technology produced a move from a performative model to a player-as producer paradigm since it has potentiated user-generated transformative uses of intellectual works. In fact, sharing, sampling, remixing and creating new derivative content through digital network collaboration platforms are today pillars of the so-called "age of remix". However, when unauthorized, such activities may constitute copyright infringement since the making available right and the right to make new derivative works are exclusive rights granted by copyright law. A restrictive exercise of exclusive rights may hinder the implementation of online platforms envisioned to facilitate access to knowledge and to potentiate the creation of new works. The present chapter analyzes the creation the importance of online communities of practice using free/open source software licenses like GNU GPL or Creative Commons Licenses as agents of an alternative and less rigid exercise of the powers granted by copyright law in favor of a freer system of creation and dissemination of creative works in the digital world.

This study aims to shed light on Turkish football forum users on the Internet from a social identity and uses and gratifications (U&G) perspective in order to reveal joint intentions among football fans online. The research model of the current study applies a uses and gratifications approach to examine whether fan motivations while using online football forums determine we-intentions among forum members. Social influence processes are also essential in the context of research on online forums, since they determine changes in attitudes and actions produced by the virtual social influence that may occur at different levels. Findings reveal uses and gratifications of football forum participation as maintaining interpersonal interconnectivity, generating entertainment and purposive value along with affective social identity construct determined we-intention among forum users.

Preface

The Tunisian and Egyptian Revolutions of 2011, which resulted in the overthrow of the governments in those countries, brought the world's attention to the potential of online communities, using social media, to effect change in significant ways. Yet, online communities existed long before the Arab Spring, operating more quietly and out the spotlight of international news, and bringing together people with common interests who believed, correctly, that they could accomplish more as a community than they could as individuals. The purpose of this book is to bring to the forefront recent research that addresses the role of online communities as agents of change and social movements.

ONLINE COMMUNITIES

The word "community" elicits various images and meanings. If you ask people about their community, they are likely to describe their neighborhood, the people who live near them. They might tell you that they belong to a community center where the neighbors can gather to celebrate occasions and use shared facilities, such as a swimming pool. Others might think you are referring to their religious community, to people with whom they have feelings of kinship because they worship in the same location and at the same time. Those who belong to a social club might think of its members as their community. In all these examples, the sense of community is created by proximity and, to some extent, shared interests.

The concept of "community of interest" broadens the definition of "community" to those who share common interests and viewpoints without the need for proximity. Before the Internet existed, creating such communities was challenging. Members of a community of interest could, perhaps, gather once or twice a year at a conference, and they could publish journals or booklets to share ideas. But, maintaining such a community was expensive, and without frequent interactions and the deep interpersonal knowledge that results from them, any sense of belonging to it was undoubtedly tenuous.

The arrival of the Internet made it possible for members of a community of interest to exchange ideas without ever having to meet in person. The ability to interact online dramatically simplified the processes of forming and maintaining such a community. In the early days of the Internet, the medium of choice for establishing connections was email and the medium for broadcasting ideas was the blog. But, the arrival of social network services (SNS), such as Facebook and YouTube, deepened and enriched the interactions that could take place, allowing for a sense of community among a community's members. According to McMillan and Chavis (1986), a sense of community has four elements: membership, influence, fulfillment, and shared emotional connection. Jenson (2012) and Koh and Kim (2003) conclude, in separate studies, that online communities fully fulfill the criteria for community.

Online communities that do not meet in a physical space are sometimes called "virtual communities" (see, for example, Tsai & Bagozzi, 2014), which is a bit of a misnomer since they are as real as neighborhood communities and often more active. The places where members of these online communities "meet" are sometimes called "virtual spaces" (see, for example, Craig et al., 2016), which is a reasonably accurate description. Unlike physical meetings, meetings in virtual places are not necessarily synchronous. But, the exchange of data, comments, and images is effective because community members know where to go to find them.

Online communities form around all sorts of interests – academic, entertainment, political, and social among others. This book is about online communities, but only, or almost only, about those whose purpose is to make a change in the world or advance a social movement. The one exception can be found in Chapter 11, which addresses how an online community created for quite another purpose, football fandom in this case, can nevertheless be a source of energy for social change.

CHANGE AND SOCIAL MOVEMENTS

There are many definitions for what constitutes a social movement. For purposes of this book, I draw on Jamison (2010: 813), James & Seeters (2014: xi), and others to define a social movement as the mobilization of human, material, and cultural resources in networks linking actors in pursuit of a common cause. Some definitions require that a social movement must oppose an elite, authoritative, or powerful force (Tarrow: 4). For this reason and because this volume explores the role of online communities in effecting any sort of social change, its title incorporates the word "change" in addition to the term "social movement."

By almost any definition, the Protestant Reformation, the American Revolution, and the Suffrage Movement in the United States are all examples of social movements. These movements predate by tens to hundreds of years the existence of online communities. Although, as these examples show, online community support is not needed for a social movement to achieve success, some researchers believe online communities can be effective agents of change, making success more likely and accelerating its pace. In support of this hypothesis, researchers have claimed that online communities are effective in organizing and coordinating protests (Segerberg & Bennett, 2011), creating a collective sense of identity (Oh et al., 2015), generating a persuasive call to action (Haug, 2013), obtaining the attention of mass media (Parmelee, 2014), creating awareness in the external community (Reuter & Szakonyi, 2015), and obtaining resources, especially funding (Hara & Huang, 2011). However, others argue that underlying economic and social conditions, not social media, are the cause of social movements and revolution (Mellen, 2012). Skeptics also note that opponents of social movements can exploit and have exploited the public nature of online discussion to identify and persecute movement leaders and neutralize their threat (Morozov, 2012). This book contributes to both sides of this debate.

The chapters of this book illustrate the many ways in which online communities have acted as agents of change in a variety of contexts. But, they also make clear that achieving change is difficult and success is not guaranteed. The following section describes the organization of the book and provides a brief description of each of its chapter.

ORGANIZATION AND CONTENTS OF THIS BOOK

The chapters of this book have been grouped into three sections. Section 1 consists of five studies exploring the role of online communities in promoting and supporting protests and demonstrations. Section 2 addresses the socio-political concerns of online communities in two very different environments, one in Mexico and one in Iran. The chapters in Section 3 explore the role of online communities as agents of another type of change that reflects personal growth and development, ranging from older adults in long term care settings discovering new ways to communicate, to the anti-consumption movement's opposition to consumerism, and the open-source publishing movement's desire to provide freedom from copyright limitations.

Section 1: Online Communities, Protests, and Demonstrations

Chapter 1: The Road to Egypt's Tahrir Square: Social Movements in Convergence, Coalitions and Networks

This chapter, by Marwa Maziad, Norah Abokhodair, and Maria Garrido, uses the context of the Egyptian Revolution of 2011 to develop and support the concept of "nodes of convergence." The authors define nodes of convergence as shared political and economic grievance as well as shared virtual and physical space. They argue that such a convergence has to be created before mass mobilization for a collective action can ensue. The authors support their contention with a detailed recounting of the events leading to the January 25 protests in Tahrir Square, Cairo, that eventually resulted in the overthrow of the Egyptian regime. Central to their case are the posts, activities, and leadership of two very different online communities, whose names, translated into English, are the "April 6th Youth Movement" and "We Are All Khaled Said." In addition to developing the nodes of convergence concept, this chapter offers a case study for how to mobilize a community in a repressive environment.

Chapter 2: Social Media Users Collectively Speak Up. Evidence from Central Asian Kyrgyz Republic

Using a collective action theory framework, this chapter, by Bahtiyar Kurambayev, presents and analyzes several examples of online community actions in Kyrgyzstan. Despite significant constraints on the media and a repressive environment, online communities were able to organize protests to successfully oppose costly projects that had been approved by the country's lawmakers. They also were able to spread information about abuses of power and government incompetence, leading to protest-inspired revolutions in 2005 and 2010, that resulted, in both years, in the abdication of the president. The chapter concludes that the success of online communities in Kyrgyzstan has positive implications for other areas of Central Asia where freedom of speech and expression are heavily restricted.

Chapter 3: Social Media Support for the Occupation of Public Schools in São Paulo, Brazil

In this chapter, Cynthia Corrêa analyzes the protests and occupations that arose in 2015 after the São Paulo State Secretariat for Education announced the closing of 94 public schools, affecting 311,000 students. Based on an in-depth case study of the first school occupied, it addresses the role that information and communication technologies and social media tools played in generating and sustaining a successful occupation protest, which then spread among the public schools in São Paulo. This study extends the findings of prior research on other occupation movements that have been initiated online by analyzing what occurred in relation to Latin American social norms and the educational environment in Brazil at the time of the occupation.

Chapter 4: Information and Communication Technologies as Drivers of Social Unrest

In a statistical analysis of time series data from 138 countries between 2005 to 2014, the research presented in this chapter, by Martha Garcia-Murillo, Moinul Zaber, and Marcio Wholers de Almeida, finds that contrary to popular belief, when controlling for economic factors, governance, and population size, the communication and information technologies used by online communities not only fail to increase social unrest, but they might actually decrease it. Interestingly, this effect is found to be greatest in those countries having the most restrictive regimes. The authors posit that this is because these technologies can help alleviate some of the problems a country may be facing by opening opportunities to people. The policy implication of these findings is that governments should increase the availability of broadband, mobile, and other networking and communication technologies to reduce social unrest and provide a better environment for its citizens.

Chapter 5: Protests, Social Movements and Media Legislation in Mexico 2012-2014

Not all online communities are successful in opposing an entrenched and powerful status quo. This chapter, by Tonatiuh Lay, describes how several online communities failed over an extended period of time to keep proposed Mexican legislation from concentrating, or at least failing to dilute, the already concentrated *de facto* powers of the Mexican broadcast media. This case study shows that the alliance between the State and traditional media can be extremely difficult to overcome. The chapter concludes with a positive outlook, noting that the State and its allies could not prevent the development of online communities nor the use and appropriation of technology for their current and future projects as a civil society.

Section 2: Online Communities and Socio-Political Concerns

Chapter 6: Political Participation in Mexico Offline and Through Twitter

In this chapter, Julio Amador and Carlos Adolfo Piña-Garcia present a study of political participation of online communities in Mexico against a backdrop of political events and political participation by the general public. It uses Twitter data as the source for quantifying the participation of online communities by region and political movement. Data gathered from other sources provide insight into the general public's electoral participation by region, interest in politics, and sources of political information. While political participation in Mexico seems to be decreasing overall, participation through Twitter seems to be increasing. In this regard, this research points towards the emergence of Twitter as a significant platform for political participation in Mexico, and illustrates how online communities, as agents of social movements can enhance political participation.

Chapter 7: The Formation of Consensus in Iranian Online Communities

This chapter, by Ali Honari, challenges the common perception that the members of online communities are predominantly oppositional users with political democratic motivations. Using a variety of online data sources, it reveals that, at least in the case of Iran, this view overlooks the diversity of users and the broad range of issues frequently and intensively discussed among them in online communities. The failure to examine a broader range of issues means that scholars have neglected how consensus forms and develops among online users on other issues. This study broadens our understanding of the current social issues and possible areas of change in Iran. It also proposes fresh methods and techniques for gathering data from online communities and analyses data extracted from the Internet to study digitally mediated social movements in repressive societies.

Section 3: Online Communities in Support of Personal Growth, Development, and Self-Actualization

Chapter 8: Connected Living for Positive Ageing

In this chapter, Helen Hasan and Henry Linger explore the value to ageing citizens of being a part of an online community. Observing that isolation is detrimental to the wellbeing of citizens as they age, this research shows how, with suitable devices and ongoing support, older people who have not previously used a computer can develop the digital capability to remain connected to family and community. This research shows the importance of taking an individualized approach to meeting the needs of each older novice user who is motivated to learn. It also demonstrates how mastering just one or two digital applications can not only enhance social wellbeing but also enable citizens to have more control of their lives and be less reliant on help from others.

Chapter 9: The Impact of Social Media on Social Movements: The Case of Anti-Consumption

Anti-consumption is the rejection of consumerism, the modern notion that satisfaction and happiness can and should be achieved through the acquisition and consumption of goods and services. This chapter, by İrem Eren-Erdoğmuş and Sinem Ergun, analyzes the role of online communities in supporting the nascent anti-consumption movement. Case studies of online anti-consumption communities in the United States and Turkey provide examples of how these communities use social media in pursuit of their goal and serve as a means for comparing and contrasting their roles in developed and emerging markets.

Chapter 10: Free and Open Source Software Movements as Agents of an Alternative Use of Copyright Law

Copyright law grants exclusive rights to the copyright owner to control how copyrighted works are shared, sampled, remixed and incorporated into new derivative content. Unfortunately, the restrictive exercise of such exclusive rights may hinder the implementation of online platforms envisioned to facilitate access to knowledge and to enable the creation of new works. This chapter, by Pedro Pina, addresses how online communities of practice are using free/open source software licenses like GNU, GPL, and Creative Commons Licenses, to act as agents of a less rigid exercise of the powers granted by copyright law in favor of a freer system of creation and dissemination of creative works in the digital world.

Chapter 11: A Social Influence Perspective on Uses of Online Football Forums: The Case with Turkish Football Fans

This chapter, by Anil Sayan, Vehbi Gorgulu, Itir Erhart, and Yonca Aslanbay, shows that apolitical online communities that exist for reasons unrelated to social movements can, when the circumstances warrant it, become forums for social action. The focus of this chapter is online forums used by Turkish football fans. It shows that the constructs of social identity and "uses and gratifications" can predict the existence of joint-intention formation among the online community. Findings reveal uses and gratifications of football forum participation as maintaining interpersonal interconnectivity, generating entertainment and purposive value along with affective social identity construct determined we-intention among forum users. Examples are provided to show how this joint intention has been turned towards political and social action.

CONCLUDING THOUGHTS

The studies in these chapters shed light on the role of online communities as agents of change in contexts ranging from highly repressive environments to supportive ones, from actions in conflict to those in play or in comfort, and from those that succeeded in their goals to those that failed. The stories are interesting and the lessons learned instructive. The authors and I hope you enjoy and profit from reading it.

Steven Gordon
Babson College, USA

REFERENCES

Craig, S. G., Hoang, E. C., & Kohlhase, J. E. (forthcoming). Does closeness in virtual space complement urban space? *Socio-Economic Planning Sciences*.

Hara, N., & Huang, B. Y. (2011). Online social movements. *Annual Review of Information Science & Technology*, *45*(1), 489–522. doi:10.1002/aris.2011.1440450117

Haug, C. (2013). Organizing spaces: Meeting arenas as a social movement infrastructure between organization, network, and institution. *Organization Studies*, *34*(5-6), 705–732. doi:10.1177/0170840613479232

James, P., & van Seeters, P. (2014). Globalization and Politics (Vol. 2. *Global Social Movements and Global Civil Society*). London: Sage Publications.

Jamison, A. (2010). Climate change knowledge and social movement theory. *Wiley Interdisciplinary Reviews: Climate Change*, *1*(6), 811–823. doi:10.1002/wcc.88

Jensen, J. L. (2012). Online communities: A historically based examination of how social formations online fulfill criteria for community. In Virtual Community Building and the Information Society: Current and Future Directions (pp. 121-134). Hershey, PA: IGI Global. doi:10.4018/978-1-60960-869-9.ch006

Koh, J., & Kim, Y. G. (2003). Sense of virtual community: A conceptual framework and empirical validation. *International Journal of Electronic Commerce*, *8*(2), 75–94.

McMillan, D. W., & Chavis, D. M. (1986). Sense of community: A definition and theory. *Journal of Community Psychology*, *14*(1), 6–23. doi:10.1002/1520-6629(198601)14:1<6::AID-JCOP2290140103>3.0.CO;2-I

Mellen, R. P. (2012). Modern Arab uprisings and social media: An historical perspective on media and revolution. *Explorations in Media Ecology, 11*(2), 115–130. doi:10.1386/eme.11.2.115_1

Morozov, E. (2012). *The Net Delusion: The Dark Side of Internet Freedom*. New York: Public Affairs Publishing.

Oh, O., Eom, C., & Rao, H. R. (2015). Research note – Role of social media in social change: An analysis of collective sense making during the 2011 Egypt revolution. *Information Systems Research, 26*(1), 210–223. doi:10.1287/isre.2015.0565

Parmelee, J. H. (2013). The agenda-building function of political tweets. *New Media & Society, 16*(3), 434–450. doi:10.1177/1461444813487955

Reuter, O. J., & Szakonyi, D. (2015). Online social media and political awareness in authoritarian regimes. *British Journal of Political Science, 45*(1), 29–51. doi:10.1017/S0007123413000203

Segerberg, A., & Bennett, W. L. (2011). Social media and the organization of collective action: Using Twitter to explore the ecologies of two climate change protests. *Communication Review, 14*(3), 197–215. doi:10.1080/10714421.2011.597250

Tarrow, S. (1998). *Power in Movement*. Cambridge: Cambridge University Press. doi:10.1017/CBO9780511813245

Tsai, H. T., & Bagozzi, R. P. (2014). Contribution behavior in virtual communities: Cognitive, emotional, and social influences. *Management Information Systems Quarterly, 38*(1), 143–163.

Section 1
Online Communities, Protests, and Demonstrations

Chapter 1

The Road to Egypt's Tahrir Square:
Social Movements in Convergence, Coalitions and Networks

Marwa Maziad
University of Washington, USA

Norah Abokhodair
University of Washington, USA

Maria Garrido
University of Washington, USA

ABSTRACT

On January 25th 2011, Egyptians revolted, thereby making history. Before the date, roads to political activism were being incrementally built towards their eventual converging on Tahrir Square. This chapter argues that "nodes of convergence," defined as shared political and economic grievances, as well as shared virtual and physical spaces, had to be created first before mass mobilization for a collective action of millions on the street could ensue. Providing in-depth examination of events leading to January 25th, this chapter offers a case study for mobilization, from which generalized theory is extrapolated about online communities' convergence, networking, and coalition building. Two main Facebook pages were studied: April 6th Youth Movement and We Are All Khaled Said-- both in Arabic. The conceptualization is built on anthropological fieldwork trips in Egypt since March 2011. This covered ethnographic participant-observations and interviewing. For evidence triangulation purposes of the "convergence effect", the authors conducted qualitative content analysis of significant posts.

DOI: 10.4018/978-1-5225-2495-3.ch001

INTRODUCTION

Six years ago, on January 25th 2011, Egyptians came out on the streets. Youth had called for protests, albeit not knowing for certain what would ensue. In an unprecedented scene, mass demonstrations against poverty, corruption, and political repression broke out and people chanted for "Livelihood, Freedom, Human Dignity, and Social Justice." In Tahrir Square, located right in the heart of Cairo, as well as in other squares nationwide, Egyptian men and women from different walks of life, religious convictions and political ideologies came together. They filled the public space under the fixated gaze of international audiences, thereby rendering "Tahrir" a global household name and an icon that stood for what it actually means in Arabic: "Liberation." As a result, on February 11, 2011, former President Hosni Mubarak was forced to relinquish power. He stepped down due to public pressure that continued for 18 days. Hastily-appointed Vice President Omar Suleiman announced that Mubarak would resign as president, turning power over to the Supreme Council of the Armed Forces (SCAF). This chapter, investigates core questions about what became known as the "January 25 Revolution"—How and why did millions converge on Tahrir Square?

CONCEPTUAL FRAMEWORK: NODES OF CONVERGENCE

In this chapter, we argue that what we call "Nodes of Convergence"— defined as shared political and economic grievances on the one hand, as well as shared virtual and physical spaces on the other— had to be created first before mass mobilization for a collective action of millions on the street could ensue.

In this conceptualization, the Egyptian Uprising is not seen as a historical event, but rather as a historical process, rooted in a long record of Egyptian activism, and projected into a political and economic future that Egyptians are still currently painting, one brushstroke at a time. However, the reasons why the Uprising has been depicted as an event will also be delineated, given the way social media[1] helped mobilize core segments of the young population, who in turn mobilized others towards the convergence on the specific date of January 25, 2011.

In news reports that came out during the process of the uprising, as well as in subsequent myriad academic studies conducted, the interplay between digital media and acts of mobilization has been recognized as essential. However, the extent of digital media's impact has also been debated. In this chapter, while we do acknowledge the nature of social media that helped construct the "Nodes of Convergence" we conceptualize, we move beyond reductionist techno-determinist enchantment with a so- called "Facebook" and "Twitter" Revolutions to ascertain the complex and dynamic online and offline political history and communication strategies, which actual members of various affiliations employed, in order to cooperate together in real and virtual life, for the purpose of inducing political and social change.

"Nodes of Convergence," we argue, were formed when specific actors—employing social media—performed tasks, communicated and publicly deliberated with various other actors including governmental, non-governmental and international organizations as well as global movements pursuing similar goals. We examine the Egyptian case study in order to highlight how this conceptual framework of "Nodes of Convergence" brought in dynamic citizen engagement and communication practices to mobilize the population.

January 25, 2011, is a significant date of Convergence because not too long before it, some Egyptian intellectuals were actually asking "Why Don't Egyptians Revolt?" In fact, that was a title of a series of articles written by Alaa Al Aswany (2010), a well-known liberal Egyptian author oppositional to the Mubarak regime, and whose name has been intertwined with the Egyptian revolutionaries. Al Aswany was rhetorically asking and analyzing in his articles why Egyptians seemed to have accepted the political stagnation of almost 30 years under the same ruler.

Yet, our contention is that just because scholars, analysts, observers, and even activist-participants like Al Aswany were not able to detect every minute underground move, this does not mean a political earthquake was not bound to occur. Before an eruption, things might seem quite stable. Actually, we argue and will illustrate in our analysis of the Egyptian case that mobilization started since 2000. The incremental build-up for massive protests was indeed taking place, albeit not as visibly. For without the logical build-up there would be no successful mobilization. There has to be a point of saturation: A tipping point. A generation that was turning thirty-something by 2010 felt that this was its moment to take action. Paired with this real-life build-up, social media platforms on Facebook and Twitter allowed organizational procedures, dissemination of information and citizen-journalism reporting on the actual days of the uprising as an "event." This match of grievances, on the one hand, and virtual and physical spaces that contain these grievances, on the other, was the convergence formula that made mass protests possible.

Certainly in hindsight, vision is 20/20 and in retrospect reasons can be more clearly seen about why and how Egyptians revolted. But in this chapter, the zoom gets closer to particular instances along the lengthy trajectory of Egyptian activism in order to find supporting evidence demonstrating how strategic networking behavior and acts of reciprocity for the purpose of forming coalitions and framing demands were actually played out by significant political actors. This resulted in convergences for successful alliance building, enabling a core of activists, who did not exceed a few hundreds, to reach out to myriad segments of society, thereby forging newly-formed societal unity against Mubarak's regime, at a much more mass-generalized level.

Only after such convergence occurred, could state-society relations be fundamentally changed, ushering a new relationship between "citizen" and "government," whose characteristics have been significantly altered since 2011, (Maziad, 2011c).

Now that the conceptual framework of "Nodes of Convergence" was introduced, in the next section, attention will be given to the literature on technology, social media, and social movements.

LITERATURE REVIEW

The Role of Technology in Global Social Change

Our research considers the problem raised by Tilly (2003) more than a decade ago regarding ways in which social movement activists have incorporated new technologies into their organizing and into their very claim-making performances:

Are new technologies transforming social movements? In what ways? If so, how do they produce their effects? How do new tactics and new forms of organization interact in 21st century social movements? More generally, to what extent and how do recent alterations in social movements result from the changes in international connectedness that people loosely call globalization?" (Tilly, 2003, p.1).

Complex Internationalism and Complex Multilateralism

James Rosenau (1999) argues that global politics and the international system of governance have transformed in two significant ways, both temporally and spatially. The communications revolution has deeply and expansively involved non-state actors in the promotion and implementation of international standards and normative behaviors (Finnemore, 1996; Risses et al., 1999), sometimes in agreement with and at other times in resistance by state institutions. As a result, the locus of political agency has become less clearly defined by state actors and more so by "mixed actor coalitions".

These coalitions emerged and proliferated as they consisted of globally networked nongovernmental organizations (NGOs), alliances of communities, and social movements (della Porta and Diani 2006; Khagram et al., 2002; Livingston & Asmolov, 2010). Thus, these non-state actors became more deeply engaged as agents of global governance. When describing this new global landscape of governance, Political Sociologist Sidney Tarrow (2005) speaks of "complex internationalism" and Robert O'Brian of "complex multilateralism" (O'Brian et al., 2000).

4

These kinds of internationalism and multilateralism represent a new arrangement of horizontal organizing, as opposed to vertical hierarchal ones. At one level, such horizontal circumstance allows for collective action within and even across nation-state borders. At another level, individuals become even more organically linked, beyond the horizontal level and into more globally rounded social networks. In the most recent cases of the Arab uprisings, such social networks became manifested online in social media such as Twitter, and Facebook.

Distant Proximities, Networks, and Scale Shifting

Another relevant aspect to our case in Egypt concerns the partial disintegration of barriers to large-scale collective action (Seigel, 2009; Livingston & Asmolov 2010). Accessing social networks, globally, alters our ways of experiencing distance and time. Rosenau (1997) conceptualizes this phenomenon as "distant proximities." Once on Facebook, the physically distant becomes close and the physically close might be alienated. Longing for and belonging to become disrupted. Thus, "local events can, through electronically enabled networks, shift to global significance (and versa-versa) without the involvement of intermediating levels of organization, such as the nation-state, and even when intermediate levels attempt to impede shifts," (Livingston & Asmolov, 2010). Tarrow, refers to this phenomenon as "Scale Shifting," and defines it as "the seamless and simultaneous presence of local events and issues at a global scale," (Tarrow, 2005 cited in Livingston & Asmolov 2010).

Scale Shifting is a core process of governance. Not only are borders penetrable and the power to narrate is diffused among various interlocutors' networks, but also affairs that were once local are now global, and global issues find local manifestation and resonance. This malleability in the focal range of issues is at the crux of scale shifting.

This notion of "scalability" or "scalable" political actions refers to the flowing interchangeability of local and global expressions of issues (Mamadou, 2004). This is relevant to how the local protests of Tunisia, became regional events for Egypt and the rest of the Middle East. And how Cairo's Tahrir Square became a site of the international gaze. So what was behind such national mobilization and global resonance?

State and Non-State Actors

With nation-states, as a political form, facing contestations regarding their total monopoly over issues of governance and with emerging competition of non-state actors, both peaceful and violent, over aspects of power, everything we know about organizations, collective action, and the distribution of information became altered.

Linvingston & Asmolov (2010) argue, that if the monopoly over information is removed and the element of fluid dissemination over new media networks is added, one sees "a new array of opportunities and constraints for scalable political action," (p. 751). A surge in information leads to administrative structures—to the degree they remain in place—that are "fluid, adaptable to shifting constraints and opportunities on a global scale, and open to rapidly formed and dissolved coalitions, movements, and networks," (p. 750). Reliance on vertical organizational structures decreases and boundaries between core organizational elements and other organizations become less rigid (Castells, 2000, 2009 cited in Linvingston & Asmolov 2010).

What conclusions can be drawn from such developments? Linvingston & Asmolov argue that if print capitalism gave rise to the nation-state of the eighteenth to twentieth centuries, as Benedict Anderson (2006) illustrates in his seminal book Imagined Communities, the new media network of global flows of images and sounds enable new forms of international organization to emerge. New communication technologies enable networked structures of global governance to emerge combining numerous state and non-state actors. These technologies not only embolden new players at the global level, they also "create non-spatial relationships, relationships not defined by geo-physical features such as proximity or bureaucratic routines, among actors in a network of transnational organization, (Linvingston & Asmalov 2010, p. 750).

New Media in the Arab World

When it comes to the Arab world specifically, some scholars view social media as the principle mobilizing force of anti-authoritarianism movements in the Middle East and North Africa (Cohen 2011; Webster 2011). In two separate studies, Diamond, Plattner and Costopoulos (2010; 2012) went beyond that, rendering these technologies "liberation technologies." Some even claimed that these technologies are shaping and shifting the fate and the face of societies. In this view, social media are seen as a democratizing means for social change (Castells, 2012; Shirky, 2008). Yet Diamond and Plattner's (2014) subsequent edited volume entitled *"Democratization and Authoritarianism in the Arab World"* qualified a lot of their initial optimism about the technology as automatic means for democratization.

From another perspective, some scholars undermined the role of social media altogether and argue that revolutions were bound to occur with or without the Internet and social media, and that Facebook and Twitter had little effect on this phenomenon (Rich, 2011; York 2011).

When it comes to contemporary Arab countries most specifically, it is clear that this part of the world has faced a lot of challenges regarding restrictions on freedoms of speech and expression, articulations of democratic governance, diversity of religious practices, and manifestations of gender roles. Many of these challenges were revealed in recent research done to investigate the use of technology during the Egyptian, Tunisian, and Libyan uprisings as well as the Syrian Civil War (Hamdy & Gomaa, 2012; Howard & Parks, 2012; Khamis & Vaughn, 2011; Mohamed, 2012).

In the title of a well-cited study by Howard et al. (2011) entitled *"Opening Closed Regimes: What Was the Role of Social Media During the Arab Spring?"* the researchers paid particular attention to innovative ways by which Arab youth appropriated social media to "open" such closed political regimes. Quantitatively creating a database of information from Facebook and YouTube as well as examining more than 3 million tweets, this study showed how online social media offered youth with newer and safer—as in more secure—opportunities to break out of their silence and participate in collective action. The study confirmed the critical role of the online communities in organizing, coordinating, and publicizing the protests. It documented a) the surge in online revolutionary conversations prior to major events on the ground, and b) the expansion of online discussions about democracy across international borders. Creating Facebook "events" inviting people to physical demonstration and subsequent live tweeting/blogging about street action became a pattern for organizing and implementing demonstrations in the field.

Of the literature that also confirms the importance of social media for social change is a study by Khamis and Vaughn (2011) that notes how Facebook enhanced the ability of activists and protestors to coordinate peaceful demonstrators, while allowing larger segments of the public to participate as citizen journalists, documenting and sharing eyewitness accounts from their cell phone images and videos. Another study by Baron et al. (2013) analyzes the different roles of Facebook during the Egyptian protests of 2011. The results of the study confirm the common findings that social networks had a crucial role in a) raising political awareness, b) mobilizing youth, and c) linking the virtual world to the physical streets.

These diverse views echo current debates on the Internet's influence on politics and democracy. In summary, Technological Determinist scholars see the Internet's proliferation as ways to develop civil society, enhance political participation, and institute democracy (Hague & Loader, 1999; Kamarck & Nye, 1999; Locke, 1998). Contrastingly, technologically averse theorists, or Social Determinists, perceive society as the actual independent force shaping technology, cultural values, social structure and/or history. In this view, actual socio-political relations are what shape societies, not a technological platform or some social media. Moreover, some go as far as determining that the Internet is currently becoming a menace to democracy, as governments and businesses use it to control users; sell their preferences for marketing purposes; and/or invade their privacies (Barber, 1996; Fox 1994), all while debasing political debates (Gutstein, 1999; Moore, 1999; Wilhelm, 2009).

Our conceptual framework and stance of the "Nodes of Convergence" is located somewhere in the middle of these two extremes of social or technological determinism. Our approach recognizes that communications technology is a medium that is acted upon by human actors with real-life issues, grievances, and demands, while recognizing that the nature of the social media—as plural of medium— are "actants," in of themselves. In this respect not only does our position echo Marshal McLuhan's mantra of the "Medium is the Message," but it also evokes Latour's (2005) terms in Actor-Network Theory (ANT), which stresses that humans and non-humans act upon one another.

Are Grievances Enough?

Following the global financial crisis in 2008, the Arab Uprisings, the Israeli housing crisis sit-in of 2011, or the Turkish Gezi Park Taksim Square Protests in 2013, the literature on social movements came to show diversified "thick descriptions" of bottom-up citizen and community-based initiatives. These are examples of issue-driven mobilizations across various causes and grievances, including economic welfare, political participation, public health, education, urban sustainable development, and children's and women's rights among other contemporary sociological perils. Moreover, current humanitarian crises, such as the Ebola outbreak and the refugee outflows, have led to extensive citizen engagement through a variety of social change communication strategies and community-driven enterprises.

Yet, causes alone are not enough for mass mobilization. Grievances regarding corruption, government oppression, rich and poor discrepancies, high costs of living, and unemployment have long been contentious issues in Egypt and other Arab countries. But grievances cannot be the sole explanations for the crescendo of the 2011 events. Throughout history, social and economic grievances, by themselves, have not engendered social movements (Buecheler, 2000). Rather, people get involved in collective action when they become aware of their affiliation with specific collectives (Wright, 2001). Thus, the level of identification with a group, rather than the actual issues, seems to be a stronger indicator of participation in collective action than grievances (Stekelenburg & Klandermans, 2007). This is when social movements and social mobilization begin to matter and have an impact.

The "Social" Aspect of Social Movements and Social Networks: Strong Ties Mobilize Weak Ties

Defining social movements, Tilly (2004) explains that they are sets of contentious performances, exhibits, and operations which ordinary people use to make collective claims. Additionally, social movements and protests can be conceptualized as peoples' networks united by shared goals or interests. Social movements indicate failure in the present societal interactions. It is a boiling point for mobilization.

The protest becomes the Sign. The medium of protesting becomes the message. A social mobilization becomes the communicated symbol to society that there has been a system failure.

Moreover, Tilly conceptualizes the repertoires of collective actions, as procedures in which "people act together in pursuit of shared interests" (Tilly 1995, p. 41). These repertoires are understood as forms of action, which are readily available to a given number of people in their context. These forms of actions have two attributes: 1) they are acquired, comprehended, sometimes deliberated upon and rehearsed by political actors, and 2) people have limited means at their disposal to perform such actions. However, the repertoire of collective action "typically leaves plenty of room for improvisation, innovation, and unexpected endings," (Tilly, 1984, p. 307). That is how strongly tied social actors mobilize weakly tied ones. The strongly tied actors manage to create "Nodes of Convergence" of grievances and physical and virtual spaces, as conceptualized above. Certainly, in an increasingly networked global society, the way it has been explicated thus far, social mobilization manifests itself in a process of interplay between online and offline communities.

The Generational Collective

In confirmation of Tilly's observations, what the cases of the Arab uprisings further illustrate is the sociological phenomenon we shall call a "Generational Collective." While revolutions need not be generational and generational protests do not necessarily become revolutions, certainly, a generational collective is larger than a sub-generational collective, and thus provides more support for revolution. In other words, something could be said about the way demonstrations can morph into a massive uprising or even a revolution and that might be in the case of the Arab uprising as having to do with the sense of political suffocation of a single authoritarian person governing for decades, as was the case in Tunisia (Ben Ali 23 years), Egypt (Mubarak 30 years), and Gaddafi (40 years). But not in Syria of Bashar Al Assad, for example, who by 2011, was in power for only 11 years, since 2000 — despite his father's earlier rule; for Father and Son proved to not be the self same person. From this perspective, the civil war continued and Bashar was not toppled, we may argue, because he had not been personally ruling for the long decades others have been.

The generational collective mobilizes an entire generation to go beyond the single figure they grew up with, not trusting in democratic procedure to replace him and with whom they feel he imposes a cap over their future. This condition did not squarely apply in the case of Bashar in Syria. Nor did it apply in the case of Taksim Square 2013 against Turkish President Recep Tayyip Erdoğan. Erdoğan, despite his manifested authoritarian tendencies, has not been in power, thus far yet, for more than 15 years.[2] This might explain why protests against Bashar in Syria and Erdoğan in Turkey did not achieve the level of buy-in that accompanied protests in Tunisia and Egypt.

Thus, while grievances are necessary they are not sufficient for mobilization. Yet, we should emphasize that collectively identified grievances are indeed necessary, in the sense that if generational collective grievances are not strong enough, there will be no "converged" upon agreement. A generation with shared memories and grievances become closely linked individuals. Core clusters of closely-linked individuals mobilizing others who are weakly-linked can help us understand how social movements depend on social networks to turn individual dissatisfaction into a mass movement of discontent (Granovetter, 1973; McAdam, 1986; Tarrow, 1998).

Social Media as Space

Observably, social media as mobilizing tools are treated, for the most part, in undifferentiated ways, neglecting to highlight the distinct technological features that allow for certain uses and appropriations in different socio-political contexts but not others. However, as Lim (2012) argues "Social media may be viewed both as technology and space for expanding and sustaining the networks upon which social movements depend," (p. 234). She adds:

The Arab revolts exemplify how online social networks facilitated by social media have become a key ingredient of contemporary populist movements. Social media are not simply neutral tools to be used or adopted by social movements, but rather influence how activists form and shape the social movements, (Lim, 2012, p.234).

In this nuanced reading of what social media are, Lim invites us to let go of expressions like "adopted" and "tools" and think of social media in more dynamic ways, where activists and social media constitute one-another. In other words, if social media have become principal components of current movements, then without them the movements would look structurally and practically different. In that respect, both Latour's Actor Network Theory—that sees non-humans objects as "actants" just as much as humans—as well as Marshall McLuhan's notion that "The Medium is the Message," apply significantly. So the media themselves influence how the social movements are shaped and performed.

Moreover, Andión, (2013) elaborates that "virtual social networks can be defined, strictly speaking, as electronic media that serve to socialize. The key difference between these media and conventional media is allowing horizontal communication, back and forth, they are interactive and therefore ideal for socializing," (p.47). In fact social media are so different from traditional media in that they are closer to a social club, a pub, or a café as in a physical place where people meet, interact and socialize. In the case of social media such socialization is virtual. Social media, therefore, are primarily a place for virtual socialization, and secondarily a platform and space of information sharing and news circulation. Again, like an actual urban café, it is where people physically meet to interact, socialize with one another, and share news about the big world or their small world, neighborhood gossip, and activism to stop or promote an initiative. For mass mobilization purposes however, following this kind of virtual organizing, actual spatial convergence must occur.

Relevant is the way Haug (2013) looks at meeting arenas as infrastructure for social movements. Our concept of "Nodes of Convergence" agrees with the idea of combining "social movements as actors" to "social movements as spaces" emphasizing the importance of face-to-face meetings and actual convergence onto a physical space like Tahrir Square or Taksim Square or all the other Midans (arenas). Haug introduces the concept of "meeting arena" as a hybrid of three forms of social order: organization, institution, and network. He argues that, "the complex figuration of meeting arenas in a social movement or protest mobilization constitutes an infrastructure that synchronizes the dispersed activities of movement actors in time and space. This infrastructure is not an entirely emergent phenomenon but is also the result of conscious decisions by organizers," (p.1). The analysis below will illustrate how the actors mobilized for the convergence on the Tahrir Square as arena.

Social Network as an Organizational Form

The seminal work of Manuel Castells' (2011) provides important contributions in delineating the nature of "Networks" as organizational forms. Up until his work, political communication was conceptualized in an "institutional" organizational paradigm. The literature addressed institutions of government, of press, of political parties, producing political messages—a sender-messages-receivers' paradigm. Yet all of this was turned upside down when organizations were being replaced, and networks started becoming the mode of operation of our time. Messages are constantly changed as they are being appropriated while circulating around the networks. This is theoretically relevant to the present study.

Coalitions and Alliances as Forces for Mobilization

Related to this chapter as well is the scholarship on coalitions and alliance building as the energy fueling mobilization. Coalitions can be loosely defined as groups of people or organizations that find each other in order to work together for one goal. When coalitions are formed, members make a long-term commitment to share responsibilities and resources. Alliances, on the other hand, generally involve forming unions or associations with other members, who form a short-term relationship to come together to achieve a specific or exact objective.

Tilly & Tarrow's (2007) conceptualization of repertoires in relation to Coalitions and Alliances, is important as they delineate social movements, "as a sustained campaign of claim making, using repeated performances that advertise the claim, based on organizations, networks, traditions, and solidarities that sustain these activities," (p. 8). Tilly (2005) further argues that

Identities belong to that potent set of social arrangements in which people construct shared stories about who they are, how they are connected, and what has happened to them... Whatever their truth or falsehood by the standards of historical research, such stories play an indispensable part in the sealing of agreements and the coordination of social interaction. Stories and identities intersect when people start deploying shared answers to the questions "Who are you?" "Who are we?" and "Who are they?" (p. 209)

Building further on the concept of strategic mobilization, Meyer and Staggenborg (2012), illustrate that social movements' strategies are the product of the interplay of structure and agency "as activists seek to respond to changing political and cultural circumstances and maximize their impact," (p. 4). The authors also argue that strategic decisions are made based on incrementally formed web of relations. These relations allow activists to make choices about how to conduct a collective action regarding demands; partners; media frameworks, resources and tactics. Three major pillars of strategic decision-making are emphasized: "the demands or claims made by collective actors; the arenas or venues of collective action; and the tactics or forms of collective action. All these choices imply the selection of particular targets or collective action." (Meyer & Staggenborg, 2012, p. 5)

This framework resonates with how we came to understand the "Nodes of Convergence" to be about the interplay between actual mobilizing actors, general grievances/demands, and the means/platforms to interact with (weakly tied) others and mobilize them through social media. The end product is some kind of "convergence" on the public demands and the "call for protests" using the social media. Without the demand, the pulse of the collective, and the general sentiment of shared grievances of the large number of people, the sheer social medium and the social media combined will not work in mobilizing people. However, once inhabited, these social media become actants, in of themselves and influence the nature of mobilization and its outcomes.

THE STUDY

Our cases in this study are derived from the public posts in the two Facebook Pages in Arabic that were considered the forces that proved instrumental in the call for protests on January 25th. The first page marks a date, April 6th, and the second carries a name, Khaled Said. The first page is titled "the April 6th Youth Movement (A6YM)," and spans varied ideologies and political orientations, commemorating the day of a General Strike that took place in 2008. The second page is "We Are All Khaled Said (WAAKS)," which portrays a consciously stated non-political position, focused instead on the humanistic side of the worth and dignity of Egyptian life. It gets its name from honoring the 28-years-old Khaled Said from the coastal city of Alexandria—a young man beaten to death in June 2010, at the hands of police agents under Mubarak's Emergency Laws.

Despite different geneses and timing, 2 years apart, the date April 6th and the name Khaled Said converged at some points, taking the Egyptian uprising one critical step closer towards being possible. This study traces the story of such convergence, while contextualizing these elements within a broader domestic political culture and in interaction with regional and international elements.

Methods

The conceptualization and theorization regarding networking and interactions in this study are built on extensive anthropological fieldwork in Egypt[3] divided into 4 timelines: In March 2011; from July 2011 until December 2011; from July 2012 until December 2012; and lastly, from July 2013 till November 2013. Fieldwork also included many subsequent fieldtrips between September 2014 and August 2016. The covered ethnographic research methods of participant-observations and in-depth interviewing was conducted with political actors, journalists, April 6th group members, and conversations during public meetings with Wael Ghonim, the admin of the page "We Are All Khaled Said," and correspondence via Facebook, and in person interviews with Ahmad Maher, Coordinator of the Facebook group "April 6th Youth Movement".

For the purpose of validity and triangulation of evidence on the convergence mechanism of both A6YM and WAAKS, the authors conducted qualitative content analysis of significant posts on the two pages from mid-2010 until January 2011. The text was analyzed to detect how the linkages between the actors were manifested in the call for protest. In order to collect Facebook posts, the authors developed an application[4] using the Facebook Graph API, which is a way for developers to access Facebook data and build applications. The application was employed to retrieve Facebook wall posts without comments. Since the current Facebook format does not enable users to browse through old posts without closing the browser, this application proved useful as it presented the posts in a bulleted format. The user needs only specify start and end dates, as well as the number of posts to be retrieved. The languages used to develop the application were HTML and JavaScript.

FINDINGS AND ANALYSIS

The Actors

The April 6th Youth Movement Page (A6YM) in Arabic

The birth of A6YM goes back to commemorating a date, where activists called for a General Strike that took place in 2008, in solidarity with the workers of Mahalla—an industrial town north of Cairo, known for its state-owned textile factories employing more than 24,000 workers and slashed for privatization. Mahalla workers, decided to strike, protesting sudden price increases of essential commodities, unpaired with equal increase in income, at the height of the global economic crisis.

Uniting with the workers, many political forces decided to back their endeavors. Facebook use was beginning in Egypt. So, two young Egyptians Ahmad Maher and Esraa Abdel Fattah[5] co-created a Facebook Group on March 23rd, and set up an "event invitation" calling it "April 6th: A General Strike for the People of Egypt," in solidarity with Mahalla's pre-existing plans for the day. The Facebook Group invitation was created for deliberation purposes, and for enacting the call for strike, which spread like wildfire. In a few days, the group reached 75,000 members rendering it the largest Arabic language group at the time. Mahalla had its strike, despite divisions among the workers' leadership regarding proceeding, due to government threats and seeming compromises that were reached to satisfy workers' demands. Nonetheless, protests ensued in the city. A few were killed, several injured, and many arrested.

While media reports were mixed about the strike's "success", the young activists who had thus far been communicating online wanted to frame the event as an unprecedented triumph. "Thus, the Facebook group members came out to get to know one another in real life, and decided to form a movement that bears the name of that day."[6] Following the movement's consolidation a Facebook Page was created in August 2008. The Page's main message was mentioned in "About me," as follows:

We are a group of Egyptian youth whose love of country brings us together with the desire to fix things. We do not call for a new group or a new party, but rather, we call on all Egyptians (individuals - communities - parties - the honest in all sectors) to converge on a single project: To awaken the people. To end unjust oppression. To remove the gang of corruption and tyranny. Our presence is everywhere in order to support the oppressed and advocate for the weak. The transformation of Egypt will not come with "asking for" or "calling for." Rather, it will materialize through real work and by providing real well studied alternatives and solutions in order to find a true alternative to achieve political, economic and social renaissance for Egypt and to provide stability and security for the Egyptian citizen, (in Arabic translated by authors; emphasis added).

On the Facebook Page, under "Employer," A6YM have specified "The Egyptian People." And under "Favorite Quote," they stated, "Our generation has the right to try. Either we will succeed, or we will offer an experience from which future generations may benefit."

From the aforementioned self-descriptions, certain characteristics can be deduced. First, there is a conscious attempt of building consensus around one aspect: Love for Egypt, apart from ideological or political differences. Second, the language used aims to unite Egyptians at the individual, community, and party levels as well as generalizing to whoever is "honest" in their patriotism. This is significant as it shows the movement founders are neither alienating the politically involved nor chastising the apolitical, thus aiming for creating a catchall entity. Third, the movement delineates specific demands that start with awakening and consciousness, and ends with stopping despotism and corruption. Finally, the phrase "our presence is everywhere" will prove pivotally true later, as the state becomes perplexed by the "April 6th" phenomenon. As one journalist put it, "No one knows exactly how big April 6th is. How many members? A few dozen? A few hundreds? Thousands? That's actually their edge. It's a matter of survival. You might think they are a few generic Ahmed, Mohamed and Mahmoud. Yet they have the ability to mobilize others and reach hundreds of thousands, and even millions," (Personal Communication, March 2011).

We Are All Khaled Said Page (WAAKS) in Arabic

This Facebook Page was established on June 10th 2010. According to its "Personal Information," the purpose is "to defend Khaled Said, God bless his soul, against all injustice to which he was subjected. God has willed it that the Page become a forum to defend every Egyptian's rights for a decent life."[7]

The Page's drive is to expose police brutality as it sheds light on issues surrounding the death of Khaled Said—portrayed as the first victim following Emergency Law's renewal.[8] The story portrayed on the Page goes as follows: Khaled Said was tortured to death at the hands of two police agents. Several eyewitnesses described how

Figure 1. Image of Khaled Said circulating online and becoming an "iconic" representation of emergency law victims

the police informants took him into the entrance of a residential building, brutally punching and kicking him until he died.

The page further elaborates:

Despite his calls for mercy.... they continued their torture until he died according to many eyewitnesses. Khaled has thus become the symbol for many Egyptians who dream to see their country free of brutality, torture and ill treatment. Many young Egyptians are now fed up with the inhumane treatment they face on a daily basis... and aspire to the day when Egyptians have dignity.

In response to this, the Egyptian state tried to discount all innocence narratives of Khaled Said, calling him a drug addict, who broke the law running shady business and who was dishonorably dismissed from the compulsory military service. They even refuted his age in the circulating image, arguing that he was much younger in it than the "adult" who actually died.

Amid two competing narratives, one initiated on WAAKS and reflected in media reports on independent and foreign media, and the other propagated on Egyptian state television and semi-official newscasters, Egyptian citizens had to make up their minds regarding whom to believe. Heated discussions continued and with it the verdict to re-open the case for further autopsy. That was the first time an alleged police torture case was re-opened due to public pressure (Gomaa, 2010).[9]

Our analysis of the Page is that it is a case of successful political marketing par excellence. There is a unifying character: The young Egyptian man. There is a brand name: Khaled Said. And there is a poignant and short message: We Are ALL that person who was beaten to death. This message was at the heart of the page's success in implicating the middle class,[10] (Abdelnasser, 2011). Hence, no longer is activism reserved for the "core few." With this Page, rather, mass politics could ensue. Marketing for a "brand" and making it "relatable" to everyone was one underlying goal for the Page's anonymous admin.

The identity of the WAAKS admin, Wael Ghonim, Head of Marketing of Google Middle East and Africa, remained concealed until February 7th 2011 when he was released by Egyptian authorities who had detained him on January 27th, following the beginning of the Jan 25th protests. He appeared on a popular Talk Show with host Mona El Shazli, for the first time that evening. In fact, for a long time other activists communicating with him were calling him "Khaled Said." They would say "I chatted with Khaled Said today and he told me this or that."[11] This simple act of being anonymous while circulating Khaled Said's name is a marketing strategy that builds "brand recognition."

Before A6YM and WAAKS Ever Existed: A Decade at a Glance 2000-2010

If A6YM and WAAKS were two converging nodes on the scene of Egyptian activism between 2008 and 2010, what other nodes had preceded them? To understand the significance of the eventual coming together and joining forces of these two actors: Ahmad Maher of A6YM and Wael Ghonim, the then-anonymous admin of WAAKS, some light should be shed on the political context preceding their crucial moment of convergence in preparation for the Jan 25th Revolution.

The 2000 Intifada

Each year of the past decade marked some significant political event, influencing Egyptians' public consciousness. The year 2000 started with Syrian president Bashar Al Assad "inheriting" the presidency from his late father Hafez Al Assad, via procedural elections, raising speculation about a similar scenario in Egypt from father Hosni Mubarak to son Gamal Mubarak.[12] The year ended with the second Palestinian Intifada. Egyptians performed their protests in solidarity with the Palestinians all while inserting their own domestic grievances.

September 11 2001 and US War on Iraq in 2003

Then September 11th attacks occurred in 2001 and with them an internal discourse regarding the strained, and in some views, politically taxing Egyptian alliance with the US. American war on Iraq and its subsequent occupation followed in 2003, which further fueled unprecedented worldwide protests.

Kefaya Movement and the Blogosphere in 2004 and 2005

Marxist journalist, blogger and activist Hossam el-Hamalawy recalls that Information Technologies had enabled coordination of protests. He says "the first invitations for protests started coming around 2000, through email." He added, "the same people who called for protests in 2000, 2001 and 2003 are the people who called for protests against the 'inheritance project' in 2004, through Kefaya, meaning Enough."[13] (el, Hamalawy, 2009; Oweidat et. al 2008, Bogad, 2005).

Hamalawy also refutes "a claim that often comes from the West, positing that Arabs only cared about Palestine while they don't care about their domestic problems." He added, "I can say for certain that people with such claims have never attended a single demonstration in Egypt! Because we always started these demonstrations with 'Palestine' and we ended them with 'Down with Hosni Mubarak!!'" (Translated by author, el- Hamalawy, 2009).

By 2004 and 2005 blogs have started to appear. There were about 30 to 40 blogs covering primarily personal matters of people expressing opinions about things happening in their lives. El-Hamalway (2009) argues, "The general sentiment was that those blogging at the time somewhat had an aversion towards politics." Yet the turning point, according to him, was on May 25th 2005, which activists called "Black Wednesday" where then-ruling National Democratic Party's "baltageya" (thugs) committed atrocities against protesters opposed to constitutional amendments that made it practically impossible for any candidates besides Mubarak and his son Gamal to run.

The presence of bloggers among the protesters at this particular event switched their interest from personal matters to sharing this very public event, through their collected images. This started what became later known as "Citizen Journalism." The idea behind this was that the "professional journalist" in big state-owned media would no longer have the monopoly over news production, (el-Hamalawy, 2009; Lim, 2004, Van de Donk et al., 2004;).

Thus bloggers' ability, in the mid-2000s, to utilize existing technological infrastructure to disseminate information, independent of mainstream media, is particularly crucial in countries with state-controlled media such as Indonesia under the Suharato regime (Lim 2004; 2006) and Egypt under the Mubarak regime (Howard, 2010; Howard et. al 2011). By 2005 privately owned independent newspapers such as Almasry Alyoum and others; as well satellite channels have emerged and started to proliferate.

Yet el-Hamalawy (2009), consistent with the theorization above, was quick to qualify that the proliferation of bloggers in 2005 and 2006 does not constitute them as "a movement," due to their diverse orientations. While using similar "media," such as Twitter, BlogSpot or Flicker, they varied considerably among themselves.

He says "People at that juncture were either living entirely in the virtual world; or mixing being on the streets, actually receiving the beating and also using the Internet; or refusing that medium entirely,"

Furthermore, Ahmed Maher of A6YM delineates the nature of streets-online dynamics in a personal communication with the author, as follows:

In 2005, there was enormous international pressure for democratization put on Mubarak. But in 2006 that pressure was lifted. Mubarak pressured us [activists] continuously and banned any street protests. This caused a withdrawal from the streets due to the pressure by the security forces; and everything became "internet activism". Everyone was blogging, videotaping. Everyone had a camera, used YouTube and such. But street protests became really scarce; they became really dangerous, (personal communication with author Marwa Maziad; translated form Arabic by the author 2012).

Thus, according to el-Hamalway's, their myriad backgrounds and dispersed interests would disband the bloggers as a collective. In agreement with this, we conceptualized that for social movements to shape up there needs be an act of "convergence" that mitigates such "disparities." Through "convergence," strands of society come together at a certain point in time to form coalitions, activate networks and frame demands that resonate with many more people outside the boundaries of the intimate clique of dedicated activists. This is consistent with Haug (2013) explicated above regarding the arenas.

Workers' Movement Gains Momentum in 2006-2008: The Birth of A6YM

On the activism timeline, 2006 and 2007 mark considerable accomplishment for Egyptian worker's movement. Protests and strikes were planned and coordinated; succeeding in obtaining raises and gains. What makes April 6th 2008 significant, was that building on the initial success of the workers' movements, young activists who had been inhabiting the virtual world, or have had a leg in that world and a leg on the street through Kefaya's protests or oppositional parties' demonstrations, could actually capitalize on a moment of "convergence" regarding basic economic demands in order to generalize the call beyond the worker's movement. That was the moment; the A6YM was conceived as such, arguably to fill the "collectivity" gap which el-Hamalawy was referring to regarding the disparate bloggers.

In the Documentary "The Silent Speak Up" (Abdelnasser, 2011), Gamal Eid, a Human Rights activist, and Tarek El Kholy, spokesperson of April 6th Movement[14], illustrated how the state intervention, warning the people against going on strike, actually backfired and spread the idea more. "Demonstrations started to come out."

On April 5th, the night before the day of the strike, anchor Tamer Amin of the highly viewed "Al Bait Baitak" talk show running on state TV read a statement from the Ministry of Interior saying that "those who will not go to work will be subjected to very harsh punishments." This kind of propaganda by the Ministry of Interior warning against the strike made people wonder: "Is there a strike?!" A lot of them looked on the Internet and found the Facebook event. And so some joined the Facebook group!

It is quite significant to note how the actors describe why more people joined the Facebook group, attributing it to the mechanism of "finding it online" based on State TV's very warning against striking. So it is almost a catch 22. Those who did not know about the invitation heard about it on state TV, went to "check", and when they liked what they saw "they joined the event". That arguably made them more motivated to give it a try and come out in demonstrations rather than ignore it. The magnitude of the success of April 6th demonstrations on the street in Cairo or other governorates besides Mahalla might have been limited but the "Ping-Pong" action-reaction mechanism between the activists and the state became a performance to be watched and vetted for by the depoliticized citizen. This is, literally and in practice, how strongly tied actors mobilized weakly tied groups.

ElBardei and "Breaking the Barrier of Fear" Strategy in 2009

Towards the end of 2009, Mohamed ElBaradei, former Director General of the International Atomic Energy Agency announced his intentions to run in the presidential elections of 2011 if the constitution were to be amended allowing for candidates to actually run. With his return to Egypt, the National Association for Change (NAC) was formed as a coalition of various political forces. It became an umbrella under which youth from all movements, liberal and conservative, be it Kefaya, independent intellectuals, or the Muslim Brotherhood, could work together to induce political change.

NAC's Information Technology team had to decide whether to show full names for those providing electronic signature in support of the ElBaredi for President Campaign. They concluded that, "if 'breaking the barrier of fear,' were to be a strategic goal, then showing the full names of individuals is essential to encourage others to do the same."[15]

That said it is important to keep in mind that by that time in 2009 Facebook had already become well integrated and combined not only with other social and traditional media, but also with other forms of information and communication such as email, SMS, leaflets, knocking doors, and physical meetings. We even note that at some point there was progression in the appropriation of social media. Facebook was the primary one, uniquely appropriated in 2008 by Esraa and later becoming the April 6th Movement's main platform. Then by 2010 El Bardei used Twitter for his first tweet about Khaled Said in June 2010. Since then, for better or worse, El Baradei became known as the "Twitter activist." The youth felt he was closer to their media of communication. But others critiqued him for his "virtuality" and not being an actual on the ground politician— even though his tweets had not been that frequent. Here we can analyze the deliberate use of social media by social actors. We can argue that social media were appropriated one by one for different purposes. As one activist interviewed indicated "you learn the news or 'what's going on, on the ground' from Twitter; but the planning and dissemination of these plans happens on Facebook."

Wael Ghonim Joins the Scene Mid-2010

Around April 2010, Wael Ghonim approached NAC to "help out" and cooperated by providing Google ad space for the Arabic word "Tagheer" or "Change" that would connect the search to NAC website.[16] By June 2010, Ghonim had taken his own individual initiative to start We Are All Khaled Said Facebook Page, while remaining an anonymous admin, calling for vigils and mobilizing protests in support of Khaled Said's rights and against police brutality.

A6YM and WAAKS: Acts of Reciprocity

By mid-2010, almost all the new actors had been positioned in the political playing field. A6YM had gained some momentum and WAAKS has already mobilized large segments of society around a humanistic cause of Egyptian dignity in the face of police brutality. The coordination, acts of reciprocity, and convergence on causes and themes of those two different mobilizing "entities," will prove instrumental in the first two months of 2011 and the subsequent episode of Egyptian history.

It is worth mentioning that "A6YM had kept a calendar of potential protest days!" as one of its member put it in an interview. A sample included Police Day on January 25th, April 6th in memory of the first General Strike, May 4th marking Mubarak's birthday, and National Day on July 23rd. The purpose "was to offer a counter-celebration of the given day and to create an opportunity for networking among online activists."

Thus, when WAAKS joined the activism scene in June 2010, complementarity of roles and distribution of tasks started to be detected and seen. That will prove crucial for the big event of Police Day January 25th 2011.

For example, a communication between Ahmed Maher of A6YM and the anonymous admin of WAAKS took place on July 8th 2010, stating that they must join forces and work towards a shared goal of awakening Egyptians. WAAKS admin, however, expressed the need to maintain his page humanistic in nature and not political. The admin wrote to Maher that he worked diligently on using We Are All Khaled Said to draw "people who are apolitical. These people do not want to feel that I'm a political organism." He added "We should be one hand Ahmad [an idiom meaning united] and our work complement one another, instead of having disagreements, where our positive energy to change Egypt turn into a negative one," Maher concurred that coordination is essential.[17]

Three weeks later, by July 29th 2010, WAAKS made its first reference to the arrest of Blogger and A6YM Member Ahmad Doma, by sharing a video of a police officer accused of beating activists at the time Doma was arrested on May 3rd 2010, protesting against the State of Emergency renewal. WAAKs posted:

This policeman beat lots of people on that date; among them is Ahmad Doma of April 6th, who led the chants. Ahmad has been charged with a fictitious case and sentenced to 3 months in prison

This status reflects an act of reciprocity, following the initial conversation between Maher and Ghonim. It also shows sustained mobilization around the central cause adopted by WAAKS, namely police brutality and Egyptian dignity. Finally, it reflects a sense of humor and sarcasm when it directly addresses the Ministry of Interior informants and calls them to task, inquiring if that policeman, beating protesters was in anyway punished for his actions.

Rigged Elections November 2010

November 2010 marked rigged parliamentary elections of historical magnitude. Against any political logic, none of the members of the Muslim Brotherhood (MB) oppositional movement had won. MB members had been running as independents due to the banning of the group, as such. In the previous parliament of 2006, however, they had won 88 seats, after political arrangements with the regime. Yet by 2010, Mubarak's ruling National Democratic Party[18] won by 97%, without a single MB affiliate. That was yet another political straw that was about to break the proverbial camel's back.

Thus, on November 26th, collaboration between A6YM and WAAKS ensued, converging on the call for a "Day of Anger." Instructions were to wear black on Friday the 26th, and peacefully protest in public squares. Both admins were aware

Figure 2. WAAKS page in Arabic asks people to "like" and share a YouTube video entitled "Scandal of beating citizens in Egyptian Demonstration," and refers to A6YM member Ahmad Doma

of the importance of "convergence." More specifically, A6YM was strategic about understanding WAAKS's popular weight due to its humanistic nature, and in terms of the number of its members. By the end of 2010, WAAKS was very close to getting 1 million likes, and accordingly it was well positioned to be the "space of convergence" and to actually call for the January 25th protests, which eventually translated into a popular uprising.

Planning for the Big Day: Jan 25th 2011

On 30th of December 2010, WAAKS admin chatted online with Ahmed Maher, suggesting a "crazy idea" to "celebrate" Police Day on Jan 25th. Maher confirmed that the year before, A6YM had indeed "celebrated" it and expressed how the police force were mad for having to work on their day off.[19] In the end, the two agreed that WAAKS can "mobilize people for the protest," handling publishing the invitation on the Page, while A6YM would handle all the logistics on the ground, given Maher's experience in spreading information, campaigning and maneuvering the police. The process of convergence, coalitions, and networking was in place for mass mobilization towards physical enactment in public arenas.

Gender

In WAAKS admin's attempts to mobilize women for the protests to come on Jan 25th, he posted a status message on December 31st saying:

Thanks to all the girls on the Page, because since started, half of the contributions have been from girls, although the total number of girls on Facebook, in Egypt, does not exceed 35%... This is evidence that they sympathized with our cause. Lots of them went down for protests and helped a lot. Suffice to say that the main Page Designer is a girl named Sarah[20]... thanks again to the most reliable Egyptian Girls!

Figure 3. WAAKS page in Arabic praises Egyptian girls

Numbers

Tying the abovementioned gender-specific mobilization to yet another more generalized one, WAAKS's admin added a glimpse of "Hope" on the 8th of January 2011, by showing statistics reflecting an increase in the number of members to 365,000 and indicating that the Page received 60 million views in 1 month. The admin then mobilized his audiences to share, saying that the faster their voice reaches additional people, the more they can turn incidents of injustice into public opinion cases—An application of a strongly tied core mobilizing a weakly tied periphery.

Figure 4. Statistics of increase in likes and views

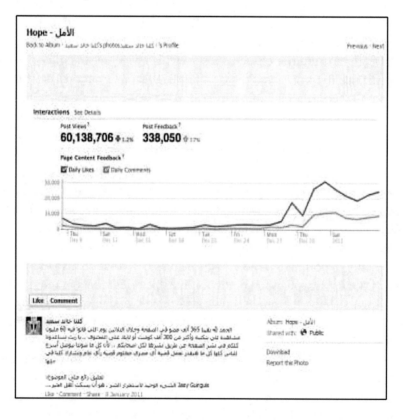

The First Call for Jan 25th Appears on WAAKS

On January 9th at 4:15, We Are All Khaled Said posted: Police Day has approached and we have to celebrate the policemen martyrs who sacrificed their lives for our security. But we also have to "celebrate" those criminal officers who kill Egyptians and torture them in police stations. We have to "celebrate" them in our special way as Egypt's youth![21]

The Tunisian Factor

As the Egyptians were setting their date, the Tunisian Revolution was simultaneously manifesting itself as an act of civil resistance. The events started on December 17th, 2010, following the self-immolation of street vendor Mohamed Bouazizi and led to the ousting of President Zine El Abidine Ben Ali on January 14th, 2011.

The demonstrations resonated with Tunisians due to many political and economic reasons. Deaths and injuries ensued, most of which were due to police and security forces acting against protesters. It is worth noting that international coverage of the protests was limited at the beginning. Yet Aljazeera was able to broadcast news, based on citizens' submissions of videos. Some Egyptian journalists and writers addressed the demonstrations, making comparisons to Egypt's situation and conceptualizing the notion of "citizen's rights" vis-à-vis Arab governments, (Maziad, 2011a). As Howard et al. (2011) argue, the Arab Spring had many causes. One of these enablers was social media and its ability to put a human face on political grievances. Bouazizi's self-immolation was one of several stories circulating on Facebook, Twitter, and YouTube in ways that mobilized the opposition to "organize protests, criticize their governments, and spread ideas about democracy," (P.1).

It is equally important to note that the Tunisian revolution also did not happen suddenly. Like the Egyptian Revolution, it had historical roots in the resistance of Tunisian civil society, the protests of Gafsa mine workers of June 2008, as well as the vibrancy of Tunisian digital activism particularly Tunisia's anti-censorship movement[22] (Randeree, 2011).

During the Tunisian protests, Egyptians online noticed that Tunisians were also using Facebook, sharing tips on managing clashes, in reaction to teargas for example. However, while Tunisia's events had started on December 17th and Maher and Ghonim started planning for Jan 25th Police Day on December 30th, i.e after the start of Tunisia's protests, there was no particular reference to Tunisia's ongoing events at the time. That illustrates two things. First, Police Day was already being planned for, discounting any particular "cascading effect" in absolute unqualified terms. Second, this reflects some nuanced decision-making strategies and actors' psychology. The main actors did not want to refer to Tunisia at the time for fear

Figure 5. January 10th: Tunisian government is making concessions under protests' pressures

that if Tunisia's protests failed, the pairing with it would demotivate Egyptians to continue on their own path.[23]

Yet, WAAKS shared one post on Jan 10th, framing the Tunisian protests in positive light as having pressed the government enough to yield certain demands.

When the Tunisians Succeeded

If, at first, it was not strategic to fully refer to Tunisia's protests until some concrete success materialized. By the time Ben Ali did flee, it became absolutely strategic to fully refer to Tunisia. On January 17th, A6YM tied Tunisia's success to that of Egypt, thereby raising confidence about the January 25th preparations. The post was: "Tunisia was liberated and Egypt will be liberated." As E. E. Schattschneider (1975) put it, the outcome of every conflict is determined by the extent to which the audience becomes involved in it, that is, by the "scope of its contagion" (p. 2). Tunisia became contagious.

10 Days to go: Posts on January 15th

As the countdown began, WAAKS's admin started mobilizing people around the theme of "capacity". Are the Egyptians able to do what Tunisians did? That became a rivalry-challenge-provoking analytic to use. It was not evoked under a pretext

Figure 6. A6YM distributed flyers saying, "Tunisia was liberated and Egypt will be liberated." They gave instructions for placing flyers in building entries, on movie theatres seats, and in the Metro.

Figure 7. WAAKS snapshot saying, "If 100,000 of us took to the streets, no-one will stand in our way. Can we?"

Figure 8. Five suggested demands for the day of protest

of animosity towards the Tunisians. Quite the contrary, the appreciation for them was tremendous. Yet the comparison itself mobilized Egyptians around national self-images along the lines of Egypt being "the Heart of the Arab world," or the "Big Sister," who must outdo her metaphorically Arab "siblings," even if the task is performing a Revolutionary Act— rather, precisely if that is the task

Discussing the Demands

WAAKS's admin, never said, "I decided something," meaning that everything was raised up for discussion and opinion solicitation. "He only suggests."[24] Here is what the admin wrote regarding the Jan 25th Demands:

I think we should only have five demands for Jan 25th so that it is easy to spread. These are my suggestions and I await your opinions: First, Ending state of emergency and releasing those detained under its pretext. Second, dismissal of Habib El Adly, Minister of Interior. Third: No running for Mubarak for another term and amendment of the constitution. Fourth, increasing governmental subsidy of essential commodities. Fifth, cancelling security censorship on all means of communication.

The Big Day of Convergence and its Aftermath

On the 25th of January Egyptian protesters chanted "Peaceful. Peaceful. Peaceful", avoiding clashes with riot police, and demonstrating maximum self-restraint and civility. Yet as President Mubarak stayed officially silent, till the end of the day, in a detached "business as usual" disposition, the protesters had already begun to construct their collective image as "constituents" urgently demanding rights.

Expectations rose and decisions to reconvene on Friday the 28th were reached. Christians and Muslims, religious and secularists, rich and poor, peasants and urbanites were to converge again on Tahrir Square, and other arenas nationwide.

Figure 9. Reference is made to the protests not being exclusively of the "Free Facebook Youth," who had sparked the Revolution. But the protests are of those struggling Egyptians, who felt the hope of seeing 100, 000 Egyptians demonstrating on Jan 25. "Tomorrow is our Date. We pray that we all do the right thing so that 1 million Egyptians go down the streets."

By now, the feeling among Egyptians had amounted to anger for being ignored by their president.

In the few following themed days, such as Friday's "Day of Anger" till Tuesday's "Million Man March", the State cut off the Internet and interrupted phone services, isolating the Egyptian people from the outside world, in what was interpreted as collective punishment. Police withdrew from the city and crime ensued. Arguably, the State pursued that in order to terrify citizens of what chaos and uncertainty would resemble, (Maziad, 2011b).

When Mubarak finally spoke four days later, citing government change, this was perceived by protesters as "too little, too late". Following that critical juncture, Mubarak could not turn back the wheel as sentiments among Egyptians had reached the point of demanding he step down. Yet Mubarak delivered another speech exhibiting no plan to resign, albeit proclaiming he will oversee constitutional reforms and will not run for another term— echoing the very demands that WAAKS had put forward.

Following Mubarak's speech, where his rhetoric reflected phrases such as "I was born in Egypt and shall die on its soil," the Egyptian people split on their degrees of sympathy, reflecting what looked like disagreements on the subsequent plan of action.

In the end, as incidents of pressures and concessions alternated, one thing became certain: There was no return to a pre-January 25th Egypt, (Maziad, 2011c).

On January 27th a WAAKS status read:

Very important: Regardless of anything that might happen even if a curfew was set. We will all go to pray the Friday noon prayers or go to Church. Then we will walk in huge marches to the public squares and sit there... even if they tried to stop us...I hope that the blood of the people who died and those arrested do not go in vain... Actually I'm already certain that the People have risen— but I just wanted to emphasize this point.

Figure 10. Detailed instructions on list of mosques and churches, at which people will congregate on Friday Jan 28th

On Cutting off the Internet

When the Internet was cut, that actually put the Egyptian movement to the test. While it took another form relying on face-to-face communication and knocking on doors, no doubt it still altered the way the movement was formed and shaped, all while attesting to the resourcefulness of actors and mass protesters who devised old ways of going about their protests. What many Egyptians said at the time was: "We had to pause and think. When our Forefathers revolted in 1919, without cell phones or Internet, how did they do it?"[25] Now, the flyer, the knock and the actual calling of a human voice saying "Enzel. Enzel." "Come Down. Come Down," to those watching a march from their balconies, became the oldest and most reliable communication media. In the end, after 18 days of protests, on February 11th 2011, Mubarak relinquished power.

Remembering Khaled Said in the Middle of it all:

Figure 11. A birthday cake, with the infamous #Jan25 falling like a rocket on Minister of Interior Habib El Aldi. The post reads: Khaled Said. His name is a description. Khaled means Eternal and Said means Happy. Eternally Happy. Today January 27th is his birthday. He would have turned 29. "We're almost there. Your rights and those of Egypt are about to come soon, Khaled."

DISCUSSION AND IMPLICATIONS

Egyptian activists interviewed for this research had affirmed that their political struggles to induce change in their political reality is nothing anomalous or shockingly new, but rather date back to the dawn of history. They are quick to remind us that Egyptian workers building tombs in Ancient Egypt went on a strike to demand better rations— an episode in human history that provides "the first known fully documented evidence of collective protest by a workforce," (David, 1996).

Yet, while the protests of the Pyramids builders were the first documented collective actions to improve economic conditions, it is important to note that when their rations increased, they went back to work, like any modern union would do. So yes, collective bargaining it was. And it is commended and shows that state-society relations are old and ingrained. But it was not a revolution. And that is why perhaps the very motto in Jan 25 of combining livelihood with freedom (political and cultural freedoms) dignity (humane treatment of one another) and social justice, might have been an ill match. That is because apparently different people were there for very different reasons. Thus, those whose economic problems would be solved or severely hurt would join or jump ship, respectively, regardless of the rest of the demands. It seems, in retrospect, that the catchall phrases didn't keep all.

Some of the activists interviewed back up their argument about the history of mobilization by fast-forwarding to the turn of the 20th century, when, in a nationwide 1919 Revolution, petition-signing was pursued for the first time in history as a political pressure tool for negotiating with the British occupation. Egyptians from all walks of life protested by signing a petition, forcing Britain to recognize Egypt's independence in 1922 and to implement a new constitution in 1923, (Fahmy, 2011).

Their point is to state that Egyptians have a long history of political mobilization that predates the Tahrir Square image upon which the world became fixated. It is in this historical legacy of political activism, popular mobilization and national legacies of collective action that Egyptians locate their January 25th Revolution.

This is actually how protesters devised yet another call for petition signing to culminate in the second uprising of June 30th 2013, against Muslim Brotherhood (MB) rule, with more than 22 million signatures gathered as an impeachment process of the post-Jan 25 first elected Former President Mohamed Morsi. This mechanism of petition signing was resorted to as Parliament had been dissolved and therefore could not perform the impeachment process. What ensued was Morsi's and MB's further clinging to power, in the name of their legitimately democratic ascent to power. But when Morsi repeated "Legitimacy" 52 times in his final speech, people were at an impasse, given that the millions protesting had hoped he would understand the magnitude of the protests, the way Mubarak did, and would call for early elections, given the pressure. When he did not, this ushered in the military intervention on July 3rd 2013 and the road map that eventually brought in Field Marshal Abdel Fattah El Sisi as a newly elected President.

Yet, in light of June 30th —as a second wave of uprisings and not simply a unilateral military coup— the military needs to be located in relation to society and to the re-mobilized segments of that society. In other words, while the dichotomy of "Military" or "Muslim Brotherhood" does exist, this binary does not squarely stand by itself or on its own. Neither is monolithic or all-powerful without other segments in society that weigh one over the other at some point, only to re-arrange the weights and weigh anew. Personal and social agency, coalitions that form and break, networks, and alliances are in flux all the time. A snapshot of political life in Egypt at any given moment reflects these oscillating arrangements.

CONCLUSION

Our conceptual framework had emphasized the importance of the cause, the grievance, the shared and converged upon element. What follows the agreed upon demands are appropriation of means and media for the purpose of creating converging events to mobilize a population. Upon detailed examination and analysis of the events, we discovered that while grievances alone are not sufficient they are indeed necessary. Yet we also discovered that while social media alone are equally insufficient, in a post-nation-state world they have become significantly impactful. Hence, the conclusion is that both grievances and arenas, virtual and physical, co-constitute one another into Nodes of Convergence for social mobilization into social movements.

Thus, while this chapter focuses on the early episode surrounding January 25 2011 and argues and illustrates that the road to Tahrir Square had been built up from coalitions and networks, actors and demands, and virtual and physical spaces that constituted "nodes of convergence" without which Tahrir Square would not have been the political spectacle it had become, it seems that this road and its nodes had already started to form much earlier than most contemporary observers might think. That is why our conceptual framework regarding "Nodes of Convergence" was defined to be about shared political and economic grievances on the one hand, as well as shared virtual and physical spaces on the other. Grievances had to be discussed in virtual and physical spaces. The creation of virtual and physical nodes of convergence to discuss shared grievances had to occur first, and among key actors engaging with social media as "actants." Under these conditions, mobilization for a collective action of millions on the street could ensue.

In today's world, institutions of various kinds flatten, become more fluid, less hierarchical, receptive to new inputs, and events become "scalable" from local to global phenomena. As we saw in the Egyptian case study and with other references to Arab countries and their uprisings, "Scale shifting has been defined as, a change in the number and level of coordinated contentious actions to a different focal point, involving a new range of actors, different objectives, and broadened claims. It can also generate a change in the meaning and scope of the object of the claim," (Tarrow, 2005, p. 121 cited in Linvingston & Asmolov 2010).

Thus, this explains why setting oneself on the journey does not mean you reach the destination. To borrow Alexandrian Poet Cavafy's metaphor for "Ithaca," this does not mean Ithaca will be paradise. The road to Tahrir did not end up in democratic heaven for Egyptians. Far from it. Mobilized they became. Converging on the Arena, they did. But consensus agreeing on subsequent steps did not materialize. The converged upon mobilization did not create newly agreed upon political structures. Rather, political institutional building did not take place. And substantive structural challenges to political institutions still exist today. Slow political processes have not ensued in political trust. And as the Muslim Brotherhood and the Military alternated their grip over power with an oscillation back and forth from a) religio-nationalism to b) secular militarism, "Al-Midan" or "The Square" that was a haven for societal harmony and acceptance is struggling to remain relevant or even alive, in the collective memory. This has proven to be even more difficult, especially in times of regional turmoil, international ideological clashes and worldwide negations of the Other, whoever it may be.

ACKNOWLEDGMENT

This research was supported by a grant from Microsoft Community Affairs to the Technology & Social Change Group (TASCHA) at the University of Washington's iSchool. A larger project on ICTs and collective action in Egypt was comprised of research team members Maria Garrido, Volodymyr Lysenko, Luis Fernando Baron, Marwa Maziad, and Norah Abokhodair.

REFERENCES

Abdel Fattah, E. (2011). Personal Communication.

Alaswany, A. (2010). Why Don't Egyptians Revolt?! In *Arabic Li mā dhā lā yathūr il-Miṣriyūn*. Cairo: Al Shuruk Publishing.

Anderson B. (2006). *Imagined Communities*.

Andión, M. (2013). Las redes sociales virtuales como medios alternativos al poder de la telecracia en México. *Revista Versión*, *31*, 114-139.

Barber, B. (1996). *Jihad vs. McWorld: How globalism and tribalism are reshaping the world*. New York, NY: Ballantine Books.

Baron, L. F., Abokhodair, N., & Garrido, M. (2013, May). Human and Political Grievances for Mobilization: Different roles of Facebook during the Egyptian Arab Spring. *Proceedings of the 12th International Conference on Social Implications of Computers in Developing Countries*, Montego Bay, Jamaica.

Bogad, L. M. (2005). Tactical carnival: Social movements, demonstrations, and dialogical performance. In J. Cohen-Cruz & M. Schutzman (Eds.), *A Boal companion* (pp. 46–58). New York, NY: Routledge.

Buechler, S. M. (2000). *Social movements in advanced capitalism: The political economy and cultural construction of social activism.* Oxford: Oxford University Press.

Castells, M. (2000). *The Rise of The Network Society: The Information Age: Economy, Society and Culture* (Vol. 1). Chichester, UK: Wiley.

Castells, M. (2009). *Communication Power.* Oxford, New York: Oxford University Press.

Castells, M. (2011). A Network Theory of Power. *International Journal of Communication, 5,* 773–787.

Castells, M. (2012). *Networks of outrage and hope – social movements in the Internet age.* Chichester, UK: Wiley.

Cohen, R. (2011, January 24). Facebook and Arab dignity. *New York Times.* Retrieved from www.nytimes.com/2011/01/25/opinion/25iht-edcohen25.html

David, R. (1996). The Pyramid Builders of Ancient Egypt: A modern investigation of Pharaoh's workforce (2nd ed.). London: Routledge.

della Porta, D., & Diani, M. (2006). Social Movements: An Introduction (2nd ed.). Wiley-Blackwell

Diamond, L., & Marc, F. Plattner. (2012). Liberation Technology: Social Media and the Struggle for Democracy. Johns Hopkins University Press.

Diamond, L., & Marc, F. Plattner (2014). Democratization and Authoritarianism in the Arab World. Johns Hopkins University Press.

Diamond, L., Plattner, M. F., & Costopoulos, P. J. (Eds.). (2010). *Debates on Democratization.* Baltimore, MD: Johns Hopkins University Press.

El-Hamalawy, H. (2009). Speech in a seminar about youth protest movements (YouTube video). http://www.youtube.com/watch?v=ZHMFPSicBCI

El Kholy, T. (2011). personal communication.

Fahmy, K. (February 17, 2012). Interview with Mahmoud Saad on Akher Alnahar TV Show (YouTube video). Retrieved from http://www.youtube.com/watch?v=RKNM4XFk-hU

Finnemore, M. (1996). *National Interests in International Society*. Ithaca, NY: CornellUniversity Press.

Fox, E. (1994). Communication media in Latin America. *Journal of Communication*, *44*(3), 4–8. doi:10.1111/j.1460-2466.1994.tb00695.x

Gomaa, M. (2010). Extracting the body of the Martyr of Emergency in Egypt. *Aljazeera.net*. Retrieved from http://www.aljazeera.net/humanrights/pages/a6fcf209-0e10-499e-ab4f-1c7454f5b05d

Granovetter, M. S. (1973). The strength of weak ties. *American Journal of Sociology*, *78*(6), 1360–1380. doi:10.1086/225469

Gutstein, D. (1999). *How the Internet undermines democracy*. Toronto, Canada: Sodart.

Hague, B., & Loader, B. (Eds.). (1999). *Digital democracy: Discourse and decision making in the information age*. London, England: Routledge.

Hamdy, N., & Gomaa, E. H. (2012). Framing the Egyptian Uprising in Arabic Language Newspapers and Social Media. *Journal of Communication*, *62*(2), 195–211. doi:10.1111/j.1460-2466.2012.01637.x

Haug, C. (2013). Organizing spaces: Meeting arenas as a social movement infrastructure between organization, network, and institution. *Organization Studies*, *34*(5-6), 705–732. doi:10.1177/0170840613479232

Howard, P., & Parks, M. (2012, April). Social Media and Political Change: Capacity, Constraint, and Consequence. *Journal of Communication*, *62*(2), 359–362. doi:10.1111/j.1460-2466.2012.01626.x

Howard, P. N. (2010). *The digital origins of dictatorship and democracy: Information technology and political Islam*. New York, NY: Oxford University Press. doi:10.1093/acprof:oso/9780199736416.001.0001

Howard, P. N., Duffy, A., Freelon, D., Hussain, M. M., Mari, W., & Maziad, M. *"Opening Closed Regimes: What Was the Role of Social Media During the Arab Spring?"* (2011). SSRN:10.2139/ssrn.2595096

Kamarck, E., & Nye, J. (1999). *Democracy.com? Governance in a networked world*. Hollis, NH: Hollis Publishing.

Khagram, S., Riker, J. V., & Sikkink, K. (2002). *Restructuring World Politics: transnational social movements, networks, and norms*. Minneapolis: University of Minnesota Press.

Khamis, S., & Vaughn, K. (2011). *Cyberactivism in the Egyptian revolution: How civic engagement and citizen journalism tilted the balance*. Arab Media and Society.

Latour, B. (2005). *Reassembling the Social: An Introduction to Actor-Network-Theory*. Oxford: Oxford UP.

Lim, M. (2004). Informational terrains of identity and political power: The Internet in Indonesia. *Antropologi Indonesia*, *27*(73), 1–11.

Lim, M. (2006). *Cyber-urban activism and political change in Indonesia*. Eastbound, 1(1), 1–19. Retrieved from http://eastbound.eu/site_media/pdf/060101LIM.pdf

Lim, M. (2012). Clicks, Cabs, and Coffee Houses: Social Media and Oppositional Movements in Egypt 20042001. *Journal of Communication*, *62*(2), 231–248. doi:10.1111/j.1460-2466.2012.01628.x

Livingston, S., & Asmolov, G. (2010). Networks and the future of foreign affairs reporting. *Journalism Studies*, *11*(5), 745-760. DOI:10.1080/1461670X.2010.503024

Locke, J. L. (1998). *The de-voicing of society: Why we don't talk to each other anymore*. New York, NY: Simon and Schuster.

Maher, A. (2012). Interview with author.

Mamdou, V. (2004). Internet, Scale and the Global Grassroots: Geographies of the indymmedia network of independent centers. *Tijschrift voor Economics en Social Geografie*, *95*(5), 48297.

Maziad, M. (2011a, January 17). The Egyptian Citizen; The Tunisian Citizen (in Arabic). *Almasry Alyoum Independent Newschapter*. Retrieved from http://www.almasryalyoum.com/node/297381

Maziad, M. (2011b, February 7). Anger and Hope (in Arabic). *Almasry Alyoum Independent Newschapter*. Retrieved from http://www.almasryalyoum.com/node/311401

Maziad, M. (2011c, February 11). Egypt: An idea whose time has come. *Aljazeera*. Retrieved from http://english.aljazeera.net/indepth/opinion/2011/02/20112714401412146.html

McAdam, D. (1986). Recruitment to high-risk activism: The case of Freedom, Summer. *American Journal of Sociology*, *92*(1), 64–90. doi:10.1086/228463

Mohamed, A. S. (2012). On the Road to Democracy: Egyptian Bloggers and the Internet. *Journal of Arab & Muslim Media Research*, *4*(2), 253–272. doi:10.1386/jammr.4.2-3.253_1

Moore, R. (1999). Democracy and cyberspace. In B. Hague & B. Loader (Eds.), *Digitaldemocracy: Discourse and decision making in the information age*. London, England: Routledge.

Abdel Nasser, Gehad. (2011). *The Silent Speak Up* (documentary). Aljazeera.

O'Brian, R., Goetz, A. M., Jan Aart, S. & Williams, M. (2000) Contesting Global Governance: multilateral economic institutions and global social movements, Cambridge: Cambridge University Press.

Oweidat, N., Benard, C., Stahl, D., Kildani, W., O'Connell, E., & Grant, A. K. (2008). *The Kefaya movement: A case study of a grassroots reform initiative*. Retrieved from http://www.rand.org/pubs/monographs/2008/RAND_MG778.pdf

Randeree, B. (2011, July 11). The Arab Spring. *Aljazeera*. Retrieved from http://english.aljazeera.net/indepth/features/2011/07/201177101959751184.html

Rich, F. (2011, February 5). Wallflowers at the revolution. *New York Times*. Retrieved from http://www.nytimes.com/2011/02/06/opinion/06rich.html

Risse, T., Ropp, S. C., & Sikkink, K. (1999). *The Power of Human Rights: international norms and domestic change*. Cambridge: Cambridge University Press. doi:10.1017/CBO9780511598777

Rosenau, J. (1997). *Along the Domestic Foreign Frontier: exploring governance in a turbulent world*. Cambridge: Cambridge University Press. doi:10.1017/CBO9780511549472

Rosenau, J. (1999). Toward an Ontology for Global Governance. In M. Hewson & J. Sinclair Timothy (Eds.), *Approaches to Global Governance Theory*. Albany: State University of New York.

Schattschneider, E. E. (1975). The Semisovereign People: A Realist's View of Democracy in America. Fort Worth, TX: Harcourt Brace Jovanovich College Publishers.

Shirky, C. (2008). *Here Comes Everybody: The Power of Organizing Without Organizations*. Penguin Press.

Siegel, D. A. (2009). Social Networks and Collective Action. *American Journal of Political Science*, *53*(1), 12238. doi:10.1111/j.1540-5907.2008.00361.x

Tarrow, S. (1998). *Power in movement: Social movement and contentious politics*. Cambridge, England: Cambridge University Press. doi:10.1017/CBO9780511813245

Tarrow, S. (2005). *The New Transnational Activism*. Cambridge: Cambridge University Press. doi:10.1017/CBO9780511791055

Tilly, C. (1984). Social Movements and National Politics. In C. Bright & S. F. Harding (Eds.), *Statemaking and social movements: essays in history and theory* (pp. 297–317). Ann Arbor: University of Michigan Press.

Tilly, C. (1995). *Popular Contention in Great Britain, 1758–1834*. Cambridge, MA: Harvard University Press.

Tilly, C. (2003). Social Movements. Enter the Twenty-first Century. *Paper presented at the conference on Contentious Politics and the Economic Opportunity Structure*.

Tilly, C. (2004). *Social Movements, 1768–2004* (p. 184). Boulder, Colorado, USA: Paradigm Publishers.

Tilly, C. (2005). *Identities*. Boundaries, and Social Ties.

Tilly, C. (2006). *Regimes and Repertoires*. University Of Chicago Press. doi:10.7208/chicago/9780226803531.001.0001

Tilly, C., & Tarrow, S. (2007). *Contentious Politics*. Colorado: Paradigm Publishers.

Van de Donk, W., Loader, B. D., Nixon, P. G., & Rucht, D. (2004). *Cyberprotest: New Media, Citizens, and Social Movements*. Routledge.

van Stekelenburg, J., & Klandermans, P. G. (2007). Individuals in movements: A social psychology of contention. In P. G. Klandermans & C. M. Roggeband (Eds.), *The Handbook of Social Movements Across Disciplines* (pp. 157–204). New York: Springer.

Webster, S. (2011, February 16). Has social media revolutionized revolutions? *World News*, *87*(15). Retrieved from http://www.jcunews.com/2011/02/16/has-social-media- revolutionized-revolutions/

Wilhelm, A. G. (1998). Virtual sounding boards: How deliberative is on-line political discussion. *Information Communication and Society*, *1*(3), 313–338. doi:10.1080/13691189809358972

Wright, S. C. (2001). Strategic collective action: Social psychology and social change. In R. Brown & S. Gaertner (Eds.), Blackwell handbook of social psychology (Vol. 4, pp. 409–430). Oxford, England: Blackwell Press.

York, J. (2011, January 14). Not Twitter, Not WikiLeaks: A human revolution [blog post]. Retrieved from http://jilliancyork.com/2011/01/14/not-twitter-not-wikileaks-a-human-revolution/

ENDNOTES

1   We adopt Howard and Parks definition of Social Media to be as follows: Social media consists of (a) the information infrastructure and tools used to produce and distribute content that has individual value but reflects shared values; (b) the content that takes the digital form of personal messages, news, ideas, that becomes cultural products; and (c) the people, organizations, and industries that produce and consume both the tools and the content.

2   If Erdoğan makes the constitutional changes he is aiming for, changing the political system into a presidential one and does get reelected for a second term, till 2024, he will have already reached the same number of years of Ben Ali. Perhaps then, the conditions would be different for a "Generational Collective" to apply.

3   All fieldwork participant-observations and interviewing were conducted by author Marwa Maziad

4   Link to the Facebook tool enabling to download bulk posts for offline use. http://groupbrowser.azurewebsites.net/

5   After co-founding the April 6th Facebook Group calling for a General Strike, Esraa was arrested and further detained by Minister of Interior's orders until April 23rd. She never formally joined the A6YM.

6   That was the description given by the admin in response to a Tunisian inquiring on January 19th 2011 what "April 6th was all about". https://www.facebook.com/photo.php?v=490566825677

7   From "Personal Information" and "About" entries on the Page https://www.facebook.com/ElShaheeed/info

8   Emergency Law had been continuously enacted under Mubarak, since the assassination of former President Sadat in 1981. Egypt is not currently governed under Emergency Laws or a State of Emergency. There are strong yet specific anti-terrorism laws, which can be critiqued for their severity, but they match the global anxiety against pervasive terrorists attacks, and are not the generalized "state of emergency," that was perpetually renewed by Parliament during the Mubarak era.

9   A comparison here is to the uproar against Beyoncé's song where she depicted American police brutality against black teenager Michael Brown. Black Lives Matter became a movement that ensued. Yet, Republican Congressman Pete King issued a lengthy 5-paragraph statement criticizing Beyonce's video. He argued, "This fable of an innocent people with their hands raised high above their heads in surrender. This fable of an innocent Michael Brown being murdered by police while attempting to surrender, which dominated the airwaves for months in 2014, has been thoroughly discredited. In simple language, it was

and is a lie from beginning to end." Quote cited in Campbell, Colin. (Feb. 8, 2016) GOP congressman releases lengthy, 5-paragraph statement denouncing Beyonce's new video. *Business Insider* www.businessinsider.com/pete-king-beyonce-formation-video-super-bowl-2016-2

[10] Blogger and journalist Ahmad Naje quoted to comment on class dynamics vis-à-vis Khaled Said's character in Gehad Abdel Nasser's Aljazeera-produced documentary: Alsametun Yatakalamun, The Silent Speak Up. Ahmed Naje is currently in prison regarding a sexually graphic novel that he wrote and whose chapters were published in Al Akhabar Al Adab, literary state-owned newspaper. He and the editor-in-chief were sued by a reader regarding the graphic nature of the novel.

[11] Interview with April 6th member.

[12] Sociologist Saad Eldin Ibrahim was the first to raise this issue publicly in a newschapter interview. He was later imprisoned on charges of fraud regarding operations of Ibn Khaldun Research Center. He argues that the charges were politically motivated due to his public discussion of presidential "inheritance" from Hosni Mubarak to his son Gamal.

[13] "Kefaya" means "Enough" and is also known as the Egyptian Movement for Change.

[14] It is important to state here that there was a rift within the April 6th Movement. Ahmed Maher had his "Maher Front" arguing that they were the core of the movement. And Tarek El Khouly started the "Democratic Front" arguing for elections within the movement to elect the new leader of the group. Maher eventually perceived El Khouly as a state agent aiming to break the movement from within. Maher was eventually jailed following the arrests after former President Morsi's ousting in 2013, and was recently released in January 2017. El Khouly is currently a Parliament Member.

[15] Personal communication with NAC IT Coordinator, conducted by author 2012.

[16] Ibid.

[17] Exchange cited in Wollman, 2011.

[18] With the struggle between the old guard of Mubarak's National Democratic Party and the new guard of the party over its leadership, Gamal Mubarak's cohort and friends, especially Ahmed Ezz, advanced. Ezz was eventually the one ultimately in the heat of criticism of such blatant elections rigging.

[19] Ibid.

[20] We learn later that Sarah is actually Wael Ghonim's American wife. But Sarah being a common Egyptian name, there were no questions raised about her identity, nationality, or family affiliation. She could have very well been an average Egyptian Sarah helping the website out.

21   Abdel Nasser, 2011. *"The Silent Speak,"* Quote of Dr. Khaled El Ghamry Professor of Linguistics.

22   Interview in Tunisia, by author Marwa Maziad with Hende Chenaoui Tunisian journalist and blogger, October 2011

23   Interview with Tarek El-Kholy of A6YM (Democratic Front), October 2011.

24   Abdel Nasser, 2011. *The Silent Speak up.* Quote of Dr. Khaled El Ghamry Professor of Linguistics.

25   Interview with April 6 member.

Chapter 2

Social Media Users Collectively Speak Up:
Evidence From Central Asian Kyrgyz Republic

Bahtiyar Kurambayev
Independent Researcher, Kyrgyzstan

ABSTRACT

An analysis of online community activities in the former Soviet Union Kyrgyz Republic shows that social media can facilitate an effective organization and expression of ideas in a constrained media system. Specifically, online users were able to collectively and successfully speak their minds when the country's lawmakers planned costly projects, ultimately causing these plans to be dropped. Also social media users facilitated spreading information about the abuses of power and government incompetence in the 2010 and in 2005 revolutions, causing presidents flee the country in both cases. These findings suggest that the internet can facilitate a broad and effective civic and political engagement. The implications of these findings in this media restricted context are discussed in relation to collective action theory.

INTRODUCTION

The purpose of this chapter is to examine the wider implications of the internet and other new communication technologies in the former Soviet Union Kyrgyz Republic (sometimes known as Kyrgyzstan). Specifically, this chapter addresses how online communities utilize these technologies in pursuit of their collective

DOI: 10.4018/978-1-5225-2495-3.ch002

goals, including revealing and opposing government incompetence and/or abuses of power (Calingaert, 2010). Overall, a great deal of research already exists about the power that online communities wield by using social media tools and the internet particularly in non-democratic countries. Studies have been published, for example, about uprisings after 2009 elections in Iran (Wojcieszak & Smith, 2014), massive political protests in Egypt (Tufekci & Wilson, 2012), the online justice movement in Guatemala (Harlow, 2012), protest mobilization in Tunisia (Breuer, Landman & Farguhar, 2014), awareness of electoral fraud in parliamentary elections in Russia (Reuter & Szaknyi, 2015) and similar examples in many other locations. A plethora of research suggests that people use the internet to engage civically and politically (Nash, 2013, Margaretts, 2013; Boulianne, 2009; L. Hoffman, Jones, & Young, 2013). This chapter extends and supports prior research by analyzing how online communities have used social media and the internet to generate public engagement and political action in the context of the semi-authoritarian republic of Kyrgyzstan.

The significance of the internet can be noted by the fact that some repressive and authoritarian state leaders who had been in power for many years or even decades were removed by force with the help of new communication technologies. People in countries headed by these repressive leaders were able to bypass official restrictions and still organize opposition (Cottle, 2011). Paris-based Reporters without Borders, a non-governmental organization dedicated to freedom of expression and information around the world, lists some of the above mentioned countries in its "Enemy of the Internet" list. This list identifies countries for their "disruption of freedom of information with propaganda, surveillance and censorship." Cottle noted that the striking factor about the massive waves of uprisings and mass protests held during the "Arab Spring" was the use of the internet to get their messages rendered, especially on social media platforms, such as Twitter, Facebook, YouTube, and blogs.

Yet, some argue that the internet can play a negative role for democratization. Morozov, for example, maintains that the internet makes it easier for dictators to control information and restrict it by sophisticated filtering and monitoring software. It also makes it easier for dictators to gather information about dissents. According to Morozov, "the present excitement about the internet and its potential role in opening up closed society is wrong because such interpretation is based on 'selective and, at times, incorrect readings of history'" (Morozov, 2012, p. xi). Furthermore, repressive governments can use both legal and technological tools to maintain control over communications and conversations on the internet and via mobile phones (Bowe, Freedman, & Blom, 2012; Calingaert, 2010). To support his argument, Morozov (2012) discussed the case of Iranian protests against presidential election result in 2009 when the "Iranian police began hunting the internet for photos and videos that showed faces of the protestors- numerous, thanks to the ubiquity of social media" (p.11). Morozov noted that police then sought public help in identifying those faces by publishing via state news outlets including television. He noted that the Iranian police were able to arrest several dozen people. He also said that "compromising the security of just one digital activist can mean compromising the security-names, faces, and email addresses-of everyone that individual knows" (p. 21).

Despite the plethora of literature about the power of online communities, little knowledge is available about Kyrgyzstan, a small country of six million people located in an authoritarian and repressive region of Central Asia that borders Russia and China. This can be explained by the fact that the internet is relatively new to the region of Central Asia. Only third of Kyrgyzstan's population uses the internet and the percentage is even lower in neighboring countries such as Kazakhstan, Tajikistan, or Uzbekistan. This is a region, according to Eric Freedman and Richard Shafer (2012), that scholars have barely touched from an academic perspective. "There is no shortage of potential research topics pertaining to the press, journalism and mass communication in the region, given globalization and the rapid changes in communications technologies, such efforts would be particularly timely" (p. 124).

The objective of this chapter is to examine the role of social media in organizing some successful protests online to demand an action from government and from others in the context of repressive Kyrgyzstan. Specifically, this chapter will address the role of social media and online communities in coordinating and mobilizing protests in 2005 and in 2010, which in both cases forced presidents to seek asylum elsewhere. This demonstrates the potential power of online communities expressing themselves in a constrained media system. This chapter also outlines a few other smaller in scale instances when Kyrgyz internet users succeeded in expressing their collective voice about social and other matters.

THEORETICAL FRAMEWORK

The theory of collective action provides support for this study because of its explanatory power in understanding contemporary social movements. Developed first by Mancur Olson in 1965 and later expanded by other scholars, the theory examines the extent to which individuals share organizational costs in pursuit of similar interests. The theory proposes that individuals are able to participate in wider civil society and democratic processes via social media "to an extent never before possible" (Nash, 2013, p. 446) because people collectively are able to accomplish more than they could acting individually. People can band together in groups online, and when they form groups, when they connect, they become powerful, both politically and economically (Barlow, 2008). The internet increases the potential and lowers the costs of obtaining information and of organizing and contributing to collective action (Bimber, 2003; Castells, 2000, 2007; Margetts, 2013). As Castells (2007) noted, social movements are not originated by technology but rather by people who use it. This theory has been widely applied to organizational analysis of various uprisings facilitated by social media around the world including against global economic crisis (Bennett & Segerberg, 2011), climate change protests (Segerberg & Bennett, 2011), mass student mobilization in Italy in 2008 (Trere, 2008), and mass protests against repressive regimes in many countries in Arab world (Cottle, 2011). Therefore, this theory is best applicable to the analysis of Kyrgyzstan as well where internet users were able to collectively speak against their own government incompetence and abuses of power.

BACKGROUND

It is important to understand the wider context of Kyrgyzstan. It was one of the 12 countries that made up Soviet Union for almost 70 years and it gained its independence in 1991. The population of Kyrgyzstan is slightly more than six million people (Kabar.kg, 2016) while 1.5 million citizens of Kyrgyzstan work in Russia as migrant workers (IRIN News, 2015) because of the poor economy in the country. Its official languages are Kyrgyz and Russian. It is listed among the lower-middle income countries in Asia (World Bank, 2015). Overall, Kyrgyzstan is one of the poorest countries (Index of Economic Freedom, 2016) and political unrests, instability and widespread corruption have hurt the already weak economy. It is so weak that it relies on foreign aids and grants to function. Parliament members drafted a law in April of 2016 to formally acknowledge that the country is in urgent need of humanitarian aid (Bengard, 2016). The judiciary system is subject to corruption, says the recent 2016 report by the Department of State of the United States about human rights. The report noted that the outcomes of some trials were predetermined and that judges paid bribes to attain their positions. Just at the time of writing this chapter, news reports said that the head of the investigative department of the Kyrgyzstan's Prosecutor's Office, Kylychbek Arpachiev, was sentenced for 14 years in prison for receiving $100,000 bribe (Organized Crime and Corruption Reporting Project, June 30, 2016). Six prime ministers resigned within the last six years in the country. The country faced the deadliest inter-ethnic clashes in its history with hundreds of people dead and almost half a million displaced as a result of violence in its southern Osh city. Given this context, Kyrgyzstan adopted a new constitution after a revolution in April 2010. The new constitution does not allow the same person to be president more than one term of five years.

Changes in Regime

Upon Kyrgyzstan's independence, this Central Asian country gained a reputation as an "island of democracy" (Anderson, 1999) because the first president, Askar Akayev, changed the country's constitution to meet international standards, promised civil and political rights and allowed some limited media freedom. "Western commentators hailed him as a bright hope for democracy in Central Asia" (BBC, April 4, 2005). However, as time passed, Akayev monopolized power, enriched his family and suppressed opposition (Hiro, 2009; Radnitz, 2010). "Independent journalism became hazardous as the Akayev government began to harass those who investigated and reported corruption and nepotism at high places, and prosecuted them under the criminal charge of insulting the president" (Hiro, 2009, p. 297). Akayev justified increasing his power by saying he had no more power than the Queen of England (Anderson, 1999). Akayev's repeated manipulation of the country's constitution (Cummings, 2008), pessimism about his governance, accusations of suppressing the opposition and media, and widespread poverty and corruption throughout the country led up to 20,000 protestors to assemble in the central square of Bishkek capital city on March 24, 2005, to demand his resignation (Hiro, 2009; Kulikova & Perlmutter, 2007) in what was termed the "Tulip Revolution." Akayev had to flee the country with his family and seek political asylum in Russia. He later accused the Bush administration for bringing him down from power because of his pro-Russia stance (Hiro, 2009).

After the 2005 revolution, the opposition declared Kurmanbek Bakiyev as interim president. He promised to eradicate corruption and conduct constitutional reform if he would be elected. He was elected with 89 percent of the vote, but forgot his promises made during the election campaigns (Hiro, 2009). Five years later, in 2010, he also was kicked out of power by popular uprisings because of a deteriorating socio-economic situation (Melvin & Umaraliev, 2011) "exemplified by ongoing poverty, rising unemployment, [and] skyrocketing utility prices" (p. 6). He fled to Belarus, where he resides under political asylum. In Kyrgyzstan, a local court sentenced him in absentia to 24 years in jail for abuse of power.

The current constitution adopted in 2010 allows absolutely freedom of expression and freedom of the press. Exercising this constitutional right, however, still remains largely restricted to Kyrgyz people because mass media outlets in the country belong to the government, private businesses, or politicians.

Traditional Media

Overall, Kyrgyzstan has approximately 160 print outlets including seven major newspapers, three of which are daily. Other media include 26 radio stations, 25 TV stations, 3 local cable networks (IREX, 2016). Online news outlets are growing but it is difficult to know exact numbers. There are seven news agencies including one state news agency, five privates and one affiliated with Russian government. The newspapers are published in various languages, including Uzbek, Russian, English, and even Chinese. One Dostuk radio on OTRK is broadcast in Uighur, Dunghan, Tatar, Polish and Ukrainian languages (IREX, 2016). Public television channel OTRK has since September of 2016 begun broadcasting movies in English language with no translation in order to promote English language in the country (Kloop, 2016).

Media Suppression

Mass media outlets in Kyrgyzstan and wider Central Asia remain "bastions of official and extra-legal censorship, self-censorship, constraints on journalists and news organization, and insufficient financial resources to support independent, and sustainable, market-based press systems" (Bowe, Freedman & Blom, 2012, p. 145). Despite the country's repression of independent journalism, Kyrgyzstan has been rated above average in the region in terms of media sustainability measured by free speech, professional journalism, plurality of news sources, business management, and supporting institutions (IREX, 2016). Specifically, Kyrgyzstan has been listed among the countries of "near sustainable" while Kazakhstan, Tajikistan are ranked among the countries of "unsustainable mixed system" while Turkmenistan and Uzbekistan are among the unsustainable/anti-press systems countries. A few private or foreign funded news outlets exist, such as the Institute on War and Peace Reporting (IWPR), Agence France-Press (AFP), Radio Free Europe/Radio Liberty (RFE/RL) and the British Broadcasting Corporations (BBC), but their journalists have to be considerate of the local context to function as journalists. In other words, they have to avoid overly critical and controversial issues to be safe and sound. This is because the overall media environment remains oppressive (McGlinchey & Johnson, 2007). Independent journalists are harassed, threatened, violently attacked, prosecuted and even imprisoned (International Research and Exchanges Board, 2013; Freedman, 2012; Freedman & Shafer, 2012; Kurambayev, 2016; Pitts, 2011). Toralieva (2014) states the environment for journalists in this country are "fearful." Some independent journalists, Toralieva notes, had to flee to elsewhere and/or seek asylum in foreign countries. Under such a restrictive environment, Kulikova and Perlmutter (2007) conclude that the internet is the only avenue for any independent voices to be heard or read in the country. In terms of the wider internet, it has become an increasingly difficult to ignore the wider freedom (or lack of it) of speech and of expression in Kyrgyzstan when analyzing the role of social media in promoting social changes. Williams (2015) also noted that online activity of internet users in Kyrgyzstan may increase the likelihood of their offline activities being observed.

Authoritarian Control Over the Internet

Authoritarian rulers understand the potential impact of the internet to wider society, including its potential to effect political change. This is why many countries heavily regulate the internet in countries like Russia, North Korea, and Myanmar. While certain countries utilize the internet for economic growth only (Calinger, 2010), others utilize this new media for dissent surveillance. For example, in Azerbaijan, activists were imprisoned for their social media posts and the government actively attempts to dissuade internet users from getting involved in politics via social media (Pearce & Kendzior, 2012). Another former Soviet Union country, Tajikistan, regularly blocks most popular social media sites including Youtube, Odnoklasniki, and all Google services including Gmail (Shafiev & Miles, 2015). Tajikistan also asserts pressure on internet users critical of the government (Transitions Online, 2013). Internet freedom in neighboring Kazakhstan has been worsening as well, with the government imprisoning activists and regular internet users for their critical comments on social media (Freedom House, 2015; Savchenko, 2016). In their study of Chinese control over the internet, King, Pan and Roberts (2013) noted that each individual site privately may employ up to 1,000 censors to comply with the government requirements on censorship. These scholars argue that the purpose of the state censorship policies is not necessarily to suppress criticism but rather to prevent collective actions associated with such criticism. Further support comes from the report of an international media organization, Internews, which in 2013 reported that China has more internet monitors than soldiers.

Internet Use in Kyrgyzstan

Overall, 28% of Kyrgyz population has access to the internet (Freedom House, 2015; Srinivasan and Fish, 2009), but the number apparently is increasing due to the wider availability of public access points. For example, some public transportation services offer free Wi-Fi connections and the Prime Minister of Kyrgyzstan Temir Sariyev[1] asserted that all schools in the country would be connected to the internet by the end of 2016 (Azattyk, 2016). Some internet cafes have world-class equipment (DeYoung, 2010). And, a special internet club provides internet access for people with disabilities (Gazeta.kg, October 22, 2015). Srinivasan and Fish (2009) noted that 8 out of 10 internet users are younger than 35 years old. Internet access can be problematic outside of major cities, but it is much better in Bishkek, the capital city (IREX, 2016). Thus, the majority of internet users are based in Bishkek (Warf, 2013).

No restrictions exist in Kyrgyzstan for anonymous internet communication (Freedom House, 2015). However, official government policy requires that every cell phone number be registered with its mobile operator, providing its user's personal information, including date of birth, residence, passport number, etc. This makes it difficult for anyone to connect to the internet anonymously. Nevertheless, it is still possible for people to buy cell phone numbers and access to the internet without providing personal information.

Even though Kyrgyzstan's internet has been described as partly free, recent incidents suggest that Kyrgyz government has been trying to increase control over what people do and say online. For example, Kyrgyz lawmaker Ekmat Baibakbaev suggested on March 9, 2016, that Kyrgyzstan internet users be restricted from accessing foreign websites (Tynaeva, 2016). Later in 2016, Aibek Isaev, head of the department of Education, Culture and Sport of Kyrgyz government Office, said that social media users in Kyrgyzstan make fun of Kyrgyz officials. He instructed the information department of the Ministry of Culture to undertake comprehensive measures to correct this situation (Akipress, July 27, 2016). On October 4, 2016, Kyrgyz lawmaker Dastan Bekeshev suggested that Kyrgyz officials be banned from accessing social media sites during work hours (Kostenko, 2016). Kyrgyz lawmaker Irina Karamushkina said on October 18, 2016, that internet users often criticize the President Almazbek Atambayev. She said that insulting the president equals insulting the nation and suggested that the ministry of national security should protect the president. During the same meeting, deputy chief of the national security Rustam Mamasadykov said that such internet users critical of the president are being identified (Mamytova, 2016). Farther support comes from Privacy International, which reported in 2014 that that the Kyrgyzstan government purchased sophisticated western technology to spy on the entire country's internet communications (Radio Free Europe/Radio Liberty, November 24, 2014). The technology, the report noted, allows any government agency to monitor and access to citizens' internet activity on a mass, indiscriminate scale. Other examples are discussed below.

On January 6, 2016, a British mine worker identified as Michael McFeat was arrested for his social media post. McFeat had worked for Kumtor, a Canadian gold mine company operating in Kyrgyzstan. On December 31, 2015, he created a Facebook post comparing local equine delicacy to a sexual organ (The Guardian, January 3, 2016). He was then deported from the country. Earlier that year, on September 10, 2015, 20-year-old Kyrgyz resident Abdulla Nurmatov was detained for 48 hours and his apartment was searched for more than three hours by Kyrgyz National Security officers for his clicking the "like" button on the popular Russian odnoklassniki social network (Ferghana.ru, September 10, 2015). Freedom House's report of 2015 said a Kyrgyz blogger was "charged with inciting national hatred" (Committee to Protect Journalists, February 29, 2012) based on his blog posts on several websites. The report from Committee to Protect Journalists said that Vladimir Farafonov criticized the Kyrgyz politics. The prosecution sought a sentence of eight years in jail, however, the judge ended up levying a fine of KGS 50,000, roughly equivalent to $800 US. In another well-known case, Azimjon Askarov. a contributor to the online based publication "*Voice of Freedom*," is currently serving life sentence after a local court found him "guilty for involvement in the murder of a police officer during 2010 clashes" (RFE/RL, 2015). But, it is widely believed that his case was politically motivated.

These above-mentioned instances demonstrate that internet "behavior" is monitored by the country's special security services. It can be explained by the fact that in 2012, the United States Agency for International Development (USAID) sponsored training for the Kyrgyz prosecutor's office on how to use and monitor social media sites as part of their jobs. The same year, the Kyrgyz State Committee for National Security set up a system to monitor the internet (IWPR, 2012). Additionally, the Ministry of Internal Affairs of Kyrgyzstan asks all social media users for help to monitor the social network sites to identify "religious extremists" (Zanoza.kg, December 22, 2015). "The Internet presents potential perils for activists and ordinary citizens living under authoritarian regimes. Oppressive governments have recently demonstrated how capable they are at using the Internet to suppress dissent and for surveillance" (Ibold, 2010, p. 524). The Kyrgyzstan government reportedly has a trolling unit as part of the presidential administration as well. The main goal of these trolls is to expose social media users in Kyrgyzstan with "correct" ideology. In other words, social media websites are used for manipulating public opinion. According to a piece posted on the citizen journalism Kloop.kg website on October 2, 2015, these trolls are instructed every day by their coordinator to spread "the right" opinions about a variety of political issues, be they global issues or domestic matters. These pro-government trolls can get paid from $200 up to $800 per month (Freedom House, 2015).

The focus of this chapter is to analyze how Kyrgyz activists and other internet users were able to use social media to organize some successful protests online to demand an action or two despite their own government's attempt to block all channels of information. Several major cases are discussed below.

SOCIAL MEDIA AS AGENTS OF POLITICAL CHANGE: THE 2005 TULIP REVOLUTION

The 'Tulip' Revolution[2] marked the first ouster of a president in Central Asia in which the internet played an instrumental role (McGlinchey & Johnson, 2007; Kulikova & Perlmutter, 2007; Warf, 2012). It began when opposition parties, claiming illegal voter manipulation, demanded the invalidation of the parliamentary election held in February 2005 and the resignation of the president. Radnitz (2012) noted that election manipulation included paying cash to buy votes and/or distributing clothing and baskets of food to needy families as well as alcohol drinks to local elders who "whose ability to influence other voters was disproportionately large" (p. 134). Protests began in the capital and quickly spread to other major cities. The government responded by attempting to block all news outlets. "Most of the domestic media were in a difficult position when reporting about the events, as no one knew whether the president was still in the country" (Kulikova & Perlmutter, 2007, p. 30). State media was confused as to who was in charge in the country and media outlets produced unreliable accounts, leading people to search for alternative sources of information on the internet (Kulikova and Perlmutter, 2007). The advocacy blog www.akaevu. net and other bloggers delivered information to people during this time of uncertainty, keeping people informed about what was happening despite the low internet penetration at the time. The blogs invited readers to engage with questions, answers and comments. Some bloggers apparently had direct access to Akayev's opponents, so they were able to report fresh stories. The major news outlets cited Akaevu.net's stories when reporting about happenings in the country (Kulikova & Perlmutter, 2007).

The Tulip Revolution of 2005 contributed to the development of new media in the country (Melvin & Umaraliev, 2011) because international organizations such as the United Nations (UN), Organization for Security and Cooperation in Europe (OSCE), Open Society Institute, Internews Network, the United States Agency for International Development (USAID) and other organizations "supplied the Kyrgyz government with the software and extensive computer and network equipment" (McGlinchey & Johnson, 2007, p. 278). They had been doing so even before the revolution of 2005. In their article, McGlinchey and Johnson (2007) note that the international community insisted that the Kyrgyz government maintain a deregulated environment for the internet. A specific example of the external contribution to the development of the internet in this Central Asian country might be that of Netherland based Hivos. Hivos funded the Kloop Media Foundation, a non-governmental organization based in Bishkek, to establish a local blogging platform (Wilkinson & Jetpyspayeva, 2012). The Kloop media foundation provided a blogging platform for locals and trained those who lacked computer and blogging skills for free of charge. The foundation targeted mostly young people. These days, Kloop Media Foundation continues to teach not only blogging but also multimedia and investigative journalism skills. "Kyrgyzstan's Tulip Revolution was hailed by many as a promising triumph of democracy" (Pannier, August 25, 2009) that succeeded with the help of the internet.

THE SECOND PEOPLE'S REVOLUTION, 2010

The second revolution occurred in April 2010 for reasons similar to the first, including wide-scale corruption, growing living expenses, and a deteriorating economy. As a result of this revolution, a president of Kyrgyzstan had to seek refuge in a foreign country for the second time in five years. Just two months before the revolution, the Kyrgyz government had decided to significantly increase utilities tariffs. For example, heating costs were increased 400%.

Social media were highly used during this political instability in 2010 because several funded projects on developing citizen journalism and new media were already underway. For example, the Open Society Institute and Transitions Online funded several blogging, discussion forums, and video hosting sites. Protests began on March 10, 2010, then spread more widely across the nation. These nationwide protests became violent and President Bakiyev imposed a state of emergency (Melvin & Umaraliev, 2011).

Twitter users were "reporting about the protests and used the hashtag #freekg to disseminate information on the demonstrations" (Melvin & Umaraliev, 2011, p. 6) while traditional media were silent about the protests as they were under the control of then president Bakiyev and his associates. The hashtag gained popularity and it became a source of information to wider audience in the country and for those who were elsewhere (Melvin and Umaraliev, 2011). "Reporters suffered violent attacks, newspapers were suspended, broadcasters were pressured to drop critical programming, and access to online news websites were blocked" (Djanbaev, 2011, para. 1). The government sought to block information about the protests but internet users circulated news via social media platforms. Social networks and online forums became key places to get information about anti-Bakiyev protests happening in the country (Melvin and Umaraliev, 2011). Bakiyev's government reportedly warned the locally popular social media site, Diesel.kg, that it needed to stay away from circulating anything that might go against the Bakiyev ruling. Diesel.kg subsequently deleted discussions about the topic (Melvin & Umaraliev, 2011, p. 6). With the support of Open Society Institute in Kyrgyzstan, the Civil Initiative on Internet Policy discussed with Twitter executives a plan to aggregate tweets about Kyrgyzstan and make the service cheaper for users there (Djanbaev, 2011, para. 6). As a result, Kyrgyzstan became the first country in the former Soviet Union to allow mobile phone users to send tweets at a reduced cost. The decision apparently migrated to other online platforms, such as blogs and even private Skype chats. Blogging project Eurasia. net, Kloop Media (kloop.kg), and Diesel Forum (diesel.kg) cumulatively had a great impact on Kyrgyzstan internet users (Melvin & Umaraliev, 2011).

KYRGYZ PARLIAMENT DROPS ITS ORDER

In 2015, internet users inundated social media platforms with their disapproval and angry comments when Kyrgyzstan's parliament announced that that it had ordered 120 new chairs at a cost of 2.6 million soms, or over US$ 38,000 (BBC, October 14, 2015) during the time when government officials consistently stated of the need to cut the government spending and optimize its budget. The BBC reported that each planned chair would cost $310 a piece. It is important to understand the context that Kyrgyzstan is one of the poorest countries in the former Soviet Union. The World Bank reports that every third resident of the country lives below the poverty line (World Bank, 2013), while it is possible that the actual number might be higher. It is especially important to note that Kyrgyzstan heavily depends on trade with Russia, which was experiencing a marked recession (Asian Development Bank, 2016) because of a significant drop in oil prices and the imposition of Western sanctions. Almost two million of Kyrgyzstan's citizens, one third of the entire working population in Russia, are migrant workers and their remittances are thought to be 30 percent of Kyrgyzstan's budget every year. So, this news of planned expensive purchase led hundreds or even thousands of internet users to share photos of their own worn out or half broken armchairs and office chairs under the #hashtags and #120armchairs. Some internet users commented saying "let us give chairs to PM, many of you might have one in a shed or garage" (BBC, October 24, 2015). Instead, the internet users suggested that the cash should be allocated to cancer treatment centers of the country to buy new equipment. After the massive online protests, the parliament cancelled the public tender and abandoned the initial plan. This is another example showing how online communities can influence lawmakers' decision making.

On December 12, 2015, the Kyrgyz Ministry of Finance announced of its plan to purchase two electronic tablets for 228,000 soms (approximately $1,500 USD) each and unspecified leather office chairs for $3,744 USD out of state budget (Ibragimov, 2016). The Ministry said that the officials should have easy access remotely to relevant information and that is why there was a need to purchase tablets. After massive online criticism by activists, journalists and ordinary internet users, the plan was abandoned as well. Radio Free Europe/Radio Liberty reported that a government investigation had been opened regarding the "unusually costly" tablet (Azattyk, December 18, 2015). No updates were available about the outcome of government investigation about whether this plan had corruption elements. Social media users commented harshly about the plan saying "government officials should get back to reality and live with current financial conditions. Do they even know that the external debt of Kyrgyzstan is almost several billion dollars?" asked social media users.

Under pressure from the public, Kyrgyzstan's Manas International Airport cancelled its planned 2015 New Year's $20,000 USD priced party for the agency. The timing of the announcement of the plan occurred when the public was discussing another airport plan to charge $15 per passenger to pay off the airport renovation and maintenance debt. As a result of this public criticism, most other state and private companies cancelled their planned lucrative New Year celebration events.

On February 24, 2016, the Russian TV channel "Russia" aired a documentary titled "Kyrgyzstan is the training field for ISIL fighters" (Кыргызстан «кузницей кадров для ИГИЛ). The TV documentary discussed the recruitment of Kyrgyz citizens for ISIS and specifically noted that Kyrgyzstan had become a source of manpower for ISIS and recruited terrorists to enter into Russia (Kloop, 2016). Social media users of Kyrgyzstan protested particularly the headline with comments saying that Russians are fighting in Syria and elsewhere as part of ISIS and that this documentary was provocative. One user identified as Alina on her Facebook page commented, "This is not politically correct to blame Kyrgyzstan and that it is the training field for terrorists. Terrorists with Russian passports are also there fighting along with ISIS." Another Facebook user identified as Temirlan asked, "Do you have any facts that terrorists from Kyrgyzstan are entering Russia. Why do you write such provocative story?" Just alone at the diesel.kg forum website, several hundred users participated in the discussion about the headline and content. Similar levels of participation in other popular social media sites were included on the official Facebook page of the Russian news outlet. But, it is difficult to estimate the amount of social media engagement in this regard. At least one activist, Burul Makenbaeva, filed a complaint about Russian news outlets to local to the local Kyrgyz "Commission for Media Complaints" (24.kg, February 25, 2016) on behalf of a local non-governmental organization "Mental Health and Society." As a result of this social media protest, the Russian TV channel website changed the headline of its documentary the following day. The headline became "How ISIS recruits terrorists: Special Report."

SOLUTIONS AND RECOMMENDATIONS

Whether the internet and wider social media tools have a positive relationship with self-expression in a media restrictive context has been controversial and much disputed within multiple disciplines. Some scholars argue that the internet has a potential to build communities and strengthen connections and advance democracy (Dijck, 2013; Gil de Zúñiga, Jung, & Valenzuela, 2012). Others assert that online communities hinder democratic debate because members of any online community have common perspectives and tend to push their own point of view while disregarding the opposing points of view (Dahlgren, 2005; Kaye, Johnson, & Muhlberge., 2012; Sunstein, 2007; Xenos, 2008). Yet, examples in this chapter about the former Soviet Union Kyrgyz Republic have suggested that the internet can provide an opportunity for collective self-expression and organization against some government policies even when all traditional media outlets are under governmental control. Although previous literature concluded that "the ability of social media to promote political opposition and organization in Central Asia remains largely speculative to date," (Bowe, Freedman, & Blom, 2012, p. 151) the Kyrgyz experience illustrates that such pessimism is not always warranted.

It is possible that the state leaders of Kyrgyzstan have been strengthening their positions in controlling what people do and say on internet platforms. In this context, the Kyrgyz government should take certain steps if it wants Kyrgyzstan to become a community-involved environment where voices of peoples are heard. For example, the Kyrgyz government could continue promoting a deregulated internet that would become a model of excellence for other countries in the region of Central Asia. Furthermore, opening up free wifi spots in major cities would be an important initiative at the state level to support internet penetration. Although it is important to acknowledge that giving people the internet with little or no regulations does not necessarily lead to democracy (McGlinchey & Johnson, 2007; Brundidge & Rice, 2009), it is necessary condition. Kyrgyzstan should not monitor social media users with the intention to manipulate the public by spreading carefully planned set of opinions and ideas via social media. In particular, the Kyrgyz government should seriously consider shutting down its "trolling unit" which is believed to exist for the purpose of influencing public opinion to serve the government officials rather than public interests.

Kyrgyz authorities could also utilize internet opportunities both for economic growth and for further democratization by "listening" to their own citizens' concerns and questions online. If they hope to achieve this objective, it is important that internet users not be imprisoned or punished for their expression of opinions. The Kyrgyzstan parliament should not legally block independent news websites, such as the well-read independent news website, ferghana.ru, for offering alternative viewpoints about happenings in the country.

The Kyrgyz government should be clear about national security concerns. It is widely believed that Kyrgyzstan authorities may misuse "national security concern" to restrict online activities of Kyrgyzstan users.

Finally, if the Kyrgyz government wants to promote a community-involved environment, it should be more willing to engage with international community in promoting internet penetration in the country. For example, international organizations or companies should be given priority in assisting with internet to local educational institutions such as schools, colleges, universities.

FUTURE RESEARCH DIRECTIONS

This chapter has examined instances when online communities in Kyrgyzstan succeeded in demanding actions from their government despite a repressive environment. However, there are several areas that researchers should focus in future analyses. For example, future studies should examine the types of civic and political engagement of Kyrgyzstan internet users. Specifically, research should address the question of how Kyrgyz internet users get engaged, such as by sharing information, commenting, or expressing their opinions about current affairs. Also, it would be interesting to examine under what conditions Kyrgyz internet users get engaged and under what circumstances they choose not to participate. Other questions include what topics or issues internet users are more concerned about and therefore more engaged. Alternatives include, for example, politics, social issues, culture, economics, and education.

CONCLUSION

The goal of this chapter was to examine and highlight examples when the internet and wider social media platforms could facilitate collective expression in the context of Kyrgyzstan. A main contribution of the study is to illustrate that internet communication technologies can promote social and political change even in a repressive environment, such as existed in Kyrgyzstan. This is because internet users were able to use the internet platforms to share important information and mobilize for common goals even when state media outlets were either silent or heavily restricted. Although the findings in this chapter may seem trivial, it is in fact crucial in terms of today's concern over the growing control of the internet for political reasons. The conclusion is that the internet has facilitated the organization of like-minded people in a media constrained environment and has enabled them to collectively speak their minds about important issues that matter them on a daily basis. This is something that would be difficult to accomplish in the pre-social media world. These conclusions have significant implications for areas of Central Asia where freedom of speech and expression are heavily restricted. The conclusions are also important in understanding how the simple computer clicks of online communities have the ability to create social and political change.

REFERENCES

Akipress. (2016). *В Интернете и соцсетях издеваются над чиновниками, — завотделом Аппарата правительства А.Исаев.* Retrieved from http://kg.akipress.org/news:1194600?from=portal&place=last

Anderson, J. (1999). *Kyrgyzstan: Central Asia's island of democracy.* Amsterdam: Harwood Academic Publisher.

Azattyk. (2015). *Налогоплательщики учат чиновников экономии бюджетных средств.* Retrieved from http://rus.azattyk.org/a/27434902.html

Azattyk. (2016). *Сариев: Все школы в 2016 году будут подключены к Интернету.* Retrieved on March 21, 2016, from http://rus.azattyk.org/archive/ky_News_in_Russian_ru/20160304/4795/4795.html?id=27588847

Barlow, A. (2008). *The blogging America: the new public sphere.* Westport, CT: Praeger.

BBC. (2005). *Profile: Askar Akayev.* Retrieved on June 29, 2016, from http://www.news.bbc.co.uk/2/hi/asia-pacific/4371819.stm

BBC. (2015). *Kyrgyzstan: Online protests over new chairs for MPs.* Retrieved on March 5, 2016, from http://www.bbc.com/news/blogs-news-from-elsewhere-34527694

Bengard, A. (2015). *Минфин передумал закупать кожаные кресла и планшеты.* Retrieved on March 5, 2016, from http://24.kg/obschestvo/25025_minfin_peredumal_zakupat_kojanyie_kresla_i_planshetyi_/

Bengard, A. (2016). *Депутаты считают, что Кыргызстан остро нуждается в получении гуманитарной помощи.* Retrieved on June 29, 2016, from http://24.kg/vlast/30204_deputatyi_schitayut_chto_kyirgyizstan_ostro_nujdaetsya_v_poluchenii_gumanitarnoy_pomoschi/

Bennett, W. L., & Segerberg, A. (2011). Digital Media and the Personalization of Collective Action. *Information Communication and Society*, *14*(6), 770–799. doi: 10.1080/1369118X.2011.579141

Bimber, B. (2003). *Information and American Democracy: Technology in the Evolution of Political Power*. Cambridge University Press. doi:10.1017/CBO9780511615573

Boulianne, S. (2009). Does Internet use affect engagement? A meta-analysis of research. *Political Communication*, *26*(2), 193–211. doi:10.1080/10584600902854363

Bowe, B., Freedman, E., & Blom, R. (2012). Social Media, Cyber-Dissent, and Constraints on Online Political Communication in Central Asia. *Central Asia and Caucasus*, *13*(1), 144–152.

Breuer, A., Landman, T., & Farguhar, D. (2014). Social media and protest mobilization: Evidence from the Tunisian revolution. *Democratization*, *22*(4), 764–792. doi:10. 1080/13510347.2014.885505

Brundidge, J., & Rice, R. (2009). Political engagement online: Do the information rich get richer and the like-minded more similar? In A. Chadwick & P. N. Howard (Eds.), Routledge Handbook of Internet Politics (pp. 145-156). New York: Routledge.

Calingaert, D. (2010). Autoritarianism vs. the Internet. *Policy Review*, *160*, 63–75.

Castells, M. (2000). Materials for an exploratory theory of the networked society. *The British Journal of Sociology*, *51*(1), 5–24. doi:10.1080/000713100358408

Castells, M. (2007). Communication, power, and counter-power in the network society. *International Journal of Communication*, *1*(1), 238–266.

Cottle, S. (2011). Media and the Arab uprisings of 2011. *Journalism*, *12*(5), 647–659. doi:10.1177/1464884911410017

Cummings, S. (2008). Introduction: Revolution not revolution. *Central Asian Survey*, *27*(3-4), 223–228. doi:10.1080/02634930802536811

DeYoung, A. (2010). *Lost in Transition: redefining students and universities in the contemporary Kyrgyz Republic*. Charlotte, NC: Information Age Publishing.

Dijck, J. (2013). *The culture of Connectivity: A critical history of social media*. Oxford, UK: Oxford University Press. doi:10.1093/acprof:oso/9780199970773.001.0001

Djanbaev, M. (2011). *Expanding Twitter's Reach in Kyrgyzstan*. Retrieved on June 26, 2016, from https://www.opensocietyfoundations.org/voices/expanding-twitter-s-reach-kyrgyzstan

Ferghana News. (2015). *Кыргызстан: В городе Кара-Суу за «религиозные лайки» в социальной сети задержан молодой человек*. Retrieved on February 21, 2016, from http://www.fergananews.com/news/23897

Freedman, E. (2012). Deepening shadows: The eclipse of press rights in Kyrgyzstan. *Global Media and Communication*, *8*(1), 47–64. doi:10.1177/1742766511434732

Freedman, E., & Shafer, R. (2012). Advancing a comprehensive research agenda for Central Asian mass media. *Media Asia*, *39*(3), 119–126. doi:10.1080/0129661 2.2012.11689927

Freedom House. (2015). *Kyrgyzstan: Freedom on the Net 2015*. Retrieved on February 22, 2016 from https://freedomhouse.org/report/freedom-net/2015/kyrgyzstan

Freedom House. (2016). *Kazakhstan: Freedom on the Net 2015*. Retrieved on October 30, 2016 from https://freedomhouse.org/report/freedom-net/2015/kazakhstan

Gazeta.kg. (2015). *В Бишкеке открылся информационно-образовательный центр для людей с ограниченными возможностями здоровья*. Retrieved on March 5, 2016, from http://www.gazeta.kg/news/kyrgyzstan/society/32463-v-bishkeke-otkrylsya-informacionno-obrazovatelnyy-centr-dlya-lyudey-s-ogranichennymi-vozmozhnostyami-zdorovya.html

Gil De Zúñiga, H., Puig-I-Abril, E., & Rojas, H. (2009). Weblogs, traditional sources online and political participation: An assessment of how the Internet is changing the political environment. *New Media & Society*, *11*(4), 553–574. doi:10.1177/1461444809102960

Guardian. (2016). *Kyrgyzstan detains Briton for 'horse penis' delicacy comparison*. Retrieved from https://www.theguardian.com/world/2016/jan/03/british-worker-kyrgyzstan-gold-mine-held-horse-penis-delicacy-comparison

Harlow, S. (2012). Social media and social movements: Facebook and an online Guatemalan justice movement that moved offline. *New Media & Society*, *14*(2), 225–243. doi:10.1177/1461444811410408

Heritage. (2016). *2016 Index of Economic Freedom: Kyrgyzstan*. Retrieved on June 29, 2016, from http://www.heritage.org/index/country/kyrgyzrepublic

Hiro, D. (2009). *Inside Central Asia: A Political and Cultural History of Uzbekistan, Turkmenistan, Kazakhstan, Kyrgyzstan, Tajikistan, Turkey and Iran*. London: Overlook.

Hoffman, L. H., Jones, P. E., & Young, D. G. (2013). Does my comment count? Perceptions of political participation in an online environment. *Computers in Human Behavior*, *29*(6), 2248–2256. doi:10.1016/j.chb.2013.05.010

Ibold, H. (2010). Disjuncture 2.0: Youth, Internet use and cultural identity in Bishkek. *Central Asian Survey*, *29*(4), 521–535. doi:10.1080/02634937.2010.537135

Ibragimov, S. (2016). *The Hashtag That Stymied Corruption in Kyrgyzstan*. Retrieved on March 5, 2016, from https://www.opensocietyfoundations.org/voices/hashtag-stymied-corruption-kyrgyzstan

Institute for War and Peace Reporting. (2012). *Kyrgyz Secret Police to Monitor Web*. Retrieved on February 21, 2016, from https://iwpr.net/global-voices/kyrgyz-secret-police-monitor-web

International Research & Exchanges Board. (2013). *Media Sustainability Index: Development of Sustainable Independent Media in Europe and Eurasia*. Washington, DC: IREX.

IRIN News. (2015). *Hope and Fear: Kyrgyz migrants in Russia*. Retrieved from https://www.irinnews.org/report/101398/hope-and-fear-kyrgyz-migrants-russia

Kabar. (2016). *We became 6 million, and growth of population of Kyrgyzstan indicates about people's confidence in the future of their country*. Retrieved from https://kabar.kg/eng/society/full/14531

Kaye, B., Johnson, T., & Muhlberge, P. (2012). *Blogging in the Global Society: Cultural, Political and Geographical Aspects*. Hershey, PA: IGI Global Publishing.

King, G., Pan, J., & Roberts, M. (2013). How Censorship in China Allows Government Criticism but Silences Collective Expression. *The American Political Science Review*, *107*(2), 326–343. doi:10.1017/S0003055413000014

Kloop. (2016). *Телеканал «Россия-24» изменил заголовок сюжета о кыргызстанцах в ИГИЛ*. Retrieved on March 5, 2016, from http://kloop.kg/blog/2016/02/26/telekanal-rossiya-24-izmenil-zagolovok-syuzheta-o-kyrgyzstantsah-v-igil/

Kostenko, Y. (2016). *В Кыргызстане чиновников хотят лишить доступа к социальным сетям*. Retrieved from http://24.kg/vlast/37746/

Kulikova, S., & Perlmutter, D. (2007). Blogging down the dictator: The Kyrgyz revolution and samizdat websites. *International Communication Gazette*, (69), 29-50.

Kurambayev, B. (2016). Journalism and Democracy in Kyrgyzstan: The impact of victimizations of the media practitioners. *Media Asia*, *43*(2), 102–111. doi:10.1080/01296612.2016.1206248

Mamytova, A. (2016). *Ирина Карамшукина: Оскорбляя президента, оскорбляете государство*. Retrieved from http://24.kg/vlast/38455_irina_karamshukina_oskorblyaya_prezidenta_oskorblyaete_gosudarstvo/

Margetts, H. (2013). The Internet and Democracy. In W. Dutton (Ed.), The Oxford Handbook of Internet Studies (pp. 421-437). The Oxford University Press.

McGlinchey, E., & Johnson, E. (2007). Aiding the Internet in Central Asia. *Democratization, 14*(2), 273–288. doi:10.1080/13510340701245785

Melvin, N., & Umaraliev, T. (2011). *New Social Media and Conflict in Kyrgyzstan.* SIRPI Insights on Peace and Security. doi:10.1037/e726612011-001

Morozov, E. (2012). *The Net Delusion: The Dark Side of Internet Freedom.* New York: Public Affairs Publishing.

Nash, V. (2013). Analyzing Freedom of Expression Online: Theoretical, Empirical and Normative Contributions. In W. Dutton (Ed.), The Oxford Handbook of Internet Studies (pp. 441-463). The Oxford University Press.

Olson, M. (1965). *The Logic of Collective Action.* Cambridge, MA: Harvard University Press.

Organized Crime and Corruption Reporting Project. (2016). *Kyrgyzstan: Former Chief Investigator Receives 14 Years for Corruption.* Retrieved from https://www.occrp.org/en/daily/5425-kyrgyzstan-former-chief-investigator-receives-14-years-for-corruption

Pannier, B. (2009). *Rethinking Kyrgyzstan's Tulip Revolution.* Retrieved on July 1, 2016, from https://www.rferl.org/content/Rethinking_Kyrgyzstan_Tulip_Revolution/1807335

Pearce, E. K., & Kendzior, S. (2012). Networked Authoritarianism and Social Media in Azerbaijan. *Journal of Communication, 62*(2), 283–298. doi:10.1111/j.1460-2466.2012.01633.x

Pitts, G. (2011). Professionalism Among Journalists in Kyrgyzstan. In E. Freedman & R. Shafer (Eds.), *After the czars and commissars: journalism in authoritarian post-Soviet Central Asia* (pp. 233–243). East Lansing, MI: Michigan State University Press.

Podolskaya, D. (2016). *Глава ОО Психическое здоровье и общество» требует от комиссии по рассмотрению жалоб на СМИ наказать Вести.ru.* Retrieved on July 1, 2016, from http://www.24.kg/obschestvo/28292_glava_oo_psihicheskoe_ zdorove_i_obschestvo_trebuet_ot_komissii_po_rassmotreniyu_jalob_na_smi_ nakazat_vestiru/

Radio Free Europe/Radio Liberty. (2014). *Report: Western Firms Help Central Asian States Spy On Citizens.* Retrieved from http://www.rferl.org/a/26701293.html

Radnitz, S. (2012). *Weapons of the Wealthy: Predatory Regimes and Elite-Led Protests in Central Asia.* Ithaca, NY: Cornell University Press.

Reuter, O., & Szakonyi, D. (2015). Online Social Media and Political Awareness in Authoritarian Regimes. *British Journal of Political Science*, *45*(1), 29–51. doi:10.1017/S0007123413000203

Savchenko, I. (2016). *Kazakhstan: The oppression of journalists and bloggers.* Open Dialogue Foundation. Retrieved from http://en.odfoundation.eu/a/7228,kazakhstan-the-oppression-of-journalists-and-bloggers1

Segerberg, A., & Bennett, W. L. (2011). Social Media and the Organization of Collective Action: Using Twitter to Explore the Ecologies of Two Climate Change Protests. *Communication Review*, *14*(3), 197–215. doi:10.1080/10714421.2011.5 97250

Shafiev, A., & Miles, M. (2015). Friends, Foes, and Facebook: Blocking the Internet in Tajikistan. *Demokratizatsiya: The Journal of Post-Soviet Democratization*, *23*(3), 297–319.

Srinivasan, R., & Fish, A. (2009). Internet Authorship: Social and Political Implications Within Kyrgyzstan. *Journal of Computer-Mediated Communication*, *14*(3), 559–580. doi:10.1111/j.1083-6101.2009.01453.x

Sunstein, C. (2007). *Republic.com.* Princeton, NJ: Princeton University Press.

Toralieva, G. (2014). Kyrgyzstan-Challenges for Environmental Journalism. In Y. Kalyango & D. Mould (Eds.), Global Journalism Practice and New Media Performance (pp. 214-226). Palgrave Macmillan.

Trere, E. (2008). Social Movements as Information Ecologies: Exploring the Coevolution of Multiple Internet Technologies for Activism. *International Journal of Communication*, *6*, 2359–2377.

Trilling, D. (2011). *Kyrgyzstan: Osh Blame Inquiry Censors Independent Media.* Retrieved on June 28, 2016, from www.eurasianet.org/node/63694

Tufekci, Z., & Wilson, C. (2012). Social Media and the Decision to Participate in Political Protest: Observations from Tahrir Square. *Journal of Communication*, *62*(2), 363–379. doi:10.1111/j.1460-2466.2012.01629.x

Tynaeva, N. (2016). *Ограничить кыргызстанцам доступ к иностранным сайтам хотят депутаты*. Retrieved from on October 28, 2016, http://knews.kg/2016/03/ogranichit-kyrgyzstantsam-dostup-k-inostrannym-sajtam-hotyat-deputaty

Verba, S., & Nie, N. H. (1987). *Participation in America: political democracy and social equality*. Chicago: University of Chicago Press.

Warf, B. (2012). *Global Geographies of the Internet*. New York, NY: Springer.

Warf, B. (2013). The Central Asian Digital Divide. In R. Massimo & G. Muschert (Eds.), The Digital Divide: The Internet and social inequality in international perspective (pp. 270-271). Academic Press.

Wilkinson, C., & Jetpyspayeva, Y. (2012). From Blogging Central Asia to Citizen Media: A Practitioners' Perspective on the Evolution of the *neweurasia* Blog Project. *Europe-Asia*, *64*(8), 1395–1414. doi:10.1080/09668136.2012.712267

Williams, W. N. (2015). Observing protest: Media use and student involvement on 7 April 2010 in Bishkek, Kyrgyzstan. *Central Asian Survey*, *34*(3), 373–389. doi:10.1080/02634937.2015.1007663

Wojcieszak, M., & Smith, B. (2014). Will politics be tweeted? New media use by Iranian youth in 2011. *New Media & Society*, *16*(1), 91–109. doi:10.1177/1461444813479594

Xenos, M. (2008). New mediated deliberation: Blog and press coverage of the Alito nomination. *Journal of Computer-Mediated Communication*, *13*(2), 485–503. doi:10.1111/j.1083-6101.2008.00406.x

Zanoza.kg. (2015). *МВД просит помочь граждан "патрулировать" социальные сети*. Retrieved on February 21, 2016, from http://zanoza.kg/doc/330299_mvd_prosit_pomoch_grajdan_patrylirovat_socialnye_seti.html

KEY TERMS AND DEFINITIONS

Central Asia: The region of Asia that consists of five former Soviet Union countries. They are: Kazakhstan, Kyrgyzstan, Tajikistan, Turkmenistan and Uzbekistan.

Democracy: This term is used to broadly refer to the conditions when people are able to elect their own representatives to form a government by holding a fair and free election.

Engagement: Refers to the definition suggested by Verba and Nie (1987) that those activities by those private citizens that are more or less directly aimed at influencing that selection of governmental personnel and/or the actions they take.

Online Communities: A group of internet users who share common interests and engage via sharing information, commenting, liking, re-posting, etc.

Semi-Authoritarian: The term broadly refers to countries where the governments allow some democratic principles to exist but also impose some authoritarian regime restrictions. For example, Kyrgyzstan allows some opposition parties and civil society to exist/function while mass media are still restricted and censored and elections are manipulated.

Social Media: Broadly defined as the tools and online platforms for socially networking and user-generated content sharing sites.

ENDNOTES

[1]   Temir Sariyev resigned as the Prime Minister of Kyrgyzstan at the time of the writing. Mr. Sooronbay Jeenbekov has been appointed on April 13, 2016, as the new Prime Minister.

[2]   It is called Tulip Revolution because some protestors held this rare mountain flower.

Chapter 3
Social Media Support for the Occupation of Public Schools in São Paulo, Brazil

Cynthia H. W. Corrêa
University of São Paulo, Brazil

ABSTRACT

Networked social movements have amplified the emancipation of protesters everywhere. In Brazil, a conflict arose after the São Paulo State Secretariat for Education announced the closing of 94 public schools, impacting 311,000 people. In response, about 30 students organized the occupation of the State School Fernão Dias Paes. Subsequently, the occupation spread to other schools. Based on a case study of the first school occupied in the city of São Paulo, this research aims to identify the role of information and communication technologies (ICTs) and social media tools in generating and sustaining the successful occupation protest of public schools in São Paulo. This chapter covers theories on demonstrations initiated online, on the social panorama in Latin America and educational issues in Brazil. It also addresses and analyzes the occupation process at this school, which reached visibility and support at national and international levels using ICTs and social media, confirming the steps of occupy movements around the world.

INTRODUCTION

In contemporary times, social movements in different parts of the globe have gained visibility and won followers and supporters, regardless of origin and geographical location due to the power of information disseminated via the Internet and supported

DOI: 10.4018/978-1-5225-2495-3.ch003

by information and communication technologies (ICTs), primarily using social networking sites. Diani (2000) identifies many reasons why computer-mediated communication (CMC) affects political activism significantly. For instance, communication technology allows setting up discussion groups for individuals interested in an issue, encouraging interaction. The World Wide Web offers the chance of making vital information for campaigners readily available from websites, and it also makes conceivable the independent existence of virtual coordination networks. In this context, Castells (2012) observes that networked social movements may well be a characteristic feature of the network society: the social structure of the Information Age. Besides, Internet social networks are autonomous spaces, largely beyond the control of governments and corporations, which have monopolized the channels of communication as the foundation of their power for decades.

In the panorama of Latin America, historically underlined by social conflicts, such as the struggle for land rights, labor exploitation, women's oppression, and the fight for the right to housing, health and education, the Internet has been adopted as an alternative instrument to publicize the concerns of social demonstrations. Consequently, social networking services have been critical mechanisms for the promotion and organization of social crusades, against the position of the mass media that often foster political and economic views of entrepreneurs and government supporters, which tends to silence the citizen's voice.

Despite the recent democratization of access to public education in Brazil, disputes in the field of public education are still commonplace. The struggles have tended to focus on the appreciation of teachers and professors, improving the quality of teaching, and the right to participate in decision-making bodies. One conflict faced by students and teachers in São Paulo, the richest state in Latin America, occurred late in the second half of 2015. It received national and international attention based on the strategic assistance of ICTs and social media triggered when the São Paulo State Secretariat for Education announced through the mass media, especially on television, the closure of 94 public schools, affecting 311,000 students who were enrolled in elementary and secondary education. To oppose the governmental resolution, about 30 students, boys and girls between 12 and 17 years-old, organized a protest that culminated in the occupation of the State School Fernão Dias Paes, in the Pinheiros neighborhood of São Paulo city in November 2015. It was the first school occupied by students in the capital that resulted in the interruption of classes and other activities.

The campaign of the social movement through social networking sites equivalent to Facebook and YouTube obtained the full attention of society, which started to contribute in various ways, such as by providing food and informal education options. Considering the high level of mobilization and empowerment of students participating, the research question proposed in this chapter is, "What was the role of ICTs and social media tools in generating and sustaining a successful occupation protest of public schools in São Paulo?" Answering this question will support the results of many other research studies that have addressed occupation related to online mobilization, for example, the Occupy Movement in New York City, the 15-M Movement in Spain and the 2011 Egyptian Revolution, from a Brazilian point of view. The idea is to observe a different cultural condition, age group, complaints to recognize some contextual differences that could be important to future protesters around the world.

This investigation has the following specific objectives:

- To present social actions around the occupation of schools that occurred in the state of São Paulo, at the end of 2015.
- To examine the strategic use of ICTs and social media in diverse situations.
- To analyze how social networking sites mobilized students and civil society, being decisive for the communication and success of the protest.

This is intended to be confirmatory research using qualitative methods, involving a descriptive study, a literature review, a document research, and collected records on social networking sites, traditional newspapers and alternative press websites. Additionally, semi-structured interviews were conducted from May to July 2016 with three student leaders of the demonstrations at the State School Fernão Dias Paes, who were also responsible for online communications with the demonstrators.

Networked Social Movements

In the social structure of the Information Age (Castells, 2012), new means of political mobilization exists. The Internet has become a critical component of insurgent political movements since it can connect people meeting face-to-face in neighborhoods and living rooms. "In a world connected live by the Internet, concerned citizens became immediately aware of struggles and projects they could identify with" (Castells, 2012, p. 158). Social movements are defined by Diani (1992) as networks of informal relationships between a multiplicity of individuals and organizations, who share a peculiar collective identity and mobilize resources and attention around conflicting issues. McCaughey and Ayers (2003) describe collective identity as a social psychological concept used to explain the relation of an individual to the group: "When a group has a strong collective identity, the movement can garner support and power because the participants feel that they are all working towards common goals, have defined opponents, and have an integrated sense of being that is incorporated into the movement ideologies" (p. 8). Shangapour, Hosseini and Hashemnejad (2011) endorse the importance of collective identities because they help to attract new members and uphold old ones. Further, new collective identities aim to change cultural codes; also, social protests create new identities that help recruit and sustain membership. Indeed, the action repertoire of political demonstrations is as full as there are social movements and activists, objectives and causes, claims and complaints (Van Laer & Van Aelst, 2010). Additionally, revolution and strikes are words directly associated with activism, terms that have in common the need for change and acting against the system.

The nature and scope of the technology influence not only the modes by which a protest communicates its aims and objectives, but also its geographical scale, structure and collective identity (Shangapour et al., 2011). Hence, where real public places do not exist, there is still a way to promote social communication. Castells (2012) affirms that networked social movements seem to be a typical feature of the networked society that is expressed by cyber activism. Cyber activism includes electronic advocacy, e-campaigning, e-activism and online organizing, using tools such as e-mails, blogs and social networking sites to publicize a cause by rapidly disseminating information that is unreachable through government and commercial news sources (Coillie, Santamaria, Redmond, & Torres, 2013).

The public engagement with the Internet reveals an assortment of activists and groups in the social and political crusade. The Internet not only acts as an instrument of mobilization and participation in traditional manners of campaigns, such as local street demonstrations, but also give these protests a further national and transnational character by quickly diffusing communication and mobilization efforts (Van Laer & Van Aelst, 2010). As reinforced by Shangapour et al. (2011), "social networks are open structures, able to expand without limits, integrating new nodes as long as they are able to communicate within the network" (p. 3). In this sense, Diani (2000) points out treating social movements as networks make the relationship between causes and their spatial location explicit: "Contemporary social movements have developed historically in parallel to the emergence of a public sphere located in specific physical and cultural spaces" (p. 387). This requirement of indicating places and cultures is one of the paradoxes of computer-mediated communication. Although communication is global, some protests need to be geographically situated to show the world the local problems.

The Internet aids and supports collective action regarding the organization and mobilization of protests and social movements. At the same time, it generates collective and unrestricted membership, increasing visibility and elevating the cause transnationally. As elucidated by Storck (2011), Egyptian activists used social media networks like Facebook, Twitter, YouTube and weblogs as gears for organizing the protest, serving as an alternative press, and for generating awareness both regionally and internationally, in the uprising in Egypt in January and February 2011. Also, to Eltantawy and Wiest (2011), "social media technologies represent an important instrumental resource that contributed to the birth and sustainability of the January 25 protests" (p. 1212). The inaugural demonstration occurred on January 25, 2011, in Cairo's Tahrir Square, convened by a Facebook page entitled "We Are All Khaled Siad", in honor of the young blogger killed after supposedly posting a video incriminating police officers. His death became a symbol of the brutal police routine against citizens (Eltantawy & Wiest, 2011). Fifty thousand people participated on the first day and, within days, they were millions in distinct places. The principal contribution of Storck's study (2011) was to prove that while having the potential to facilitate and accelerate political mobilization, the Internet is a dialectical force that should not be treated merely as a liberator or oppressor. In Egypt, online communication helped to engage people in the movement at first, but shortly afterwards, the government effectively blocked access to the Internet. Regardless of the blockade, demonstrators continued to communicate with the networks initially created.

In turn, Vallina-Rodriguez et al. (2012) and Sampedro and Lobera (2014) demarcated as a milestone of cyber activism in Spain the eruption of the 15-M Movement in the 2011 elections. Indeed, for Sampedro and Lobera (2014), "Spain pioneered the presence of 'online multitudes' or 'cybermultitudes' in 2004, when the population reacted to the electoral manipulation of the 11th March terrorist attacks" (p. 3). At that moment, digital technology played a key role in the ability to self-organize and in creating collective action without formal structures. Already in 2011, Spanish activists used Facebook and Twitter to gain adherents and to combat the prevailing situation, whose discussion gave birth to the collective *¡Democracia real, Ya!* (DRY). Then, members of DRY convoked public demonstrations to be held on May 15, 2011, in more than fifty cities across Spain (Vallina-Rodriguez et al., 2012): "The protesters used Twitter as a channel for discussing their position and organizing themselves. A broad movement was born; whose members call themselves '*Los indignados*' ('The Indignant')" (p. 62). In this case, Twitter and Facebook were the leading communication platforms for spreading the messages of the protesters, who had free access to organize the revolution online. To Sampedro and Lobera (2014), online multitudes appear to produce a new public space for crusades, which takes in a broad range of campaigners and citizens. For the authors, *Los indignados* is an expression of a sociopolitical dissatisfaction shared by millions of Spaniards, bringing together people with different social and political viewpoints. At the same time, the 15-M Movement promotes a plural space where new political action and discourse emerge.

The Occupy Movement that began on September 17, 2011, in New York City, is another significant example of how activism can take place online and move offline, to occupy physical places (Coillie et al., 2013). More interesting is the fact that Occupy Wall Street was born digital (Castells, 2012). Besides, participants utilized social media tools, particularly Facebook and Twitter, to interact, collaborate, coordinate, and debate ideas, to mobilize a huge number of people, starting in New York City and circulating the globe. This example demonstrates how social networking sites expand a movement's visibility, being fundamental to gaining support locally and globally. In summary, to Coillie et al. (2013) "social networks provide a platform to engage with other people and join forces in a mutual cause" (p. 3). In fact, nowadays it is unimaginable to think about local and exclusive triggers, since actions and impacts are felt miles away, especially if the subject involves essential human rights and democratic principles.

To Van Laer and Van Aelst (2010), perceiving that political and economic influence has progressively moved to the international level is crucial. The Internet has allowed social movements to follow this transition and to operate globally. What the authors emphasize as an advantage is the possibility that civic groups with few resources can mobilize public attention against a far more powerful contestant more efficiently and self-reliant than in the past. Another aspect to keep in mind is that the real world and the online world now act jointly and work in parallel (Coillie et al., 2013).

THE BRAZILIAN EDUCATIONAL CONTEXT

With the publication of "*As veias abertas da América Latina*" [Open Veins of Latin America], Galeano (1971) showed some features of 500 years of economic exploitation and political domination in all Latin American nations, which were subdued in different periods of history in diverse ways. The greatest legacy of this long period of oppression and curtailment of social rights is still present in the desires and the actions of those who understand that most people must obey and abide by a dominant minority. This subordination must be accepted and naturalized among the dominated majority. This balance of power is still present in Brazilian sectors, through the conservative political parties and the financial system that dominates this country (Galeano, 1971). These power relations also act on the part of the middle-class with low levels of education who are easily manipulated by the power of mainstream media, which control and shape public opinion.

Considering the production of knowledge on social movements in the field of education in different spheres - whether in relation to university research, with the knowledge and conflicts of public school, or a student demonstration - there are yet few studies that "articulate the Brazilian production to other Latin American countries, principally with those who underwent military regimes" (Gohn, 2011: 333-334). Gohn (2011) highlights the role of social protests related to education as "sources and production agencies of knowledge", justifying the importance of the school environment for the exercise of participation since this environment produces the civic learning for involvement in society and establishes the relationship between school and community.

Also, emphasizing the status of the school-community relations, Spósito (2002) defends the democratic management in school as a precondition for widespread participation. The author believes the autonomy of the community can only be established by creating exchange experiences between members of the school community, by decentralizing decision-making processes and intervening in existing hierarchical relationships. According to Spósito (2002), for the management and the process of participation to produce an effect on the school environment, "a profound change in organizations related to education: in federal, state and municipal levels" (p. 50) is required. Then, the community made up of parents, teachers and students would be heard and felt to be a valued part of the school.

A study by Silva (2002) investigates the contributions of public schools for the foundation of a democratic citizenship. This analysis is grounded in the experience of four Brazilian schools that showed essential conditions for the implementation of an educational project with this bias, allowing the participation process. Among its needs, the author stresses the institutional support and the development of a government policy, the experiences of democratic management, and a "pedagogical project oriented to the formation of citizenship" (p. 9), which can be put into practice and considers the educator to be a significant element in this process.

But a school committed to training for citizenship, in the context of a democratic management, should pay attention to the education needs of teachers to be able to work with aspects such as autonomy and citizenship. In this sense, Freire (2005) deals with the construction of knowledge and the links to be established between educator and student. The author declares "respect for the autonomy and dignity of each person is an ethical imperative and not a favor that may or may not give each other" (p. 66).

Patta and Valle (2015, online), researchers in the field of education studying the struggle for quality public education, presented one of the first records in the free press on the school reorganization act in the state of São Paulo in 2015. In an interview with student leaders of the movement, the authors investigated students' motivations to fight for their school, and their view of politics, politicians and political parties. Patta and Valle concluded (2015, online), "to paint the walls, to wash bathrooms and weed courtyards that were not receiving proper maintenance, besides showing high organizational skills, commitment, creativity and consciousness, they revealed their strength." The students took upon themselves the role of key stakeholders in their future and made visible the neglect and irresponsibility of the government towards the area.

Nassif (2015, online), who interviewed two leaders of school occupation, declared "for many of the boys, the rebellion was not just a bet on life, but a challenge of death." The commitment and seriousness of the movement that started with high school students were nothing more than an exercise of citizenship. The school occupation displays the efficiency of their pedagogy of participation. Feeling that they were protagonists, the students showed their true anxieties to the world. It was an unexpected event, the most important product of a demonstration which had simply aimed to prevent students from being relocated to other schools without consultation (Nassif, 2015). This event confirms the thought of Gohn (2011) that "struggles for education have a historical character, are procedural, occur, therefore within and outside schools and other institutional spaces" (p. 346). In other words, the battle for education always involves struggles for rights and part of the construction of citizenship, which still shows fragile and under construction in Brazil.

METHODOLOGY

This is a confirmatory study using qualitative methods, including a descriptive study, a literature review, and document research covering reports from the São Paulo State Secretariat for Education, and collected records on social networking sites, traditional newspapers and alternative press websites. The literature review addressed ICTs, collective identity concepts, networked social movements, the Brazilian power structure, the relationship of Brazilian public schools with their community, social conflicts in Latin America, social protests, and participative and democratic school management.

Semi-structured interviews were conducted from May to July 2016 with three student leaders of the movement who were also responsible for the online communications with the demonstrators. The respondents will be referred to as students A, B and C to preserve their identities. The purpose of the interviews was to collect data and opinions from these students about the influence of ICTs and social media, such as applications for mobile devices, to the success of their campaign. A content analysis following Bardin (2006) was used to analyze documents, online publications, and data obtained during the interviews with the student leaders.

For the content analysis, Bardin (2006) suggests that, following the step of pre-data analysis (detailed and careful exploration of the material), the analysis will be based on the interpretation of the manifest content of each document, every speech, associated with the theoretical framework to support the analysis. Thus, the pre-data analysis step was performed with the purpose of systematizing and highlighting the ideas that have arisen repeatedly in the interviewees' reports, as well as in news circulated by different media. After the systematization of ideas, it proceeded to the proper interpretation of papers and statements made relating to the literature reviewed, which allowed the analysis and observation of the strategic use of ICTs and social media in the occupation of the *Paulistas* schools.

RESULTS AND DISCUSSION

Understanding the Dispute

Presented here are the official version of the school reorganization act, released by the government and traditional mass media, and the version of the students who resisted in the process. In the authorized version, a statement entitled "The São Paulo reorganization and the new school model" announced the closure of public schools, which proposal would be put into practice at the beginning of 2016. This information was published on the website of the State Secretariat for Education on September 29, 2015. The reason given by the then Secretary of Education was that the plan would provide "the best education for students that would be separated by cycles and transferred to other schools" (Voorwald, 2015, online). For analysts of public educational policy (Rodrigues, 2015, online), oblivious to the problems of the education system and without presenting any data that could justify such a measure, the Secretary of Education, Mr. Herman Voorwald in a public document, alleged that Brazil had suffered a steady reduction in enrollment in public schools. Thus, the drop in school enrollment combined with a disordered urban sprawl in different regions would require the design of a new network of schools to serve a population in transformation and looking for change. "The government Geraldo Alckmin starts from this month a historical movement in the teaching units focusing on building a new school model and improving the quality of education", said the Secretary (Voorwald, 2015, online).

This event, coupled with the continuous procedure of devaluation and abandonment of public schools during the previous 25 years, led to the mobilization of students in a school in the west zone of the city of São Paulo. The central problem that stimulated the conflict between the students and the local government was the fact the closure plan had been decided without establishing any dialogue of discussion with the school community. As justification, the governor of São Paulo said that schools to be closed were considered idle. Hereafter, thousands of students would be relocated to schools in nearby regions. This action, named by the mass media as the "school reorganization act," surprised and displeased students, teachers, families and many sectors of civil society.

To protest the decision of the São Paulo State Secretariat for Education, about 30 young students decided to confront the harsh measure. They organized a resistance movement that culminated in the occupation, on the first fortnight of November 2015, of the State School Fernão Dias Paes, located in the district of *Pinheiros*, in the city of São Paulo. They left their homes to stay full-time on the premises of this school.

Early in the occupation, the state government of São Paulo attempted to disqualify the student cause through the mass media demanding the depredation of public property, influencing the audience. Despite the actions reported by the mainstream media to discredit the protest in support of the governor, the local community, composed of merchants, intellectuals, and neighborhood groups, started to collaborate with students. To sustain and protect them and to express their empathy, support, and adherence to the movement, people began to donate food, hygiene items, cleaning supplies, and materials for school maintenance.

From that first occupation, in less than a fortnight, dozens of schools were occupied by students throughout the state of São Paulo. At the end of November, the number of occupied schools exceeded a hundred. The success of such mobilization was due chiefly to the extensive communication stratagems through social networking services and use of several ICTs, employing the main slogans: *Não tem Arrego*! [No chance!] (Figure 1), and *Ocupe a sua Escola*! [Occupy your school!].

Figure 1. Students' protest with slogans
Source: https://www.facebook.com/OcupaFernao/photos/a.1717702621797266.1073741829.171715
1681852360/1723994597834735/?type=3&theater

While traditional mass media, aligned to the São Paulo State Secretariat for Education, had tried to legitimize the discourse of the school reorganization act and persuade public opinion against the students' movement, the complaint was being spread on social media and by the alternative press. Every day, the movement acquired new supporters, a phenomenon inspired by the notion of collective identity (McCaughey & Ayers, 2003), powerfully working in the context of the groups formed in social networks by Shangapour et al. (2011). Apart from this, it was evident that social networking tools continued to fulfill their function of disseminating information to the public, at the local, national and international levels, and acting as a partner for the alternative press, repeating the steps of successful occupy protests around the world (for instance, the Occupy Movement in New York City, the Spanish 15-M Movement and the 2011 Egyptian Revolution).

Over time, the absence of dialogue between the state and students made the crusade grow even more. In fewer than 20 days, more than 100 public schools in the state of São Paulo were occupied (Figure 2).

In the view of the alternative press, in response to new occupations, the government initiated a major repression, threatening the students, and using the military police to physically assault and even arrest them (CartaCapital, 2015, online). Many

Figure 2. Protesters and supporters encourage students
Source: http://jornalggn.com.br/tag/blogs/escolas-ocupadas?page=1

arrests and scenes of violence were reported by the alternative media and on social networks, catching the attention of students from different Brazilian states, and prompting intellectuals and students from other countries to embrace the cause of the São Paulo students.

Mobilization Stratagems

When asked about promoting the occupation of the School Fernão Dias Paes, the interviewee A, an 18-year-old girl, reported that after October 26, 2016, students and some teachers gathered in the streets in support of small protests contrary to the government action. Although campaigns occur timidly in São Paulo, they decided to go to the Department of Education to seek clarification on this process. Despite failing to receive any explanations or justifications from the administration, student A said that the group felt more encouraged after watching a video of Chilean students who had occupied their schools. At that moment, 30 students resolved to stay in the State School Fernão Dias Paes, closing it for its everyday activities. The group was composed of teenagers, boys and girls, aged 12 and 17, who with the support of parents left their homes to live 24 hours a day at the school (Figure 3).

Subsequently, the students created different commissions with rotating functions every week, such as communication, information, cultural activities, security, cleaning and feeding. They decided to create a page on Facebook to be the official channel of communication. "At first, we were locked in the school and had a laptop connected to the Internet, which represented the line of communication. Thus, arose the idea of creating a Facebook page that would be our own media," commented the interviewee B. The page also allowed the population to receive information without having to go to the school. For the student C, the adoption of social networking sites and other electronic communication channels to articulate, to set up meetings and to publicize events via Facebook in the early stages was natural because they are a very connected generation: "From the beginning, social media have always been presented as part of the movement." Such a determination to work with social media tools to organize a crusade is a recurring practice among various demonstrations, as mentioned by Vallina-Rodriguez et al. (2012), Castells (2012), Storck (2011), and Eltantawy and Wiest (2011). This assessment also confirms the results of Storck's study (2011) about the 2011 Egyptian Revolution, when activists used a variety of social media channels as mechanisms to organize the protest and to produce mindfulness locally and globally.

Soon, the page named *Escola de Luta Fernão Dias Paes* [Fernão Dias Paes Resistance School] served as an essential tool in the fight, both to boost the protest and to deliver quotidian information, attracting public attention. It also functioned to keep in contact with other schools and broadcast content for the media. In the

Figure 3. Occupation of the School Fernão Dias Paes
Source: http://jornalggn.com.br/tag/blogs/escolas-ocupadas?page=1

words of student B: "The page of our school grew very fast, in less than a month there were already about ten thousand registered. It was critical because people knew the information source and how to contact us, independent of the occupation. So, the page is the sound basis for communication." In November 2015, the Facebook page of the School Fernão Dias Paes had recorded more than 10,000 likes. In fact, the demonstration organizers decided that all schools should create their respective pages on Facebook, as a standard communication tactic. To interviewee B: "It had to be something easily replicable, and that everyone could do."

One committee of information was created to bring information into the school, and another communication commission was charged with divulging information to the public, since on the first two days of occupation, more than two thousand people were accompanying the protest outside the school. After two weeks, the connection to the Internet was cut. Next, the two committees (information and communication) had come together, and people with access to the Internet by mobile phone were responsible for contacting supporters and updating facts on electronic communication channels, such as social media and other ICTs, including mobile applications.

Initially, the students used radio communication from the first to the last gate of the school, but rapidly they stopped using it because the police could track them. It is believed that many students had their phones tapped during the resistance period. These episodes confirm Storck's (2011) assertion that the Internet is a dialectical force that should not be perceived as either a savior or a persecutor medium. This assertion holds as well for more traditional technologies, like radio transmission, since the authorities tracked these modes of communication as well to reprimand the demonstrators. As a result, students abandoned technological solutions in preference to less-traceable pamphlets and even letters to establish external communication.

The commission of cultural activities, through the Google Docs service, a digital tool for editing text in shared mode, invited teachers, former students and people from civil society to donate classes and to hold cultural events and non-formal education activities during the occupation throughout the state of São Paulo (Anpuh, 2015). In accordance with interviewee A, a diversity of themes was offered by the public that had or no relation to the content traditionally developed at school.

Likewise, applications for mobile devices, such as Telegram, Messenger and WhatsApp, were used to create groups to organize activities in school and to manage external activities, as street demonstrations. In Telegram, a group called "the command" was created for the exchange of messages between several schools. In Messenger, groups were exclusive to members of the same school. WhatsApp was set up for distinct groups, such as support and spokespeople, among others. Internal communication within the movement was also frequently accomplished by word of mouth, for fear of having information leakage. The protest schedules were informed personally and disseminated through coded messages in mobile applications. These coordination and management activities support the findings of Sampedro and Lobera (2014) about how digital technologies can play a fundamental role in the capacity to self-organize and create collective action without established structures.

Contributions of ICTs and Social Media

Assuredly, social networking tools were significant factors in expanding the movement's visibility, an advantage well explained by Castells (2012) when dealing with the Occupy Wall Street movement. They were most effective in denouncing police repression and other abuses at the schools. As student C reported, "On one occasion, the police beat the students. We recorded videos with mobile phones and shared them on our official Facebook page, via YouTube and WhatsApp. We sent the material to the alternative press, such as to the broad network of collectives called *Jornalistas Livres* [Independent Journalists], who posted it on their page, which went viral" (Figure 4). For the diffusion of the students' campaign, the

Figure 4. Student 12-year-old beaten by the policeman
Source: *http://bemblogado.com.br/site/fechamento-das-escolas-tenho-12-anos-e-ja-aprendi-o-que-e-repressao-professor-alckmin/*

independent communication channels on the Internet had a strong presence in the daily reporting of occupation as it occurred, principally in *Mídia Ninja* [Ninja Media], *O Mal Educado* [The Uneducated], *Bem blogado* [Well blogged], and *Jornalistas Livres*. Activists' usage of social media as an alternative press again confirmed Storck's (2011) findings. In the case of students from São Paulo, the online channels acted as an alternative to the mass-media coverage and were sources of information for the free press.

Social media played an instrumental role in the empowerment process. Meanwhile, traditional mass media, especially television, misrepresented the reasons for the protest. For instance, in an occupied school in the city of Osasco, where the students were forcibly removed, some drug traffickers invaded the school and stole equipment. The first television news bulletins reported that the students were responsible for the crime. "Via social media, they displayed testimonials from students saying they were not involved in the robberies in this school", said student C. Student B commented that the press used the images provided by the students, however, the bias of the news had always been favorable to the government and condemning of the students' movement. This demonstrated the traditional role of the dominant communication conglomerates in Latin American countries, as pointed out by Galeano (1971). Student B also emphasized that social media were vital to the spread of the protest in the vision of the students since the mainstream media did not fulfil this function. The sharing of violent images worldwide through Facebook and YouTube was decisive for the governor of the state of São Paulo to suspend the proposition to close the schools. The state, students, and São Paulo prosecutors agreed that discussions on the proposed closure of schools would be held throughout the year 2016.

Student C remarked that another crucial role of ICTs and social media was contributing to the organizational aspect of the crusade, which continues to this date to hold meetings and create new pages. Several pages exist on Facebook, such as *Não fechem minha escola* [Do not close my school], and *Caravana Secundarista* [The high school caravan], among many others created across the country, to help propagate the movement's actions. Although the protest started in São Paulo, it has diffused throughout Brazil and students follow it and keep in contact with one another via social media. "If it were not for social networking sites, you would not be interviewing me now. Even my family had a wrong view of the demonstration because of the press. If not for our voices, texts, photos and videos, the movement would not have received so much support", summarized student C. As illustrated by these comments, the support of social media tools was vital to the birth and sustainability of this protest, as it was to the Revolution in Egypt in 2011, as described by Eltantawy and Wiest (2011).

Finally, for the respondents, social media contributed to making the cause internationally recognized. Throughout the occupation, the Paulistas students kept in touch with Argentinian, French, Italian, Chilean and South African students that shared similar experiences in their respective nations. Others occupied their schools in solidarity with the students from São Paulo, despite many barriers. As the case of high school students at Liceo Statale Virgilio in Rome, who knew of the conflict through Facebook, marched in support of the struggle of the Brazilian students and sent, through social media, the message: "accomplices and solidarity with the struggles in the whole world." And the endorsement received was not only of international students. For example, workers also occupied a factory and released a poster in support of the school. As expressed by Sampedro and Lobera (2014) relative to the 15-M Movement in Spain in 2011, online crowds seem to generate a new public space for causes, bringing together activists and citizens with different backgrounds, values and beliefs. By social media, students received international encouragement from notorious experts, such as the well-known geographer and writer, David Harvey, and still were interviewed by influential newspapers. This is a clear sample of the potential of electronic communication, especially via social media, for the fomentation of groups based on identification processes inspired by a collective identity (McCaughey & Ayers, 2003; Shangapour et al., 2011; Coillie et al., 2013), perspective that acquires an increasingly transnational character in today's world (Van Laer & Van Aelst, 2010).

Occupation as Pedagogy

Reflecting on the leading role of young students in political decisions and the struggle to guarantee social rights (Figure 5), it is easy to agree with the Patta and Valle (2005) that the students took on the responsibility to display to Brazil and the world the neglect of education by local authorities and government. In addition, they set an example of organization, with well-defined and fulfilled tasks, managed collectively, with the basic objective of promoting the improvement of the quality of teaching. As highlighted by Nassif (2015), the seriousness of the movement led by high school students was a full exercise of citizenship. The occupation also demonstrated the value of participation as a pedagogical tool.

In the campaign undertaken by high school students in the last three months of 2015, it was experienced some findings of Gohn (2011), emphasizing that struggles for education issues have a historical character, occurring, in and out of schools and spread by institutional spaces. Further, this kind of action embraces fighting for some basic rights in defense of the citizenship construction, which unfortunately follows breakable and under development in nations as Brazil.

Figure 5. Student surrounded by police barrier (Text on the student's shirt: "I have in me all the dreams of the world")
Source: http://jornalggn.com.br/tag/blogs/escolas-ocupadas?page=1

Another substantial result of the students' movement against the school reorganization act in 2015 was to clarify to civil society the lack of interest of state leaders in the construction of a school based on democratic management, able to promote dialogue and, consequently, the transformation of school practices (Spósito, 2002; Silva, 2002). Lastly, with the episode of the occupation, the students indicated the desire to negotiate and to strive for the maintenance of the public school, in a systematic way to protect their rights. This behavior demarcates the aptitude and the students' intelligence, demonstrating the relationship in the classroom should be reviewed since it must be respected the autonomy and dignity of each person. Also, Freire (2005) confirms that educational practice deals with the production of knowledge founded on an exchange between educator and student.

CONCLUSION

This study supports and confirms the results of numerous research studies that have addressed the role of online mobilization in supporting and strengthening demonstrations and occupations. Analysis of the nearly three-month occupation of the State School Fernão Dias Paes in São Paulo has made it possible to identify the stratagems used for social actions. Communication systems performed a fundamental role in distinct aspects, such as organization, mobilization, communication and dissemination of information, particularly online. Based on electronic communication channels created by students on Facebook, YouTube, Google Docs and mobile applications as Telegram, Messenger, and WhatsApp, the occupation strategies quickly been spread to students at other schools facing analogous conditions. Social networking sites were vital to guarantee the right to free expression and the ability to broadcast news of students' struggles for a quality public education.

Due to the capacity of social media mobilization to generate collective identities (McCaughey & Ayers, 2003; Shangapour et al., 2011; Coillie et al., 2013), as with many occupy movements, this research found that people came together regardless of transnational interests. The aggregation potential of a network with global dimensions deserves the attention of those advocating for local causes. Triggers that can arise locally, such as the occupation of the State School Fernão Dias Paes, in São Paulo, or born-digitally, such as in the Occupy Movement in New York City (Coillie et al., 2013; Castells, 2012) can achieve worldwide support and attention.

For the diffusion of the students' position, the independent communication channels (alternative or free press) on the Internet were essential to the daily reporting of occupation as it happened. In contrast, traditional media misinformed the public about the actions of students to preserve the status quo of state power (Galeano, 1971). Facebook has constituted a fundamental and critical tool for the organization and visibility of the protest. Each school located in a different sub-region of the city created its own page to report general activities. Through these pages, many people came to support the campaign, for instance, school communities, artists, intellectuals and students' movements in other countries that have taken the defense of the interests of São Paulo students.

The ongoing conflicts on the streets recorded by students from São Paulo and divulged on social media had given the movement international recognition that received the support of students, workers and intellectuals around the world. Social media were decisive in changing the opinions of the Brazilian public, which was initially influenced by television news programs and unaware of the dimensions and implications of the school closure proposal. On the other hand, this study also confirms that the Internet's force is dialectical (Storck, 2011), enabling authorities to identify student leaders and forcing them to resort to other means of communication.

As with similar networked social crusades in Egypt, Spain and the United States of America, the success of the protest in the state of São Paulo was due in significant part to the allies recruited by the disclosure of information facilitated by ICTs and social networking tools. As mentioned, the dissemination of violent images globally via Facebook and YouTube was important for the governor of São Paulo to suspend the proposed closure of schools. The idea is to involve the São Paulo Department of Education, the whole school community (students, parents, and teachers) and sectors of civil society fighting for a quality public education in Brazil. This is an attempt to put into practice widespread participation (Spósito, 2002) and democratic citizenship (Silva, 2002) in the decision-making process.

This study is limited regarding the number of students interviewed (three) and the number of schools to which those students belong (one). A larger study, involving several schools in the state, would be beneficial, as it would enable comparisons on a range of actions of each student group and their associated successes and outcomes.

REFERENCES

Anpuh - Associação Nacional de História. (2015). Apoie uma escola ocupada: doe uma aula. Retrieved from http://site.anpuh.org/index.php/2015-01-20-00-01-55/noticias2/diversas/item/3106-apoie-uma-escola-ocupada-doe-uma-aula

Bardin, L. (2006). Análise de Conteúdo. Edições 70. Lisboa.

CartaCapital. (2015). Em vídeos e fotos, a repressão da PM aos estudantes secundaristas. Retrieved from http://www.cartacapital.com.br/blogs/parlatorio/em-videos-e-fotos-a-repressao-da-pm-aos-estudantes-secundaristas-8726.html

Castells, M. (2012). *Networks of Outrage and Hope: Social Movements in the Internet Age*. Cambridge, UK: Polity Press.

Coillie, C. V., Santamaria, L., Redmond, S., & Torres, A. (2013). *Online Activism. The transformation of the 'Public Sphere', and the creation of collective political identities around activism in the digital age – the case of the 'Occupy' movement. Project work*. Roskilde: Roskilde University.

Diani, M. (1992). The concept of social movement. *The Sociological Review, 40*(1), 1–25. doi:10.1111/j.1467-954X.1992.tb02943.x

Diani, M. (2000). Social Movement Networks Virtual and Real. *Information Communication and Society, 3*(3), 386–401. doi:10.1080/13691180051033333

Eltantawy, N., & Wiest, J. B. (2011). Social Media in the Egyptian Revolution: Reconsidering Resource Mobilization Theory. *International Journal of Communication, 5*, 1207–1224.

Escola de Luta Fernão Dias Paes. Facebook page. Retrieved from https://www.facebook.com/OcupaFernao/?fref=ts

Freire, P. (2005). *Pedagogia da Autonomia: saberes necessários à prática educativa*. São Paulo: Paz e Terra.

Galeano, E. (1971). *As veias abertas da América Latina*. RJ: Paz e Terra.

Gohn, M. da G. (2011). *Teorias dos movimentos sociais. Paradigmas clássicos e contemporâneos*. São Paulo: Loyola.

McCaughey, M., & Ayers, M. D. (2003). *Cyberactivism: Online Activism in Theory and Practice*. New York, NY: Routledge.

Nassif, L. (2015). Os estudantes paulistas em uma aula inesquecível de brasilidade. Retrieved from http://jornalggn.com.br/noticia/os-estudantes-paulistas-em-uma-aula-inesquecivel-de-brasilidade

Patta, C., & de Valle, V. S. (2015). Ocupações, luta da periferia? Retrieved from http://www.carosamigos.com.br/index.php/artigos-e-debates/5667-ocupacoes-luta-da-periferia

Rodrigues, C. (2015). Desinformação sobre reorganização cria boataria e pânico. Retrieved from http://www.cartaeducacao.com.br/reportagens/desinformacao-sobre-reorganizacao-cria-boataria-e-panico/

Sampedro, V., & Lobera, J. (2014). The Spanish 15-M Movement: A consensual dissent? *Journal of Spanish Cultural Studies, 15*(1-2), 61–80. doi:10.1080/14636204.2014.938466

Shangapour, I., Hosseini, S., & Hashemnejad, H. (2011). Cyber Social Networks and Social Movements. *Global Journal of Human Social Science*, *11*(1), 1–17.

Silva, A. M. M. (2002). *Escola pública e a formação da cidadania: possibilidades e limites. 222f. Tese (Doutorado em Educação)*. Universidade de São Paulo, São Paulo: Faculdade de Educação.

Spósito, M. P. (2002). Educação, gestão democrática e participação popular. In Bastos, J. B. (Ed.), Gestão democrática. Rio de Janeiro: DP&A, SEPE.

Storck, M. (2011). *The Role of Social Media in Political Mobilisation: A Case Study of the January 2011 Egyptian Uprising* [Unpublished master dissertation]. University of St Andrews, Scotland.

Vallina-Rodriguez, N., Scellato, S., Haddadi, H., Forsell, C., Crowcroft, J., & Mascolo, C. (2012). *Los Twindignados: The Rise of the Indignados Movement on Twitter. Proceedings of the 2012 ASE/IEEE International Conference on Social Computing and 2012 ASE/IEEE International Conference on Privacy, Security, Risk and Trust*. Washington, DC. doi:10.1109/SocialCom-PASSAT.2012.120

Van Laer, J., & Van Aelst, P. (2010). Cyber-protest and civil society: The Internet and action repertoires in social movements. In Y. Jewkes and Yar, Majid (Eds.), Handbook of Internet Crime (pp. 230-254). Abingdon, UK: Willan Publishing.

Voorwald, H. (2015). A reorganização paulista e o novo modelo de escola. Retrieved from http://www.educacao.sp.gov.br/noticias/a-reorganizacao-paulista-e-o-novo-modelo-de-escola

KEY TERMS AND DEFINITIONS

Democratic Management of School: Participatory process of society, family, teachers, students and operational staff in the planning and management, administrative and teaching in a public school.

Geraldo Alckmin: A Brazilian politician affiliated to the Brazilian Social Democratic Party (PSDB) and current governor of São Paulo.

Herman Voorwald: A Brazilian professor and politician. Secretary of the São Paulo State Education dismissed on December 4, 2015.

Networked Social Movement: Social demonstration broadcasted with the support of social networking tools.

The Occupation Movement of Schools in the São Paulo State: The fighting of the students against the measure of the closure of public schools proclaimed by the São Paulo State Secretariat for Education.

Paulista: Adjective to refer to a person or thing originated in the state of São Paulo, Brazil.

Pedagogical Project: Proposals and educational actions, teaching and learning activities, which will be implemented, evaluated and reorganized by a public or private school in each period.

Protagonist Youth: Teenager participation in actions that go beyond the areas of their personal interests manifested at school space, and in the various spheres of social-community and political life.

São Paulo State Secretariat for Education: Agency responsible for managing the network of public schools of the São Paulo State, Brazil.

School Community: Meeting members of a society composed of parents, students, teachers, community leaders and operational staff who share the school environment.

The School Reorganization Act: The proposal of closing 94 public schools announced by the São Paulo State Secretariat for Education in October 2015.

State School Fernão Dias Paes: The first public school occupied by the students in the capital in November 2015, located in *Pinheiros* neighborhood, West Zone of São Paulo city, Brazil.

Chapter 4
Information and Communication Technologies as Drivers of Social Unrest

Martha Garcia-Murillo
Syracuse University, USA

Moinul Zaber
University of Dhaka, Bangladesh

Marcio Wohlers de Almeida
State University of Campinas – UNICAMP, Brazil

ABSTRACT

Information and communication technologies (ICTs) are alleviating frictions associated with the gathering and distribution of information, as well as reducing transaction costs related to the identifying, monitoring, and coordination of citizens dissatisfied with certain government policies. We conducted a random-effect logit tests based on a uniquely developed panel dataset of 138 countries from 2005 to 2014 to determine, ceteris paribus, whether or not ICTs play a role in facilitating changes to the status quo that gravitate against government policies. We found that ICTs although it can reduce hysteresis, the tendency to remain passive, inertia, is stronger. In addition, because ICTs are multi-purpose technologies they also support other beneficial economic and political activities which can explain why we don't see greater evidence of social unrest with these technologies. The literature on social unrest provide some clues about this phenomenon. People are willing to engage in these movements but it appears that only during a crisis.

DOI: 10.4018/978-1-5225-2495-3.ch004

INTRODUCTION

The goal of this chapter is to understand why information and communication technologies (ICTs) can be a powerful tool for citizens to protest against what they perceive to be unjust. We focus on the attributes of ICTs that are able to reduce friction in information gathering and distribution, as well as reduce the transaction costs of searching for information and or people, monitoring their behavior, and coordinating participation among similarly concerned citizens. These attributes, we believe, can facilitate and enhance the emotional connections that people have with the problems they face. This century has seen, much more tangibly, the manner in which these technologies have facilitated, to a certain extent, social movements such as the Arab Spring in the Middle East, the Occupy and the Black Lives Matter movements in the U.S. and *Los Indignados* in Spain, among others. We believe that ICTs are opening virtual public spheres where the members of civil society are able to engage with peers and, at times of distress, to organize to protest against their governments.

Many scholars have studied social unrest and have tested different hypotheses to try to elucidate the causes of these movements. The main contribution of this paper is to make connections between neuroscience (in particular the emotional connections that are needed for people to get engaged in a social protest) and economics (in particular the manner in which fundamental concepts such as information friction and transaction costs are significantly reduced by ICTs), while also taking into consideration the contributions of the social sciences (in particular the factors that contribute to unrest). From this analysis, we find that, indeed, ICTs contribute to social manifestations of discontent.

Using data from the World Bank and other international organizations, we constructed a model to empirically determine if information technologies, specifically mobile devices and Internet access, lead to greater social unrest.

In addition to ICTs, we included three control factors that previous scholars have identified as contributors to a society's need to protest. These are: economic factors (income per capita), governance, and the size of the population.

LITERATURE REVIEW

Explaining Social Unrest

Social unrest can have different manifestations. It can be displayed in violent and uncontrolled ways, in more planned and organized public protests, and even in the form of nonviolent resistance, which, we believe, in the future may even take place exclusively online. There is a large body of scholarly work about social unrest.

Regarding social unrest specifically, Castells (2013) notes that social neuroscientists have shown that social change involves individual or collective actions that have emotional motivations. The main emotions involved in social change are fear, which results in precautionary behaviors such as withdrawal, and anger, which acts as a trigger to action. In other words, emotions push individuals towards action, which, with others, can evolve into collective action.

Castells' (2013) ideas about the role of emotional motivation in social change is supported by the social psychological theory of protest. Van Stekelenburg and Klandermans (2013), for example, have provided a sound literature review on social psychological issues explaining peoples' reasons for protesting. The authors stress that group-based emotions, including anger, are important motivators of protest participation.

The literature about protests has found that individuals are relatively slow to respond to the problems they face. There is, therefore, a delay between a problem and a reaction from citizens. Scholars have modeled the process in terms of movement from a passive state, when civil society is not engaged, to an active state, which can involve street protests, for example. This swift passage from passive to active is shown in Figure 1, which represents the delay or reluctance that people show before they decide to get involved. F1 is the point at which people are no longer satisfied with the problematic situation they are facing and decide to act. They remain active until things get better at point F2, when it is no longer justifiable or necessary to remain active.

This phenomenon is getting greater attention in other fields like economics, where, for example, Liu, Hassanpour, Tatikonda, and Morse (2012) describe how a network of individuals may or may not be willing to participate in collective action, depending on their level of risk and the number of other people engaged. For people to get engaged, they need to know that their discontent is shared by other people, and they must be willing to join in. Under an oppressive regime, nobody wants to be involved in an unsuccessful attempt to protest against their government, as this can result in severe retaliations, such as those experienced in Turkey after a failed coup attempt in July of 2015.

In this study, we were concerned only with the first part of the sigmoidal curve, as we were mainly interested in the factors that lead a society to move from passive to active, from idleness to protest, in the presence of perceived economic or political problems. In this respect, we believe that ICTs may shorten the time it takes, and the frequency with which people wait, to get organized. Hysteresis, which is the tendency to remain constant in spite of changes in the environment, is analogous to the delay that we see in societies before they are willing to get engaged more

Figure 1. Public attitude versus perceived seriousness of the problem. (Adapted from Scheffer, Westley, & Brock, 2003)

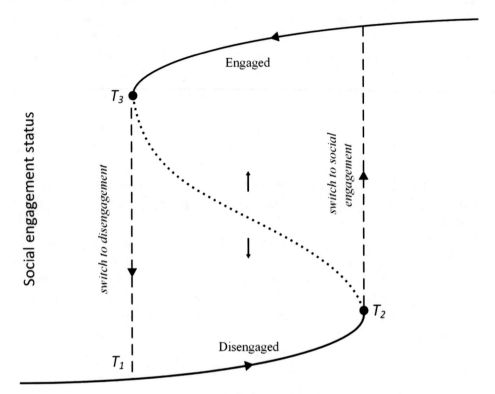

Level of social discontent

visibly when faced with a problem. As Kuran (1991) explains, in the absence of information about other's people's concerns, each risk-averse citizen, falsifies his/ her preference until a threshold is reach when people are willing to display their private preferences and get engaged in a public protest. We may thus find that ICTs reduce hysteresis, meaning the tendency to maintain the status quo, due to the ease with which they can make people aware of problems.

It is clear that research about social movements points to two key elements that prompt people to get involved: the dissatisfaction that they feel about a situation and an emotional connection to dissatisfied others that may prompt them to act. According to Jovanović, Renn, and Schröter (2012), social unrest is an expression of collective dissatisfaction, where the intensity of the protest depends on the level and nature of the social discontent.

Pappas and O'Malley (2014) identified four groups of causes that can lead people to take to the streets to express their dissatisfaction: economic, cultural, socio-ideological, and state-related.

There are examples in the literature that support Jovanović, Renn, and Schröter's definition. In Argentina in 1993, for example, government employees rioted and burned three government buildings, as well as the houses of local politicians and government officers. Scholars who studied the event found that the government employees had not been paid in more than three months; moreover, instances of corruption, nepotism, and police repression had led to "psychological states of indignation, frustration and/or resentment" (Auyero, 2003, p. 121).

Today, we see, potentially, more instances of this type of abuses, not necessarily because there are more of them but because ICTs have made them more public globally.

Dewey, Kaden, Marks, Matsushima, and Zhu (2012), for example, documented seven of the Arab Spring uprisings, all of which show that economic and government-related problems contributed to these social protests.

Regarding state motivators for unrest, Tunisia, Egypt, Yemen, Jordan, Bahrain, Syria, and Morocco were all governed by authoritarian regimes, and many lacked free elections and/or had restrictions imposed on the creation of new parties. In addition, they lacked transparency and showed little respect for the rule of law and the protection of civil liberties. Corruption was also prevalent in many of these countries. In Egypt, for example, President Mubarak was believed to have accumulated between $40 USD and $70 USD billion and business associates close to his son to have accumulated $1 billion USD (Jack, 2011). Similarly, people in Tunisia, Syria, and Yemen were outraged at the level of corruption and nepotism displayed by their governments.

Given this more recent evidence, we believe that information and communication technologies, as explained below, can also contribute by reducing the frictions associated with information gathering and distribution, and by reducing the costs of searching and monitoring other people's reactions and coordinating social action, making these manifestations of discontent more salient.

In isolation it is difficult for people to find out whether their discontent with government is shared and if other people are willing to protest, and could lead, we believe, to many fewer instances of social unrest.

As we will describe in the next section, ICTs can incite a faster transition from passive to active participation, due to the fact that the tipping or threshold point is reached sooner because these technologies are available to enable people to communicate and share information.

The Role of ICTs in Helping Citizens Get Organized

Previous generations faced challenges when trying to make policy changes or changes in government. These citizens did not have the tools needed to find and share information about government incompetencies, for example, nor did they have the means to coordinate their efforts against perceived injustices. ICTs have, however, improved information and access.

ICTs are "a diverse set of technological tools and resources used to communicate, and to create, disseminate, store and manage information" (Blurton, 1999). However, technology alone is not, per se, a solution to society's problems; it is the people who own them and the manner in which they use and apply them. ICTs allow people to access information and to communicate with one another, facilitating more informed decisions.

There are several reasons why ICTs can be particularly effective in coordinating people for the purpose of expressing their collective dissatisfaction with their government (Kaur & Tao, 2014): (1) ICTs are interactive, so that they can facilitate conversation, not only between two people, but among many simultaneously; (2) they are permanently available, barring any government blocks – once a population has acquired mobile phones or has access to the Internet, these tools are available to them anytime they need them; (3) they aren't bound by geography and have, in fact, a global reach, which means that social movements can coordinate and bring together people from all corners of a nation, or even the world; (4) the actual costs, as well as the transaction costs, of communication have decreased significantly, making it affordable for most people.

In his book *Networks of Outrage and Hope*, Castells (2013) highlights ten characteristics of social movements that are particular to this Internet age. The movements: (1) are networked using the Internet and wireless devices that allow for mass communication with powerful images; (2) are horizontal networks that create a sense of fellowship that helps to overcome fear and find hope, while facilitating and encouraging cooperation; (3) are triggered by a spark of outrage in a spontaneous manner; (4) become viral due to the easy dissemination of information on the Internet, which is reinforced by the demonstration effect of other social events; (5) convert indignation into an autonomous entity, which usually happens through decisions made in a space of autonomy; (6) are self-reflexive and constantly question what they want, with a governance structure that can help them avoid the pitfalls of failed movements; and (7) are generally nonviolent. However, (8) they tend to occupy public spaces to pressure political authorities and business representatives, and (9) they rarely have a focus, except in cases of rebellions against dictatorial regimes. They have many and varied demands, in order not to produce an organization or leadership, because agreements proceed from their collective decisions and detailed protest plans, and (10) they intend to transform the state but not radically change it.

These technologies are thus able to create links among people who lacked them prior to their prevalence and use in society. They expanded the "neighborhood" to reach all corners of the globe and multiply the number of channels that people have to distribute or obtain information.

We know from experimental research in psychology that people are highly influenced in their actions by the actions of others (Latane & Darley, 1968). It is clear, thus, that knowing what others are doing will influence a person's behavior. Before ICTs were more widely available, it would have taken much longer for a person to know what fellow citizens were feeling about their government. Today, the public has many tools for communicating with people they don't know. With a few keystrokes, a person can easily share information on practically any topic or event. Mobile phones, for example, allow people to connect to others through blogs, Facebook postings e-mail, tweets and SMSs. On the Internet, they can find limitless information, and with a broadband connection, they can make, share, and access videos.

We may thus find that the inertia (hysteresis) or reluctance that people may feel about getting involved can be eased by their getting to know, through these technologies, that there are many peers as dissatisfied as themselves.

ICTs as a communication resource affect people's perceptions due to a reduction of both information friction and transaction costs. Information friction stems from the limited information that the population has about the preferences and concerns of their fellow citizens. Reductions in transaction costs include a reduction of the cost of searching, which in the case of protests means both for information about a problem and for people who may have similar negative perception about it, a reduction of monitoring costs, which, for social unrest to happen, means knowing about the amount of people who may also feel discontent about a specific problem, and a reduction of coordination costs of participating in public demonstrations about the issues of concern. In the past, people had to dedicate time and resources looking for information that was spread through means such as radio, TV, newspapers, and word-of-mouth. Today it is much easier, due to the fact that people can simply subscribe to news, follow tweets or Facebook posts, and read at their leisure. This cursory awareness is, in fact, a form of monitoring that takes little effort. Coordination is another factor that has significantly changed with the spread of ICTs. In this respect, we made an important distinction that does not appear in the literature. We divided ICTs into coordination and information technologies, with cell phones being primarily a coordination tool, and the Internet primarily an information tool. Because cell phones convey short messages with basic information, people can quickly get information about the location and time of an organized event. However, if they need more in-depth information about an issue, they will find it more convenient to do it through a broadband connection, with a larger screen that allows them to navigate to multiple sources.

Information technologies, with their ability to reduce information friction and transaction costs, also enable leaders to emerge much faster. An opinion leader who finds an audience can quickly acquire a large number of followers through likes and the spreading of links to the leader's site. These leaders, as Scheffer et al. (2003) indicate, can precipitate a rapid shift in opinion.

If one looks back at work on group processes in the literature, such as the book edited by Berkowitz (1978), we find that decentralized groups, in which information is distributed and accessible to everyone, are more productive (Shaw, 1964). At the time Shaw was writing about this, we find that without these technologies the amount of information and coordination that a person could handle significantly limited the size and activities of a group. From an information-handling perspective, previously, the problems of noise and distribution were significant because there were no tools like these, and the size of the groups was consequently limited, but with these technologies, groups can correct mistakes (also they can be larger), and provide unlimited access to information flows. In sum, ICTs are able to reduce information friction when larger groups of people need to coordinate their work.

Today, even traditional media outlets have moved to the digital realm, creating what Wilson calls a media "ecosystem," a closely knit network of information producers where entities public, private and, we would argue, citizens, participate (Palmer & Perkins, 2012) These new digital information outlets have opened spaces for participation, openness, and knowledge/content creation (Palmer & Perkins, 2012).

Given the unique characteristics of these technologies, there has been greater interest in studying their role in the policy field. Lopes (2014), for example, explores the impact of social media on social movements. Using a data set that includes economic, social, and political conditions, she uncovers a relationship between those conditions and social media. Using Internet penetration as a proxy variable for social media, she found, is a strong predictor of protest activity. From this, she concludes that social media is the "latest and most revolutionary tool in the formation of social movements" (p. 5).

In fact, although there is some evidence that these technologies are not sufficient to produce social unrest (Dewey et al., 2012), some recent studies suggest that social media, which is made possible by ICTs, may have contributed to the Arab Spring (Ghannam, 2011). Thus, we expect that, given the political instability related to poverty, education, and governance factors, ICTs may lead to greater instability because people can more easily organize. From an economic perspective, this would mean an upward shift in the relationship between ICTs and protests as ICTs become more widely accessible to a population.

Figure 2. Average subscription to mobile phones per 100 and fixed broadband subscription per 100 (in logarithmic scale) over the years 2005 to 2014. Data Source: ITU

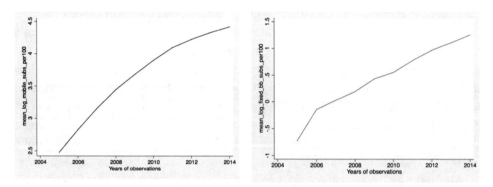

Figure 3. Increase in reports of social unrest over the years 2005 to 2014. Data Source: (Democracy, 2016)

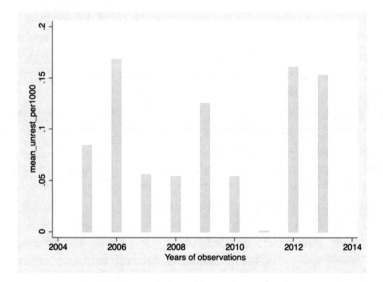

Figure 2 shows the increase in average subscriptions of both mobile phones and broadband, and Figure 3 provides an early indication of the growth in social unrest that has been experienced around the world over the last ten years.

Twitter was founded in 2006, and the great recession happened in 2008. We see a slight increase in social unrest just before the crisis and then a significant increase two and a half years later. These two graphs require additional scrutiny, which is the focus of the empirical analysis.

Beyond statistics, we find cases of the impact of ICTS even in a country like China, where citizens face severe limitations on their civil liberties. An example of the manner in which ICTs are becoming an important information mechanism for people to mobilize is described by MacKinnon (2009), who discusses the case of Guo Baofeng, a blogger who was arrested in 2009 by police on suspicious rape charges. At the time of his arrest, he sent a tweet that led to bloggers' organizing to get him released. One set up a campaign to get hundreds of people to mail postcards to the detention center where Mr. Guo was being held. Others organized fundraising to pay for his defense. These efforts eventually led to his release two weeks later. As MacKinnon explains, if this event had taken place ten years earlier, few people would have known of it at all through the traditional media, much less the public at large in real time.

Similarly, in 2001 in China, ICTs contributed to a social movement following an explosion at a school that killed 41 people in Jiangxi Province. The initial official report had blamed the blast to a single person. Using the Internet, parents at the school contradicted the government's explanation, explaining instead that the explosion was caused by school children who were forced to work constructing firecrackers on the school grounds. Although the government deleted many of these postings, enough remained to eventually lead to an unprecedented official apology by Zhu Rongji, then Prime Minister (Kalathil & Boas, 2010; C. Smith, 2001).

In Indonesia, as Lim (2003) explains, warnets (public rooms with computers) were the main source for "forbidden" information. The mailing list *Apakabar*, founded by an American, John McDougall, forwarded Indonesian-related news all over the world, including messages about corruption by Suharto and his cronies, and contributed to the online emergence of the Indonesia Communist Party (PKI). Furthermore, Indonesian students abroad coordinated through an e-mail-based newsletter, *Suara Demokrasi* (voice of Democracy). All of these channels of communication eventually contributed to the fall of President Suharto (Kalathil & Boas, 2003)

As these cases show, ICTs create spaces where citizens can express their contentions with government and feel free to criticize it. The relationships that ICTs can foster among families, friends, other people with similar interests, and civil society organizations generate spontaneous or coordinated efforts aimed at protesting a government's inability to respond to the needs of the population.

In addition to facilitating protests, ICTs also expand human emotions. ICTs, Castells (2013) believes, create horizontal networks that feed movements in both local and global dimensions, producing enthusiasm that strengthens social mobilization intentionality. It is the Internet, he argues, that turns untreated responses into movements of political importance.

In light of the preceding discussion, we wish to test the following hypothesis:

H1: ICTs are likely to increase social unrest.

While we are interested in the role of ICTs, it would be unrealistic to ignore other factors that can contribute to the emergence of these movements. Because of this, our econometric analysis includes economic factors, political factors (specifically, governance), and the size of the population as control elements that can contribute to a society's need to protest.

Other Factors That Contribute to Social Unrest

Social unrest is not an isolated phenomenon; because of this, our empirical analysis includes other factors found in the literature, described below. Figure 4 presents these additional variables.

Figure 4. Theoretical model of factors influencing social unrest

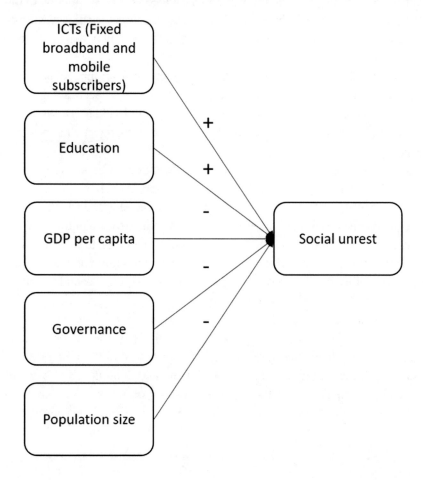

Economic Factors

In 1970, Gurr published the book *Why Men Rebel*, in which he argues that when people are negatively affected by economic factors, such as a general economic recession or more specific feelings of deprivation, it can lead to frustration, and thus, aggression.

Economic conditions such as depressions and crises that lead to austerity measures can negatively affect employment opportunities and wages. Other scholars (Bohlken & Sergenti, 2010; Brandt & Ulfelder, 2011) have also found that a country is likely to experience social unrest when its economic growth is slow, while the contrary is true when its economy is growing. A similar result was found among European countries, where instances of social unrest increased when public spending as a percentage of GDP decreased, and the probability of protests almost doubled when these cuts reached 5% of GDP.

The 2008 "Great Recession" led to citizen protests. In some countries, these continued for months, while in others they dissipated relatively quickly. In the U.S. and the U.K., for example, Roberts (2013) explains, people ceased their manifestations of discontent due to quantitative easing that limited the extent to which the recession affected them.

Roubini (2011) warned about social unrest coming from inadequate economic responses to market forces. For instance, firms' cutting jobs because of inadequate consumer demand. This rational decision on the part of individual firms is destructive to society at large, and, if it is not dealt with well by governments, can generate widespread discontent.

We need to be concerned about these manifestations of discontent because of the impact they have on a country's economy. Justino (2005), for example, found a correlation between social unrest and reductions in economic growth. She argues that frequent episodes of civil unrest significantly reduce the potential for economic growth and poverty reduction. In short, civil unrest can lead to poverty. However, it is also true that poverty induces civil unrest. The magnitude of recent social and political instability in many developing countries has brought social conflict to the forefront of modern development economics.

In his book *The End of Protest - How Free-Market Capitalism Learned to Control Dissent*, Roberts (2013) presents an analysis of the factors that lead to social protest. He states that unrest is an intrinsic part of the free market model, a problem identified earlier by thinkers like Polany and Schumpeter. These authors, Roberts (2013) states, noted the natural tendency of loosely regulated markets to create discontent. However, in the United States and England, unrest emerged during the Great Recession, the worst economic crisis in a generation, but not to the extent expected, because these countries developed new methods for reconciling the neoliberal disdain for democratic politics with the immediate need to avert a total economic meltdown.

In the 19th century, politics were routinely shaped by mass action on the part of citizens in the form of strikes, demonstrations, marches, and riots. Currently, preventing crowds into mass action depends on the effectiveness of democratic institutions to give expression to public frustration about the economy (Roberts, 2013).

One of the aims of protesters since the financial crisis has been to point out the ways in which the democratic process has been undermined during the neoliberal age and to denounce democratic institutions that have been captured by well-heeled interests. In others words, the institutions that are supposed to function as the vehicle for responding to public discontent have been hobbled so that they cannot do this properly.

More recently, Della Porta (2015) presents a broad perspective analyzing social unrest under the conditions of income concentration, unemployment, and under-unemployment. She makes a distinction between the salariat, such as the 29th century's industrial workers, and the precariat. These, she argues, constitute the main participants of social unrest and encompass people without formal employment and social protection, as well as disadvantaged youth. She also explores the influence of neoliberalism and its crises on protest movements. In this respect, she argues that the precariat is reinforced by neoliberal policies that reduce social protections in favor of pro-market solutions.

Social movements do not begin only because of social inequality or political despair. They also require an emotional mobilization triggered by outrage and hopes for a possible change. They are fueled by movements in other parts of the world whose successes have been spread by the Internet.

The 1993 riot in Argentina occurred in Santiago del Estero, where almost a third of the population at the time was unable to satisfy basic needs. The city had the lowest income level and the lowest life expectancy (Auyero, 2003). When a population is living with incomes at or below the poverty line, it is reasonable to expect that, feeling pressure, they will protest to influence the government to change their circumstances (Alesina & Perotti, 1996). They have nothing to lose so that they decide to demonstrate, or even engage in acts of terrorism (Abadie, 2006). As their income increases, they grow busy with their lives, and, being a bit more satisfied, they may be more reluctant to protest, leading to greater political stability. We should thus expect that as income increases, so should stability.

We thus tested the following hypothesis:

H2: The lower the GDP per capita, the more likely social unrest.

Governance

An efficient and effective state is open, transparent, and accountable to the population (Theobald, 2002). Poor governance affects the poor, which can in turn push citizens to the streets to call for the prosecution of corrupt behavior.

Poor governance can potentially have two effects on the likelihood of protests. On one hand, it can be a powerful motivating factor that can lead people to protest when they realize how poor policy decisions and corruption are affecting their country, and them personally. For example, poorly paid, or even unpaid, government employees can take advantage of their positions to "sell favors" in the form of government services and to commit even more serious offences, such as selling weapons to drug cartels or approving lucrative public work contracts. The main concern is when money is diverted from the economy at the hands of public officials to illegally supply public services.

Governments that profit from the status quo will try to limit protest, resist any changes and simply put in place cosmetic solutions that lead the population to think that something is being done, while, in reality, the problem persists. In addition, given the personal benefits that these individuals receive and the power they hold, they can delay or block changes in government (Magee, 1989).

Examples from many countries provide evidence of a link between social unrest and ineffective or corrupt governments. In China, for example, Sun (1991) attributes to government corruption the 1989 protests in Beijing. Also in China, Chen (2000) attributes labor protests to corruption and the ineffectiveness of state enterprises that systematically eroded salaries and subjected workers to coercive labor controls.

Similarly, Lippman (2014) explains how protests in Bosnia-Herzegovina, which resulted in several torched government buildings, could be traced to pervasive government corruption in the country, and in India, the actions of Anna Hazare, who began a protest fast against public corruption, and ultimately died, was the starting point for the Hazare Movement, which resulted in protests in many sectors of the economy.

Even in a world where citizens have greater access to ICTs, governments play an important role in the success that citizens may have in using these tools to get organized. In this respect, Lessig has indicated that governments can regulate the Internet through the technical code that runs the network or through their laws and regulations (Lessig, 1999).

This is not more evident than in China, where the government decided in 1996 that connections to the Internet were going to be arranged through a two-tier system, where users connect to a first level of servers, which in turn connects to a second tier of servers controlled by the state (Kalathil & Boas, 2010). Similarly, as described by Kalathil and Boas (2003) in Saudi Arabia and the United Arab Emirates, the government uses technology that blocks both pornographic and political sites. Studies of other countries, like Egypt and Turkey (Kalathil & Boas, 2003), indicate that censorship of participation happens when governments make very public crackdowns against the use of ICTS that have political or socially inappropriate content.

In this study, we thus tested the following hypothesis:

H3: Poor governance in a country will lead to higher instances of social unrest.

METHOD AND DATA DESCRIPTION

Using data from the World Bank and other international organizations, we assembled panel data that tested the impact of ICTs on political stability through the variables of income, governance, and size of the population.

To analyze the data, we used a panel dataset from 2005-2014 encompassing 128 countries from 2005 to 2014. The dataset is unique in that it was constructed by merging data from various sources. The appendix provides a more detailed description for each of the variables, summary statistics and correlations among the variables. The data come from:

- The World Bank database, which provided us with data on GDP per capita, education enrollment and population. We used log transformations of both the GDP and population variables;
- The International Social Science Resource, produced by Witold J. Henisz, who constructed the Political Constraint Index Dataset (POLCON III), where POLCON = 0 means minimum constraint, or the most unstable political environment, and POLCON = 1 means maximum constraint, or the most stable political environment. POLCON III is an attempt to measure political constraint, that is, to recognize underlying political structures and measure their ability to support credible policy commitments (National Bureau of Economic Research, 2015). This is also our proxy variable for governance;
- The International Telecommunication Union, where data on broadband subscriptions and mobile subscriptions are available. We used the log of both broadband subscribers per 100 in the overall population and mobile subscribers per 100 in our estimations;

- The Freedom house, that reports the press freedom index of the countries of the world. The index is a numerical score calculated from evaluating the "legal environment for the media, political pressures that influence reporting, and economic factors that affect access to news and information (Freedom House, 2016)".
- The University of Illinois Urbana-Champaign which provided the dependent variable unrest, which represents a weighted conflict index taken from its Civil Unrest Data (Cline Center for Democray, 2016). The variable that indicates unrest is termed domestic9 in the estimation – it is a weighted index of the number of reports of protest in the country in question. The weighted index is based on reports of assassinations, general strikes, guerrilla warfare, government crises, purges, riots, revolutions, and anti-government demonstrations.

Tables 1 and 2 present the regression results of the cross-national panel regression conducted on the variable *social unrest*. We have used a level-log linear model to ascertain the impact of the explanatory variables on unrest variable. The model helps to reduce the effect of possible outliers and also handles the non-linear relationship between the dependent variable and some of the independent variables. Using log makes the relationship non-linear while still preserving the linear nature of the model.

The general model for the estimation is given below:

$$Unrest_{it} = \beta_0 + \boldsymbol{logICT}_{it}\beta_1 + \boldsymbol{Politic}_{it}\beta_2 + \boldsymbol{logDemographic}_{it}\beta_3 + +\varepsilon_{it},$$

Where *i* indicates countries, *t* indicates years, *unrest* is a variable that indicates number of protests (in thousands) in a country in a given year, the vector *ICT* stands for the explanatory variables: log of mobile (log_mobile_subs_per100) and broadband subscriptions (log_fixed_bb_subs_per100). *Politic* indicates the political structure variable (polcon3). *logDemographic* indicates the demographic variables, GDP per Capita PPP (log_gdp), *Population* (log_pop). *logEducation* indicates educational enrollment. Finally, ε_{it} indicates the error for that observation.

ANALYSIS OF RESULTS

The model (1) described in the previous section was scrutinized with the help of a cross national time series data. Econometric estimations of such datasets may have systematic differences among coefficients. In order to reduce country specific biases, fixed effect (FE) estimation methods are often used. Along with country specific

Table 1. Regression results by region

VARIABLES	1	2	East Asia and Oceania 3	South Asia 4	Middle East 5	Africa 6	Europe 7	North America 8	South America 9
	unrest per1000	unrest per1000	unrest per1000	unrest per1000	unrest per1000	unrest per1000	unrest per1000	unrest per1000	unrest per1000
polcon3	0.07	-0.01	0.36**	0.10	0.21	-0.24	0.08*	0.14***	-0.03
	(0.056)	(0.083)	(0.149)	(0.067)	(0.142)	(0.267)	(0.045)	(0.054)	(0.052)
log_gdp	0.04**	0.07*	-0.09**	0.02	0.02	0.19**	-0.02	-0.02*	0.02
	(0.018)	(0.037)	(0.045)	(0.039)	(0.035)	(0.079)	(0.017)	(0.010)	(0.024)
log_pop	-0.02**	-0.14***	-0.04***	-0.01	-0.03	-0.11**	-0.01	-0.00	0.01
	(0.010)	(0.028)	(0.014)	(0.005)	(0.028)	(0.054)	(0.009)	(0.001)	(0.006)
log_education enrollment	0.09	-0.30	0.70	-0.17**	-0.53	0.59	-0.77**	0.36**	0.06
	(0.177)	(0.290)	(0.758)	(0.084)	(0.437)	(0.567)	(0.379)	(0.164)	(0.442)
log_fixed_bb subs_per100	-0.02***	-0.04***	0.02	-0.01	-0.00	-0.10***	-0.01	-0.00	-0.02***
	(0.006)	(0.010)	(0.019)	(0.016)	(0.014)	(0.031)	(0.005)	(0.004)	(0.007)
log_mobile subs_per100	-0.01	0.00	-0.01	0.01	0.02	-0.09**	-0.01	-0.01	-0.01
	(0.008)	(0.013)	(0.030)	(0.008)	(0.021)	(0.038)	(0.008)	(0.006)	(0.008)
t	0.01***	0.01**	-0.01	-0.00	0.01	0.06***	0.01***	0.00***	0.00
	(0.003)	(0.004)	(0.010)	(0.008)	(0.007)	(0.018)	(0.002)	(0.001)	(0.003)
Constant	-0.03	1.79***	1.53***	-0.04	0.17	-0.19	0.25	0.21**	-0.23
	(0.249)	(0.584)	(0.500)	(0.420)	(0.597)	(1.307)	(0.215)	(0.105)	(0.221)
Observations	1,233	499	129	57	161	213	462	41	170
R-squared									
Number of cn	132	116	13	7	19	29	41	4	19

Standard errors in parentheses
*** $p<0.01$, ** $p<0.05$, * $p<0.1$

Table 2. Regression results by freedom index

VARIABLES	freedom 1 10	freedom 2 11	freedom 3 12	freedom 4 13	freedom 5 14	freedom 6 15	freedom 7 16
	unrest per1000	unrest per1000	unrest per1000	unrest per1000	unrest per1000	unrest per1000	unrest per1000
polcon3	-0.02	0.11	-0.08	0.33	-0.11	-0.01	3.39*
	(0.029)	(0.066)	(0.148)	(0.229)	(0.282)	(0.055)	(1.948)
log_gdp	-0.01	0.01	0.01	-0.03	0.21	-0.01	0.48***
	(0.011)	(0.033)	(0.043)	(0.102)	(0.167)	(0.011)	(0.151)
log_pop	-0.00	0.00	-0.03	-0.08	-0.16*	0.00	-0.09
	(0.003)	(0.013)	(0.018)	(0.055)	(0.085)	(0.007)	(0.088)
log_enrollment	0.28	0.29	0.44	0.21	-0.56	-0.14*	1.40
	(0.273)	(0.213)	(0.368)	(0.823)	(0.905)	(0.077)	(1.711)
log_fixed_bb_subs_per100	0.00	-0.01	-0.01	-0.04	-0.05	0.00	-0.18***
	(0.004)	(0.008)	(0.016)	(0.025)	(0.038)	(0.005)	(0.060)
log_mobile_subs_per100	0.00	-0.01	0.00	0.05	-0.15*	0.00	-0.12*
	(0.006)	(0.014)	(0.017)	(0.038)	(0.083)	(0.007)	(0.065)
t	-0.00	0.01	0.01	-0.02	0.07***	-0.00	0.11***
	(0.001)	(0.005)	(0.008)	(0.014)	(0.025)	(0.003)	(0.043)
Constant	0.11	-0.10	0.39	1.47	0.86	0.14	-3.42
	(0.109)	(0.384)	(0.517)	(1.282)	(2.052)	(0.150)	(2.573)
Observations	482	175	160	106	82	160	68
R-squared							
Number of cn	48	31	36	33	21	30	13

Standard errors in parentheses
*** $p<0.01$, ** $p<0.05$, * $p<0.1$

105

biases, a time series estimation may also have time specific biases. More specifically, many of the occurrences of unrest around the world may be due to global events at a specific time of a specific year. We therefore introduce a variable 't' to capture any time specific effect. In order to ensure the appropriateness of the use of FE method we conducted a Hausman test. A statistically significant p-value of the test indicates there may be a systematic difference in the coefficients, and we should prefer the fixed-effects ("within") model rather than include the random-effects ("between") model. However, in the case of the datasets we have employed, the p-value was not found to be significant. Hence we had to assume RE method over FE method. This is particularly important for variables such as Population and GDP per Capita, because they do not change much and hence would be dropped if fixed effect is assumed. Hence all the estimations in tables 1 and 2 use random effect model. In this context we would like to emphasize that, there is not much difference in both the direction and magnitude of the independent variables in RE and FE methods.

Tables 1 and 2 summarize the findings of the estimate. Estimation 1 is the cross country analysis consisting of the countries in the world that are in the dataset while estimation 2 only covers the country-year pair that do not have any 0 value for the unrest variable. Estimation 2 therefore has fewer observations and it is useful to understand the impact of the independent variables on the estimations 3-8 that are over various regions of the world. Estimation 3 is of countries in East-Asia and Oceania, estimation 4 is of south Asian countries, estimation 5 is of Middle Eastern countries, estimation 6 is of African countries, estimation 7 is of European countries, estimation 8 is of North American countries, and estimation 9 is of South American countries. Estimations 10-16 are respectively of countries grouped according to their Freedom House press freedom index. Here 1 indicates countries where press has greatest freedom while 7 indicates countries that have the least press freedom. The breakdown into these seven categories is done by Freedom House so we kept the same groupings to maintain the structure of the data.

The estimations indicate that the ICT variables of both mobile and broadband are significant and they show a negative impact on the weighted unrest index. This is contrary to what we had hypothesized. The results indicate that an increase of fixed broadband subscriptions may be associated with a decrease in the unrest index. A 1% increase in broadband subscribers results in a 2 to 4% decrease in the value of the unrest index for all countries. In Africa, the decrease is around 10% and in South America it is around 2%.

We find the same result for the mobile variable where the coefficient is significant, specifically Africa, where countries with higher penetration of mobile telephony seem to have fewer reports of unrest. This indicates that all things being equal, the more people who subscribe to the Internet via fixed broadband the less likely the country will experience unrest.

While these models capture governance in general we wanted to determine if one variable in particular, freedom of expression, could help us understand the impact of ICTs on social unrest. This is because the ability of the population to express their discontent depends on whether or not their governments allow it or repress it. This is why our second set of models clusters countries not by region but by the freedoms (1 = most free, 7 = least free) these populations are granted. Table 2 shows those results. It should be noted that for many countries their respective value changes almost every year as press freedoms changes.

The results are almost identical to the previous models where the we find that a higher penetration of broadband leads to a reduction of instances of social unrest particularly in those with the most restrictive regimes where improvements in broadband can result in a 18% decrease in social unrest.

The mobile results are similar. In the most restrictive countries we find reduced social unrest. There is a 7% reduction in social unrest due to mobile improvements in countries with a freedom index of 5 and there is an 11% reduction for countries with a freedom index of 7. We believe that these lower instances of social unrest may be due to a lesser reporting of unrests in the least free countries.

All of these findings contradict our central hypothesis, which prompted us to search for additional research on the subject. Previous work on social unrest does not include information and communication technologies but some of those works can give us some clues about the role of ICTs with respect of social unrest.

We believe that two things can be happening. First ICTs are multi-purpose technologies, which means that they indeed reduce information frictions and transaction costs but this is true for many other activities including for example the ability to start a business or access to government services, for example. Broadband affords countless activities, from education to entertainment. Because of this, access to broadband can also provide access to many other resources, many of which are not related to social unrest. In fact, it is possible that having broadband access at home provides relief from other afflictions. It is also a door to educational and business opportunities that can help alleviate some of a country's economic and political problems.

Broadband penetration entails significant fixed costs which means that in order for a country to improve broadband access to the population it needs to be able to have reached a level of economic prosperity that can afford such infrastructure.

This may indicate that as wealthy societies mostly enjoy better fixed broadband connectivity, the effect of broadband is in a sense the effect of economic prosperity. However, as table 1 shows, higher GDP per capita PPP is associated with a higher value of unrest index. This indicate that in countries that have similar GDP per capita PPP, the country that has better fixed broadband connectivity will see less unrest. The estimations show that contrary to popular belief, digital connectivity is not one of the enablers of social unrest.

The literature on social unrest also provides other clues regarding the negative effect of ICTs on social unrest. (Mancini & O'Reilly, 2013) for example argue the opposite to what we hypothesized, that ICTs could be used to effectively prevent violence and conflict but they also acknowledge the importance of other measures to that aim. More importantly the work that the OECD (Renn, Jovanovic, & Schröter, 2011) did on social unrest focuses on specific events to explain these civic manifestations. The study highlights specific events such as the Greek economic crisis, environmental disasters such as Hurricane Katrina or the H1N1 flu as triggers to public protest. This approach is similar to the one that (T. Smith, 2013) took which focused exclusively on food prices. These works point to a reality that exhibits much more difficult conditions. What does this mean within the context of the theory we proposed in the paper? It appears that the level of inertia that we see is much greater than what we had anticipated, meaning that willingness to engage in social unrest requires much harsher conditions before people feel that public demonstrations are warranted. Similarly, these technologies also afford other benefits which can help counteract the potentially negative circumstances that the society may encounter. These two factors combined may thus help explain why we don't see greater instances of unrest with the greater penetration of these technologies.

Among the control variables, we found the log of population to have a negative effect on the number of protests. Again we may be seeing the effects of inertia but these countries may also experience more free riders where many of them are simply not engaged expecting others to do so.

Of the economic variables, the log of GDP per Capita was found to be significant and negative for North America and Oceania, which includes China, Japan and Korea as well as many island countries. This, as expected, means that as the per capita income of the population increases, they are more satisfied with their government and thus less likely to engage in social protests. In Africa, GDP per capita is significant but positive. This could mean that circumstances are improving but not to their satisfaction.

As regards the governance variable, the results tables also shows that the variable *Polcon* (0 indicates most politically unstable, 1 indicates most politically stable) is significant for some regions only. For North America, Europe and Oceania countries that have experiences of social unrest, when the political circumstances improve social unrest increases. It should be noted that over the period of study these regions have experienced significant economic changes with the reduction of manufacturing jobs due to both trade and automation, stagnant income and increased income inequality, which may explain why, in spite having good governments, they show increasing social discontent.

The variable education was, significant and negative, which means that improvement in education can result in reduced instances of social unrest. The exception is North America where an increase in educational enrollment increases social unrest. This may reflect the conflicted relationship that the public education system has in both the US and Mexico where funding in many areas is considered inadequate.

The time variable is seen to have a positive impact on the unrest variable indicating that reporting of unrest is increasing over time.

POLICY IMPLICATIONS AND CONCLUSION

This paper examines the relationship between ICTs and social unrest. Our main hypothesis was that ICTs can lead to more social unrest because they reduce information friction, which can help citizens gather and distribute relevant information, reduce the transaction costs of finding fellow citizens who may feel equally dissatisfied, and also reduce the coordination costs of getting organized. These technologies, we believed, reduce the natural inertia people have for getting engaged under conditions where information is lacking. However, we have found that contrary to our belief, ICTs do not seem to increase social unrest, or at least not exclusively. This finding does not invalidate the central premise that ICTs reduce both information frictions and transaction costs. Rather, what we might be seeing is that more engaged social interaction may reduce uncertainty which may dissuade people from taking to the streets for minor reasons.

Of the two technologies, broadband, which we expected to contribute to social unrest is found to be associated with reduced reports of social unrest. This, we believe is because this general purpose technology can help alleviate some of the problems a country may be facing by opening opportunities to people. In addition, as mentioned in the theory section, before people are willing to engage in social protest there is a certain level of inertia; only when they see others concerned with similar problems protesting are they willing to participate. These results indicate that inertia was stronger than expected and other literature points to much more serious events pushing people to the streets.

From a policy perspective, the fact that ICTs are not associated with a higher level of social unrest implies that governments should not limit their use, as some governments have tried to do. Instead, investing in infrastructure such as broadband can help improve the economic and political conditions of a country. The adoption of ICTs can in fact positively affect the economic development of a nation. They could also contribute to the strengthening of democratic processes. Opportunities for policy engagement through government sites, improvements in governance through e-government initiatives, and improvements in the economic circumstances of the population through online education and business are tools that governments can use to advance the wellbeing of their populations and reduce social unrest.

Educational policy raises far-reaching issues. Increasing the education level of a country leads to productivity gains and by doing so expands the possibilities for economic growth. However, as people become more educated, they are more likely to become aware of injustices and will thus be more likely to protest, leading to more unrest and instability. This is because education provides the tools to look at information with a more critical eye whereas ICTs might lead some to emphasize viewpoints with which they are already familiar.

It is important to stress that capitalism will continue to raise income concentration, unemployment, and under-unemployment. Taking into account increments in the use of ICTs, these conditions may have the potential to lead to social unrest but only under catastrophic circumstances. If governments do not wish to spawn protest movements, it is necessary for them to prevent them through adequate economic policies or to properly respond to crisis.

This study is a first attempt to empirically ascertain the impact of ICTs on social unrest. Further analysis – of more granular datasets at the national level, for example – can help us understand the roles that these technologies play when there is widespread discontent among people.

REFERENCES

Abadie, A. (2006). Poverty, political freedom, and the roots of terrorism. *The American Economic Review*, *96*(2), 50–56. doi:10.1257/000282806777211847

Alesina, A., & Perotti, R. (1996). Income distribution, political instability, and investment. *European Economic Review*, *40*(6), 1203–1228. doi:10.1016/0014-2921(95)00030-5

Auyero, J. (2003). Relational riot: Austerity and corruption protest in the neoliberal era. *Social Movement Studies*, *2*(2), 117–145. doi:10.1080/1474283032000139742

Berkowitz, L. (1978). *Group processes*. New York: Academic Press.

Blurton, C. (1999). New directions of ICT-use in education. Retrieved from https://goo.gl/6SgGxV

Bohlken, A. T., & Sergenti, E. J. (2010). Economic growth and ethnic violence: An empirical investigation of Hindu-Muslim riots in India. *Journal of Peace Research*, *47*(5), 589–600. doi:10.1177/0022343310373032

Brandt, P. T., & Ulfelder, J. (2011). Economic growth and political instability.

Castells, M. (2013). *Networks of outrage and hope: Social movements in the internet age*. John Wiley & Sons.

Chen, F. (2000). Subsistence crises, managerial corruption and labour protests in china. *China Journal (Canberra, A.C.T.)*, *44*(44), 41–63. doi:10.2307/2667476

Cline Center for Democracy. (2016). Civil unrest monitoring - dataset. Retrieved from http://www.clinecenter.illinois.edu/data/speed/

Della Porta, D. (2015). *Social movements in times of austerity: Bringing capitalism back into protest analysis*. Cambridge, UK: John Wiley & Sons.

Democracy, C. C. f. (2016). Civil unrest monitoring - datasets. Retrieved from http://www.clinecenter.illinois.edu/data/speed/

Dewey, T., Kaden, J., Marks, M., Matsushima, S., & Zhu, B. (2012). The impact of social media on social unrest in the arab spring. *Final report prepared for Defense Intelligence Agency* Retrieved from https://goo.gl/pT0Pgi

Freedom House. (2016). Freedom in the world. Retrieved from https://freedomhouse.org/report-types/frcedom-press

Ghannam, J. (2011). Social media in the Arab world: Leading up to the uprisings of 2011. Retrieved from https://goo.gl/a6KuSC

Gurr, T. R. (1970). *Why men rebel*. Princeton, NJ: Princeton University Press.

Jack, G. (2011). Understanding the revolutions of 2011. *Foreign Affairs*, *90*(3), 8.

Jovanović, A. S., Renn, O., & Schröter, R. (2012). *Social unrest*. OECD. doi:10.1787/9789264173460-en

Justino, P. (2005). Redistribution and civil unrest. Retrieved from https://goo.gl/KYkc6c

Kalathil, S., & Boas, T. C. (2003). *Open networks, closed regimes: The impact of the internet on authoritarian rule*. Washington, DC: Carnegie Endowment for International Peace.

Kalathil, S., & Boas, T. C. (2010). *Open networks, closed regimes: The impact of the internet on authoritarian rule*. Washington, D.C.: Carnegie Endowment for International Peace.

Kaur, H., & Tao, X. (2014). *Icts and the millennium development goals*. New York: Springer. doi:10.1007/978-1-4899-7439-6

Kuran, T. (1991). Now out of never: The element of surprise in the east european revolution of 1989. *World Politics, 44*(1), 7–48. doi:10.2307/2010422

Latane, B., & Darley, J. M. (1968). Group inhibition of bystander intervention in emergencies. *Journal of Personality and Social Psychology, 10*(3), 215–221. doi:10.1037/h0026570 PMID:5704479

Lessig, L. (1999). *Code: And other laws of cyberspace*. New York: Basic Books.

Lim, M. (2003). From real to virtual (and back again). In K. C. Ho & R. Kluver (Eds.), *Asia. Com: Asia encounters the internet* (pp. 113–128).

Lippman, P. (2014). Bosnia-herzegovina protests a response to post-war corruption, impoverishment. *The Washington Report on Middle East Affairs, 33*(3), 29–30.

Liu, J., Hassanpour, N., Tatikonda, S., & Morse, A. S. (2012). Dynamic threshold models of collective action in social networks. *Paper presented at the 2012 IEEE 51st IEEE Conference on Decision and Control (CDC)*. doi:10.1109/CDC.2012.6426657

Lopes, A. R. (2014). The impact of social media on social movements: The new opportunity and mobilizing structure. Retrieved from https://goo.gl/Jb1OS3

MacKinnon, R. (2009). Book review: The power of the internet in china: Citizen activism online. *Far Eastern Economic Review,* September.

Magee, S. P. (1989). *Black hole tariffs and endogenous policy theory: Political economy in general equilibrium*. Cambridge University Press.

Mancini, F., & O'Reilly, M. (2013). New technology and the prevention of violence and conflict. *Stability: International Journal of Security and Development, 2*(3), 1–9.

National Bureau of Economic Research. (2015). Data. Retrieved from http://www.nber.org/data/

Palmer, N. A., & Perkins, D. D. (2012). Technological democratization: The potential role of ict in social and political transformation in china and beyond. *Perspectives on Global Development and Technology, 11*(4), 456–479. doi:10.1163/15691497-12341236

Pappas, T. S., & OMalley, E. (2014). Civil compliance and political luddism: Explaining variance in social unrest during crisis in Ireland and Greece. *The American Behavioral Scientist, 58*(12), 1592–1613. doi:10.1177/0002764214534663

Renn, O., Jovanovic, A., & Schröter, R. (2011). Social unrest. *OECD.* Retrieved from http://www.oecd.org/governance/risk/46890018.pdf

Roberts, A. (2013). *The end of protest: How free-market capitalism learned to control dissent*. Cornell University Press.

Roubini, N. (2011). The instability of inequality. *Project Syndicate*. Retrieved from https://www.project-syndicate.org/commentary/the-instability-of-inequality

Scheffer, M., Westley, F., & Brock, W. (2003). Slow response of societies to new problems: Causes and costs. *Ecosystems (New York, N.Y.)*, *6*(5), 493–502. doi:10.1007/s10021-002-0146-0

Shaw, M. E. (1964). Communication networks. *Advances in Experimental Social Psychology*, *1*, 111–147. doi:10.1016/S0065-2601(08)60050-7

Smith, C. (2001). China backs away from initial denial in school explosion. Retrieved from https://goo.gl/AHjpTv

Smith, T. (2013). Food price spikes and social unrest in Africa. *CCAPS Research Brief*(11).

Sun, Y. (1991). The Chinese protests of 1989: The issue of corruption. *Asian Survey*, *31*(8), 762–782. doi:10.2307/2645228

Theobald, R. (2002). Containing corruption. *New Political Economy*, *7*(3), 435–449. doi:10.1080/1356346022000018775

Van Stekelenburg, J., & Klandermans, B. (2013). The social psychology of protest. *Current Sociology*, *61*(5-6), 886–905. doi:10.1177/0011392113479314

APPENDIX

Table 3. Description of the variables used

Variable	Description
domestic9	Weighted conflict index
unrest_per1000	Weighted conflict per 1000
polcon3	Political Condition Index (POLCON = 0 most hazardous and POLCON = 1 most stable political environment.)
log_gdp	log of gdp per capita
log_pop	log of total number of inhabitants
log_fixed_bb subs_per100	log of fixed broadband subscribers per 100
log_mobile subs_per100	log of mobile subscribers per 100
enrollment	School enrollment, primary (gross), gender parity index (GPI)
log_enrollment	log of School enrollment, primary (gross), gender parity index (GPI)
pressfreedom	PR, and Freedom Rating Score Explanation: (1 = most free and 7 = least free)
region	Regions of the world
year	Years of observations

Table 4. Summary statistics

Variable	Obs.	Mean	Std. Dev.	Min	Max
domestic9	2349	721.75	2953.76	0	85625
unrest_per1000	2340	0.11	0.62	0	14.35
polcon3	2357	0.28	0.20	0	0.72
log_gdp	2680	8.76	1.30	5.47	11.63
log_pop	3165	15.18	2.34	9.15	21.04
log_fixed_bb_subs_per100	2316	0.03	2.92	-9.94	4.55
log_mobile_subs_per100	2829	3.36	1.93	-5.55	13.24
enrollment	2253	0.96	0.08	0	1.33
log_enrollment	2251	-0.04	0.09	-0.83	0.29
pressfreedom	2773	3.33	2.15	1	7
region	2880	4.03	1.88	1	7
year	3235	2007	4	2000	2014

Table 5. Correlation Matrix

	domestic9	polcon3	log_ gdp	log_ pop	log_ fixed bb subs_ per100	log_ mobile subs_ per100	log enrollment	Press freedom	region	year
domestic9	1									
polcon3	-0.04	1								
log_gdp	-0.09	0.29	1							
log_pop	0.25	0.06	-0.12	1						
log_fixed_ bb_subs_ per100	-0.07	0.34	0.83	-0.07	1					
log_mobile subs_per100	-0.05	0.28	0.66	-0.14	0.72	1				
log_ enrollment	-0.10	0.16	0.41	-0.01	0.46	0.35	1			
pressfreedom	0.08	-0.62	-0.50	0.09	-0.50	-0.3958	-0.2897	1		
region	-0.09	0.18	0.21	-0.26	0.22	0.18	0.14	-0.33	1	
year	0.06	-0.10	-0.02	0.01	0.30	0.36	0.03	0.13	-0.05	1

Chapter 5

Protests, Social Movements and Media Legislation in Mexico 2012–2014

Tonatiuh Lay
Universidad de Guadalajara, Mexico

ABSTRACT

The objective of this chapter is to describe and analyze the use of ICTs by social movements in Mexico in their attempt to keep proposed legislation from concentrating, or at least failing to dilute, the already concentrated power of the Mexican media. These technologies not only have been a means of organization and synchronization for protests and mobilization, but also, before restrictions in Mexican law, served as alternative media for citizens to obtain more truthful information and make use of their right to communicate.

INTRODUCTION

In today's world, due to digital convergence, the technological possibilities for the optimization of the radioelectric spectrum have expanded. Frequencies have multiplied increasing opportunities for participation and quantity of content. Ideally, given a greater supply of information, participating citizens should have opportunities to make better decisions and, ultimately, have a positive impact on democracy. However, the conditions to achieve this end in Mexico have never been granted as

DOI: 10.4018/978-1-5225-2495-3.ch005

rights for citizens. On the contrary, communication and information have remained in the hands of private companies almost since the birth of radio and, subsequently, television. Through mechanisms of influence (manipulation) on citizenship, these groups, above all *Televisa*, the largest Spanish-speaking broadcasting company, have been able to accumulate power.

The combination of such manipulation with the authoritarian exercise of State power and limitations in sources of information have for many years inhibited the development of groups of civil society, a concept that will also be defined later. However, Internet and social media have allowed these groups to begin to act with greater freedom.

The development, use and appropriation of ICTs has strengthened the organization and, in some cases, the mobilization, of different groups and social movements. In particular, groups interested in media and telecommunication legislation were attentive to the need to reform the regulatory framework and demand the rights and participation in the spaces that could be created due to digital convergence.

The objective of this chapter is to describe and analyze the use and appropriation of ICT by groups and social movements in the context of discussions on broadcasting and telecommunications legislation in Mexico. The chapter is constructed in three sections. The first addresses the concepts of civil society and *de facto powers*, which are critical to understanding the struggle over media power. The second setion provides some background on the state of Internet use and ICT infrastructure in Mexico. The third section describes how the broadcasters in Mexico have made an alliance with government entities to achieve legislation that is favorable to their interests to the detriment of other actors and competitors and, significantly, to democracy itself. This section is divided into a section on the background of the so-called *"Televisa Law"*, followed by the description and analysis of the radio and telecommunications policy of the current government of Enrique Peña Nieto, as well as the reactions and actions of the groups that seek a democratization of the media.

We describe here a complex phenomenon that cannot be understood in the romantic sense of the traditional Western media's depiction of the "Arab Spring". The Arab Spring was portrayed as a situation where virtual social networking platforms allowed people to organize and overthrow their governments. Actually, the local context and the social organization of the citizens of those North African countries were such that virtual networks played an important, but not exclusive, role in their success.

CENTRAL CONCEPTS

Civil Society

According to Alberto Olvera (2010), the term "civil society" puts us in a controversial and polysemic space, because it is a category used in different ways by political, business, academic, class and even some social groups. Jonathan Fox adds that "most explanations of collective action and civil society-building are either state or society-driven. On the society side, there is the 'historical determinist' explanation of social capital formation, including some who stress social structure and others who take values and cultures as givens." (Fox, 1996: 1089). Although the term was used by Marx in the nineteenth century to refer to the sphere of needs (the market sphere and their networks of constitutive social relations), it was Gramsci, who in the twentieth century used the concept of civil society to differentiate it from political society and refer to a social and cultural sphere of construction and organization of autonomous social networks (Olvera, 2010).

Kenneth Newton (2001) observes that, ideally, civil society is supported by a dense network of voluntary associations and citizen organizations, whose community relations generate trust, cooperation and a high level of commitment and civic participation among citizens. This creates the conditions for social integration, public awareness and action, and thus democratic stability. But even this author points out that survey research fails to support some of the basic claims of this theory (Newton, 2001, p. 201), and affirms that "the concept of civil society refers to a social context in which there is a broad range, great diversity, and high density of social networks and formal and informal social organizations. It is a contextual property of societies in which individuals live, not a characteristic which individuals carry around with them" (Newton, 2001, p. 208).

In Mexico in the 1990s, non-governmental organizations (NGOs) comprised a visible and autonomous social sector with critical capabilities. These groups are recognized as civil society, "as there is a historical conceptual association to link NGOs with civil society, basically by the idea of space for autonomy in a society that cannot develop autonomous spaces in other areas of society itself "[1] (Olvera, 2010).

But perhaps Olvera's most interesting contribution to the discussion of the concept of civil society is that they are able to affect the public agenda. This characteristic differentiates them from those organizations of volunteers that only dedicate themselves to carry out assistance actions.

Finally, for the Brazilian federal government, an organization of civil society is defined differently. According to the Federal Law to Promote Activities Undertaken by Organizations of Civil Society (2004), it must be a legally constituted corporation (moral person) and non-profit group (Article 2, paragraph g, and article 3); to receive government support, it must meet one of the 17 activities listed in Article 15, as well as being registered in the Federal Register of Civil Society Organizations (Article 7). However, this definition includes many non-profit groups that do not meet our definition, which requires them to have their proposals and demands discussed on the public agenda.

De Facto Powers

The concept of *de facto powers* that we try to define here does not have a precise translation in English. In Spanish, the concept is "Poderes fácticos" which means "Factual powers" but the translator translates it as "real power" or simply as "power" as if the word "factual" was unnecessary. So we decided to use the word *"de facto"*, if only to provoke academic discussion on this concept. We follow the lead of Enrique Sanchez Ruiz (2009), who differentiated *de facto powers* from *de jure powers*. This does not mean that they are illegal or illegitimate, just that they are not granted by law. Most of the time it is not necessary to impose them by force. Rather, it is enough to express, or even suggest their interests for them to become a reality. The key is the ability to control external resources.

One of the first texts where the term *de facto powers* appears is from Jose Maria Riaza Ballesteros (1983), in discourse about the Spanish realty. He refers to two social actor powers: The Church and the Armed Forces. Although Riaza does not define the concept, he describes eight cases where these *de facto powers* become visible. This visibility does not mean that they had been previously invisible, because both the Church and the army are actors who have been present in the life of any Latin American state.

The first reference to *de facto powers* in Mexico was a combination of theoretical and academic reflection with empirical evidence, when Mexican researchers such as Enrique Sánchez Ruiz, Alma Rosa Alva de la Selva, Javier Esteinou or Jacqueline Peschard, explained[2] the process of discussion and approval of the amendments to the Radio and Television Federal Law (LFRyT) and Telecommunications Federal Law (LFT) in the House of Representatives at the end of 2005.

In this regard, Jacqueline Peschard commented that today we use the concept *de facto powers* to refer those, people or entities, whom without being part of the institutionalized power, have the power to condition the exercise of the action of the Mexican state, when not to threaten or neutralize it (Peschard, 2006). Meanwhile, O'Donnell identified economic groups, entrepreneurs, the financial sector, drug traffickers and the media, as users of *de facto powers*. These interest groups, says O'Donnell, function as powerful lobbies. The financial sector and the media in the last decade have been the interest groups with the greatest success in limiting the decision power of governments (O'Donnell, 2004, p. 159).

Table 1. Differences between public and media powers

Public Powers	Media Powers
They act representing the collective interests of the nation and the common good.	They represent particular or personal interests.
Its legitimacy comes from a democratic election by the people through the ballot, except the Judiciary, which is appointed by the Executive with ratification of the Senate.	They acquire their power through economic and technological concentration.
Ideology of democracy and the modern state.	Business freedom and freedom of expression.
Constitution and the rule of law.	The form and transmission control everyday reality.
Three branches of government (executive, legislative and judicial) with representatives and specific locations.	Informal powers with no specific location.
Independent powers among them.	Monopolist form.
Processes required to have transparency and accountability (The Executive at least once a year before the Legislature).	They are not subject to any accountability procedure.
They are renewed periodically. Executive Branch: Six years; Legislature: Congress 3 years Senate six years; Judiciary: 15 years.	They are not renewed periodically and the award is hereditary.
They give institutional form to the state.	They try to replace the formal powers and point out that the modern state is expendable to govern, and is only recognized as an entity to manage .

As for the media, its *de facto power* resides in its ability to manipulate information, which directly influences the perception of citizens. This is not a simple situation. The possibility of convincing an electorate that a position or a political party is the best option was the most important reason for the Mexican political class to accept the writing of the reform of the LFRyT and the LFT by *Televisa*, which will be described below.

According to Javier Esteinou (2008), the differences between public authorities and the media powers are as follows:

INTERNET USE AND INFRASTRUCTURE IN MEXICO

According to the 12th Study on the Habits of Internet Users in Mexico, conducted by the Mexican Internet Association (AMIPCI, 2016), Internet users in Mexico totaled 65 million (this figure represents 59 percent of Mexico's population), mainly in the age groups of 13 to 18 (19%), 19 to 24 (17%), 25 to 34 (20%) and 35 to 44 (15%). The three main uses of the Internet are for use of virtual platforms and social networks (79%), email (70%) and information searches (64%).

The four main devices through which users connect to the network are smartphones (77%), laptops (69%), PCs (50%), and electronic tablets (45%). In 2016, access to social networking platforms ranked first among Internet applications and email ranked second, with 79% and 70% availability respectively. While the AMIPCI study shows a projection of what the user will do on the Internet in the future: take online courses (37%), shop online (33%), and access social networks (31%), it does not explore the digital divide situation.

The use of virtual social networks, in line with technological development and convergence, has become an excellent resource for media communication. It offers the possibility of bringing those who share the same project or ideology together, with the technological advantage that such an approach enables the response to be massive and immediate. This means that one of the greatest potentials of social network service platforms is their ability to maintain the organization of almost any large event in synchronous time. It should be clear, however, that a social movement is not defined merely by the use of these programs and services, but by the ideas it represents and the citizen participation to support it. In other words, social movements exist by the affinity to a community of people for the various topics and mechanisms to carry them out, and not by the mere fact of using a social network service platform, such as Facebook, Twitter, or YouTube.

However, the value of social media tools to social movements is unclear, even to academics in Mexico. Some declare that they are skeptical of the ability of social network services to generate a new dynamic of political debate, "as these spaces are dominated by the same interests that capture traditional electronic media, and politicians have no responsibility to answer when questioned" (Camacho, 2011). Others point out that they are light and reactive communicative processes where there is very little thought and even though there is a deliberation, it is composed mostly by occurrences and pointless comments so that we do not necessarily become better informed and more active citizens. A third perspective is that "the use of new technologies cannot bring a genuine change in the social structure created for being a technology at the service of capitalism" (Castillo, 2012). Although this latter position seems to be very radical, it is perhaps the one that is exemplified by those seeking to liberalize Mexican media, as described in the next section of this chapter.

Beyond the potential or the "dangers" that the platforms could represent, academic interest must lie in answering the question of under what criteria and perspective citizens use them. A second academic interest should be the description and analysis of activism through digital platforms. In the case of Mexico, they have allowed the creation of new communities in virtual spaces that pursue common causes, identify with each other and share the same goals. These platforms have enabled exchanges in points of view, consensus building and coordination processes within a group, along with the effective management of information and contacts (Azuela and Tapia, 2013).

Until September 2014, Mexico had experienced two major social movements that had made significant use of ICT. The Zapatista movement, which emerged in 1994, which has based much of its communication strategy on the Internet, even before the advent of virtual platforms for social networking; and the social movement *#YoSoy132* created in 2012, which will be addressed in the next section.

MEDIA LEGISLATION AND SOCIAL MOVEMENT RESPONSES

Televisa Law

In 2001 the determining factor that initiated the idea of revising and updating the legislation of electronic media was the arrival to the Presidency of the Republic, after 70 years, of an opposition party. The new President, Vicente Fox, saw media communication as a staunch ally of the old regime, which therefore had to change. Fox instructed then Interior Secretary Santiago Creel to initiate a consultation to achieve this objective.

In March 2001 the Bureau of Dialogue for comprehensive reform legislation of electronic media was appointed. For the first time, one of the members was a representative of civil society, who represented more than 50 organizations interested in the subject. They had to run against the interests of large broadcasting groups, especially *Televisa*. This and the change of the position of President Fox, who began supporting the media, made the efforts of the Bureau of Dialogue fail. However, the civil society organizations continued to work until a citizens' initiative was drafted and presented to the Senate in November of that year (Lay, 2012).

Since the Constitution does not contemplate the figure of citizen initiatives, a group of senators endorsed and presented it as their own to the Senate. The judgment process was boycotted by *Televisa* and politicians involved with this company. However, due to technological advances and the digital transition, an update to the media and telecommunications legislation was needed. *Televisa* chose to compose a new reform initiative, which was presented in November 2005 by two supporter senators. This is the origin of the *"Televisa Law"*.

In a legislative process that lasted ten days, the proposed reform was approved. It then passed to the Senate the media senators and others, who were given support in the media for political purposes, approved the bill without any change in March 2006 (Lay, 2012).

The last legal resource to oppose the reform was an appeal for unconstitutionality to the Supreme Court of Justice (SCJN), which was presented in May 2006 and would not be decided until July 2007. In an unprecedented ruling, the Court overruled the articles that benefited *Televisa* and the major broadcasting companies in Mexico. However, although the Senate appointed a bureau to discuss the reforms required by the LFRyT and the LFT, and presumably succeeded in drafting an initiative, no official initiative was ever presented and the issue slowly died down. The organizations that were created to achieve the reform goals also dissipated.

Two populist initiatives were formed over time to address media legislation. The first was the *Frente Nacional para la democratización de los medios* (National initiative for media democratization), formed on February 20, 2008 with the aim of getting legislators to discuss and approve the amendment to the LFRyT and LFT during regular session. The proposed strategy was simple: The citizens themselves would have the task of "reminding" each senator member of the relevant committees and thoroughly discussing with them the importance of an objective. This task was to be achieved by sending daily emails and messages to the legislators' cellphones. The *Frente Nacional* would be given the assignment of informing the public about this process and collecting signatures of support for referral to the senators. But the regular session came to an end without discussing the subject. Reforms were not on the agenda again until 2010.

The social movement *#YoSoy132* adopted the democratization of the media in their list of demands on May 23, 2012. Their aims read, "... our movement seeks the democratization of the media in order to ensure transparent, plural information and minimum standards of objectivity to promote awareness and critical thinking" (YoSoy132, 2012).

One of #YoSoy132's achievements was that the Federal Competition Commission (CFC) authorized them to be an observer in the bidding process of the third and fourth broadcasting television network. However, this promise was never fulfilled. On September 18, 2012, #YoSoy132 unveiled an initiative to democratize the media, and on February 26, 2013 they presented it to the press, but no legislator endorsed it. Nevertheless, this movement achieved what the National Electoral Institute (INE) could not: that *Televisa* and *TV Azteca* transmit the second debate of the presidential candidates, and the transmission of a third one under its organization. In 2013 this movement began to be diluted.

A second initiative called Citizen Democracy and Media Coalition, led by the Mexican Association of Right to Information (AMEDI) was organized on May 28, 2012 (Lay, 2014, p. 29). It had an adherence of over a hundred civic organizations, with the following objectives:

1. Conduct a legislative reform that limits grabbing media, promote the pluralism in social, public, indigenous, and community media. This is due to the fact that commercial broadcasting has become a conglomeration of companies that

combine different frequencies. They have several radio stations or television channels. Likewise, the commercial media have not only historically neglected the public, community and indigenous media, but also the independent commercial and local commercial broadcasters, who consider competition in the advertising market.

2. Create a true digital agenda, which includes universal access to broadband for all citizens. Integrated digital television policy that ensures access and redistribution of the new digital dividend. At this point, one of the objectives of the digitization is the optimization of the frequencies, since where before a signal was carried, now several can fit. Civil society has called for the new signals to be distributed to different entities and bodies that promote plurality of content, even if the commercial media wants these for themselves.

3. To safeguard journalistic work, with effective measures to end impunity against journalists and media, ensuring their rights and that media companies take their work and training and comply with obligations toward information workers. This issue becomes important in a context where journalism became a dangerous profession not only because of the violence and drug trafficking in our country, but also because of the censorship of the state governments themselves for journalistic work, in addition to the subcontracting model which some media undertook.

4. Ensure the strengthening of national, regional and local independent domestic production, as well as full respect for the rights of the hearings and priority sectors for the country: children women and indigenous people.

However, for reasons of the federal election that year, the issue no longer prospered. The demands of society members were simply ignored in comparison to the benefits granted by the government to *Televisa* during the last two years of President Calderon's administration. Some examples are the famous Bidding 21, which granted *Nextel-Televisa*, for just 180 million pesos, a portion of the radio spectrum with a market value of more than five billion pesos, the delivery of two strands of dark fiber optic from the State Federal Electricity Commission (CFE), and the approval of *Televisa-Iusacell* merger, among other benefits.

During the Calderon government the impediment to *Telmex* (the local telephone company of Mexico) to provide broadcasting services has remained as a strategy to prevent competition within the sector, which has benefited *Televisa*. This has been achieved by creating and sustaining of the *Telebancada* in Congress, named that way because the legislators who integrate the Commission of Communications (in the Senate) and Radio, television and Film (within the House of Representatives) keep a fairly close relationship with large broadcasting groups in the country. Some of this representatives and senators worked for the broadcasting companies and others own radio stations. Senator Ninfa Salinas, for example, is the daughter of the owner of *TV Azteca*, the second largest commercial TV station in Mexico).

Virtual Social Networks and Mobilizations in Mexico

The *#YoSoy132* movement originated as a response to the press attempts to discredit the protests of March 11, 2012 at the Universidad Ibero-Americana against the candidate Peña Nieto. The media had reported that participants were not students of that institution but *porros (undercover thugs)* serving the candidate of the left. In response, students recorded a video and uploaded it on *YouTube*, where 131 students showed their credentials. The name *#YoSoy132* would be adopted after a citizen expressed solidarity with the students and attributed herself be number 132. Subsequently the movement noted the following objectives (Lay, 2012, p. 113):

First: We are a people's movement unrelated to any political party and constituted by citizens. As such, we do not express any signs of support for candidate or political party, but we respect the plurality and diversity of the members of this movement. Our desires and demands focus on the defense of freedom of expression and the right to information to Mexican citizens, with the understanding that both elements are essential to form a conscious and participatory citizenship.

By the same token, we promote an informed and reflected vote. We believe that in the current political circumstances, abstention and null votes are ineffective to advance the construction of our democracy actions. We are concerned about the democratization of the country and as such, we think that a necessary condition for it involves the democratization of the media movement. This concern stems from the current state of the national press and the concentration of media in fewer hands.

Second: #YoSoy132 is an inclusive movement that does not represent a single university. Their representation depends solely on the people who join this cause and that are articulated through university committees. In essence, our movement seeks the democratization of the media in order to ensure transparent, plural information and minimum standards of objectivity to promote awareness and critical thinking. With this reason we: Demand real competition within the sector of the media, particularly with regards to television duopoly consisting of *Televisa* and *TV Azteca*.

In general, the demands focus on the establishment in all media (radio, television and print media) of instruments that protect the public interest. This includes continuous access to the Internet as constitutional right and the safety of the members of this movement, who are freely expressing themselves throughout the country be ensured and, in particular of journalists who have been affected by violence. In addition, we express our absolute solidarity with people who in recent days have been repressed for expressing their ideas in different states of the republic.

Specially, as an immediate demand, we call for immediate transmission on national television of a debate of candidates for the Presidency of the Republic. Finding this not as an imposition for a privileged audience, but as a way to guarantee the right for everyone to choose to see it or not, whom today do not even have that possibility.

On May 28, Emilio Azcarraga Jean, Chairman of the Board of Directors of *Televisa* responded to the request. In a message posted on Twitter he said "in *Televisa* young people are listened to", so he agreed to the transmission of the second presidential debate on Channel 2. The next day, Ricardo Salinas Pliego, Chairman of the Board of Directors of *TV Azteca*, said it would also be broadcasted on Channel 13.

Not satisfied with the information that citizens could get about the candidates to cast their vote, *#YoSoy132* asked for the realization of a third debate, which was rejected by the Federal Electoral Institute (IFE), under the justification that they were only required to carry out two debates. For this reason, the group decided to organize it with its own resources.

#YoSoy132 convened the four presidential candidates to a debate at the Office of the Commission on Human Rights of the Federal District. The candidate of the right-wing National Action Party, Josefina Vazquez Mota, leftist Andres Manuel Lopez Obrador and Gabriel Quadri, from the New Alliance Party responded. Peña Nieto decided not to participate in the convened debate and expressed that "there was no guarantee of neutrality as *#YoSoy132* had undertaken a project against my person" (Rojas, 2012).

The debate was broadcasted exclusively online through the *Google* platform because the traditional media decided only at the last minute to participate. But, the contract with *Google* gave it exclusivity. For some analysts, the above meant a triumph for the youth and the movement, while opponents stressed the technical failures of transmission.

Subsequently, the movement entered the dynamics of the electoral contest. Along with other social organizations they held a series of protests called *Anti Peña Nieto*, which reached up to 64,000 demonstrators gathered in Mexico City (May 19) and were conducted in multiple cities in Mexico[3] and two abroad[4]. Likewise, through the Hashtag *#OcupaTelevisa*, which had no relation to Occupy Wall Street and its derived movements, it was summoned to the peaceful takeover of *Televisa* for 24 hours, which held about 10 thousand people in the facilities of the television station on Avenida Chapultepec, from the 26th to the 27th of July 2012.

The speech given justified the actions of the siege and the battle plan of the movement, which took up the democratization and transformation of the media. Towards the end of the Joaquin López-Doriga news TV show, on June 26, in a barely 20 second note and without audio, a note was posted about the event that took place outside the facilities. At 23:00 pm that day *#OcupaTelevisa* was a global trend, but at 23:30 it "magically" had ceased to be.

The *taking over* also took place at the facilities of *Televisa* in Acapulco, Aguascalientes, Cancún, Cuernavaca, Chetumal, Chihuahua, Ensenada, Guadalajara, Hermosillo, Monterrey, Poza Rica, Puebla, Querétaro, San Luis Potosí, Tampico, Tijuana, Veracruz and Zacatecas. They also surrounded the premises of *TV Azteca* in León, and the daily El Sol de Durango and Diario de Xalapa (Alfaro, 2012).

Despite accusations of electoral fraud and vote buying by the Institutional Revolutionary Party, Peña Nieto was declared the winner of the election. Faced with a crisis of legitimacy, one of the first actions of the now President of the Republic was to convene opposition to a covenant called *Pacto por México* (Pact for Mexico), to carry out various actions and reforms "for the country". In an apparent inclusion policy, the new government promised to the movement *#YoSoy132* they would be an observer in the process of bidding for the new broadcast networks, which did not happen.

Peña Nieto's Broadcasting and Telecommunications Policy

On March 11, 2013 the issue of broadcasting and telecommunications legislation became important. President Enrique Peña Nieto presented an initiative to reform various articles of the Constitution on telecommunications. While some voices felt that it was far from being a true change to democratize the sector, others supported what they called "first steps towards a new stage".

However, the above seemed impossible due to the context of the sector. Let us remember the delivery of infrastructure to *Televisa* and allied companies in the aforementioned Tender 21, the delivery of CFE's dark fiber wires, the authorization of merger of telecommunications companies, and the creation of Telebancada in the Federal Legislative Power.

For this reason, more than a democratization for the sector, the reform represented a possibility of legitimization for Peña Nieto. The government's strategy was well prepared: First, an initiative was sent to reform the Protection Law (Ley de Amparo), with which the legal form of the suspension of the contested act was removed; and secondly, Elba Esther Gordillo, the leader of the National Union of Education Workers, was apprehended, accused of embezzlement. With these actions the Government showed muscle to the *de facto powers*.

Overall the initiative was intended to prepare the arena for the new competitive game after the digital transition and create the Federal Telecommunications Institute as regulator of the sector. In a legislative procedure known in the jargon as "fast track," the initiative was approved only ten days later, with some modifications on the *Must offer* and *Must carry* terms, reciprocity in the percentage of investment for foreigners, and extending from 120 to 180 days the period to bid for two new national TV broadcasters. As a constitutional amendment, it required the approval of at least half plus one of the legislatures of the states, which was achieved in June of that year.

The next step would be the adjustment of the secondary legislation, which at this time was made up of the LFRyT and the LFT. But by this time the *Pact for Mexico* had already dissolved. as the opposition had understood that the government only used it for legitimizing boosting the *peñista* reforms, but without the intention of genuine deliberation.

Therefore, there was no unity in the opposition to boost draft legislation to be a counterweight to the government's proposal. The representative of the Party of the Democratic Revolution, Purificación Carpinteyro, presented on October 15, 2013, the initiative Regulatory Law of Articles 2, 6, 7, 27, 28 and 105 of the Constitution, on rights to free access to information, the information and communications technology and public telecommunications services and broadcasting.

On the 28th of October the AMEDI presented through senators Javier Corral, Silvia Garza, Manuel Bartlett, Alejandra Barrales and Zoé Robledo, the proposed Initiative of Federal Telecommunications and Broadcasting Law (LFTyR). Even *#YoSoy132* unveiled a proposed initiative to amend Articles 2, 3, 7, 27, 41, 73, 76, 78, 89 and 132 of the Constitution with the aim that "the media serve the people and not only meet business functions" (Camacho, 2013), but this did not have the same fate as the AMEDI proposal and was not adopted by any legislator.

This was perhaps one of the last proposals from *#YoSoy132* focused on media legislation and its goal of achieving an impact on the democratization of the media. This meant the gradual fragmentation of the movement, where some cells remain active and others became part of different social movements.

In February 2014, AMEDI started exerting more pressure on the issue of media legislation. Two activities of great interest to the topic were initiated: creating a campaign called "*No more power*" in reference to *Televisa*, *TV Azteca* and *Telmex*, referring to them as *de facto powers* which should no longer invade the faculties of public policy; and the call to discuss the proposed legislation, which concluded with the drafting of 30 points, which include some of the following:

1. To strengthen the social role of broadcasting, in order to transcend the discretionary compliance that currently identifies it, and to introduce parameters of this nature in telecommunications;
2. To expressively list the rights of audiences and users of the services of telecommunications.

3. Ensuring the Federal Telecommunications Institute sufficient authority to regulate, promote and monitor public telecommunications services and broadcasting, to ensure the exercise of the fundamental rights of freedom of expression, right to information and right of access to technologies information and communication. The Interior Ministry should not maintain their current roles in overseeing audiovisual content.
4. Define an effective standard of accountability, that besides guaranteeing transparency of the pubic management regulatory body, allows social participation through the Consultative Council;
5. Establish a simplified procedure for granting concessions for public and social use, while for commercial use, it must be determined that the bidding process will be the only way of concessioning, excluding the economic aspect as a decisive factor to determine the winner, in such a way that the process does not deprive an exclusively profitable interest;
6. Pertinently regulate the must offer and must carry services for the benefit of the consumers.

On February 28, the daily *El Financiero* unveiled elements of a draft of secondary legislation, without specifying whether it was a previous or current version. Highlighted there were several setbacks, such as alterations to the funding for community radios, as well as the return of faculties to the Interior Ministry, which had already been granted to the Federal Telecommunications Institute (IFT) and the Federal Electoral Institute (IFE). In this regard, AMEDI reacted by disclosing its position and pointing out the elements of contradiction within the spirit of the constitutional reform itself.

The Federal Telecommunications and Broadcasting Law Initiative

Just over 100 days after the constitutional deadline of 180 days to issue secondary legislation, on 24 March 2014 the Federal Government presented its Federal Telecommunications Act and Broadcasting initiative. But, this initiative contradicted the Constitutional Reform of 2013, ignored human rights violations, and strengthened *Televisa*, so academics and actors called it the *"Peña-Televisa Initiative"*.

The testimony of Mony de Swaan, who was the President of the Federal Telecommunications Commission, days before leaving office in that agency, noted that the initiative project contained 375 articles, and amended more than a dozen related laws (de Swaan, 2014, p. 44). According to Beatriz Solís Leere (2014) that document was sent by the Legal Department of the Presidency of the Republic, to *Televisa*. The result was the initiative Peña presented to the Senate.

According to the AMEDI, the initiative of the Federal Executive did not take into account that the constitutional reform recommended public media autonomy, financial management, guarantees of citizen participation, and allowed financing options. It also attributed to the Secretariat of Communications and Transportation the IFT faculties.

In addition to the above, the initiative contained an inequitable regime of concessions in their terms and conditions of use. It required that the real-time geolocation on any type of communication device be disclosed at the request of competent authorities (Art 189 and 192). It forced the telecommunications licensees to block, inhibit or reverse temporarily telecommunications signals during critical events and places for public and national security at the request of the competent authorities (Article 197). And, it delayed the conclusion of the terrestrial digital transition until 2017, when the Constitution had marked it in December 2015 (Art Sixteenth transitory).

In this situation, the Mexican Communication Researchers Association (AMIC) and the National Council for Education and Research of Communication Sciences (CONEICC), as well as instances of academic, and various citizen groups, mostly students, responded accordingly, organizing forums and discussion groups to spread the subject matter, as well as writing articles in magazines, newspaper columns and media interviews.

Meanwhile, student and youth organizations employed more dynamic information strategies through virtual platforms, convening and organizing protests and calling to discussions panels. While civic and academic organizations addressed all aspects of controversy with the initiative, young people`s actions were more specific to Internet related matters.

The Amedi and CONEICC published their first newspaper spread on March 28, where they made clear the need to reformulate the initiative to preserve the public interest. The AMIC unveiled its position on April 1, pointing out aspects of concern in the areas of telecommunications, copyright, content, broadcasting, public media and social use, gender equality, the Internet, and network neutrality.

The press, blogs and journals in politics and communication, gave wide publicity to the views and positions regarding the initiative, especially in the first week of April. After the analysis of the proposal, the public opinion widely criticized the attitude of Peña Nieto, especially in regards to the Internet (García, 2014; Robles, 2014), and the violation of the Constitution (Álvarez, 2014). Movements mainly consisting of young people, such as *#YoSoy132*, *#YoSoy131* and *#Somosred*, created through technological tools on April 21, tweeted using the hashtag *#EPNvsInternet*, which became a global trend by noon that same day. (El Informador, 2014)

On April 22nd a ruling of the Joint Committee on Communications and Transport, Radio, Television and Film, and Legislative Studies was published, with the draft decree of the LFTyR and the Public Broadcasting System Law. Due to the various pressures on the initiative, National Action Party Senator Javier Lozano presented the draft of a "conciliatory" opinion, but it was not a real proposal for change and only switched controversial contents around. As a result, it was rejected not only by the commissions but also by his own political party.

One of the last citizen actions before the end of the regular session in the legislature, was the creation on Saturday April 26 of a human chain running from the official presidential residence of Los Pinos to *Televisa* headquarters. Rather than being a massive event, the chain had the symbolic purpose of representing citizens who had not been taken into account in the agreements between the Presidency of the Republic and *Televisa*.

The Process of Approval and Enactment

Although there was a real excitement among stakeholders in the field, after stumbling through the intervention of Senator Lozano the legislative discussion continued, advancing to the Senate. In the session of the Communications Commission on July 3, the draft opinion was approved with 25 votes in favor and 5 against. The next day, the draft opinion was presented for discussion in the full Senate. After a 17-hour day, it was approved by 80 votes in favor and 37 against. Among the arguments that were forwarded to approve the initiative were the following benefits: the end of charges for long distance calls, telephone portability, the creation of two national television channel stations as well as a television channel of the Mexican State, the addition of two new carriers of cellular phone services, the creation of a public internet network, mechanisms for access to broadcasting content for people with disabilities, and the end of officialdom in the public media.

Following the protocol referred to in Article 72 of the Constitution, the dictum was sent as a bill to the Chamber of Representative. In an express process, on July 7, at a meeting and without discussion or revision, it was approved at the Committee of Radio, Television and Film by 34 votes in favor, 12 against and one abstention.

The next day, a plenary session was held, which addressed the issues of preponderance, interconnection rates, the *Must Carry* and *Must offer*, government surveillance and the limitation to community broadcasting. Again without discussion, most of the representatives rejected the 549 reservations that had been made by the legislators of the National Action Party, the Democratic Revolution Party, the Labor Party, the New Alliance Party and the Citizens' Movement Party. Thus, in a span of 20 hours, the legislation was approved with 390 votes in favor, 129 against and one abstention.

On July 14, at the ceremony of enactment, President Peña Nieto said that the act would ensure free Internet access for all Mexicans, online freedom of expression and net neutrality (Vargas, 2014). To complete the process, the law was published in the evening edition of the Official Gazette of the same day.

The senators and house representatives who had denounced the contradictions of the initiative and had voted against it sought to bring an action of unconstitutionality, but acknowledged they did not have enough votes to carry it out. In the Senate an action of unconstitutionality required 44 votes, but only 37 legislators had voted against the law (Montalvo, 2014), while in the Chamber of Representatives 165 votes were needed, when they had managed only 129. Thus, the probability of undertaking the demand was in the hands of the National Human Rights Commission (CNDH) and the Federal Institute of access to Information (IFAI).

Only the IFAI showed interest in studying the case. Due to the specialty of their area they could have started the action of unconstitutionality for violating the right of access to information and protection of personal data, which was implied in Articles 30, 189 and 190 of the Act (Montalvo, 2014b). However, in plenary session of this institute, four of the seven commissioners voted against, arguing that such items were not in violation of the Constitution.

The CNDH made no statement on the matter, which was criticized by academics and civil society organizations, although the Commission had previously demonstrated opacity regarding violation of human rights issues. Only the Plenum of the Federal Institute of Transparency and Access to Public Information, Protection of Personal Data and Accountability of Mexico City (InfoDF) voted unanimously to direct the application to the Court (Montalvo, 2014c), delivering it by the deadline of August 13. But the Court rejected it, two days later asserting that the InfoDF had no authority to challenge laws that had not been approved by the Legislative Assembly of the Federal District (Mexico City).

With this, the trust that several academics and society groups had placed on the 2013 constitutional reform and the 2014 creation of secondary legislation ended. Ultimately, instead of allowing social development through access to information and the media, the new laws granted greater power to the largest radio, television and telecommunications corporations and increased restrictions on the rights of citizens, communities and indigenous peoples to own and operate their own media systems. The construction of public policy on telecommunications and broadcasting was, as pointed out on several occasions by opposing legislators and online communities, a process where it summoned all, heard some, but ignored them all.

CONCLUSION

In Mexico, the government appeared to encourage openness and discourse, but in practice its operation was closed. The aims of the movements and organizations around the telecommunication and broadcasting legislation were not achieved to a great extent for this reason. Even when the government called for everyone to participate, it only listened to some and ignored others. However, government action could not prevent the development of these groups nor the use and appropriation of technology for their current and future projects as a civil society.

Unfortunately, the victory of the *de facto powers* in the telecommunication and media law meant not only allowing them to continue their expansion projects on the channels of information and communication in Mexico, but also forced the State to continue dismantling the few media resources in the hands of indigenous communities, urban, rural and so-called public media. In fact, in the last three years the government dismantled 37 community radio stations in the country. The concept of public media was misrepresented in the law and recognized as pertaining only to the media in the hands of the state institutions and public universities, but under strict institutional and pro-neoliberal control, which contradicted UNESCO's definition of public media.

As far as social protest is concerned, the state found a way to criminalize and neutralize it by Articles 189 and 190 of the LFTyR, which the Court validated in 2016. In addition, the Initiative Federal Law to Prevent and Punish Crimes Responsible Computing, also known as *Fayad Act*, in reference to its author, Omar Fayad, sought to criminalize certain uses of the Internet and virtual social networks.

This case provides a counterbalance to other cases where online communities used ICT and social media successfully to achieve their goals. Future research needs to address how the characteristics and ICT use of social movements, their goals, the context in which they act, and the strength of *de facto* powers, affect their success.

REFERENCES

Alfaro, A. (2012). En otras 12 ciudades se realizaron manifestaciones contra *Televisa*. Retrieved from http://www.jornada.unam.mx/2012/07/28/politica/004n1pol

Álvarez, C. (2014, March 31). EPN, ¿su iniciativa viola la Constitución? Diario El Financiero.

AMICPI. (2016). *Hábitos de los usuarios de Internet 2016*. México: Amipci.

Azuela, M., & Tapia, M. (2013). *Construyendo ciudadanía desde el activismo digital*. México: Alternativas y Capacidades.

Cabrera, R. (2014, April 7). La iniciativa Telecom es la más regresiva desde que Internet existe en México. Animalpolitico.com. Retrieved from http://www.animalpolitico.com/2014/04/la-iniciativa-de-telecom-es-la-mas-regresiva-desde-que-internet-existe-en-mexico/#ixzz2zXy9GsmF

Camacho, F. (2011). Las nuevas tecnologías de la información hacen más vulnerables a ciudadanos. Retrieved from http://www.jornada.unam.mx/2011/10/19/politica/012n2pol

Camacho, F. (2013). Presenta #YoSoy132 iniciativa para la reforma de los medios. Retrieved from http://www.jornada.unam.mx/2013/02/27/politica/022n1pol

Castillo, M. (2012, May 9). Mesa de debate Tecnología y lucha social. *Proceedings of the Tercer Congreso Nacional Multidisciplinario*, CUCSH-UDG.

De Swaan, M. (2014). Telecomunicaciones, el sector de las promesas incumplidas. *En Voces de Alerta: la contarreforma de Peña Nieto en telecomunicaciones y radiodifusión.*

El Informador. (2014). Hashtag #EPNvsInternet se vuelve tendencia mundial en Twitter. *El Informador.* Retrieved from http://www.informador.com.mx/mexico/2014/524189/6/hashtag-epnvsinternet-se-vuelve-tendencia-mundial-en-twitter.htm

Esteinou, J. (2008, May 8). *"Políticas públicas en comunicación", Ponencia, panel: Políticas Públicas en Comunicación. Proceedings of the 20th Encuentro Nacional AMIC '08.* Monterrey, Nuevo León: Universidad Autónoma de Nuevo León.

Esteinou, J., & Alva, A. (2009). *La "Ley Televisa" y la lucha por el poder en México.* México: UAM.

Fox, J. (1996). How does civil society thicken? The political construction of social capital in rural Mexico. *World Development, 24*(6), 1089–1103. doi:10.1016/0305-750X(96)00025-3

García, F. (2014). Enrique Peña Nieto contra el Internet. *Nexos en línea.* Retrieved from http://www.redaccion.nexos.com.mx/?p=6176#sthash.SviUc2QV.dpuf

Lay, T. (2012). *Legislación de medios y poderes fácticos en México 2000-2012.* México: Universidad. de Guadalajara.

Lay, T. (2014). Frentes para la democratización de los medios. Revista Zócalo, 171(14).

Melucci, A. (1992). Che cosa è "nouvo" nei "nouvi monimenti social"? *Sociologia*, *26*(2-3), 271–300.

Montalvo, T. (2014). En el Senado, sin votos para acción de inconstitucionalidad contra la Ley Telecom. Retrieved from http://www.animalpolitico.com/2014/07/en-el-senado-sin-votos-para-accion-de-inconstitucionalidad-contra-ley-telecom/

Montalvo, T. (2014b). Hoy vence el plazo para acción de inconstitucionalidad contra la Ley Telecom. Retrieved from http://www.animalpolitico.com/2014/08/vence-el-plazo-para-accion-de-inconstitucionalidad-contra-la-ley-telecom/

Montalvo, T. (2014c). InfoDF interpone acción de inconstitucionalidad contra Ley Telecom; Ifai declina recurso. Retrieved from http://www.animalpolitico.com/2014/08/el-ifai-discute-presentar-accion-de-inconstitucionalidad-contra-ley-telecom/

Newton, K. (2001). Trust, social capital, civil society, and democracy. *International Political Science Review*, *22*(2), 201–2014. doi:10.1177/0192512101222004

O' Donnell, G. (2004). La Democracia en América Latina. El debate conceptual de la democracia. Hacia una democracia de ciudadanos y ciudadanas. Bases empíricas del informe. Programa de las Naciones Unidas para el desarrollo, Perú.

Olvera, A. (2010, October 25-26). *El desarrollo de la sociedad civil en México. Participación en el Coloquio El desarrollo de la sociedad civil en México: un enfoque multidisciplinario.* México: UNAM.

Peschard, J. (2006). *La democracia ayer y hoy. A cuarenta años de La democracia en México de Pablo González Casanova. Ponencia presentada en el homenaje a Pablo González Casanova.* México: Instituto de Investigaciones Sociales, Universidad Nacional Autónoma de México.

Radcliffe-Brown, A. (1996). *Estructura y función en la sociedad primitiva.* Barcelona: Península.

Riaza, J. (1983). La democracia y los poderes fácticos, en *Revista Fomento Social*, *152*, 427-434.

Robles, J. (2014). La guerra abierta de Enrique Peña Nieto Contra Internet. *Vice.com.* Retrieved from http://www.vice.com/es_mx/read/la-guerra-abierta-de-enrique-pena-nieto-contra-internet

Rojas, M. (2012). Peña no asistirá a debate convocado por #YoSoy132. *Radioformula.com.* Retrieved from http://www.radioformula.com.mx/notas.asp?Idn=248481

Sánchez, E. (2009). *Poderes fácticos y gobernabilidad autoritaria. La "Ley Televisa" como estudio de caso, en: Alma Rosa Alva, y Javier Esteinou (Coord), La "Ley Televisa" y la lucha por el poder en México.* México: UAM.

Solís Leere, B. (2014) Intervención de Beatriz Solís en reunión con la Amedi. Guadalajara, Jalisco.

Vargas, R. (2014). Peña Nieto promulga la Ley Federal de Telecomunicaciones y Radiodifusión. Diario La Jornada. Retrieved from http://www.jornada. unam.mx/ultimas/2014/07/14/pena-nieto-promulgara-hoy-la-ley-federal-de-telecomunicaciones-y-radiodifusion-5219.html

YoSoy132. (2012). Primer comunicado de la Coordinadora del Movimiento YoSoy132 (Manifiesto). Retrieved from https://es.wikisource.org/wiki/Primer_comunicado_ de_la_Coordinadora_del_Movimiento_YoSoy132_(Manifiesto)

ENDNOTES

[1]   Throughout this chapter, quotations, such as this, from texts written in Spanish have been translated into English by the author.

[2]   You can read this discussion in the text *La "Ley Televisa" y la lucha por el poder en México* (Esteinou & Alva, 2009).

[3]   Aguascalientes, Cancún, Ciudad Satélite, Coatzacoalcos, Colima, Córdoba, Cuernavaca, Culiacán, Chihuahua, Guadalajara, Huatusco, Irapuato, León, Manzanillo, Mazatlán, Monterrey, Morelia, Oaxaca, Orizaba, Pachuca, Puebla, Puerto Vallarta, Querétaro, Saltillo, San Cristóbal de las Casas, San Luis Potosí, Tampico, Tapachula, Taxco, Tejupilco, Tlaxcala, Toluca, Torreón, Tuxtla Gutiérrez, Veracruz, Villahermosa, Xalapa y Zacatecas.

[4]   New York and London, where the team of *Televisa* News was reached by a demonstration after a transmission of the Olympics. Demonstrators disrupted a recording outside the Saint James Park stadium, where moments before the national team had participated.

Section 2
Online Communities and Socio-Political Concerns

Chapter 6

Political Participation in Mexico Offline and Through Twitter

Julio Amador
Imperial College London, UK & Pollstr, UK

Carlos Adolfo Piña-Garcia
IIMAS UNAM, Mexico

ABSTRACT

We used survey data and collected data from the online social network Twitter between October 5, 2015 to November 9, 2015 to provide an overview related to political participation in Mexico. With the former we provided a qualitative assessment of participation by examining electoral participation, participation between regions, interest in politics and sources of political information. With Twitter data, we described the intensity of participation, we identified locations of high activity and identified movements including agencies behind them. We compare and contrast participation in Mexico to its counterpart in Twitter. We show that participation seems to be decreasing. However, participation through Twitter seems to be increasing. Our research points towards the emergence of Twitter as a significant platform in terms of political participation in Mexico. Our study analyses the impact of how different agencies related to social movements can enhance participation through Twitter. We show that emergent topics are important because they could help to explore how politics becomes of public interest.

DOI: 10.4018/978-1-5225-2495-3.ch006

INTRODUCTION

Academics generally agree that political participation is quintessential for democracy. Not only does political participation serve as the main conduit with which the public expresses their opinion, but it also establishes an important link between the public, the state and its institutions. In spite of its importance, there is a view amongst researchers suggesting that political participation has decreased in recent decades. The lack of participation is visible through the decrease in turnout during election periods, the growth of negative sentiments towards politicians and their parties, and the decline in engagement in civic associations (Norris 2002).

Even if political participation seems to be decreasing, the emergence of new agencies, such as online social networking sites, pose the possibility that political participation is shifting away from traditional practices and moving towards online ones. In fact, as the use of online social networks has become mainstream, their role as agents for social change has increased (Gonzales–Bailon, Borge-Holthoefer J., Rivero, A. & Moreno Y., 2011). The use of online social networks in events ranging from the spread of political news to election campaigns and protests has demonstrated their importance in the context of fomenting social change.

The growing importance of online social networks as a catalyst of social change has sparked an increasing interest in studying them. Studies increasingly use online crawling of social networks for data collection. Mining social signals from online social networks provides quick knowledge of real-world events (Roy & Zeng, 2014). In fact, areas of social network analysis are now expanding to different disciplines, not only in data mining studies, but also in computational social science; i.e., user behavior. Thus, the availability of unprecedented amounts of data about human interactions from different social networks opens the possibility of using this information to leverage knowledge about the diversity of social behavior and the activity of individuals (Weng, Flammini, Vespignani, & Menczer, 2012; Lu & Brelsford, 2014; Thapen & Ghanem, 2013; Piña-García, Gershenson, & Siqueiros-García, 2016; Piña-García & Gu, 2013). In particular, the focus of social data analysis is essentially the content that is being produced by users. The data produced in social networks is rich, diverse and abundant, which makes them a relevant source for data science (Ferrara, De Meo, Fiumara, & Baumgartner, 2014; Weikum et al., 2011).

Twitter is one of the most studied online social networks. This social media platform provides an efficient and effective communication medium for one-on-one interactions and broadcast calls (e.g., for assistance or dissemination and access to useful information). In Twitter users post messages that are limited to 140 characters known as tweets. In addition to this, users can follow other accounts they find interesting. Unlike the case with other social networks, the relationship does not have to be mutual. As of 2014 Twitter produces around 500 million tweets per day and has 271 million regular users (Serfass & Sherman, 2015).

Because Twitter is used to share information, opinions, and online petitions, the social network provides us with an important source of data useful to analyze online political participation in Mexico. With this in mind, our aim is to compare and contrast offline political participation in Mexico to online political participation in Mexico in Twitter and assess possible paths for how the emergence of new technologies could promote political participation.

In order to do so, the authors compared survey data to qualitatively assess political participation, interest in politics and sources of political information in Mexico. In the following lines it will be presented a descriptive visualization on electoral turnout and regions with the largest level of participation. Moreover, it will be provided an overview on the most important sources of political information in Mexico and forms of political participation other than voting. Next, it will be used a corpus of over 150,000 tweets (dataset) related to the president of Mexico, Enrique Peña Nieto. Additionally, the authors present graphics that will give us an idea of how frequently people participate with political content in Twitter, their locations and what sort of conversations they have on Twitter. Data visualizations will allow to identify different online protests in the Mexican territory. Thus, visualizations about the level of political engagement in three online protests will be provided. The authors do this by considering, first the number of tweets, second, the duration of the protest, and finally, the way in which different actors interact in the protest. In this regard, this study contributes by providing a description of political participation in Mexico by describing the methodology used to systematically collect tweets related to political engagement, particularly those related to the president of Mexico, Enrique Peña Nieto, and by comparing and contrasting offline political participation in Mexico to online political participation in Mexico in Twitter.

From the qualitative inquiry into survey data, the authors observe that even if political participation is different between regions in the country, national levels of political participation in Mexico are decreasing. This comes together with the fact that interest in politics is relatively low and only peaks when there are large political events such as presidential elections. Moreover, it can be seen that Mexicans only engage politically in activities that do not require large amounts of interaction, making Twitter a relevant agency for political participation. Finally, it is possible to observe that Mexicans' main source of political information is television with other sources of information lagging well behind e.g., magazines and newspapers. Interestingly, new sources of political information have emerged such as the Internet and online social media in terms of political information. Hence, the authors turn to study Twitter, the most influential microblogging service.

A preliminary exploration on political participation in Mexico through Twitter shows that participation levels between regions differ to those in the survey data. This finding underscores a weakness of Twitter data: that it is not representative of the overall population. Specifically, in Mexico, there is no widespread access to Internet and the use of Twitter is not common among those with access. With this caveat in place, it can be seen that political participation in Mexico seems to increase in our time window (October the 5th and November the 9th, 2015). Nevertheless, it is also driven by political events. The latter allowed the authors to identify political movements. It was observed that in those movements where there is a large organization leading a discussion, political participation lasts longer than in those where there is not. This intrinsic characteristic underscores the importance of organizations as enhancers of political participation in Mexico through Twitter.

This study is related to the research carried out by Almond and Verba (1963) on political attitudes and civic culture, Norris (2002) on political participation in Mexico, Somuano (2011) on organized civil society and democracy in Mexico and a recent study led by Instituto Nacional Electoral [INE] (2014) on the status of political participation in Mexico.

In their seminal work, Almond and Verba (1963) find that people in Mexico were proud of their political system and willing to participate in it. However, political participation was the lowest when compared to other countries. Voter turnout in Mexico trails below the Latin American average (Norris, 2002). For instance, in countries like Uruguay voter participation in the last 30 years has been well above 80% (IDEA, 2016). In relation to this, Almond and Verba (1963) conclude that in Mexico, even if people aspire to participate, there are generalized levels of cynicism and marginalization within the population.

In a more recent study, Norris (2002) finds that even if political participation has increased since Almond and Verba's (1963) study, the trend is not clear. On the one hand, when compared to similar Latin American countries, election turnout in Mexico is below average. Also, in Mexico there is a lower than average participation in protests and social movements and there is a low level of trust and approval on political institutions. On the other hand, Mexicans seem to participate slightly more on community associations.

Somuano (2011), through a deep investigation on the role of civil associations in political participation in Mexico, suggests that such associations do not encourage wide spread participation. Rather, participation is limited to a specific sector of the population. This, in turn, questions the role of civil associations as an enabler of political participation in Mexico.

A 2014 cross-sectional study commissioned by the National Electoral Institute (2014), or INE for its acronym in Spanish, finds that in Mexico, low levels of trust towards other persons and authorities translate into low levels of political participation. Such lack of trust is found on low levels of participation in social networks beyond family, friends and neighbors and a generalized disenchantment towards democracy (INE, 2014).

Almond and Verba (1963) and Norris (2002) provide a starting point for this research through a description of the state of political participation in Mexico. In this manuscript, was used these authors' views on the state of political participation as a benchmark to what the authors will find in survey and Twitter data. As such, this research provides an update to the state of political participation in Mexico and, to the best of our knowledge, adds the first comparison to online participation through Twitter in Mexico. Moreover, this research identifies promoters of online political participation. This complements Samuano's (2011) view of civil associations by highlighting the role of Change.org as promoter of political participation online.

METHODOLOGY

Given that the main aim of this study is to describe political participation in Mexico, the authors turn to survey data and collect data from Twitter to satisfy three objectives: First, to explore and examine traditional ways of political participation; Second, to spot shifts in sources of political information. Third, to assess and investigate non-traditional ways of political participation. In this context, the authors refer to political participation as any activity through which individuals express their own opinion with the goal of exerting influence regarding political decision-making.

Survey Data

In this manuscript, two different surveys to gauge political participation in Mexico were explored. On the one hand, the authors use Election Day turnout data first, from the Federal Electoral Institute, or IFE, and then from the National Electoral Institute (INE, 2014). From these sources turnout for parliamentary and presidential elections between 1964 and 2015 were obtained. Moreover, the authors obtained Election Day turnout for each of the states in Mexico between 1991 and 2009. On the other hand, data from the National Survey on Political Culture and Citizenship, or ENCUP (2016) was considered. This survey examines characteristics and practices of political culture in Mexico. This survey also consists of a National representative sample of the population in Mexico, ages 18 and older. Data is available for the years 2001, 2003, 2005 2008 and 2012 (http://www.encup.gob.mx/en/Encup/Bases_de_datos). In relation to ENCUP (2016), the authors began by examining traditional measures of political participation such as attending political meetings, signing letters, calling authorities, participating in civil associations, contacting representatives and political parties and, where available using the Internet and online social media to access political information. In this regard, INE data provides a view of voting as a way of exerting political influence, whereas ENCUP data presents a different activities individuals may take to exercise political influence. Next, the authors inquire on the sources of political information of the population. Finally, for the years where present, political participation in non-traditional ways such as online activism and social networks are presented.

Twitter Data

Given the nature of this study, it is worth briefly discussing the ethical, legal, and social implications of using Twitter data to conduct research. The tweets that were collected through the public Twitter API are subject to the Twitter terms and conditions. Thus, the privacy policy used by Twitter indicates that users consent to the collection, transfer, manipulation, storage, and disclosure of data to the public i.e., data can be used to conduct this exploratory analysis. This study analyzed only tweets that were completely public (i.e., no privacy settings were selected by the user). Thus, there was no expectation of privacy by the user (McIver et al., 2015).

The authors collected publicly available tweets related to the president of Mexico, Enrique Peña Nieto, and his personal Twitter username, also known as Twitter handle, @EPN. The data was collected from October 5, 2015 to November 9, 2015 via the Twitter streaming API (https://dev.twitter.com/streaming/overview). These tweets are openly available to the public on the web which implies that protected tweets will not be picked up. Consequently, their use for research is typically thought not to raise any ethical concerns. Twitter provides a continuous stream of public information. It does so by allowing millions of people to broadcast short messages known as "tweets". In this context, people can "follow" others to receive their messages, forward or "retweet" ("RT" in short) tweets to their own followers, or mention ("@" in short) others in tweets. People often label tweets with topical keywords or "hashtags". A hashtag is a convention among Twitter users to create and follow a thread of discussion by prefixing a word with a "#" character. Thus, Twitter tracks phrases, words, and hashtags that are most often mentioned and regularly post them under the title of trending topics.

The collected sample consisted of 150,000 tweets published by 46,399 users that emerged during the observed time window. This sample was stored for further analysis. It is important to note that this data collection contains information such as user ID, date and time that the user account was created, the screen name or alias, the number of followers, time when a tweet was posted, the tweet itself, language, device used to post the tweet (source), and the user-defined location. It should be highlighted that approximately 1% of all tweets published on Twitter are geo-located.

Figure 1. Voter Turnout for Federal Elections. Turnout for Presidential Elections is represented in orange. Turnout for Parliamentary Election (i.e., Deputies and Senators) is represented in blue. Source: National Electoral Institute (INE, 2016).

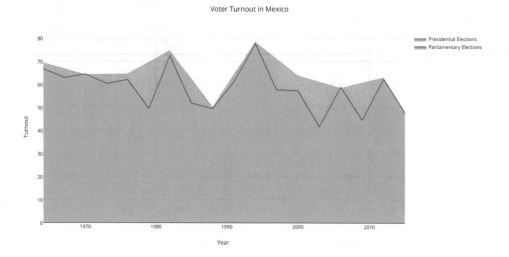

This is a very small portion of the tweets, and it is often necessary to use the profile information to determine the tweet's location (Kumar, Morstatter, & Liu, 2013).

Tweets are the basic atomic building block of all things in Twitter. Given that the text of the status update (the tweet itself) includes embedded data such as: retweet, hashtags and mentions these features were extracted to improve our exploratory approach.

RESULTS

A first approach to political participation is to explore the most basic role of the citizen in a democratic society: election of their representatives. In Mexico, Federal elections call citizens forward to vote for the election of a president every six years, election of senators every six years and the election of deputies every three years. As a simplification, the authors refer to election of deputies and senators as parliamentary elections. Voter turnout on Election Day for both, presidential and parliamentary elections are depicted in Figure 1.

Markedly, presidential elections have the highest turnout. However, when presidential elections and parliamentary election coincide, Election Day Turnout appears to be the same. Turning a particular attention to participation patterns, turnout appears to fluctuate around 65% of the population. Notice that, as Norris

Figure 2. Average Voter Turnout for Parliamentary Elections between 1991 and 2009. Source: National Electoral Institute (INE, 2016).

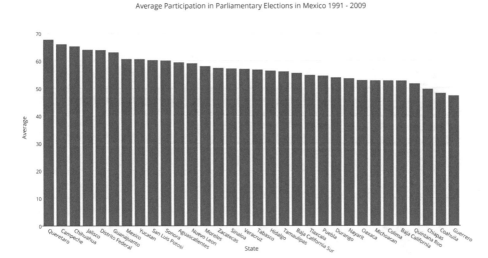

(2002) points out, there is not a clear pattern for participation levels between 1964 and 2015. But, if attention is focused to the most recent 20-year timespan, INE (2016) survey data shows a clear decline in electoral participation. This result reinforces Norris's (2002) findings on political participation.

To delve deeper into this period, in Figure 2 average participation levels in parliamentary elections for every state in Mexico between 1991 and 2009 are plotted. Given that participation level in presidential elections is higher, parliamentary elections should provide a lower bound for Election Day turnout between these years.

Figure 2 shows that there is around a 10% difference between participation levels in Queretaro, the state with the highest levels of participation and Guerrero, the state with lowest level of participation. Noticeably, the four states that host the largest urban concentrations in Mexico, Distrito Federal, Estado de Mexico (Mexico), Jalisco and Nuevo Leon, do not show the largest levels of political participation. The political community argues that political participation goes beyond the election of representatives (Norris, 2002). Activities such as protests, joining civil associations and writing letters may be also considered forms of participation. Thus, Norris (2002) found that the levels of this form political participation are, on average, larger in Mexico than in similar countries of Latin America. In order to assess these forms of participation, Figure 3 compares average participation levels between 2001 and 2012 in political meetings, writing or signing letters calling for action, calling or

Figure 3. Average Political Participation Levels in Non-Electoral Activities between 2001 and 2012. Source: National Survey on Political Culture and Citizenship (ENCUP, 2016).

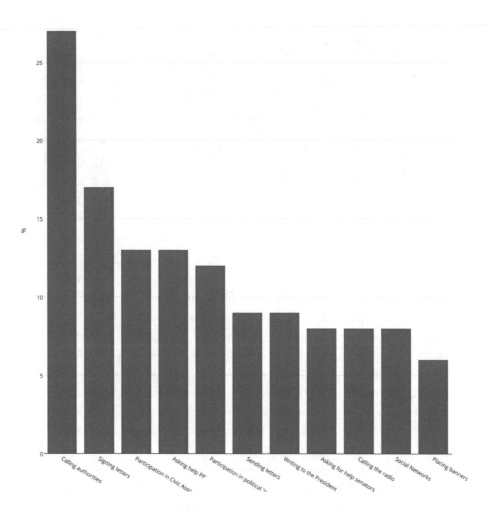

Political Participation in Mexico

contacting representatives, participating in civic associations and, more recently, new forms of participation such as engaging in interaction in online social networks.

From Figure 3 it is possible to notice that activities that do not involve deep social interaction, such as calling authorities and signing letters, are the ones that show highest levels of participation. Next, activities involving larger amounts of social engagement, such as asking to help political parties, participating in civic associations and participating in political meetings are presented. Finally, there are

Figure 4. Political Participation Levels in Non-Electoral Activities in 2012. Source: National Survey on Political Culture and Citizenship (ENCUP, 2016).

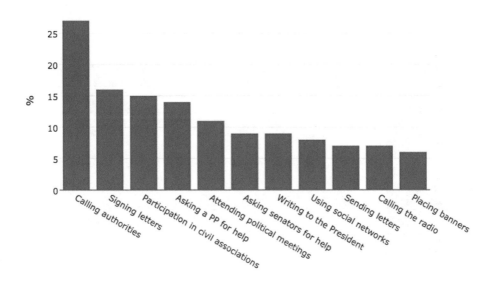

Political Participation in Mexico

mostly activities that involve the largest level of social and political engagement such as sending letters, writing to the President, asking senators for help, calling the radio and placing banners.

The emergence of new ways of participation such as online social networks suggests that agencies through which political participation is channeled might be changing. It is sufficient to notice that, even if the ENCUP (2016) started tracking participation in online social networks in 2012, the level of participation in online social networks is comparable to the average level of participation of people calling the radio. In order to underscore the importance of new outlets in participation, we plot in Figure 4 political participation levels in non-electoral activities in 2012.

Notice that channels of participation such as sending letters, writing to the President and calling the radio appear to lose ground to new agencies such as social networks.

Important for political participation are also the sources of political information. As technology evolves, new sources of political information emerge. In Mexico, even if access to the Internet is not widely spread, the Internet and platforms that are powered through it, such as online social networks, have become an important source of information. As a reflection of its importance, the ENCUP (2016) began tracking the population that accessed political information through them from 2008. In 2012, the survey began tracking the population that accessed political information

Figure 5. Average Sources of Political Information between 2001 and 2012. Source: National Survey on Political Culture and Citizenship (ENCUP, 2016).

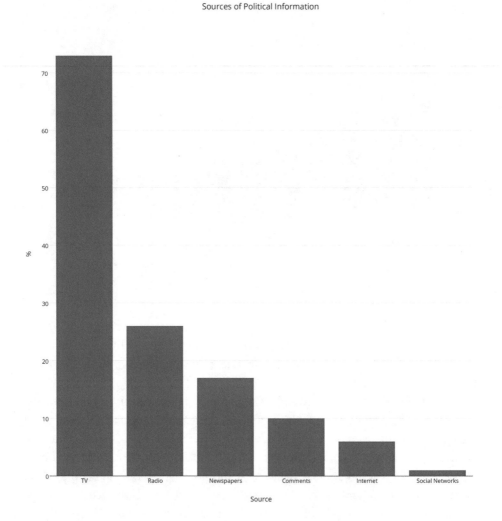

via online social networks. Figure 5 depicts the most important sources of information between 2001 and 2012.

It can be seen from Figure 5 that television is the most important source of political information in Mexico, more than twice the number of people reported obtaining political information from television than they did from radio or newspapers, the second and third most relevant sources of political information. In contrast, less than 10% of the population reported word-of-mouth, the Internet and online social networks as their source of information.

Figure 6. Sources of Political Information in 2012. Source: National Survey on Political Culture and Citizenship (ENCUP, 2016).

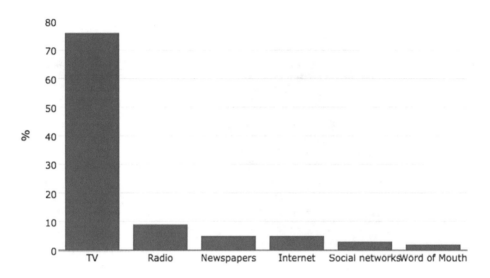

However, it is important to note that ENCUP (2016) began reporting the Internet as a source of information only in 2008 and online social networks in 2012. Figure 6 shows 2012 levels on the usage of different media as sources of political information.

Even though television, radio and newspapers prevail as the main source of political information, the Internet and social networks have already surpassed comments from word-of-mouth communication. It is interesting to note that by 2012, the same proportion of the population reported newspapers and the Internet as their main source of political information. Moreover, it should be noted that the proportion of people that reports online social networks as their source of political information is close to the proportion that said word-of-mouth comments were their main source of information.

The figures shown earlier seem to suggest emergent patterns. First, in Mexico the level of interest in politics is low, which correlates and, maybe, translates into a decrease in the levels of political participation in the last 20 years. Second, even though Mexicans participate politically in activities other than voting, such activities appear to be limited in their level of social and political engagement. Third, in recent years the sources of political information that Mexicans have access to have been disrupted by the emergence of the Internet and online social networks. An example of this is the online social protest #YoSoy132. This protest was mainly organized

Figure 7. General awareness of #YoSoy132. Source: National Survey on Political Culture and Citizenship (ENCUP, 2016).

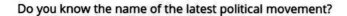

Do you know the name of the latest political movement?

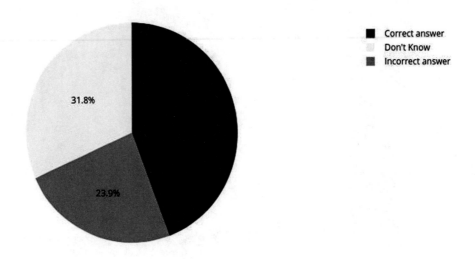

by university students and began as opposition to the now president of Mexico, then candidate of the Institutional Revolutionary Party, or PRI for its acronym in Spanish, and the alleged biased coverage the mainstream media in Mexico had of the 2012 general election. In order to assess the impact of the online social protest, Figure 7 shows the proportion of Mexicans that knew about the protest.

It is interesting that even though less than 5% of the population reported using online social networks as their source of political information, around 44% of the total population were aware of #YoSoy132. The diffusion of #YoSoy132 into mainstream media such as television, newspapers and the radio stresses the power of online social communities to transcend the barriers of the online world into the offline one.

Twitter has become a common place for political discussion (Bruns and Burgess, 2011). In particular, the flexibility of online social networks offers the possibility of interacting and sharing information from different points of view. This inherent characteristic allows anyone with a mobile phone to join a protest or mobilization through Twitter. However, it should be noted that Twitter is just a channel of communication, not a mechanism to initiate a real social mobilization. Examples can be found in countries such as Tunisia, Egypt and Yemen, where revolutions have been coordinated through online social networks. As the data from ENCUP (2016) shows, Mexico is no exception. With the goal of comparing traditional expressions

Figure 8. Daily Frequency of Tweets Related to Enrique Peña Nieto.

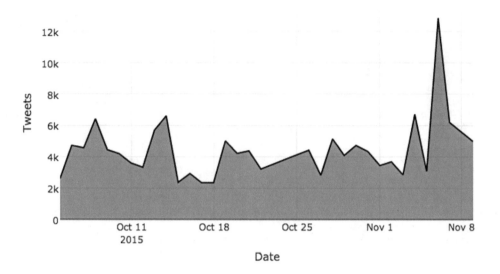

of political participation with its online counterpart, we now describe the data from the Twitter API to explore patterns in online political participation.

Following the structure of the analysis above, we begin by looking at the level of political participation in Twitter. In order to gauge online interest in politics, a possible approach is to visualize the daily frequency of tweets related to Enrique Peña Nieto, as shown in Figure 8.

A second approach to proxy political participation in Twitter is to visualize the number of tweets generated in the country. As Twitter has become a valuable tool to track and to identify patterns of mobility and activity, the authors examine and capture all locations where our collected tweets were posted. According to Kumar et al. (2013), approximately 1% of all tweets published on Twitter are geo-located i.e., users can optionally choose to provide location information for the tweets they publish. This is a very small portion of the Tweets, therefore, it was decided to use the profile information of the tweet's originator to estimate the origin of the tweet. We used the geographical coordinates related to the place where the tweet's originator resides. The geographical coordinates were obtained through the API of Twitter. Recall that in this context political engagement is proxied through tweets mentioning the president of Mexico Enrique Peña Nieto. Figures 9 and 10 provide a geographical heat map from the collected data aimed to quickly identify regions of

Figure 9. A geographical heat map showing the distribution of tweet locations around the world.

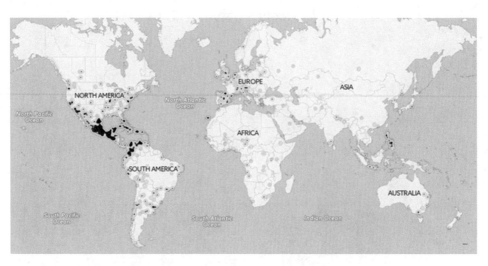

Figure 10. A geographical heat map showing the distribution of tweets in Mexico.

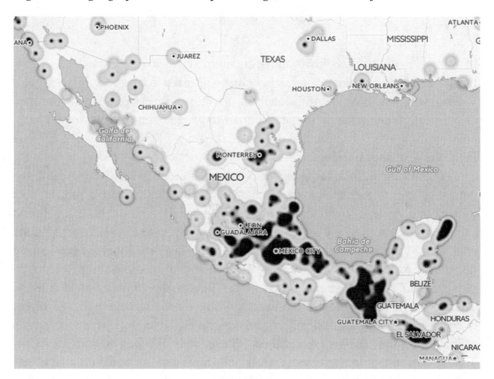

high density of tweeting activity. In this case, the color scheme denotes blue color to indicate low activity and red color to indicate high activity. Thus, it is possible to see that the central region of Mexico is the one with the highest level of political engagement.

To obtain more precise information about which places had the highest level of political engagement in Mexico, the geographical coordinates to identify political engagement by region in the country were used. Figure 11 shows that, different from what ENCUP (2016) data suggest at a national level, Mexico City and Monterrey are regions with the largest level of political engagement through Twitter. Queretaro, Veracruz and Quintana Roo follow them. All of the latter have participated with more than a 1000 tweets each. Puebla, Tabasco, Baja California Sur and Jalisco had a level of participated with less than a 100 tweets. It is important to note that the

Figure 11. Regions with the highest level of political engagement in Twitter.

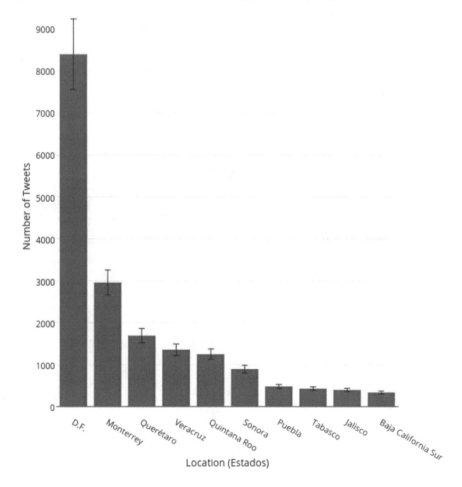

levels of political participation in Twitter may be affected by a plethora of factors and, hence, provide only a glance of the way online political participation looks like.

Having described the most active regions in terms of political participation and having visualized the way in which political participation developed, the authors analyze the way in which people participate through Twitter. As in traditional expressions of political participation, online social activism can take different forms. In Twitter political participation involves engaging in the online social network through tweets. Particularly, Pearce W., Holmberg K., Hellsten I. and Nerlich B. (2014) point out that Twitter users engage with others by addressing users in a conversation through the "@" sign and by generating conversational tags through the use of hashtags (see below). In order to identify political participation in Twitter, the authors begin by building a mentions network. In Figure 12, users are described through nodes. If user i mentions user j in her message, a link is drawn between node i and node j. The size of the node represents the number of times the node has been mentioned.

Through the visualization of the network it is possible to assess active users in the Twitter mention network. It can be seen that users @EPN, @DeniseDresserG, @Change_Mex, @SinEmbargoMX and @AristeguiOnline are the most mentioned

Figure 12. Network of political participation in Twitter.

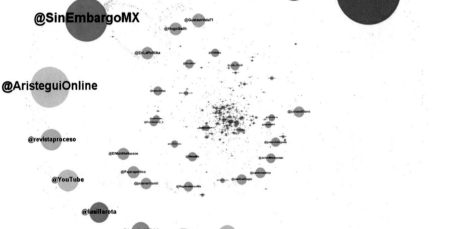

in the sample. This first approximation is useful to categorize the important users within the network. The first category are news agencies, which are represented by @SinEmbargo and @AristeguiOnline. The second category are online social activism groups and social activists, represented by @Change_Mex. Finally, the third category is represented by political pundits like @DeniseDresserG.

Users in Twitter typically organize themselves around specific interests, such as a sports team or hobbies, which facilitates interactions with other users who share similar preferences. These users classify their tweets using topic-specific "hashtags" (Olson & Neal, 2015). Tweets that contain hashtags entities are inherently more valuable in terms of embedding extra information and bridging knowledge (Russell, 2013). With this in mind, it is possible to identify the online communities that are related to the president of Mexico, Enrique Peña Nieto. Figure 13 shows the most used hashtags in the sample.

Figure 13. Top 10 most prevalent hashtags related to Enrique Peña Nieto.

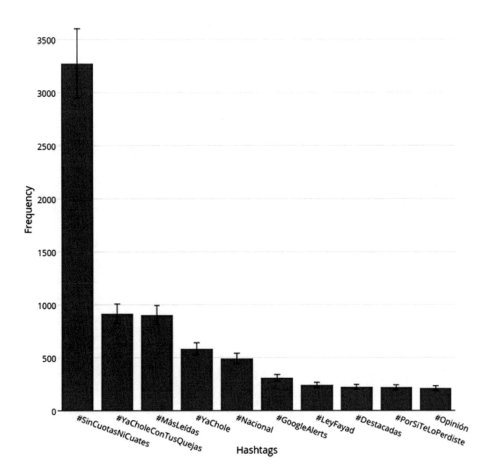

From Figure 13, it is possible to identify the most prevalent hashtags appearing in tweets in the data collection. These topics are as follows: #SinCuotasNiCuates, #YaCholeConTusQuejas and #LeyFayad. The first one is related to an online petition that intends to stop Enrique Peña Nieto from nominating people close to him to the highest court in Mexico: the "Suprema Corte de Justicia" (Supreme Court of Justice). The second hashtag is related to a TV spot that intended to communicate to the viewers that people are tired of complaints against the government. The third hashtag is related to a law proposal put forward by Omar Fayad. The so-called "Ley Fayad" (Fayad's Law) intended to restrict online freedom of speech.

To compare the intensity of political participation within these online communities, we plotted in Figure 14 the daily frequency at which users tweeted. As can be appreciated, the conversation around #SinCuotasNiCuates persists throughout the

Figure 14. Tweeting frequency through time by online community.

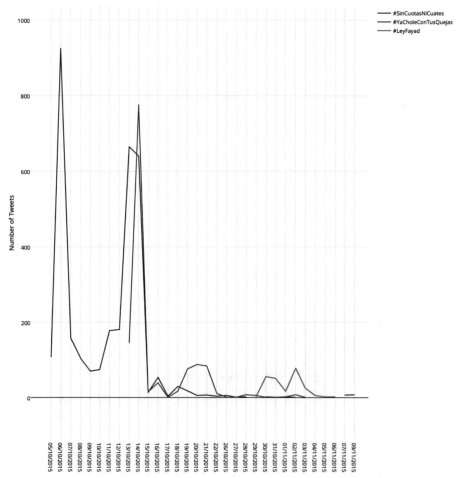

Figure 15. Mentions Network of the online community #SinCuotasNiCuates.

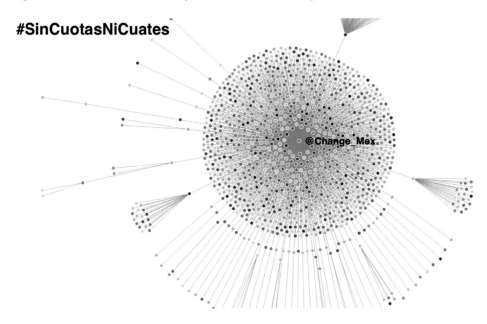

duration of the mining. However, this hashtag has a participation level of 10 tweets or more only during the first ten days of its emergence: from October the 5th to the 19th, 2015. Online community #YaCholeConTusQuejas, on the other end, is present from October 13th through November the 3rd. Nevertheless, this community has a participation level of ten tweets or more only between October the 13th and the 22nd. Finally, #LeyFayad persists between October the 29th and November the 9th, 2015. But this community has a level of participation higher than 10 tweets only until November the 3rd, 2015.

It should be highlighted that there are peaks on Twitter participation once the topic emerges. To further analyze the way in which these communities develop, different agencies within communities were explored. In order to do so, the mention network by community was provided. In this case, it was shown that every user through a node within the network and their interactions through ties to other nodes. The main goal of this figure is to identify different patterns of social interaction within these communities.

Figures 15, 16 and 17 allow to identify large differences on the way in which people participate within different online communities. It can be seen in Figure 15 that within #SinCuotasNiCuates there is a user that is being mentioned by most of the other users. This is Change.org, the online social activism website. In contrast, in Figures 16 and 17, there are different users that concentrate mentions but in a smaller scale. These users are political pundits such as Julio Astillero (@julioastiller) and

Figure 16. Mentions Network in the online community #YaCholeConTusQuejas.

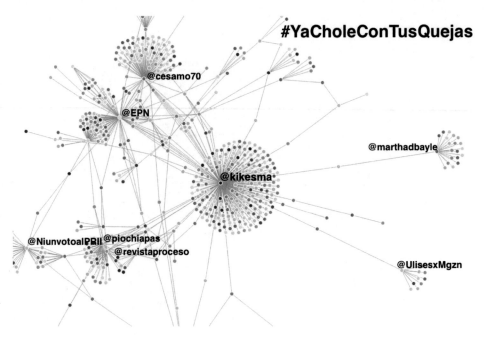

Figure 17. Mentions network for the online community #LeyFayad.

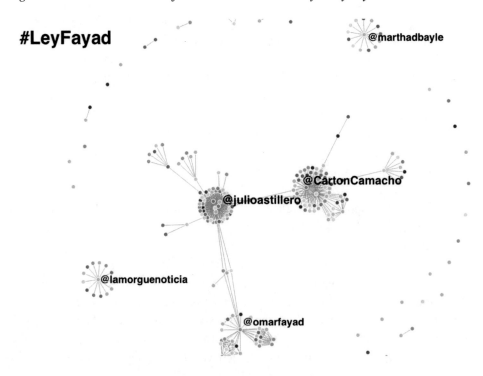

Camacho (@CartonCamacho), and social activists such as "Enrique D." (@kikesma) and different news agencies just like the magazine Proceso (@revistaproceso).

DISCUSSION

Figures in the Results section, together with a study by INE (2016) show that political participation in Mexico appears to have decreased in recent years. When looking for possible explanations, results above seem to suggest that the more people have to interact with others in person, the less likely they are to participate. This assertion seems supported through Figures 3, 4, and 5, where survey data shows that forms of participation that involve interacting with others are the less popular. In the same context, obtaining political information from sources that involve social interaction appear to be the less sought-after.

However, the emergence of new sources of information, such as the Internet and forums in which people can share ideas, such as online social networks, puts forward the possibility that political participation is being facilitated by these new forums. As survey data suggest, the proportion of the population using these forums as a source of information or to participate in political conversations is still small. Nevertheless, the high levels of information flows that are often used by individuals who share political information on Twitter suggest that political participation within this platform is vibrant.

In this study, the authors performed an extensive observational analysis of the patterns of political participation on a sample of tweets. The results reflect differences in identifying political activity delivered by Twitter. Thus, these results reveal high levels of information flows that are often used by individuals who share this type of information on this platform. According to the results obtained, the topical exploration was able to effectively identify political tweets and clusters that are formed around temporally similar preferences.

It is important to note that the levels of political participation in Twitter are very different between regions. The authors identify regions of high density of tweets, where most of the users are geographically located and share information. In this context, the central region is the one with the highest level of participation and the northern region is the one with the lowest. Moreover, differences in the level of regional offline and online political participation makes evident political participation on Twitter i.e., online social networks are still restricted by levels of adoption.

It could be seen that Twitter facilitates interaction amongst different actors that feed political participation in Mexico. For example, it was possible to see through the visualization of online social networks that politicians, social activists, pundits and the media are some of the most active participants. However, different users interact with others in different ways (Cha, et al., 2012). The latter is probably due to the diverse levels of participation in the different communities. Participation in #SinCuotasNiCuates for instance was centralized and directed through Change.org, which might explain why the lifespan of the community and participation levels within the community were so high. In contrast, participation in #YaCholeConTusQuejas and #LeyFayad was shared among other types of users. Most likely, this fragmentation caused lower levels of participation.

Taken together, this study underscores the potential of using social media for encouraging political participation in Mexico. In particular, it seems that the role of associations, such as Change.org, is essential to promote online political participation. However, the findings of Somuano (2011) put forward a word of caution about these associations, as their involvement may not be as inclusive as one might wish. Moreover, in a country such as Mexico where access to the Internet is not widespread, tools like online social networks provide only a small means for encouraging political participation.

It is important to underscore that, according to Morales, Borondo, Losada, & Benito (2014) the data taken from Twitter are not necessarily representative samples of the outside world, meaning that it cannot be generalized from these findings to the whole population. Therefore, these data must be interpreted with caution since all the information collected from this study is mainly based on the Twitter response service, i.e., Twitter users are a sample that may not be representative of the general population and it is possible to find some inconsistencies in terms of the outcomes retrieved through our data crawler.

In addition, caution was taken to ensure its validity of the information gathered in this study. This type of data is observational and, as such, no cause-and-effect relationships can be assumed. Their tweets will not show up via any publicly accessible Twitter location search method. This represents a gap in the data. However, the authors do not believe that these gaps, noises and inaccuracies completely degrade the value of the data. Similarly, some people may participate in Twitter but choose to disable location on their mobile devices and also leave their location empty in their Twitter profile. Data for this group will not be present either.

CONCLUSION

This manuscript examines online and offline political participation in Mexico. Through the use of survey data, our study underscores the low levels of interest Mexicans have in politics. This level of interest is reflected in a low level of political participation. In particular, levels of political participation are dependent on both the election cycle and regions within the country. Moreover, this study has shown that

Mexicans receive political information mainly from television, with other sources of information such as newspapers, radio, the Internet and online social networks well behind. In terms of political participation, this study has found that generally as the level of personal interaction needed to take part in political action increases, participation seems to decrease.

The emergence of new technologies, such as Twitter, facilitate social interaction to levels never seen before. Therefore, the authors consider the importance of examining the way in which political participation in Twitter is compared to levels of political participation offline. In the sample of tweets, it was found that the general level of online political participation seemed to increase. However, political participation online appears to be different from offline political participation. These differences should be taken with caution because the Twitter sample may not be representative of the Mexican population.

It was shown that people participated in three online protests: #SinCuotasNiCuates, #YaCholeConTusQuejas and #LeyFayad. These protests differed in their content, duration and agencies involved. Particularly, it was noticed that the duration of the protests may well depend on the agencies involved e.g., #SinCuotasNiCuates was organized around @Change_Mex which most likely organized the debate online. This contrasts with #YaCholeConTusQuejas and #LeyFayad, where the online protests where not organized. This lack of organization might have well contributed to their lack of staying power.

Taken together, this study demonstrates the potential of using social media analysis to develop insight into how users share political views, and opens the possibility of understanding and comparing public participation on various scales. Moreover, this research has also shown that emergent topics related to politics in Mexico are important because they could help to explore how political participation becomes of public interest.

Because most of our analysis is exploratory, it poses questions for future research. Such questions include "How do the agencies contribute on the emergence and duration of online protests?" and "How does online social activism translate into offline activism?"

REFERENCES

Almond, G., & Verba, S. (1963). *The Civic Culture: Political Attitudes and Democracy in Five Nations* (S. Publications, Ed.). doi:10.1515/9781400874569

Bruns, A., & Burgess, J. (2011). The use of Twitter hashtags in the formation of ad hoc publics. *Proceedings of the 6th European Consortium for Political Research (ECPR) General Conference 2011*, University of Iceland, Reykjavik.

Bruns, A., & Stieglitz, S. (2012). Quantitative approaches to comparing communication patterns on Twitter. *Journal of Technology in Human Services, 30*(34), 160–185. doi:10.1080/15228835.2012.744249

Cha, M., Benevenuto, F., Haddadi, H., & Gummadi, K. (2012). The World of Connections and Information Flow in Twitter. *IEEE Transactions on Systems, Man, and Cybernetics. Part A, Systems and Humans, 2*(4), 991–998.

Encuesta Nacional Sobre Cultura Política y Prácticas Ciudadanas-ENCUP. (2016). Bases de Datos. Retrieved from http://www.encup.gob.mx/en/Encup/Bases_de_datos

Ferrara, E., De Meo, P., Fiumara, G., & Baumgartner, R. (2014). Web data extraction, applications and techniques: A survey. *Knowledge-Based Systems, 70*, 301–323. doi:10.1016/j.knosys.2014.07.007

Gonzalez-Bailon, S., Borge-Holthoefer, J., Rivero, A., & Moreno, Y. (2011). The Dynamics of Protest Recruitment Through an Online Network. *Scientific Reports, 1*(197). PMID:22355712

Instituto Nacional Electoral. (2014). Informe País Sobre la Calidad de la Ciudadanía en México.

Instituto Nacional Electoral. (2016). Sistema de Consulta de la Estadística de las Elecciones Federales. Retrieved from http://www.ine.mx/documentos/RESELEC/SICEEF/principal.html

International Institute for Democracy and Electoral Assistance-IDEA. (2016). Voter Turnout Database. Retrieved from http://www.idea.int/vt/index.cfm

Kumar, S., Morstatter, F., & Liu, H. (2013). *Twitter data analytics*. Springer.

Lu, X., & Brelsford, C. (2014). Network structure and community evolution on twitter: Human behavior change in response to the 2011 Japanese earthquake and tsunami. *Scientific Reports, 4*. PMID:25346468

McIver, D. J., Hawkins, J. B., Chunara, R., Chatterjee, A. K., Bhandari, A., Fitzgerald, T. P., & Brownstein, J. S. (2015). Characterizing sleep issues using twitter. *Journal of Medical Internet Research, 17*(6), e140. doi:10.2196/jmir.4476 PMID:26054530

Morales, A., Borondo, J., Losada, J., & Benito, R. (2014). Efficiency of human activity on information spreading on twitter. *Social Networks*, *39*, 1–11. doi:10.1016/j.socnet.2014.03.007

Norris, P. (2002). La Participación Ciudadana: México Desde Una Perspectiva Comparativa. In Avances y Retos en el Desarrollo de la Cultura Democrática en México. Instituto Federal Electoral.

Olson, R. S., & Neal, Z. P. (2015). Navigating the massive world of Reddit: Using backbone networks to map user interests in social media. *PeerJ Computer Science*, *1*, e4. doi:10.7717/peerj-cs.4

Pearce, W., Holmberg, K., Hellsten, I., & Nerlich, B. (2014). Climate Change on Twitter: Topics, Communities and Conversations about the 2013 IPCC Working Group 1 Report. *PLoS ONE*, *9*(4), e94785. doi:10.1371/journal.pone.0094785 PMID:24718388

Piña-García, C. A., Gershenson, C., & Siqueiros-García, J. M. (2016). Towards a standard sampling methodology on online social networks: Collecting global trends on twitter. *Applied Network Science*, *1*(1), 1–19. doi:10.1007/s41109-016-0004-1

Piña-García, C. A., & Gu, D. (2013). Spiraling Facebook: An alternative metropolis-Hastings random walk using a spiral proposal distribution. *Social Network Analysis and Mining*, *3*(4), 1403–1415. doi:10.1007/s13278-013-0126-8

Roy, S. D., & Zeng, W. (2014). *Social multimedia signals*. Springer.

Russell, M. A. (2013). *Mining the social web: Data mining Facebook, twitter, LinkedIn, google+, GitHub, and more*. O`Reilly Media Inc.

Serfass, D. G., & Sherman, R. A. (2015). Situations in 140 characters: Assessing real-world situations on twitter. *PLoS ONE*, *10*(11), e0143051. doi:10.1371/journal.pone.0143051 PMID:26566125

Somuano, F. (2011). *Sociedad Civil Organizada y Democracia en México*.

Thapen, N. A., & Ghanem, M. M. (2013). Towards passive political opinion polling using twitter. Proceedings of the BCS SGAI SMA 2013 the BCS SGAI workshop on social media analysis (p. 19).

Weikum, G., Ntarmos, N., Spaniol, M., Triantafillou, P., Benczur, A. A., Kirkpatrick, S., & Williamson, M. (2011). Longitudinal analytics on web archive data: it's about time! Proceedings of CIDR (pp. 199-202).

Weng, L., Flammini, A., Vespignani, A., & Menczer, F. (2012). Competition among memes in a world with limited attention. *Scientific Reports*, 2. PMID:22461971

KEY TERMS AND DEFINITIONS

Big Data: A term for large data sets where most of the challenges are related to analysis, data curation, sharing, storage and visualization.

Computational Social Science: Refers to the academic sub-discipline concerned with computational approaches to the social sciences i.e., computers are used to model, simulate and analyze social phenomena.

Hashtag: Is a type of label or metadata tag used on social network and microblogging services which make it easier for users to find messages with a specific theme or topic.

Political Participation: It refers to the different mechanisms for the public to express opinions and exert influence.

Social Media: A technology based on computers and mobile devices that allow posting and sharing information and images through virtual communities.

Social Networking: An online platform that is used by people around the world to interact through social relations with other people who share similar preferences.

Twitter: A social networking service where users post and interact with tweets that are restricted to 140 characters.

Chapter 7
The Formation of Consensus in Iranian Online Communities

Ali Honari
Vrije Universiteit Amsterdam, The Netherlands

ABSTRACT

For several years now, the role that digitally mediated social movements and online communities play in challenging authoritarian regimes in the Middle East and North Africa has been extensively debated. The focus of attention on the political use of the Internet shapes conventional wisdom that political issues are widespread in online communities in these contexts and that the users are predominantly oppositional users with political democratic motivations. Using fresh methods and techniques to gather a variety of online data, this chapter argues and reveals that, at least in the case of Iran, this view selectively overlooks the diversity of users and the broad range of issues frequently and intensively discussed among users in online communities. The failure to examine a broader range of issues means that scholars have neglected how consensus forms and develops among online users in other issues. This study broadens our understanding of the current social issues and possible areas of change in Iran through investigating a more comprehensive frame of the Iranian web.

INTRODUCTION

Shocking political and social developments in the Middle East and North Africa (MENA) region, from the emergence of Iranian Green Movement to Arab Uprisings, have heightened the need for understanding agents of change in those societies. Much of the political upheavals were credited to the Internet, in particular newly more personalized digitally mediated social movements which "have frequently been larger;

DOI: 10.4018/978-1-5225-2495-3.ch007

have scaled up more quickly; and have been flexible in tracking moving political targets and bridging different issues" (Bennett & Segerberg, 2012, p. 742). One global quantitative study using country-year data demonstrates that unlike in democracies, internet use has paved the way for the occurrence of protests in authoritarian regimes (Ruijgrok, 2016). It is commonly argued that the Internet, by reducing costs and risks, facilitates participation of people as well as coordination and mobilization of protests (Earl & Kimport, 2011; Shirky, 2008) resulting in the intensification of protests in repressive societies (Farrell, 2012). On the other hand, critics contend that 'real' change in repressive societies requires hierarchical networks with strong ties formed on trust, which are absolutely absent on the Internet (Gladwell, 2010).

Whether from internet enthusiasts (Shirky, 2008; Earl & Kimport, 2011; Howard & Hussain, 2013) or from a more critical view (Morozov, 2010; Gladwell, 2010; Harlow & Guo, 2014), explaining the role of the Internet in social change in repressive contexts entails understanding of online activism (Zuckerman, 2014), in other words, the process of participation in digitally mediated social movements. Klandermans and Oegema (1987, p. 519) distinguished four steps in this process: "becoming part of the mobilization potential, becoming target of mobilization attempts, becoming motivated to participate, and overcoming barriers to participation." The first step, becoming a potential participant, involves the formation of consensus on goals and means of participation (Klandermans, 1988). The process of consensus formation concerns unplanned construction and convergence of meaning in social networks and subcultures. People validate information by discussing their issues of interest and comparing their interpretations from an event or issue with others. In fact, the process of consensus formation fertilizes the ground for participation in social movements. Thus, consensus formation, as the initial process, must be understood fully as the main condition of realizing the larger framework in the debate on the role played by the Internet in social movements.

In societies where expressing critical views is likely to be punished by the government, and mass media are suppressed and censored, online communities have increasingly become important venues where autonomous, or even anonymous discussions take place (Howard & Hussain, 2013; Al-Rawi, 2014). In this chapter, online communities refers to a collectivity of people who communicate with each other (Malinen, 2015) and actively engage in discussions in a defined web-based online service (online platform). The Internet offers a space, at least for some, to engage in conversations and spread information that can be hard to trace by government officials (Tufekci & Wilson, 2012; Lim, 2012). When people perceive lower levels of repression, the likelihood of sincere expressions of political beliefs and emotions increases, which makes preference falsification (Kuran, 1997) less likely (Farrell, 2012). In fact, in those societies, consensus forms and develops through generating and sharing content and discussing a variety of issues within online communities (Bennett & Segerberg, 2012).

Yet, a more comprehensive understanding of the web that captures the broad range of issues around which consensus forms suffers. So far, little attention has been paid to the political issues that are discussed among and expressed by ordinary citizens in online communities of repressive societies. For several years now, the role that digitally mediated social movements and online communities play in challenging authoritarian regimes in the Middle East and North Africa has been extensively debated (Howard & Hussain, 2013; Farrell, 2012; Lynch, 2011). Particularly the use of the Internet during the 2009 Iranian Green Movement protest and Arab uprisings in 2011 focus attention to political use of the Internet (Segerberg & Bennett, 2011; Aday, Farrell, Lynch, Sides, Kelly, & Zuckerman, 2010). Thus, the term 'Twitter revolution' in Iran and 'Facebook revolutions' in Egypt shaped conventional wisdom and expectations about the concerns and interests of Internet users in repressive societies. There is a widely accepted belief about the Internet in those societies that political issues are widespread in online communities, and that users are predominantly oppositional users with political democratic concerns. Studies relying on these assumptions are prone to neglect how consensus forms among online users in other issue areas. Therefore, the existing literature neglects or ignores various areas of interest to Iranian users and overlooks indirectly political issues and possible areas of change resulting from activities among the Iranian online communities (Honari, 2015). This poses a challenge for understanding the agency of social change in repressive societies. If one is to obtain the fullest possible understanding of the role of the Internet in society, to have a comprehensive view of the wide range of interests and topics and the diversity of Internet users, there is a substantial need to offer a more inclusive picture and vision of the web in these societies.

Methodologically speaking, most studies have gathered data from Twitter and other internationally well-known platforms of social networking instead of collecting data from local online platforms (Honari, 2015; Akhavan, 2013). In particular, there is a lack of research on local Iranian platforms despite their widespread popularity among Iranian users.

Taken together, while scholars have called for paying more attention to digitally mediated social movements, particularly in the authoritarian contexts (Lynch, 2011; Farrell, 2012; Earl & Kimport, 2011; Golder & Macy, 2014), studies on such societies still suffer from theoretical and methodological drawbacks: (a) little attention has been paid to the indirectly political areas of the web, (b) most studies have examined only a nonsystematic selection of topics and websites and (c) there is a lack of research on local platforms, despite their widespread popularity (Honari, 2015).

This study explores the different issues that are currently being discussed in Iranian online communities. Using a variety of online data, the study is also an attempt to present a broader picture of Iranian online communities to provide fullest possible understanding of the agents of change through the Internet. Equally important, this chapter proposes some methods and approaches for gathering data from online communities and analyzing data extracted from the Internet to understand repressive societies. It can be applied in any society of control with minor contextual adjustments.

Iran is a unique and important case in the Middle East for studying digitally mediated social movements through the Internet. While in terms of freedom of expression and press freedom Iran remains one of the most repressive countries in the world (Iran: Freedom of press the 2014, 2014; World press freedom index 2014, 2014) its growth of Internet penetration rate is amongst the highest in the Middle Eastern countries (Honari, 2015).

The remainder of this chapter proceeds as follows. In the next section the Internet in Iran will be addressed. Then, the procedure of research, methods and the data will be presented. It will be followed by the results section. Finally, in the conclusion and discussion part, the findings will be put into context and practical implications of this research will be discussed.

BACKGROUND: INTERNET IN IRAN

In 1992, Internet access in Iran was provided for the first time. Since then, the Iranian government has taken steps to expand and develop its telecommunications and informatics infrastructure (Sreberny & Khiabany, 2010). Nevertheless, while the development of Iran's Internet infrastructure enabled the number of people with access to the Internet to rise rapidly since the late 1990s, reports repeatedly reveal that the Iranian Internet -- in terms of limits on content, obstacles to access, and violations of user rights -- is ranked among the least liberated in the world (Kelly, Troung, Earp, Reed, Shahbaz, & Greco-Stoner, 2013). Internet service providers (ISPs) in Iran must obtain a license from the government, and to do so must meet official governmental restrictions by using software that blocks users from accessing forbidden URLs. Nevertheless, there is a rather large Internet service market in Iran and the Internet penetration rate is amongst the highest in the Middle East and has increased significantly over the last few years (see Figure 1 and Figure 2).

The Iranian government conducts vast and intensive filtering measures over the Iranian Web, in terms of both content restriction and access to websites. This goes far beyond simply blocking access to particular websites and services (MacKinnon, 2013). After the 2009 Green Movement protests, "increasingly complex surveillance and monitoring techniques, complementing technical filtration tools with legal frameworks and information manipulation" were adopted by the government (After the Green Movement: Internet controls in Iran 2009-2012, 2013). Despite the wide-

Figure 1. Internet penetration growth in Iran and in comparison with other counties in MENA region. The data of World Development Indictors is used for this diagram.

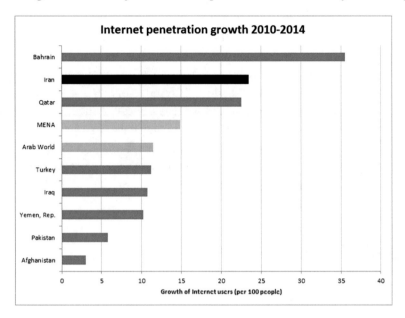

Figure 2. Internet penetration growth in Iran and in comparison with other counties in MENA region. The data of World Development Indictors is used for this diagram.

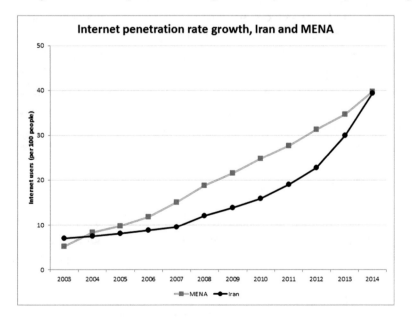

ranging and sophisticated filtering system in Iran (Internet filtering in Iran, 2009), large numbers of Iranian websites are highly responsive (i.e., blocked sites are still functioning) and the Iranian web is fresh (i.e., sites have been recently updated) (Rogers, Weltevrede, Niederer, & Borra, 2012). Moreover, the appearance of blocked blogs demonstrates that the Iranian web has an active "censorship circumvention culture" (Rogers, Weltevrede, Niederer, & Borra, 2012). Monitoring is accepted by users as what ordinarily happens (Abadpour & Anderson, 2013). While a majority of Iranian users often encounter blocked websites, most of them had heard about tools that help circumvent blocked websites, and they have easy access to such tools (Wojcieszak & Smith, 2014). In fact, despite the disruption of access to the Internet, users are not persuaded to abandon their activities (Abadpour & Anderson, 2013) and the filtering does not have any influence on users' access to the demanded websites (Rasouli & Moradi, 2012).

METHOD

Research Design and Procedure

The research proceeded in three main stages. In the first stage, I selected influential platforms within the boundaries and scope of the Iranian web. I then proposed the best sampling strategy for each platform. In the second stage, I extracted the relevant data from the selected platforms. In that stage, web scraping was used as the technique for the automated collection of online data. In the third stage of the study, I conducted analyses to identify major online communities and the issues that are most frequently discussed among users in each online community. In this stage I further investigated these issues to obtain data on correlates in terms of discussants' socio-economic characteristics and location, as well as by platform or community. Based on the profiles of user accounts, I break down the extracted data into user traits, to the extent possible.

Sampling Strategies

The first step in sampling has been to identify the influential online communities most likely to attract a diversity of Iranian users and to include diverse content generated by them. To have a comprehensive sample that represents a wide range of interests and topics and consequently a diverse group of Iranian Internet users, the most challenging issue is demarcating the Iranian national web (Rogers, 2013). As Earl (Earl, 2013) points out, sampling design, including sampling frame (i.e., identifying cases at risk of being studied) and sampling method (i.e., how cases from the sampling frame are drawn), is crucial for online studies on political issues. Studies relying on presuming a frame are prone to the production of desirable answers, and enormous bias by concealing other frames (Gamson, 2004, p. 245). In the sampling process we should have minimal preselection and pre-assumption.

A recent thorough literature review (Honari, 2015) concluded that the three main sectors of the Iranian web, which cover the main areas of interests and activities of Iranian users, are the blogosphere, social networking sites (SNSs), and news sources. For the purposes of this research the last is excluded from the sampling frame, as the content is generally not directly user driven, leaving a focus on the blogosphere and SNSs. Within SNSs, I examine both filtered and unfiltered platforms, with an emphasis on the most popular platforms, along with Balatarin which is highly user driven. Less widely used SNSs, like Twitter, are excluded. A specific sampling strategy is chosen for each platform on the basis of its nature. The main platforms that are focused on are listed in Table 1.

Data and Sample

Iranian Blogosphere (Blogistan)

There is a consensus that Iranian blogosphere "Blogistan" contributed to the opening up of society by enabling a political voice, particularly to Iranian youths during the last decade (Bucar & Fazaeli, 2008). Wojcieszak, Smith, and Enayat (2012) have shown that a considerable portion of Iranian Internet users are engaged in writing (8%), reading (42%), or commenting on (18%) blogs. A few studies on Iranian users show the variety of interests and issues in their blog posts (Wojcieszak & Smith, 2014; Honari, van Stekelenburg, & Klandermans, 2014; Sreberny & Khiabany, 2010), although most studies on the Iranian blogosphere have only been carried out on political blogs (e.g. Golkar, 2005; Jansen, 2009). In order to understand the blogosphere, one blog service provider has been chosen for identifying a sample of blogs and extracting all contents that bloggers on that platform produced in the

Table 1. Main platforms for data gathering

	Platforms	Filtering (Inside Iran)	Sector
1	Facebook	Blocked	OSN
2	Cloob.com	Accessible	OSN
3	Balatarin	Blocked	OSN (social news aggregator)
4	Tebyan	Accessible	OSN (social news aggregator)
5	Persianblog	Accessible	Blogosphere

course of the research. For this study, I chose Persianblog (http://persianblog.ir). Persianblog, which was launched in 2005 (Sreberny & Khiabany, 2010), is the oldest blog forum in Iran. Today, Persianblog is the third most important blog service provider in Iran; it hosts 9.3 million pages.

I identified blogs by extracting the feed of the "latest updated pages" on the Persianblog home page (http://persianblog.ir/). My software automatically saved the URLs of all blogs that were updated in one week from 11th August until 17th August 2014. By doing so, I identified 5,224 individual blogs from Persianblog. Then, all the contents of these blogs over two weeks were saved for later analyses.

Online Social Networking Sites (SNSs)

Over 85% of Internet users in Iran access SNSs such as Facebook and Google+ (Tabnak, 2012). Social networking is the most significant activity that Iranian Internet users are engaged in (Abadpour & Anderson, 2013). After the widely disputed Iranian presidential election in June 2009, SNSs played an important role in sharing ideas and spreading information and news among Green Movement supporters (Honari, 2013; Baldino & Goold, 2014; Rasouli & Moradi, 2012; Rahimi, 2011a), and also in "catching global media attention and raising human rights concerns" (Sohrabi-Haghighat & Mansouri, 2010). It is worth mentioning that using SNSs in Iran for political purposes is not limited to any particular political views (Abadpour & Anderson, 2013).

- Blocked in Iran

Facebook is the most popular SNS among Iranian users. Students use Facebook more than other social groups in Iran. A recent survey of social communication students in four main Tehran universities (n=325) found that the vast majority (92.3%) use SNSs, particularly Facebook (Rasouli & Moradi, 2012). Facebook in Iran represents an emerging frame for a new kind of activism (Rahimi, 2011a). Very close to the disputed 2009 presidential election, "Facebook rapidly expanded into a political forum" (Rahimi, 2011a, p. 8). Then, in the midst of post-election protests, Facebook was extensively employed by the Iranian Green Movement activists for mobilization (Honari, 2013) and "online broadcasting of offline events" (Rahimi, 2011b). Using Facebook as a platform for the mobilization attempts of Green Movement activists was also actively encouraged by Facebook itself (MacKinnon, 2013).

In June 2014, I used Netvizz applications to extract data from the Facebook platform (Rieder, 2013). To have a systematic sample of Iranian Facebook pages and avoid selection bias, I focused on popular Iranian Facebook pages. To do so, I began with an initial sample of the 233 top Facebook pages (all Facebook pages with more than 100,000 members in June 2014). Top Facebook pages were chosen based on Pagebaan (http://pagebaan.com/top). Using this initial sample, I traversed their links to other Iranian Facebook pages two steps deeper (initial sample → 1st step linked → 2nd step linked). I then removed all international Facebook pages and kept only Iranian Facebook pages. By Iranian Facebook pages I mean pages which are in Farsi or/and pages whose members are mostly Iranians. I also removed the Facebook pages with less than 14,000 members, as they are not significant on Iranian Facebook. This process resulted in a pool of 3,511 active Iranian Facebook pages. From the Facebook pages, in addition to their links to each other, I extracted following variables:

- **Like Count:** The number of likes that the page has received or the number of members.
- **Talking about Count:** The index that shows the actual number of users who are engaged in and interacting with the page.
- **Category:** The category of Facebook page, which is assigned by the administrator or the creator of the page.

Some descriptive data about the pool of Facebook pages is shown in Table 2.

After identifying the active Facebook pages, I mapped them based on their links to each other. By mapping the network of this pool, I detected the main communities and the main clusters of Facebook pages. Finally, I broke down the data extracted from the selected Facebook pages and looked at their categories and also the top issues within them.

Balatarin.com is one of the most well-known social news aggregator websites in Iran. On Balatarin, which is similar to digg.com, users submit the best links of interest to other (Iranian) internet users around the world. Once a link acquires enough positive votes, it is moved to the top of the front page ('hot posts' page). I gathered the data from this page, assuming that it represents the interests and concerns of Balatarin users. All the content of posts on this page and other relevant objects were captured automatically by software over the course of the data gathering (from 30th June 2014 to 10th August 2014).

Table 2. Descriptive data About Facebook pages

	N	Minimum	Maximum	Mean	Std. Deviation
Like Count	3,510	14,001	2,985,228	113,258.46	187,690.745
Talking about count	3,510	0	779,380	5,290.86	19,342.482

I measured the following variables from each post:

- **Number of Votes+:** The number of positive votes that the post received.
- **Number of Votes-:** The number of negative votes that the post received. This shows the extent to which the post is disputable.
- **Number of Clicks**: The number of post views shows the extent to which the post attracted Balatarin's audiences.
- **Number of Comments**: The number of comments shows the extent to which the post elicited user discussion.

Balatarin has about 35,000 users and half a million visitors per month (in 2012). Users are active in seven categories: society, politics, science/ technology, sports, art/literacy, entertainment, and economy. During the post-election events of 2009, Balatarin was one of the most influential Iranian social networks for the Iranian Green Movement (Sreberny & Khiabany, 2010; Honari, 2013), and it is one of the most popular social news aggregators blocked inside Iran.

- Accessible in Iran

SNSs accessible in Iran, such as Facenama.com (Alexa traffic rank: 7/ users: 435,000), aparat.com (Alexa traffic rank: 16), cloob.com (Alexa traffic rank: 18/ users: more than 850,000), and Tebyan.net (Alexa traffic rank 28/ users: 222,000) are among the most popular and frequently visited online platforms in Iran (Alexa ranks are retrieved in November 2014). I chose cloob.com and Tebyan; two of the most important SNSs accessible in Iran. The sampling strategy for cloob.com and Tebyan, is similar to that applied to Facebook and Balatarin.

Cloob.com is the most popular and oldest social network in Iran. Cloob users have their own profile pages, as on Facebook, and any user can share or reshare others' entries. They are also able to comment on each other's posts. In Cloob, there are 23,695 'clubs' that people are members of according their interests or needs. Clubs in Cloob are similar to Facebook pages/groups and are categorized into 22 categories.

I extracted the data of clubs in detail in June 2014. To obtain an appropriate sample of users, using Excel's random number generator, I randomly selected a certain number of users from the top 10 Clubs in each of the categories. All in all, I randomly selected 8,652 users from 220 clubs. From the profile of sample users, I gathered self-reported sociodemographic variables. Occupations, Education level and Place of residence were manually coded by a research assistant and randomly rechecked by me. Information that has not been reported by users or was not possible to understand and code is categorized as missing data. The list of variables and categories is shown in Table 3. The profile data reveal that Cloob users live mostly

Table 3. The list and information of demographics variables of Cloob users

Title	Categories	N	Mean	SD.
Gender	1 male; 2 female	8,651	1.4886	
Age		5,167	24.9145	6.1886
Marital Status	1 single; 2 married	8,652	1.1150	
Religion*	Muslim, Christian, Zoroastrian, Jewish	8652		
Education Level*	1 Under Diploma; 2 Diploma; 3 One Year College; 4 Bachelor's Degree; 5 Master's Degree; 6 PhD and more	7596		
Occupation*	1 Employer/manager; 2 Professional; 3 Manual worker; 4 Farmer; 5 Member of armed forces; 6 Culture, art and literature, 7 Journalist, politician, etc.; 8 Governmental employee; 9 Non-governmental employee; 11 Self-employed; 12 Academic; 13 Other, 14 Unemployed; 15 Student; 16 Employee; 17 Teacher; 18 Engineer, industry, etc.; 19 Professional workers	4352		
Place of Residence	1 inside Iran; 2 outside Iran	7,596	1.0072	
City of Residence*	1 Tehran; 2 Large cities (Capital of provinces); 3 Other smaller cities; 4 Towns and Villages	6116		
Province of Residence*	1 Alborz; …; 31 Zanjan	8652		

Note: * For the detail see Appendix 1

inside Iran and are distributed across the country. In comparison to international social networking websites such as Facebook and Twitter, Cloob users are younger and not limited to highly educated and high socio-economic status people.

Tebyan is a highly popular and richly informative website which is run by the Islamic Propagation Organization (Saazeman-e tablight-e eslami). A part of the website is the Tebyan Social Network which is similar to Balatarin and functions as a social news aggregator. I extracted all the posts that were shared by Tebyan users in July and August 2014. Over four weeks (weeks 27, 30-32), I extracted the data of 15,164 posts which were submitted by users. The number of positive (mean=7.36) and negative (mean=0.08) votes, as well as full text and publication date and time of the posts, are gathered from the data of Tebyan as well. In Tebyan, as in Balatarin, posts that get enough votes (45) convert to 'hot' posts and move to the top of the hot posts page. Over the course of the research 284 posts got more than 45 likes and moved onto the hot page. I focus on hot posts as they are filtered by the votes of users and represent the demands and interests of users.

RESULTS

In this section I present results from each of the online communities/platforms individually. Then I combine findings into a larger picture in the conclusions section.

Iranian Blogosphere (Blogistan)

From the 5224 blogs that I identified from Persianblog, about 10% (556 blogs) were randomly selected to be Manually coded. The coding was performed by a research assistant and it has been randomly checked by me. The sample of blogs is categorized based on the content of the last three posts of the blog. Figure 3 shows the relative size of each category of blog. The most prevalent issue that is discussed by blogs hosted by Persianblog is Personal/Diaries (about 25%). Bloggers shared their daily experiences with blog readers. They often tell the stories and often just express their feelings with a photo or short sentences. Another major category among blogs is entertaining issues. These blogs mostly publish posts that includes links for music, funny quotes and photos. The education and learning category surprisingly is the third most prevalent category among blogs. The issues addressed in these blogs are as diverse as cooking, Quran, accounting software, health and beauty.

Figure 3. Post categories in Persianblog

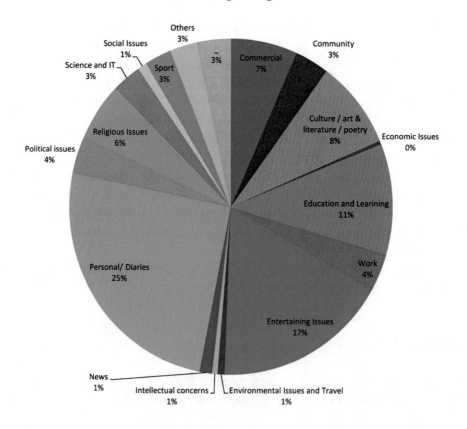

Online SNSs Blocked in Iran

Facebook

To understand the most popular issues among Facebook pages, I first identified the top Facebook pages based on the number of likes and number of talking about (the number of users who are engaged in and interacting with the Facebook pages). As one can see from Table 4, the majority of the most popular pages are in the Musician/Band category. These pages are the official or fan pages of singers. The only exceptions are two TV channels and a music website.

Analyses based on talking-about count shows, however, users interact mostly with the diverse categories of Facebook pages from singers and comedians to a campaign against mandatory Hijab.

Most Frequent Categories

Among the pool of Facebook pages, I found 147 distinct categories. Figure 4 shows the most frequent categories among Facebook pages and the descriptive data for each category. About 20 percent of Facebook pages have been categorized as community pages. After community pages, musician/band, public figure and book, in turn, are the most frequent Facebook pages. Among the top 30 categories, the category of TV channel consists of 22 Facebook pages and has the highest mean of likes (380,349) and also highest mean of Talking about (34,432).

Table 4. The most liked Facebook pages

	Label	Category	Like count	Talking about count
1	Arash	Musician/band	2,289,852	18,787
2	Ebi	Musician/band	2,262,613	127,251
3	Manoto TV	TV channel	2,167,821	261,379
4	Shadmehr Aghili	Musician/band	2,050,104	192,738
5	YAS	Musician/band	1,877,205	13,086
6	Golshifteh Farahani	Public figure	1,785,684	15,036
7	Dariush Eghbali	Musician/band	1,771,840	39,469
8	BBC Persian	Media/news/publishing	1,719,282	177,128
9	Siavash Ghomeishi	Musician/band	1,672,773	134,581
10	Radio Javan	Entertainment Website	1,647,621	61,161

Figure 4. Frequency of categories of Facebook pages

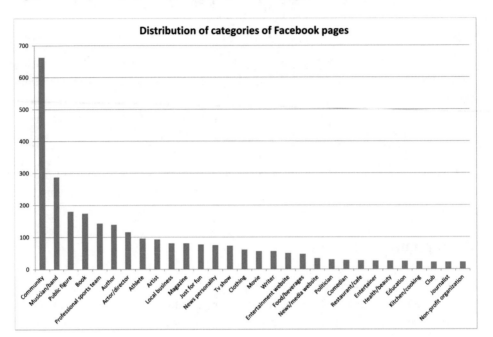

Community Detection and Clustering Analyses

Although the distribution of categories of Facebook pages gives us a general view of what Iranian Facebook pages are most frequently about, the information is too broad to fully understand the issues and the interests that are provided with these pages. To better identify the issues which are discussed in and the interests which are represented by these Facebook pages, I attempted to map out the Iranian Facebook pages and take a close look at the clustering of Facebook pages. I define Facebook pages as nodes and their likes to each other as links (or edges). By doing so, I am able to detect the main communities and main clusters within the Facebook pages network. I assume that common interests and shared demands link Facebook pages together through likes and result in clustering patterns of Facebook pages network.

From 3,510 Facebook pages I removed 413 isolated Facebook pages (the pages which do not have any link with other pages). Using the rest of the pages I mapped out the network. I used the Modularity routine in Gephi software, a network analysis software, to detect communities and compartmentalize the network into sub-networks (or communities). The community structure reveals 27 distinct communities in the Facebook pages network. By decomposing the network to sub-networks, clusters within each community become identifiable. Details of the main communities and clusters are presented in Table 5.

The main and largest community is that of entertaining and life style pages. The main clusters in this community are pages comprising entertaining issues, jokes, funny quotes and love and marriage tips. Also in this community, users are more engaged in the page providing Persian music and videos. The second popular community encompasses Facebook pages related to fashion and beauty, cooking, and some educational pages providing tips and instruction for photography, decoration,

Table 5. The main communities and clusters in the network of Iranian Facebook pages

	# nodes	% total nodes	# edges	Page with Max. like	Page with Max. Talking about	Main clusters
1	598	17,04%	3,424	Parazit (TV Show)	Persian Music (Music/Band)	Entertaining, joke, fun, love, romantic tips and quotes
2	535	15,24%	3,554	(tabloids)	Fashion and Beauty (Education Website)	Beauty and fashion, Education of cooking, photography and handicrafts, decoration, guidance to better life
3	315	8,97%	1534	Christian Ronaldo (athlete)*	Iran Volleyball National Team (professional sports team)	Sport
4	311	8,86%	1,211	Arash (Musician/Bands)	AMIR TATALOO, Rapper (Musician/Band)	Musician, bands and music websites
5	298	8,49%	1,191	Press TV (Media/news/publish.)**	Ebrahim Nabavi, politician and comedian (author)	Politicians, Green Movement websites, Fake celebrities' Facebook pages
6	295	8,40%	1,304	Sohrab Sepehri, poet (Public Figure)	Minimals for life (Author)	Authors, literature, poet, art (music), Charities
7	271	7,72%	755	BBC Persian (Media/News/Publish.)	My stealthy Freedom in Iran (Community)	News websites, informative websites, scientific and health news, oppositional human rights websites, psychology magazines
8	110	3,13%	260	Hot Pictures (News personalities) – Learn English (Book)	Hot Pictures (News personalities)	Animals lovers, tourism, environmental, tabloids, (celebrities) photos
9	108	3,08%	272	Manoto TV (TV Channel)	Manoto TV (TV Channel)	Ancient, history and nationalism, and Satellite TV channel
10	86	2,45%	176	(Writer)	Dr. Hossein Elahi Ghomshe ei (Public Figure)	Fun, troll
11	46	1,31%	322	We hate crab users(Community)	Crab Facebook Figures (Public Figures)	Girls and boys, teenagers flirting
12	38	1,08%	267	Iran Art & Architecture (Community)	Molana, poet (Author)	Poet, Art and Architect, Quran
13	25	0,71%	328	Molana, poet (Community)	Molana, poet (Community)	Poem, poet
14	474	13,50%				

Note: * The first one is a Facebook page which is not related to this community (tabloids)

** The first one is Golshifteh Farahani public figure but it was employed by a group of dissidents to spread political news.

handicrafts etc. The cluster of pages which are tabloids and gossip magazines are also in this community. The politician community is the fifth largest community. It consists of three types of Facebook pages: Politician Facebook pages such as that of Javad Zarif, foreign minister, grassroots-driven pages which were mostly created in the midst of Green Movement protests, and some Fake celebrities' pages which is used for the political purposes. Fake Facebook pages are active under the name of some celebrities, however, they are not administrated by the very celebrities. These pages mostly share political posts.

Balatarin.com. On average, 4,720 posts were moved to in the 'hot page' of Balatarin per day over the period of research (from 30th June 2014 to 10th August 2014). Partitioning the posts into categories reveals that social and political issues are the most prevalent issues that attract users in Balatarin. An exception is the last week of June during the World Cup matches when that sport was the most popular category among hot posts.

Zooming on in each category reveals that the prevalent issue in terms of getting votes is social issues, and the least is economic. The posts relating to political issues get more votes than others and entertaining issues get fewer. The issues that are most discussed in Balatarin are social issues, which has the highest mean number of comments, while the least discussed is science and technology. The most controversial posts are related to political issues and the least controversial are about art and literature. The most popular posts for the general audience of Balatarin are entertaining posts, which get more clicks than other posts, while the least popular ones are economic issues. For further details on the categories see Table 6.

To understand the issues that were discussed in each category more deeply, I identified words that are more frequently used in the content of posts in each category. Figure 5 shows the ten most used words in each category. I can see from

Table 6. The number of posts and votes in Balatarin by categories

	# posts	votes + (mean)	votes - (mean)	Comments (mean)	Clicks (mean)
Social	**1,180**	52.7	2.1	4.9	547
Economic	376	32.6	1.2	0.7	427
Entertaining	600	26.6	1.0	1.4	**844**
Political	988	**59.2**	**2.7**	**5.9**	469
Art&Lit	576	31.8	0.6	0.9	497
Sci&Tech	590	41.7	0.7	0.6	447
Sport	409	32.4	1.2	0.9	628
TOTAL	4,720	52.7	2.1	4.9	547

Figure 5. Word frequency of posts of each category in Balatarin

Social	Economic	Entertaining	Political	Art & Literature	Sci. and Tech	Sport
Women	State	Photo	Gaza	Photo	How	Iran
Gaza	economic	Cartoon	ISIS	Film	Facebook	World Cup
Tehran	economics	Comic	Iraq	Simin Behbahani	Google	Football
Prison	price	new	Israel	melody	use	Ali Karimi
ISIS	million	Iran	Prison	song	World	Volleyball
Israel	oil	video	Rouhani	picture	Invent	National Team
Gender	Country	episode	state	Life	users	Nekounam
Sentence	Rouhani	world	Khamenei	Women	Internet	League
Execution	Bank	women	I. Republic	Turkish	Samsung	Brazil
Iraq	Bazar	lady	(House) arrest	Series	Galaxy	Ali Daei

the figure which issues are most discussed in each category over the course of research. In social and political issues users were more concerned about Gaza and ISIS in that time. Women, gender issues and state repression are other issues that were discussed in both categories. The Entertaining category also consists of photos, cartoons and videos.

The issues that attract users clearly depends in part on global and local events (offline) and circumstances. Therefore, it is wise to observe changes in word occurrences over time. I focused on four weeks from June to August. Figure 6 presents the number of posts in each category per week. The word frequency shows how the World Cup was dominant in the first week, then in the next two weeks the Gaza crisis and Palestine and Israel conflict, and in the last week ISIS was the most prevalent issues (Figure 7).

Online SNSs Accessible in Iran

Cloob. In cloob.com, clubs are categorized into 22 distinct categories. Table 7 shows the number of clubs in each category. As can be seen from the table, the most frequent category among clubs is Art and Entertainment.

By extracting data from the profile pages of a random sample of club members, I attempted to find significant correlations between demographic variables and the categories that users are most engaged in. To do so, I conducted a one-way ANOVA

Figure 6. Number of posts in each category per week

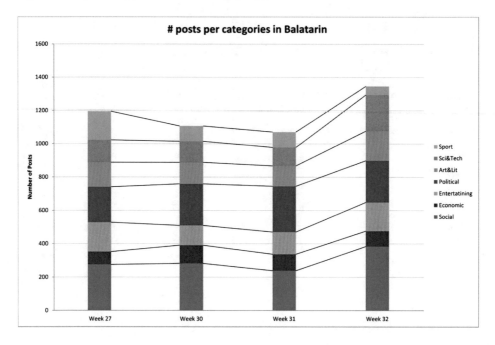

Figure 7. Word frequency in each week within the contents of Balatarin hot posts

Week 27	Week 30	Week 31	Week 32
World Cup	Gaza	Gaza	ISIS
Match	Israel	Prison	Rouhani
Iraq	Tehran	Women	Simin (Behbahani)**
ISIS	People	World	Iraq
Brazil	Sentence	Israel	Prison
America	Ali Karimi	State	Gaza
Tehran	Execution	Woman	Woman
TV	Women	Saba (Azarpeik)*	Tehran
Rouhani	Football	War	Death
Football	World	Rouhani	Turkey
Khamenei	Prisoner	Tehran	America
University	Rouhani	Rights	HRA***
State	ISIS	Newspaper	Attack

statistical test to compare the effect of socio-economic traits on the categories that users are engaged with.

The results show that almost all demographic variables and socio-economic traits significantly affect categories. The test showed that differences in age, gender,

Table 7. The frequency and percentage of categories of clubs in cloob.com

	Categories	# of clubs	%
1	Art and entertainment	2646	11,2%
2	Public Figures	2411	10,2%
3	Schools, universities and graduates	2348	9,9%
4	Marriage and Love	2136	9,0%
5	Countries, cities and regions	1551	6,5%
6	Related to cloob.com	1509	6,4%
7	Religion and Beliefs	1176	5,0%
8	Computer, Internet and Electronics	1052	4,4%
9	Sports and Games	956	4,0%
10	Literature, History and Culture	874	3,7%
11	Society and social sciences	842	3,6%
12	Fashion and Beauty	542	2,3%
13	Technology and Engineering	436	1,8%
14	Related to other websites	383	1,6%
15	Companies, organizations and associations	381	1,6%
16	Sciences	376	1,6%
17	Work, Employment and Career	356	1,5%
18	Travel	284	1,2%
19	Education and learning	265	1,1%
20	Food, Home, Family	215	0,9%
21	Health and Disease	174	0,7%
22	Others	2780	11,7%
	Total	23693	

marital status, education level, and city of residence were all statistically significant. (See Table 8 and Appendix 2)

I find that the users involved in technology and engineering are more often male than female, while users of food, home and family categories are more often female. The category of education and learning attracts more single users than married ones. In terms of age, users this category are the youngest in the category of technology and engineering, and the oldest in the category of society and social sciences. Users who are more interested in art and entertainment and science live in smaller cities than users who are interested in work, employment, and career related issues. More highly educated users of cloob.com are more involved in technology and engineering clubs, unlike less educated users who are concerned about education and learning.

Table 8. ANOVA test summary for cloob.com users

Variables	F (21, 8630)
Place of Residence	1,524
City of Residence	2,111**
Gender	3,657***
Marital Status	2,056**
Age	4,058***
Education Level	7,434***

Note: * p<.05, ** P<.01, *** P<.001

Tebyan

Posts that are shared in Tebyan get votes from other users. Similar to other platforms, there are many posts that are not interesting for other users so they receive few votes. Since I am interested in most popular posts, I focus on only hot posts which have received more than 45 votes. Partitioning the posts into categories reveals that religious issues and moral messages are the most prevalent issues that attract users in Tebyan. Religious issues are highly prevalent in week 27 as it was during Ramadan. Figure 8 presents the number of posts in each category per week and the changes over time.

Zooming on in each category reveals that the prevalent issue in terms of getting votes is foreign affairs issues, and the least is moral message. The foreign affairs posts in the period of the research were more related to Gaza crisis and brought emotionally driven votes. The posts relating to political issues get more negative votes than others and religious issues get fewer. This means the most controversial posts are related to political issues and the least controversial are about religious issues. (see Table 9)

The word frequency shows how the Ramadan was dominant in the first week, then in the next week the Gaza crisis, and in the last two week discussing the role of women and men and women relationship was the most prevalent issues (Figure 9).

SUMMARY OF FINDINGS

In this section, I first summarize the issues that I have identified in online communities. Then, I compare online communities/platforms in terms of issues that are most prevalent. In the last part of this section, I will conclude with discussing some limitations and implications of the study.

Figure 8. The number of hot posts in each categories per week in Tebyan

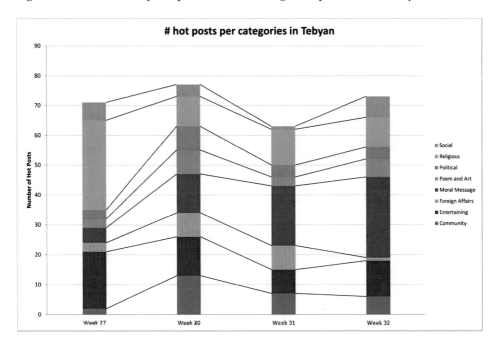

Table 9. The number of posts and votes in Tebyan by categories

	# posts	votes + (mean)	votes – (mean)
Social	18	83.1	1.1
Religious	62	80.0	0.0
Political	19	85.2	**1.4**
Poem and Art	20	77.2	0.8
Moral Message	**65**	75.7	1.1
Foreign Affairs	20	**89.1**	0.3
Entertaining	52	78.0	0.8
Community	28	79.4	0.5
TOTAL	284	79.6	0.7

Figure 9. Word frequency in each week within the contents of Tebyan hot posts

Week 27	Week 30	Week 31	Week 32
God	Ali	Woman	Woman
Ramadan	People	Imam	Man
Heart	Palestine	Islam	God
Fist	Gaza	Women	Martyrs
Pray	Imam	Reza	Men
Street	Mohammad	Man	Imam
Allah	God	Sin	Allah
Mohammad	Heart	Penitence	Life
Imam	Allah	Chamran	Love
Worship	Girl	Tebyan	Israel

Issues: Platforms

Personal issues are discussed and expressed in blogosphere. Findings show that 25% of blogs are created for the purpose of sharing personal experiences, telling routine stories, discussing personal concerns, getting advice and confabulating. Some bloggers discuss the personal issues within a broader context of the Iranian society. These blogs attract higher educated and more socio-political active audiences. Families issues, marital problems, affairs/marital infidelity, women matters, parenting problems, romantic relationships, work related problems are most frequently discussed in personal issues blogs.

Contrary to the general expectations, political issues are not widespread on social networks, neither are they limited to oppositional users. The current study found that political issues are prevalent in discussions in Balatarin, however, not in other platforms and online communities. Only four percent of blogs hosted by Persianblog.ir are about political issues. Consistently, in cloob.com, only 3.6% of clubs are categorized as society and social sciences, which includes also political related clubs. The political Facebook pages are not in the list of most popular pages. While the Facebook pages that belong to musicians/bands, athletes, artists and even authors have from 500K to 2M likes, the most popular politician Facebook page has about 400K likes. Nevertheless, the political community of Facebook pages is the fifth largest community among other clusters of Facebook pages. It contains about 8.5% of Facebook pages which is considerably large. It is important to note that the salience of political issues and the political topics in all platforms depend on global and local events and circumstances. In contrast to Balatarin, political 'hot' posts of Tebyan, which are 6% of total hot posts, are in favor of conservatives.

Entertaining issues is the most highly demanded category of issues overall. Entertaining issues is the second largest category of blogs hosted by Persianblog. ir, the largest community of Facebook pages, the most frequent category of clubs in cloob.com and the third most prevalent issue of hot posts in Balatarin – after social and political issues - and Tebyan – after moral and religious issues. It includes topics as diverse as jokes, fun messages/pictures, music tracks, video movies and topics related to life style of youth.

Issues related to social problems and concerns of people in society are frequently discussed on the Iranian Web. These issues are not only discussed in the social issues category but are also reflected in contents of other categories. In the blogosphere only a very slight portion of blogs can be categorized as social issues. However, discussions of social problems are found in other blogs that belong to other categories, particularly in personal/diaries. Social issues that mostly attract audiences and are frequently discussed among users in all platforms are women issues, environmental issues, inequality and poverty, social immorality, and children problems. Women's issues are discussed not only by people that want to improve women's situation in society, but also by people that resist any change in women's situations. However, what I found frequently in blogosphere and other communities, except Tebyan, is the fight for equality for women in society.

The findings of the current study reveal that one of the issues that most appeal the Iranian users is educational issues. A considerable number of online communities/ groups provide users with some training programs, educational information and consulting services. Some of these communities/groups are specifically created for educational and learning purposes, which are categorized as educational issues in our analyses; however, in almost all other categories and issues I found a large number of groups that are partly allocated to training and teaching users. English language, cooking, health and beauty, psychological issues are some of topics that elicited the greatest demanded for training and education.

Our findings indicate science and technology is one of the interests of users. While in blocked platforms, such as Balatarin, discussing science and technology is dominated by Internet security, tips for circumventing filtering, and ICT, in other platforms science and technology encompasses a wide range of issues; from instructions on using gadgets and electronic devices to medical breakthroughs. Religious issues, sport, cultural issues, art, literature, and work related issues, are other issues that are frequently discussed among users on the Iranian Web.

Comparisons

Accessible vs. Blocked Platforms (Cloob.com - Facebook)

Comparing Clubs in cloob.com and pages in Facebook shows that issues that attract most users are to some degree the same in both platforms. However, there are some differences in the prevalence of issues. Despite the large number of areas of overlap in the views and opinions that are expressed in both platforms, there are a number of areas of disagreement. Most importantly, there is a major divergence on the issue of politics, religion, and social morality. While there is a clear tendency towards democracy, secularism and political change among political Facebook pages, the views presented in political-social clubs in cloob.com were so diverse that one cannot derive a meaningful pattern. On social morality, on the one side, among majority of Facebook pages tolerance, equality and human rights are important values drives discussions, on the other side in cloob.com religious beliefs are central to the discussions.

In cloob.com there are a considerable number of communities related to cities and regions that are not remarkable in Facebook pages. Similar to Facebook pages, public figures, musicians, politicians shaped a large community of fans and clubs in cloob.com. However, there are a large number of actresses/actors, musicians, politicians that work inside Iran who only have clubs/pages –particularly verified ones - in cloob.com, but not in Facebook. As compared to cloob.com, Facebook pages are more dominated by political issues.

Oppositionists vs. Conservatives in Online Communities (Balatarin - Tebyan)

Based on the findings of this research, it is clear that political and social issues are discussed more in oppositional online communities (Balatarin as an example) than in conservative online communities. Furthermore, one finds an overwhelming occurrence of moral and religious issues among government-based online platforms (Tebyan as an example). Figure 10 indicates the differences and similarities in the issues that attract most attention in both platforms (Tebyan and Balatarin). There is also a major divergence on political issues between two groups of people. Interestingly, the position of women in society and the relationship between women and men is a prevalent topic of discussions in both platforms. Furthermore, over the course of this research, discussions in both platforms were influenced by global events, namely the Gaza crisis and ISIS.

Figure 10. Comparison between the categories of hot posts in Balatarin and Tebyan

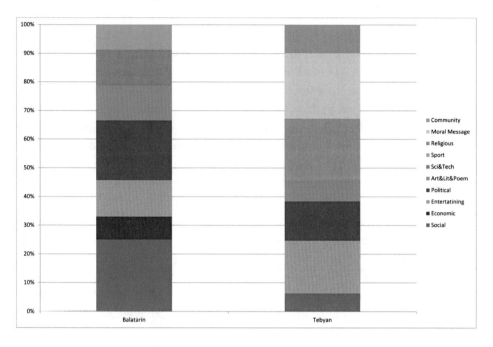

Users and Issues

This study suggests that in general the users of the Iranian Web encompass a relatively wide spectrum of people in terms of socio-economic traits. Data extracted from the users of cloob.com also shows that demographic variables and socio-economic traits significantly affect the issue of interests of each communities. In cloob.com, which is an accessible online platform, users are geographically widespread. Its users are also not limited to higher-educated people. I found that women are more interested in educational issues and discuss more about women's matters than men, while men are more often discussing engineering and technical issues. Women are also more concerned by social issues than men.

DISCUSSION AND CONCLUSION

This study was designed to lay a foundation for a broader understanding of digitally enabled social movements as agents of social change in Iran. Therefore, I attempted to capture the social issues that are most frequently discussed through online communities. A comprehensive frame of the Iranian web is offered that led to a systematic sample of online communities. From the main sectors of the Iranian web, which cover the main areas of interests of Iranian users, I identified and selected online platforms which are most likely to attract a diversity of Iranian users. The most obvious finding to emerge from this study is that the issues that are discussed among Iranians through online communities are diverse in terms of views and interests, and a wide range of issues and topics are being discussed online. However, different issues are prevalent in different online communities and online platforms. These findings broaden our knowledge about the role these communities potentially play in effecting social change. The study reveals that the formation of consensus is taking place in different issues and areas of interests among Iranian users. This can serve as a base for future studies on Iranian digitally mediated social movements that address different issues. Future research should therefore concentrate on the investigation of social, environmental, women issues-driven social movement activities through the Iranian online communities.

Steps towards participation in social movements not only require very different activities, but they also require different theories of analysis (Klandermans & Oegema, 1987). Accordingly, understanding digitally mediated social movements requires the important distinction between the different steps in the processes through which people participate in the movement. This study provides insights into the initial process of consensus formation, which breeds potential participants in social movements. Although this study focuses on the social concerns of Iranians, the methods that were introduced can be employed for other societies. Overall, this study strengthens the idea that we can understand social phenomena in repressive contexts through the online behavior of Internet users.

Similar to other studies, this research also faces 'the challenge of generalizing from online to offline' (Golder & Macy, 2014). This research approach recognizes that those Iranians who go online may not be representative of all Iranians; in other words, they are not entirely "ordinary." The research did, nevertheless, target ordinary internet users in the sense that it looked at a diversity of users, rather than focusing on activists, opposition figures, public figures and the like. It did this by examining online platforms that have been shown to be widely popular among Iranians. In addition, demographic data are not readily available for all users, so I could not make statistically weighted inferences about either those whose posts were being studied or their relationship to the larger population in the way a conventional social study based on population sampling might do so. One source of weakness in this study could be the remarkable transition in Iranian Internet usage. Over the past two years, since this study was designed and performed, Iranians have seen incredible developments in Mobile Internet penetration which resulted in a boom in instant messaging apps use among Iranians. The author acknowledges this ongoing change. Further research may explore the formation and development of consensus through instant messaging apps such as Telegram and WhatsApp.

REFERENCES

Abadpour, A., & Anderson, C. (2013). *Fights, adapts, accepts: Archetypes of Iranian Internet use*. Iran Media Program.

Aday, S., Farrell, H., Lynch, M., Sides, J., Kelly, J., & Zuckerman, E. (2010). *Blogs and bullets: New media in contentious politics*. Washington, DC: United States Institute of Peace.

Akhavan, N. (2013). *Electronic Iran: The cultural politics of an online revolution*. New Brunswick, NJ: Rutgers University Press.

Al-Rawi, A. (2014). Framing the online women's movements in the Arab world. *Information Communication and Society*, *17*(9), 1147–1161. doi:10.1080/136911 8X.2014.889190

Baldino, D., & Goold, J. (2014). Iran and the emergence of information and communication technology: The evolution of revolution? *Australian Journal of International Affairs*, *68*(1), 17–35. doi:10.1080/10357718.2013.840263

Bennett, W. L., & Segerberg, A. (2012). The logic of connective action: Digital media and the personalization of contentious politics. *Information Communication and Society*, *15*(5), 739–768. doi:10.1080/1369118X.2012.670661

Bucar, E. M., & Fazaeli, R. (2008). Free speech in Weblogistan? The offline consequences of online communication. *International Journal of Middle East Studies*, *40*(3), 403–419. doi:10.1017/S0020743808080999

Earl, J. (2013). Studying online activism: The effects of sampling design on findings. *Mobilization: An International Quarterly*, *18*(4), 389–406.

Earl, J., & Kimport, K. (2011). *Digitally enabled social change: Activism in the internet age*. Cambridge, MA: MIT Press. doi:10.7551/mitpress/9780262015103.001.0001

Farrell, H. (2012). The consequences of the Internet for politics. *Annual Review of Political Science*, *15*(1), 35–52. doi:10.1146/annurev-polisci-030810-110815

Gamson, W. A. (2004). Bystanders, public opinion, and the media. In D. A. Snow, S. A. Soule, & H. Kriesi (Eds.), *The Blackwell companion to social movements* (pp. 242–261). Malden, MA: Blackwell.

Gladwell, M. (2010, October4). Small change: Why the revolution will not be tweeted. *New Yorker (New York, N.Y.)*.

Golder, S. A., & Macy, M. W. (2014). Digital footprints: Opportunities and challenges for online social research. *Annual Review of Sociology, 40*(1), 129–152. doi:10.1146/annurev-soc-071913-043145

Harlow, S., & Guo, L. (2014). Will the revolution be Tweeted or Facebooked? Using digital communication tools in immigrant activism. *Journal of Computer-Mediated Communication, 19*(3), 463–478. doi:10.1111/jcc4.12062

Honari, A. (2013). From virtual to tangible social movements in Iran. In P. Aarts & F. Cavatorta (Eds.), *Civil society in Syria and Iran: Activism in authoritarian contexts* (pp. 143–167). Boulder, CO: Lynne Rienner.

Honari, A. (2015). Online social research in Iran: A need to offer a bigger picture. *CyberOrient: The Online Journal of Virtual Middle East, 9*(2).

Honari, A., van Stekelenburg, J., & Klandermans, B. (2014). *Socio-Political Participation in Iran: 2013 Election Data set.* Retrieved from http://IranPolPartResearch.org

Howard, P. N., & Hussain, M. M. (2013). *Democracy's forth wave? Digital media and the Arab Spring.* New York, NY: Oxford University Press. doi:10.1093/acprof:oso/9780199936953.001.0001

Internet filtering in Iran . (2009, June 16). Retrieved from Open Net Initiative. Retrieved from https://opennet.net/research/profiles/iran

2014.　*Iran: Freedom of press the.* (2014). New York: Freedom House.

Kelly, S., Troung, M., Earp, M., Reed, L., Shahbaz, A., & Greco-Stoner, A. (2013). *Freedom on the net 2013: A global assessment of Internet and digital media.* Freedom House.

Klandermans, B. (1988). The formation and mobilization of consensus. *International Social Movement Research, 1,* 173–196.

Klandermans, B., & Oegema, D. (1987). Potentials, networks, motivations, and barriers: Steps towards participation in social movements. *American Sociological Review, 52*(4), 519–531. doi:10.2307/2095297

Kuran, T. (1997). *Private truth, public lies: The social consequences of preference falsification*. Cambridge, MA: Harward University Press.

Lim, M. (2012). Clicks, cabs, and coffee houses: Social media and oppositional movements in Egypt, 2004–2011. *Journal of Communication, 62*(2), 231–248. doi:10.1111/j.1460-2466.2012.01628.x

Lynch, M. (2011). After Egypt: The limits and promise of online challenges to the authoritarian Arab state. *Perspectives on Politics, 9*(2), 301–310. doi:10.1017/S1537592711000910

MacKinnon, R. (2013). *Consent of the networked: The worldwide struggle for Internet freedom*. New York, NY: Basic Books.

Malinen, S. (2015). Understanding user participation in online communities: A systematic literature review of empirical studies. *Computers in Human Behavior, 46*, 228–238. doi:10.1016/j.chb.2015.01.004

Morozov, E. (2010, May/June). 19). Think again: The Internet. *Foreign Policy, 179*, 40–44.

Oprn Net Initiative2013*After the Green Movement: Internet controls in Iran 2009-2012*.

Rahimi, B. (2011a). Facebook Iran: The carnivalesque politics of online social networking. *Sociologica, 3*.

Rahimi, B. (2011b). The agonistic social media: Cyberspace in the formation of dissent and consolodation of state power in postelection Iran. *Communication Review, 14*(3), 158–178. doi:10.1080/10714421.2011.597240

Rasouli, M. R., & Moradi, M. (2012, October). Factors affecting the production of contents in Social Networks. *Olum-e Ejtemaei, 55*, 57–66.

Reporters without Borders2014World press freedom index 2014.

Rieder, B. (2013). Studying Facebook via data extraction: the Netvizz application. *Proceedings of the 5th Annual ACM Web Science Conference* (pp. 346-355).

Rogers, R. (2013). *Digital methods*. Cambridge, MA: MIT Press.

Rogers, R., Weltevrede, E., Niederer, S., & Borra, E. (2012). *National Web Studies: Mapping Iran Online*.

Ruijgrok, K. (2016). From the web to the streets: Internet and protests under authoritarian regimes. *Democratization*. doi:10.1080/13510347.2016.1223630

Segerberg, A., & Bennett, L. W. (2011). Social media and the organization of collective action: Using Twitter to explore the ecologies of two climate change protests. *Communication Review*, *14*(3), 197–215. doi:10.1080/10714421.2011.5 97250

Shirky, C. (2008). *Here comes everybody: How changes happen when people come together*. Penguin Books.

Sohrabi-Haghighat, M. H., & Mansouri, S. (2010). Where is my Vote? ICT politics in the aftermath of Iran's Presidential Election. *International Journal of Emerging Technologies and Society*, *8*(1), 24–41.

Sreberny, A., & Khiabany, G. (2010). *Blogistan: The Internet and politics in Iran*. London: I.B. Tauris.

Tabnak. (2012, October 11). Retrieved from http://bit.ly/1ecbBo7

Tufekci, Z., & Wilson, C. (2012). Social media and the decision to participate in political protest: Observations from Tahrir Square. *Journal of Communication*, *62*(2), 363–379. doi:10.1111/j.1460-2466.2012.01629.x

Wojcieszak, M., & Smith, B. (2014). Will politics be tweeted? New media use by Iranian youth in 2011. *New Media & Society*, *16*(1), 91–109. doi:10.1177/1461444813479594

Wojcieszak, M., Smith, B., & Enayat, M. (2012). *Finding a way: How Iranians reach for news and information*. Iran Media Program.

Zuckerman, E. (2014). New media, new civics? *Policy and Internet*, *6*(2), 151–168. doi:10.1002/1944-2866.POI360

APPENDIX 1: DESCRIPTION OF CLOOB.COM USERS

Figure 11. Occupation of sample users

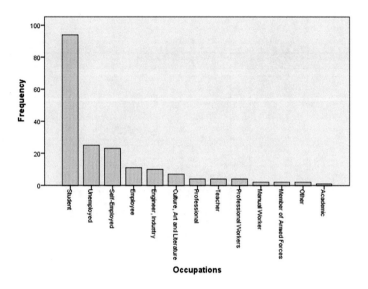

Figure 12. Province of residence of sample users

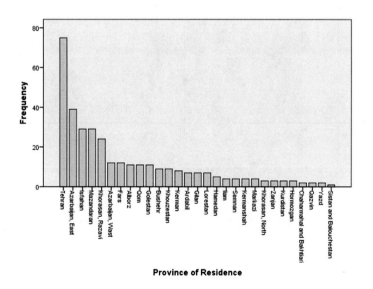

Figure 13. City of Residence of sample users

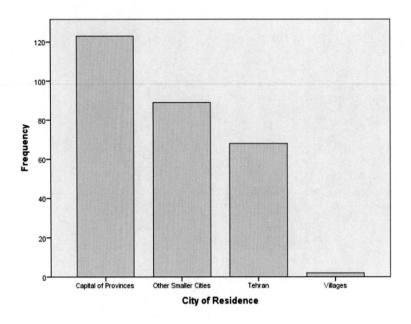

Figure 14. Marital status of sample users

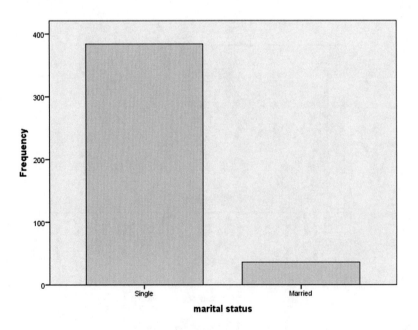

Figure 15. Education level of sample users

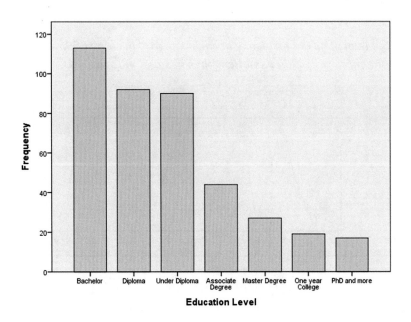

APPENDIX 2: MEANS OF VARIABLES
PER CATEGORY IN CLOOB.COM

Figure 16. Mean of city of residence in each category in cloob (Tehran = 1; Capital of other provinces = 2; Other smaller cities = 3 and villages = 4)

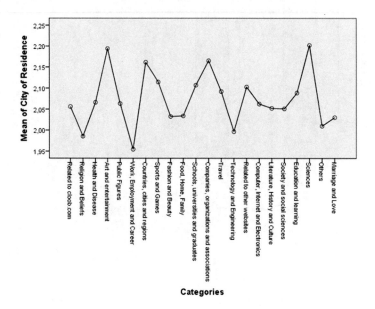

Figure 17. Mean of gender in each category in cloob (Male = 1; Female = 2)

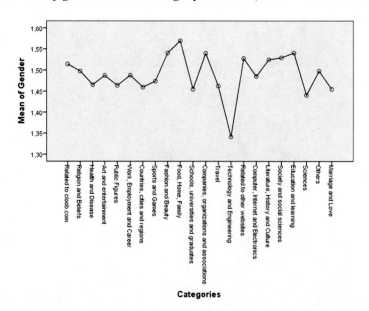

Figure 18. Mean of marital status in each category in cloob (Single = 1; Married= 2)

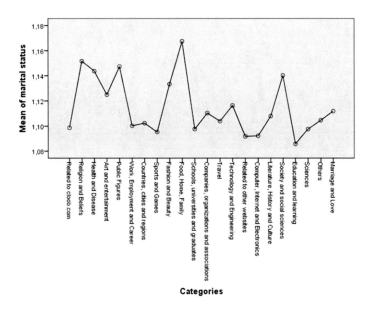

Figure 19. Mean of users' age in each category in cloob

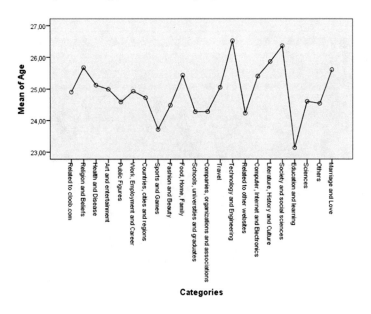

Figure 20. Mean of registration periods by month in each category

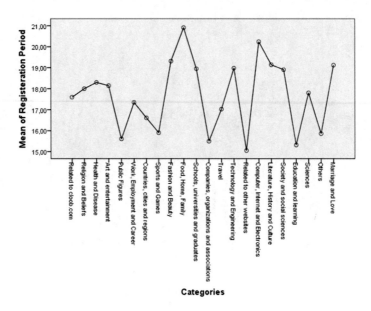

Figure 21. Mean of place of residence in each category (Inside Iran = 1; Outside Iran =2)

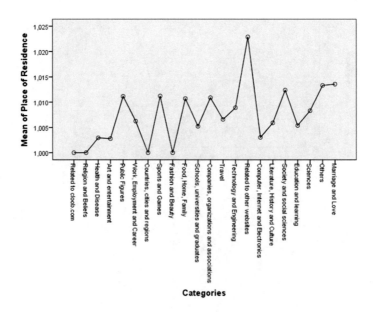

Figure 22. Mean of educational level in each category (1 = Under diploma and 7 = PhD and more)

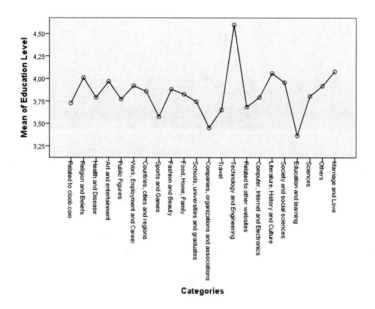

Section 3

Online Communities in Support of Personal Growth, Development, and Self-Actualization

Chapter 8
Connected Living for Positive Ageing

Helen Hasan
University of Wollongong, Australia

Henry Linger
Monash University, Australia

ABSTRACT

This chapter proposes that social use of digital technologies can play a useful role in meeting the social and economic challenges posed by the ageing populations in developed countries. Many citizens become increasingly isolated as they age and this has a detrimental impact on their wellbeing. The authors present research which shows how, with suitable devices and ongoing support, older people can develop the digital capability to remain connected to family and community. They can also engaged in activities that give meaning to their lives. The research shows the importance of taking an individualized approach to meeting the needs of each older person who is motivated to learn and of making this learning fun. It also demonstrates how mastering just one or two digital applications can not only enhance social wellbeing but also enable citizens to have more control of their lives and be less of a burden on others.

INTRODUCTION

Along with many other changes in developed economies, the changing demography of ageing populations presents challenges to health, economic and social systems (Christensen et al., 2009). Although many older citizens, i.e. those over 65 years of

DOI: 10.4018/978-1-5225-2495-3.ch008

age, are digitally literate, others can face challenges in adjusting to demands of the digital age although new forms of digital technologies can provide opportunities for positive ageing (Denvir et al., 2014). It should be acknowledged that as people age, they may need more assistance to attend to the demands of daily living (Seidel et al., 2011). Older citizens who can no longer cope at home require institutional residential care. However, care in these institutions is costly and demand for places can outstrip supply. In Australia, as in many other developed countries, one aspect of the aged care policy is to provide services that enable people to remain living in their own homes for as long as possible (Aus Govt., 2010). There is a growing number of public, private and community organizations that provide home services to meet their needs. Whether in care or at home, many of their older clients are becoming increasingly isolated as they are no longer able to get out as they once could (Grenade & Boldy, 2008). In similar circumstances, younger people would use digital devices to stay occupied and connected but less of the current cohort of older citizens have this capability. However, with suitable support and more useable technology, this can change so that participation in online activities and communities can enhance the social wellbeing of older people.

This chapter presents evidence of these positive developments from an investigation into how older citizens are learning to use Information and Communications Technology (ICT) to remain connected to, and engaged in, the community as well as access to stimulating activities online. On the one hand, the research reveals the diverse challenges that people face in developing and maintaining digital capability as they age. On the other hand, it has uncovered the many benefits of participation in online activities and communities that contribute to positive ageing. Of particularly interest are (1) the variety of online community activities in which older people can engage with a little guidance and support; (2) the attributes of social and emotional wellbeing that can be enhanced through this online engagements and (3) evidence of the synergies that exist between online and offline engagement. Having the capability for connected living through online social engagement has the potential to radically enhance positive ageing and revolutionize the efficacy of the social and economic systems of aged care.

The objectives of the chapter are to (1) increase current knowledge, from the literature and the findings of the authors' research, on older citizens' use of ICT; (2) establish the efficacy of social ICT use in overcoming effects of isolation, (3) put forward a practical program of services that could be provided for older people to set up and use ICT, and (4) encourage more attention to this issue and motivate more research in the area.

BACKGROUND

The societal challenge facing developed countries is the adverse impact on the health, economic and social systems of ageing populations (Harvey & Thurnwald, 2009). The economic consequences of this demographic challenge are high on the agendas of government, business and non-government organizations. A smaller workforce must provide for a growing number of retirees who are increasingly dependent on health care and general living services (Aus Govt., 2010). While attempts are made to meet this challenge, older citizens are becoming increasingly isolated, either because they are less mobile in their home environment or because they move into an aged-care facility, often far removed from their family, friends and familiar community (Wells & Herd, 2013).

Problems of Isolation

It is common for isolation to increase with age. For those still living at home, this can be the result of environmental barriers, such as unsafe neighborhoods, inaccessible housing and inadequate resources for socializing (Cohen-Mansfield et al., 2016). Grenade and Boldy (2008) note that, while the evidence is inconclusive, isolation and loneliness within residential settings may be even greater than it is for older citizens living in the community due to reduced social support. Isolation is also associated with boredom and inactivity due to increased lack of mobility; recent losses of family and friends, as well as mental health issues, such as the loss of role that comes with retirement from work, shame and fear (Cohen-Mansfield et al., 2016).

Isolation is known to have negative impacts on social and emotional wellbeing that can lead to severe problems such as depression (Luo et al., 2012). Of particular concern are the many studies (e.g. Nikmat et al., 2013; Cornwell and Waite, 2009; Luo et al., 2012) that have revealed strong correlation between social disconnectedness and physical and mental wellbeing. Many aged-care policies assume that, because older people have ceased working, they are at risk for becoming mentally inactive and unproductive (Norrie, 2012; Perlman, 2004). However, there is a large body of evidence that remaining active, socially connected and emotionally satisfied is a major contributor to health and wellbeing (Netten et al., 2012; Diene & Chan, 2011; Hagan et al., 2014). WHO (2001), for example, sees active ageing in terms of the health, independence and productivity of older people. Positive and productive ageing can improve social and emotional wellbeing in the best interests of both society and the individual (Kaye et al., 2003).

Problems of Access

Research, such as that by Olsson & Viscovi (2016), has identified inequalities of access to online information and services within the older population of contemporary ageing societies. Lack of access to ICT excludes many older people from its benefits. Choudrie et al. (2013) have shown that, as governments strive to replace conventional service delivery with e-government, many of the older demographic are missing out. This is also true of access to online banking (Diniz et al., 2011) and health information (Heart & Kalderon, 2013). The practical aim of our research is to inform on ways to redress these inequities of access through an open program of digital capability development for older citizens who have previously lacked access to online services and other benefits. In Australia, where our research was conducted, the government emphasizes the use of online services such as my.gov.au and myagedcare.gov.au which assumes that all citizens should have access to such online services.

Computer Capabilities of Older Citizens

There is an assumption among many in the aged-care sector that older people have a limited level of digital literacy and little potential to actively engage online (ADHA, 2011; Chadwick, 2011). Even relatively recent studies have found that many older citizens do not have access to digital technologies such as email, Skype, productivity tools and social media, or have the relevant skills to use them (Lelkes, 2013; Taylor, 2011; Hakkarainen, 2012). It is widely accepted that even well-motivated older people have a range of physical, cognitive and motivational traits and computer-awareness that together impact on their potential to develop sufficient skills to use digital technology effectively (Burgess et al. 2012). However, some recent research has reported growing acceptance of digital technology by older people (Chen & Chan 2011; Xie 2008; Niehaves & Plattfaut 2014; Zheng, 2015). Improved technology, such as new tablet computers, is playing a role in this acceptance (Tsai et al., 2014).

Research on ICT in Aged-Care

Most research efforts to date on the topic of ICT and aged-care are aimed at improving, and lowering the cost, of health and medical outcomes for older citizens (Hilty et al., 2013). ICT-based patient monitoring, remote consultations with health professionals and other telemedicine programs are introduced so that older citizens can remain living in their own homes for longer thereby reducing the demand for costly residential aged-care facilities (Nikmat et al., 2015). Such ageing in place programs ignore the social needs of older citizens that are critically important to their wellbeing and quality of life (Burgess et al., 2012).

In contrast, research conducted by the authors over the past two years has investigated how ICT can broaden the range of social activities and communities available to people as they age (Hasan & Linger, 2016). The research described in this chapter examines the challenges and opportunities faced by isolated older citizens when they use ICT and engage online.

Communities and Ageing in Place

As we conducted the research we observed the concerns of family and caregivers for the wellbeing of those who choose to age in place. On further investigation we became aware of many grassroots endeavors to support older citizens in a mixture of local and online communities for mutual support. In Australia, this includes the Australian Seniors Computer Clubs (http://www.ascca.org.au), Tech Savvy Seniors (https://www.telstra.com.au/tech-savvy-seniors) and University of the Third Age Online (http://www.u3aonline.org.au/). These programs combine the learning of ICT with mutual support, fun and personal development for positive ageing. Internationally, ground-breaking models of support for those ageing in place include the UK's My Ageing Parents website (https://myageingparent.com/) and the Village movement in the USA (http://www.vtvnetwork.org). Our research aims to give older citizens the confidence and skills to participate in the online components of these communities.

Attributes of Wellbeing

One challenge to the research design, when investigating the impact of ICT use, is to determine how to monitor outcomes among the cohort of participants. Improving wellness of older citizens is a primary motivation for such research. Wellbeing is normally associated with people's experience of their quality of life (QOL) determined by the satisfaction with their lives and a sense of personal development in their particular social context (NEF, 2013). Two prominent QOL assessment regimes are the World Health Organization's QOL index (WHOQOL) and the French subjective QOL profile (SQLP). While both are well-respected, Carr and Higginson (2001) advise against their general use because wellbeing "is determined by an individual's perceptions of their position in life taken in the context of the culture and value systems where they live and in relation to their goals, expectations, standards, and concerns" (p. 1358). During the research reported here we became aware of a new approach to measuring social care-related QOL (SCRQoL). The ASCOT project of community care in the UK (Netten et al., 2012) identified seven domains of wellbeing among older adults receiving community care services as shown in Table 1. While their

Table 1. Seven Domains of Social Wellbeing for older adults at home (Netten et al., 2009)

Domain	Explanation
Accommodation cleanliness and comfort	The service user feels their home environment, including all rooms, is clean and comfortable
Personal cleanliness and comfort	The service user feels he/she is personally clean and comfortable and looks presentable or, at best, is dressed and groomed in a way that reflects his/her personal preferences
Food and nutrition	The service user feels he/she has a nutritious, varied and culturally appropriate diet with enough food and drink he/she enjoys at regular and timely intervals
Safety	The service user feels safe and secure. This means being free from fear of abuse, falling or other physical harm and fear of being attacked or robbed
Occupation	The service user is sufficiently occupied in a range of meaningful activities whether it be formal employment, unpaid work, caring for others or leisure activities
Control over daily life	The service user can choose what to do and when to do it, having control over his/her daily life and activities
Social participation and involvement	The service user is content with their social situation, where social situation is taken to mean sustaining meaningful relationships with friends, family and feeling involved or part of a community should this be important to the service user

research (Netten et al., 2012) shows that the first four domains (Accommodation, Personal Cleanliness, Food and Nutrition, Safety) are well served by care packages in the UK, Australia and presumably in other developed countries, the next three domains (Occupation, Control, Social Participation) are not.

As noted by researchers, quantitative measurement of wellbeing among older citizens can be difficult. Research in this area shows that limited, and even conflicting, results have come from studies that use surveys or experiments with older participants (Hagan et al., 2014). For this reason, the research described in this chapter, adopted an inductive approach to identify themes and patterns of positive outcomes from the online activities and communities in which participants chose to engage.

THE RESEARCH

The motivation of the research presented here is to determine how ICT can help alleviate adverse consequences of isolation by reconnecting older citizens to family and community, as well as enabling them to remain mentally and emotionally active members of society. Thus, the research aims to investigate:

1. In what ways do motivated older citizens learn to use appropriate ICT.
2. How ICT use can help improve the social and emotional wellbeing of isolated older citizens.

Some exploratory interviews and focus groups with relevant stakeholders revealed the extent and complexity of the problem and the challenge of using empirical research methods for this type of investigation. These insights were similar to the experiences of other researchers in this area (Fokkema and Knipscheer, 2007; White et al., 2002; Naumanen and Tukiainen, 2007). In order to pursue these aims, a multifaceted research agenda was undertaken involving action research and case studies.

For the action research component, interventions were conduct in three aged-care facilities over the two-year period of the project (Davidson et al., 2004). The interventions consisted of the provision of what the facilities labeled computer kiosks. The kiosks consisted of a few computers set up in a corner of the recreation room, supplemented by weekly sessions of training and ongoing support. The research interventions were always adapted to the needs, capabilities and circumstance of each individual participant. To support these interventions the researcher and tutors made considerable effort to create a happy, fun and relaxed environment to make this complex context safe-fail, time-paced, diverse and tolerant of dissent. In other words, older citizens did what they could with the technology, learnt at their own pace, were able to laugh at their mistakes, but most importantly they set the learning agenda. Moreover, each participant was able to use the devices they felt most comfortable with, either a laptop or an iPad.

Data collection consisted of observations of the use of ICT by older citizens. Computer tutors at each weekly session in the kiosk made notes of their observations and presented these at bi-monthly meetings with the authors. This method follows the inductive approached of Xie (2007) and Ng (2007) and the informal methods of data collection and analysis used by Savago et al. (2013), Naumanen and Tukiainen (2007) and Winstead et al. (2013) in similar studies. Data was collected from the weekly sessions as well as from ad hoc emails and Skype calls with participants by the authors over the two-year period of the project.

In addition a series of informal case studies were also conducted among older citizens who reside at home, either alone or with a caregiver (usually their spouse). The authors were, from time to time, invited to provide computer assistance to some aged-care clients who resided in their homes with the help of community services. Using a similar approach to the class observations, notes were kept on their challenges and achievements.

As the research progressed, themes began to emerge from the records that were kept. Once saturation was reached and no new themes were forthcoming, the results were summarized and now presented as findings from the research.

FINDINGS

After two years of research, a stable set of themes emerged from the ongoing inductive analysis of recorded notes. Following some general observations from the research, the themes are illustrated by examples of observed practice.

General Observations

Staff in the aged-care facility, and even family members, were skeptical that any of the residents would join our program, although many of the latter wanted us to succeed. A degree of ageism was detected when people implied that older residents would never learn to use digital technologies. In this respect, we can report that while most of the participants did not become computer experts, they did learn to engage online in ways that greatly improved their lives.

Over the two-year period, records were kept of observations of thirty participants, aged from their early 60s to late 90s, and who are still continuing with the program. In addition, three participants died during the period of the research while many others attended for short periods of time as they were confident to continue alone. Others only attended briefly because they lost interest. On-going participation in the program was completely voluntary and every effort was made to make it an enjoyable, positive experience. Time and again, it was noted how important it was to match the technology to the user and for participants to learn on the device they would continue to use. For some complete novices, the intuitive iPad interface was immediately enticing; for others who saw the computer as a way to remain a productive member of society, the iPad was seen as a frivolous toy and a laptop was preferred. Equally it became apparent that participants needed to use the technology for activities of their own choosing. Most of them started with just one activity, among those described below and persisted with it for many weeks before trying something new.

Emergent Themes of Use

Once the data analysis reached saturation, wellbeing was described by the emergent themes of: connection, being occupied, self-sufficiency, self-worth/esteem, productivity, personal development, being in control, and enjoyment. These themes are described below and illustrated with a pertinent example.

- **Connection**: In addressing the detrimental effects of isolation, using ICT to get connected is paramount. Being able to connect to family is the most common request of new participants. One of our first computer kiosk participants was in his mid-eighties and had been moved from an independent self-care arrangement into secured high-care due to multiple health issues. While the other high-care residents had varying degrees of dementia, he did not but was restricted by the lock-down constraints where people with dementia were not allowed to leave the facility at will. After just weeks in this unit, he contacted us to say that he had become increasingly depressed at having no one with whom he could carry on a normal conversation. He heard about our project from other low-care and self-care residents and asked to be involved. He soon learned the basics of ICT and was able to re-establish connections with his daughter who lived interstate. They had become estranged but when they communicated via email they sorted out the difficulties that arose when they had tried to converse by phone. Before he died he was able to ensure that she would be well provided for. Re-establishing his connection with his daughter had completely changed his attitude to life.

- **Being Occupied**: Older people often have plenty of time on their hands and little to do. When it is not possible to connect with others, ICT provides many ways that isolated people can do something meaningful with their time on their own. As one example, many of the participants used a word processor to write stories both fiction and non-fiction. Some even publish their efforts online. Another example that had become increasingly popular involved participants who took up genealogy and spent hours working on their family tree. One particular participant had advanced dementia and hovered around some of the kiosk sessions, expressing mild interest. He became intrigued when someone started playing Patience on an old desktop computer that had been given to the facility but was not connected to the Internet. He learnt to switch on the computer and the research program set up a large icon on the desktop that enabled him to get started by double clicking on the icon. He would sit there and play for hours often laughing to himself when he won. The nursing staff were delighted that he was occupied and even though it may provide some stimulation for his brain.

- **Self-Sufficiency**: One of the comments that most of the participants made from time to time was their desire to do things for themselves and not have to rely on others. A participant who lived at home had limited mobility because he needed a wheelchair. He was very computer savvy with up-to-date equipment and good Internet access. He did not go out much but did attend the local Senior Citizens Association meetings when transport was provided. He was happy to give advice to people he met there on computer issues and had set up a Facebook group where those who live alone at home can ask for help online. One of the people he has helped was interviewed as part of the research program. When asked how she coped when a severe storm had closed local transport and other facilities she said that they all kept in touch on Facebook and made sure everyone was OK. Thus, a whole community of house-bound older citizens had developed a degree of self-sufficiency.

- **Self-Worth/Esteem**: Despite assurances that they had made progress with their computing skills, many of the participants expressed a view that they are dummies compared with younger people. Unfortunately, this attitude is often reinforced by ageist comments from others. The research program endeavored to engender a sense of accomplishment when participants mastered some aspect of ICT. One example where this was particularly effective was a resident in an aged care facility who was younger than other residents; being in her 60s. Her need for care was debilitating obesity and she had no family or friends to act as caregiver. She never had visitors and had very low self-esteem. She was relatively computer savvy but could not afford a computer or internet access. Participating in the research she borrowed one of the iPads the program provided and enrolled in several online courses on various topics. As her confidence grew, she began to attend some of the weekly kiosk sessions and was pleased when other residents asked for her help.

- **Productivity**: Many participants write very well. With some basic instruction participants learnt to use a work processor. The oldest participant was 97 but could still function well. He tires after an hour but has no real physical problems and only mild cognitive issues when using a computer. He used very early computers before he retired from work. He was not attracted by the iPad but when he was given access to an old laptop he wanted to use it to write his memoir. He came to each session, had learnt to use the rudiments of Word and has produced several pages of text describing his life as an airline pilot. It is fascinating reading. But he needed help to research relevant details on the Web as he had trouble remembering the name of places he wants to write about. The authors are trying to convince him to self-publish his writings online but he remains reluctant. His effort inspired other to undertake similar activities.

- **Personal Development**: A few participants discovered massive, open, online courses (MOOCs) and arranged a program of online courses on topics of interest that they previously had no time or opportunity to study.

- **Being in Control**: Many participants struggled to deal with the confusing array of services that influence their lives such as banking and social security. One participant was not very mobile and left all such matters to her husband who had died recently. She does not have any close family or friends that she can really trust to manage her affairs. In the kiosk sessions she had learnt to do many of the things that worry her online. She could check her bank

Table 2. Alignment of the Themes with the relevant ASCOT Domains

ASCOT Domain	Themes arising from the Research
Occupation	being occupied, productivity, personal development
Control over daily life	self-sufficiency, being in control
Social participation and involvement	connection, self-worth, enjoyment

account, pay bills and do other transactions. She felt more in control and no longer worried that others may be taking advantage of her position.

- **Enjoyment**: Entertainment is provided for residents in aged care but there is not a great deal of variety. Residents argue about which channel to watch on the community TV or which movies to show. Access to streamed entertainment on individual devices gets around this limitation and provides access to many forms of entertainment. A couple of self-care women participants who came to the weekly classes expressed their desire to travel but they could not afford to do so. They just came to the kiosk sessions in order to surf the Internet to plan where they would go if they could. They loved to do virtual tours of towns, museums, historic sites and gardens all over the world.

The single premise, that is consistent with the amalgamation of these themes, is improved wellbeing among isolated older citizens that stems from engagements in online communities and activities. In order to strengthen this proposition, the themes arising from the research, as illustrated above, are compared with the ASCOT domains of Occupation, Control, and Social Participation (Netten et al 2012). Table 2 demonstrates the alignment of the research themes with the ASCOT domains.

MAIN FOCUS OF THE CHAPTER

The four main objectives of the chapter, set out in the Introduction, are now revisited with a view to explain how each is addressed by the interpretation of the research findings.

Understanding the Use of ICT by Isolated Older Citizens

Research into the use of ICT by older citizens has previously had mixed findings although more recent publications show that ICT use among older citizens is increasing, particularly with the advent of more intuitive tablet devices. Older users can be challenged by decline in their physical and mental abilities that comes with ageing. Older people may have issues with eyesight, manual dexterity, and processing of information. These may require adaptations in learning strategies and even in the design of new technologies to accommodate this. Additionally, older citizens are hindered by their lack of awareness of the opportunities afforded by use of the ICT and Internet for personal and social activities.

The research reported in this chapter found that, while not every older person could or would want to develop the capability to engage with ICT, all should be encouraged to try. The critical factor is that everyone, but particularly older citizens, has different challenges, experiences, needs, interests and situations. It is therefore important not to have a one size fits all approach to the use of ICT but rather to treat each new user as a unique case and find out what they could potentially learn to do that would make a significant difference to their life. The themes that emerged from the research have been illustrated by typical examples showing what types of activities were accomplished by individual participants.

A few participants engaged in activities that did not involve others or Internet access. This included playing games and typing stories. However, in most cases, a whole new world was opened up to participants who learnt to access the Internet for social engagement, self-development and productive ways of occupying their time.

As will be discussed in more detail below, things found to be essential to successful use of ICT were (1) to learn on the device that would continue to be used; (2) to match the choice of device and activity to each participant; (3) for the majority of users who engaged in activities on the Internet, to make sure that Internet access was ubiquitous, fast and cheap; (4) that ongoing help was available and (4) the learning environment was always fun and supportive.

The Benefits of the Social Use of ICT by Isolated Older Citizens

A specific aim of the research was to answer the question "how can ICT use help improve the social and emotional wellbeing of isolated older citizens". This question was addressed by the research findings as a set of themes and supported by other studies, specifically the alignment of the themes with three of the ASCOT Domains of wellbeing as listed in Table 2. The ASCOT team had investigated the value of community services provided to older citizens who remain living at home rather than going into aged-care facilities as their ability to care for themselves declines. Their research (Netten et al. 2009, 2012) shows that basic care services of accommodation maintenance, personal cleanliness, food and nutrition, and safety are provided and improve wellbeing. However, services in the other domains of occupation, control of daily living and social participation are not commonly provided nor are they effective when these community services are provided. Most clients of community care services are no longer able to drive a car or catch transport to go out to shop or take advantage of other community facilities. They thus become isolated, no longer able to do many of the meaningful activities they once could or maintain many of their social contacts. As they became more reliant on others they lost control of many aspects of life.

The findings of the research described in this chapter show how quality of life (wellbeing) can greatly improve in the domains of occupation, control of daily living and social participation with the use of ICT and the Internet. Online banking and other services give back control to older citizens who can no longer get to the local branches. A digital device connected to the Internet provides endless opportunities for meaningful things to do and people with whom to engage. With a capability to use ICT, isolated older citizens can look forward to each day on a road to positive ageing.

One concern about encouraging older citizens to engage online is that this will replace personal contacts that previously happened face to face. Anecdotal evidence shows that in many cases engaging online can lead to opportunities to meet in person with people originally met in cyberspace.

A Program of Service to Support ICT Use by Isolated Older Citizens

The research program originally conducted in aged-care facilities has provided in depth understanding of the processes involved as older people develop the capability to use ICT for their social wellbeing. The research provides insights that can inform others who want to set up similar programs in their aged-care facilities. These insights are formulated as a practical community service that is now being provided for older people to set up and use ICT at home. The guidelines for this service involve the following four steps:

1. **Get the Right Technology:** Many people already have a computer or have access to one. They may just need to have it set up and be provided with help to learn to use it for what they want and need. If they don't have a computer, or have one that is not suitable, maybe they need advice on what would be suitable and within their budget.

2. **Get Connected to the Internet:** This is where many older citizens need most help and advice. There is increasingly free WIFI in public places and even some aged-care facilities. There are different home options that vary in price and suitability. Older citizens need someone trustworthy and reliable to help find them find the right option for them.

3. **Get Some Introductory Lessons:** There is a need to learn basic computing skills on the computer the older person will continue to use. What they learn needs to suit their capability, needs and interest.
4. **Get Ongoing Help as Needed:** Everyone will inevitably need some way to get appropriate ongoing help if they get stuck. There are commercial IT help services for those who can afford it or establish a set of volunteers for those who can't afford commercial services. Most problems can be solved by someone with basic IT skills, plenty of patience and humor. The older person needs to find the right person for them, maybe a family member, neighbor or student on a community service program.

Promoting Adoption and Expansion of the Program

The findings of this research have been presented at several conferences and workshops both in the academic world and in practical settings of aged care. Other aged care facilities are setting up similar programs and those responsible for the care of older citizens are supportive of such a service.

The authors are seeking support and partners to help establish a social business to provide a community service following these steps.

SOLUTIONS AND RECOMMENDATIONS

This research has both academic and practical contributions. On the academic side, it adds to the growing body of literature on the ICT use by older people. This literature is published in several disciplines including gerontology and information systems. However, there is little research into the link between ICT use and wellbeing among the isolated older citizens. This could be the topic of further ground breaking research as it would have profound implications for improving aged care from the perspectives of health, social and economic systems. The productive use of ICT by older citizens could reduce the burden of the ageing population on government services and finances as they could manage their own affairs and remain healthier through enjoyable and meaningful social engagement. It could also keep older people involved in society as workers and volunteers as many useful tasks can now be done online. For example, one of our participants was able to get some paid employment proof-reading student assignments. This economic value would be worth investigating further.

Some of the systematic challenges encountered during the research concerned overcoming the culture of ageism in the aged-care industry where workers and managers did not think that any of their clients could ever use computers. It was also difficult to convince managers of aged-care facilities that providing free Wi-Fi was good business that would save money as residents required less assistance and oversight when they could manage their affairs and entertain themselves online.

From the practical side this project has resulted in two applications that could be implemented in aged-care. One is establishing Web Kiosks in aged care facilities to help develop ICT capability for residents. The other is a community service program to be delivered to people who choose to remain in their own homes as they age This research project would suggest that providing a program of assistance for home resident older citizens to use ICT, as outlined above, would be a cost-effective policy as well as greatly improving the wellbeing of these older citizens.

FUTURE RESEARCH DIRECTIONS

This research has explored a topic which is difficult to investigate with traditional empirical methods. The changes observed happen slowly as older people with little understanding of ICT gradually acquired the capability for the activities that interested them. Over this time, participants' wellbeing will be affected by many factors. Indeed aspects of their physical and mental wellbeing may decline and that may mask the changes in social wellbeing due to ICT use that we are trying to ascertain. As some researchers have noted (Fokkema and Knipscheer, 2007; White et al., 2002; Naumanen and Tukiainen, 2007) more can be learnt through research that takes an approach based on observation and inductive interpretation as used in the research described in this chapter. However, future research with more, and possibly younger, participants may take a more empirical approach that identifies more specific changes in wellbeing that arise from ICT programs.

Another avenue of research may investigate the development of new digital technologies that suit the needs of older people. This would be a growing market in ageing populations.

It would also be appropriate if more research was undertaken to better understand the contribution of social programs to the overall wellbeing of isolated older citizens in conjunction with bio-medical interventions and traditional community care services related to the basic ASCOT domains of accommodation, nutrition, cleanliness and safety. One aspect of such studies could be to assess benefits of using ICT and the Internet for social wellbeing, in the context of broader social programs addressed by the ASCOT research. The additional cost incurred in the provision of ICT capability to older citizens would need to be compared to the costs of bio-medical and traditional community care services.

CONCLUSION

Four objectives were set out in the introduction to the chapter. These objectives have been met as follows:

1. The first objective was to increase current knowledge on older citizens' use of ICT. Both the literature presented as background to the study and the research itself have recognized multiple factors that affect the use of ICT by older citizens in terms of physical, mental and awareness issues. However, the literature also show how older people are increasing their use of ICT and the research presents ways that older people are using various applications to improve their wellbeing across several themes.
2. The second objective was to establish the efficacy of social ICT use in overcoming effects of isolation. Most of the beneficial use of ICT by participants in the study involved not only use of ICT but also interactions on the Internet. These interactions were with others, particularly family and friends. It also provides older citizens with more control over their lives through, for example, online banking, and more ways to meaningfully occupy their time, such as creating their family tree. These activities all contribution positively towards overcoming effects of isolation.
3. The third objective was to put forward a practical program of services that could be provided for older people to set up and use ICT. The section on solution and recommendations emphasizes the practical program of services that stems directly from the research study to provide isolated older people the capability to set up and use ICT.
4. The fourth objective was to encourage more attention to this issue and motivate more research in the area. It is hoped that readers of the chapter are encouraged to pay more attention to this issue, act in ways to assist older people in their ICT use and to conduct more research in the area.

For the authors, this research was most rewarding when they could see the wonder in the faces of older people who discovered the Internet for the first time. Many of the participants obtained great joy from things that the rest of us take for granted: downloading a picture of grandchildren, skyping with family members overseas, seeing their old community on Google maps or finding old family records in archives of old newspapers.

REFERENCES

ADHA. (2011) Older Australians and the Internet: bridging the digital divide. *National Seniors Productive Ageing Centre* (NSPAC). Retrieved from http://nationalseniors. com.au/be-informed/research/productive-ageing-centre

Aus Govt. (2010) *Australia to 2050: future challenges* Retrieved from http://archive. treasury.gov.au/igr/igr2010/report/pdf/IGR_2010.pdf

Burgess, L., Hasan, H., & Alcock, C. (2012) Information Systems for the Social Wellbeing of Senior Australians, *Proceedings of ISD2012*, Prato, Italy

Carr, A., & Higginson, I. (2001). Are quality of life measures patient centred? *BMJ (Clinical Research Ed.)*, *322*(7298), 1357–1360. doi:10.1136/bmj.322.7298.1357 PMID:11387189

Chadwick, A. (2011). Explaining the Failure of an Online Citizen Engagement Initiative: The Role of Internal Institutional Variables. *Journal of IT & Politics,* 8, 21–40.

Chen, K., & Chan, A. (2011). A review of technology acceptance by older adults. *Gerontechnology (Valkenswaard)*, *10*(1), 1–12. doi:10.4017/gt.2011.10.01.006.00

Choudrie, J., Ghinea, G., & Songonuga, V. N. (2013). Silver surfers, e-government and the digital divide: An exploratory study of UK local authority websites and older citizens. *Interacting with Computers*. Retrieved from http://iwc.oxfordjournals.org/content/early/2013/02/06/iwc.iws020.ful

Christensen, K., Doblhammer, G., Rau, R., & Vaupel, J. W. (2009). Ageing populations: The challenges ahead. *Lancet*, *374*(9696), 1196–1208. doi:10.1016/S0140-6736(09)61460-4 PMID:19801098

Cohen-Mansfield, J., Hazan, H., Lerman, Y., & Shalom, V. (2016). Correlates and predictors of loneliness in older-adults: A review of quantitative results informed by qualitative insights. *International Psychogeriatrics*, *28*(04), 557–576. doi:10.1017/S1041610215001532 PMID:26424033

Cornwell, E., & Waite, L. (2009). Social Disconnectedness, Perceived Isolation, and Health among Older Adults. *Journal of Health and Social Behavior*, *50*(1), 31–48. doi:10.1177/002214650905000103 PMID:19413133

Davison, R. M., Martinsons, M. G., & Kock, N. (2004). Principles of Canonical Action Research. *Information Systems Journal*, *14*(1), 65–86. doi:10.1111/j.1365-2575.2004.00162.x

Denvir, C. J., Balmer, N. J., & Pleasence, P. (2014). Portal or pot hole? Exploring how older people use the information superhighway for advice relating to problems with a legal dimension. *Ageing and Society*, *34*(04), 670–699. doi:10.1017/S0144686X12001213

Diene, E. & Chan, M. (2011) Happy People Live Longer: Subjective Well-Being Contributes to Health and Longevity. In *Applied Psychology: Health and Well-Being*.

Diniz, E., Birochi, R., & Pozzebon, M. (2012). Triggers and barriers to financial inclusion: The use of ICT-based branchless banking in an Amazon county. *Electronic Commerce Research and Applications*, *11*(5), 484–494. doi:10.1016/j.elerap.2011.07.006

Fokkema, T., & Knipscheer, K. (2007). Escape loneliness by going digital: A quantitative and qualitative evaluation of a Dutch experiment in using ECT to overcome loneliness among older adults. *Aging & Mental Health*, *11*(5), 496–504. doi:10.1080/13607860701366129 PMID:17882587

Grenade, L., & Boldy, D. (2008). Social isolation and loneliness among older people: Issues and future challenges in community and residential settings. *Australian Health Review*, *32*(3), 468–478. doi:10.1071/AH080468 PMID:18666874

Hagan, R., Manktelow, R., Taylor, B., & Mallett, J. (2014). Reducing loneliness amongst older people: A systematic search and narrative review. *Aging & Mental Health*, *18*(6), 683–693. doi:10.1080/13607863.2013.875122 PMID:24437736

Hakkarainen, P. (2012). No good for shoveling snow and carrying firewood: Social representations of computers and the internet by elderly Finnish non-users. *New Media & Society*, *14*(7), 1198–1215. doi:10.1177/1461444812442663

Harvey, P., & Thurnwald, I. (2009). Ageing well, ageing productively: The essential contribution of Australias ageing population to the social and economic prosperity of the nation. *Health Sociology Review*, *8*(4), 379–386. doi:10.5172/hesr.2009.18.4.379

Hasan, H., & Linger, H. (2016) How Social use of Digital Technologies by the Elderly Enhances their Wellbeing. *Journal of Educational Gerontology*. Retrieved from http://www.tandfonline.com/doi/full/10.1080/03601277.2016.1205425

Heart, T., & Kalderon, E. (2013). Older adults: Are they ready to adopt health-related ICT? *International Journal of Medical Informatics*, *82*(11), e209–e231. doi:10.1016/j.ijmedinf.2011.03.002 PMID:21481631

Hilty, D. M., Ferrer, D. C., Parish, M. B., Johnston, B., Callahan, E. J., & Yellowlees, P. M. (2013). The effectiveness of telemental health: A 2013 review. *Telemedicine Journal and e-Health*, *19*(6), 444–454. doi:10.1089/tmj.2013.0075 PMID:23697504

Kaye, L., Butler, S., & Webster, N. (2003). Towards a Productive Ageing Paradigm for Geriatric Practice. *Ageing International*, *28*(2), 200–213. doi:10.1007/s12126-003-1024-6

Lelkes, O. (2013). Happier and less isolated: Internet use in old age. *Journal of Poverty and Social Justice*, *21*(1), 33–46. doi:10.1332/175982713X664047

Luo, Y., Hawkley, L. C., Waite, L. J., & Cacioppo, J. T. (2012). Loneliness, health, and mortality in old age: A national longitudinal study. *Social Science & Medicine*, *74*(6), 907–914. doi:10.1016/j.socscimed.2011.11.028 PMID:22326307

Naumanen, M., & Tukiainen, M. (2007) Guiding the Elderly into the use of Computers and Internet – lessons taught and learnt IADIS. *Proceedings of the International Conference on Cognition and Exploratory Learning in Digital Age(CELDA '07)*.

NEF. (2013) *Social Indicators: Individual* Retrieved September 30 2013 from http://www.proveandimprove.org/meaim/individuals.php

Netten, A., Burge, P., Malley, J., & Potoglou, N. (2012). Outcomes of social care for adults: Developing a preference-weighted measure. *Health Technology Assessment Reports*, *16*(16), 1366–5278. PMID:22459668

Netten, A., Burge, P., Malley, J., Potoglou, N., Brazier, J., Flynn, T., & Forder, J. (2009) Outcomes of Social Care for Adults (OSCA): Interim Findings. *PSSRU Discussion Paper.* Retrieved from http//:www.PSSRU.ac.uk

Ng, C. (2007). Motivation among older adults in learning computing technologies: A grounded model. *Educational Gerontology*, *34*(1), 1–14. doi:10.1080/03601270701763845

Niehaves, B., & Plattfaut, R. (2013). Internet adoption by the elderly: Employing IS technology acceptance theories for understanding the age-related digital divide. *European Journal of Information Systems*, *23*(6), 708–726. doi:10.1057/ejis.2013.19

Nikmat, A., Hawthorne, G., & Al-Mashoor, S. (2015). The comparison of quality of life among people with mild dementia in nursing home and home care—a preliminary report. *Dementia (London)*, *14*(1), 114–125. doi:10.1177/1471301213494509 PMID:24339093

Norrie, J. (2012). Loneliness on the rise as our cities atomise. *The Conversation.* Retrieved http://theconversation.edu.au/loneliness-on-the-rise-as-our-cities-atomise-6068

Olsson, T., & Viscovi, D. (2016). Remaining divides: Access to and use of ICTs among elderly citizens. In *Politics, Civil Society and Participation: Media and Communications.* Retrieved from http://www.researchingcommunication.eu

Perland, D. (2004). European and Canadian studies of loneliness among seniors. *Canadian Journal on Aging, 23*(2), 181–188. doi:10.1353/cja.2004.0025 PMID:15334817

Seidel, D., Brayne, C., & Jagger, C. (2011). Limitations in physical functioning among older people as a predictor of subsequent disability in instrumental activities of daily living. *Age and Ageing, 40*(4), 463–469. Retrieved October 10 2013 doi:10.1093/ageing/afr054 PMID:21609999

Taylor, A. (2011) Social Media as a Tool for Inclusion, Research Report, Canada.

Tsai, H., Shillair, R., & Cotten, S. (2014) Social Support and 'Playing Around': An Examination of How Older Adults Acquire Digital Literacy with Tablet Computers. *Proceedings of the TPRC2014 Conference.*

Wells, Y., & Herd, A. (2013, November). Congregate Housing: Impacts on quality of life and social participation. *Proceedings of the Grey Expectations Ageing in the 21st Century AAG Conference*, Sydney.

White, H., McConnell, E., Clipp, E., Branch, L. G., Sloane, R., Pieper, C., & Box, T. L. (2002). A randomized controlled trial of the psychosocial impact of providing internet training and access to older adults. *Aging & Mental Health, 6*(3), 213–221. doi:10.1080/13607860220142422 PMID:12217089

WHO. (2001a). *Health and ageing: A discussion paper.* Geneva: World Health Organization.

WHO. (2001b). *Active ageing: From evidence to action.* Geneva: World Health Organization.

Xie, B., & Jaeger, P. (2008). Computer training programs for older adults at the Public Library. *Public Libraries*, (Sept/Oct), 52–59.

Zheng, R., Spears, J., Luptak, M., & Wilby, F. (2015). Understanding Older Adults Perceptions of Internet Use: An Exploratory Factor Analysis. *Educational Gerontology, 41*(7), 504–518. doi:10.1080/03601277.2014.1003495

KEY TERMS AND DEFINITIONS

Action Research: Is a form of applied research that is iterative, rigorous and collaborative, using informed interventions to develop a solution to a practical problem that is of value to the people with whom the researchers are working, while at the same time developing theoretical knowledge of value to a research community (Davison et al., 2004).

Aged-Care: Systems of services (both public and privately operated) that provide support to frail and aged citizens, including assistance with day-to-day living in intensive forms of specialized residential care and independent living arrangements in the community.

Ageism: Prejudice or discrimination on the grounds of a person's age particularly noticeable in attitudes that older people are not able to learn to use computers.

Bio-Medical Interventions: A group of treatments and therapies which are designed to stop, or at least reduce, the effect of physical and mental health problems in people often without reference to their social and cultural contexts.

Community Services: Are delivered by local nonprofit, government, and community-based organizations and designed to improve the quality of life for community residents, particularly low-income individuals, the disabled and people otherwise disadvantaged.

Isolation: Is a situation where a person is deprived of all social contact with an absence of communicative interaction. Loneliness and depression can be consequences of isolation.

Older Citizen: Most developed world countries have accepted the chronological age of 65 years as a definition of a senor or older citizen.

Quality of Life (QOL): Is a broad multidimensional concept concerned with the general well-being of a person or society in terms of health and happiness, rather than wealth. QOL usually includes subjective evaluations of both positive and negative aspects of life.

Social Wellbeing: Is a sense of involvement with other people and communities. It is not just about being happy or content, but also about being actively engaged with life and with other people.

Chapter 9
The Impact of Social Media on Social Movements:
The Case of Anti-Consumption

İrem Eren-Erdoğmuş
Marmara University, Turkey

Sinem Ergun
Marmara University, Turkey

ABSTRACT

The primary objective of this chapter is to analyze the support of social media for social movements within the context of the anti-consumption movement. Social media have proved to be strategic for initiating, organizing and communicating social movements. The anti-consumption movement is a trend of the postmodernism era that has not yet reached a large following. A secondary aim of this chapter is to analyze the similarities and differences in the support of social media for the anti-consumption movement between one developed and one emerging market. To achieve this goal, a content analysis was employed to analyze Facebook accounts of anti-consumption online communities in the USA and Turkey. The findings show that social media can be the right medium to increase coverage of social movements in society. Additionally, the online institutionalization and decentralized organization of the online community as well as stable social media sharing help support non-radical social movements like anti-consumption.

DOI: 10.4018/978-1-5225-2495-3.ch009

INTRODUCTION

Social media, defined as "activities, practices, and behaviors among communities of people who gather online to share information, knowledge, and opinions using conversational media" (Safko & Brake, 2009, p.6), is a new platform through which extensive consumer interaction occurs. Its ease of use, speed and anonymity make social media a tool where people can express themselves freely and influence each other comprehensively (Peattie & Peattie, 2009). This enabled interactivity among individuals on social media has changed online communication dramatically and drawn interest in academia to study its effects from business and sociological perspectives. For example, the Arab Spring fueled interest on how social media triggers protests and social movements. However, the extant literature and studies are not yet sufficient to understand the relationship between social media and social movements, so more studies on the subject are needed (Boulianne, 2015).

The aim of this paper is to add to the extant literature on how social media and online communities support social movements using the context of the anti-consumption social movement. Anti-consumption is the rejection of consumerism. Consumerism is a byproduct of modernism and modern way of living, in which standardization of culture, media, products, ideas and way of living are praised (Hakansson, 2014). Consumerism is based on acquisition and consumption of goods and services, and achieving satisfaction and happiness in return. Postmodernism was a reaction to modernism, and appeared as a revolutionary alternative (Rosenau, 1995). The post-modern world is based on impression management, accepting alternate and innovative ways of personal identification (Podesta & Addis, 2005). Thus, anti-consumption appears as a trend among some post-modern individuals to define their personal images (Yüksel & Mirza, 2010). The contributions of this paper are to help identify anti-consumption as a social movement and to illustrate how social media have lent support to the movement by uniting individual anti-consumption attempters under one platform as a community. A related contribution of the study is to illuminate the similarities and differences between the anti-consumption movement on social media in a developed and an emerging market.

To achieve the aim of the study, this paper is organized as follows. First, a background on social movements, the intersection of social movements and social media are presented, followed by a discussion of development of anti-consumption as a social movement and social media's influence on the movement. Then a content analysis of selected Facebook accounts of online communities on anti-consumption in developed and emerging markets were done to snapshot the current situation of the movement on social media. Findings of the research are discussed, followed by solutions and recommendations. A conclusion is provided after some recommendations for future research directions.

BACKGROUND

In this section, a basic literature review about the impact of social media on social movements is provided. Support of social media for the diffusion of information about, and the activation and operational process of social movements is explained to furnish a clear understanding of the phenomenon. The section begins by defining and explaining what is meant by social movements, and proceeds by discussing how and why social media affect social movements.

Social Movements

Social movements have become important actors in our everyday life as they both initiate social change and are created by social change (Delia & Diani, 2006; Tilly, 2004). They are described as communities that are made up of people and organizations that aim to change social order (Bauermeister, 2014; McAdam & Snow 2010; Snow et al., 2007). Social movements comprise an extended battle for authority between opponents and power holders (Tilly, 2004). The end goal of social movements is ultimately achieving social change. Social movement actors include organizations and individuals who make social problems visible by spreading their complaints and concerns through collective action (McCarthy & Zald 1987; Snow et al., 2007). For example, veganism is a social movement and PETA is a social movement organization that supports the movement.

Aberle (1966) identifies four kinds of social movements (alternative, redemptive, reformative, and revolutionary) based on who the movement attempted to change and how much change is advocated by the movement. Alternative social movements attempt to change the individual at a minimum amount, whereas redemptive social movements again attempt to change the individual but at radical levels. Alcoholics Anonymous, for example, is a redemptive social movement, working as a support group for recovering alcoholics. Even though alternative and redemptive social movements happen at an individual level, reformative and revolutionary ones happen at a larger level aiming to change the society or a part of the society. Reformative social movements happen at a broader group or societal level, but call for minor changes, can scale down demands if necessary or agree to share powers with others. An example of reformative social movement is advocating tougher restrictions on drunk driving. Revolutionary social movements, on the other hand, are much more radical and fundamental. Total prohibition of alcoholic drinks, for example, is a revolutionary social movement. Methods of work may also change among movements. As such they can be either peaceful or violent. Their influence range can also vary between being global or local (Boundess, 2016).

Traditionally social movements were created and occurred in physical places. A movement usually started in one geographic location and then if it is successful in that location, it spread to other places. However, lately tweets on the streets are also a common way of organizing for social movement protests. Social media act as a platform for assembling individuals or groups around occupied places such as Cairo's Tahrir Square, New York's Zuccotti Park or Taksim Gezi Park (Gerbaudo, 2012). Thus, for today, the impact of social media cannot be dropped off the map if there is a successful social movement. In the Digital Age, social media becomes an important resource for successful movements (Rolfe, 2005). Virtual space enables social movements to emerge, spread, gather support, and be organized regardless of geographical location (Hollenback & Zinkhan, 2006). Although social media and related technologies are not primarily created for social movement and activism purposes, social media are the most common platform for advocates to be informed about and participate in online or offline social movements (Brodock et al., 2009). Previous research showed how social media played an important role in the collective actions in different parts of the world, such as the overthrow of the governments in Egypt and Tunisia (Boulianne, 2015; Lynch, 2011) or the Umbrella Movement in Hong Kong (Lau et al., 2016).

To sum up, social movements can be said to emerge due to various factors including economics, institutional and social contexts. The interaction effect of these factors, rather than a single variable, enables the formation of a social movement. Therefore, it would be misleading to propose that social movements are a result of social media usage. However, the support of social media for social movements is obvious and undeniable (Lopes, 2014).

Why and How Social Media Helps Social Movements

Social media are an active part of our lives. According to Bullas (2014), the percentage of all Internet users that are active on social media is 72%. 71% of social media users prefer to use a mobile device, which makes social media more accessible anytime and anywhere in return. The Digital Yearbook developed by Global Web Index (We Are Social, 2016) states that 3.419 billion people all around the World use the Internet; that there are 2.307 billion active social media users. Facebook is the biggest social media platform with over 1.15 billion Facebook users. Facebook is followed by Twitter with over 550 million registered users. Pinterest and Instagram are also influential social media channels which are becoming increasingly popular. Other social media platforms include LinkedIn, YouTube, Tumblr, Vine, Slideshare and many others (Bullas, 2004; Akçay, 2011). Therefore, it is not surprising that social media affects every aspect of individuals' lives, including their activism as well.

Since the Battle of Seattle in 1999, the first partly electronically organized social movement, Internet technologies developed as a new strategic platform for social movements. The developments of social media in the last decades raised the importance of this platform for social movements. The social media features of speed, convenience, ease of forming a community, and anonymity are its most important discriminators from traditional media and enhance its ability to support social movements (Hollenback & Zinkhan, 2006). The Internet and social media provides fast, easy and cheap access which is not limited by time, space or distance (Castells, 2001; Juris, 2005). Individuals are able to log on to a community website any time anywhere, and are able to get the most current updates instantly and share their own information. Furthermore, they tolerate more culturally diverse friends online than offline as long as they gain some contribution from them (Hollenback & Zinkhan, 2006). When online, the values and beliefs of individual members become more important than their social life, where they come from or how much money they have. Finally, a virtual anonymous identity enables individuals to express their ideas more freely and do things normally they would not do in their social life. The feeling of no one would ever know helps members not to refrain and hold things back (Hollenback & Zinkhan, 2006).

Stein (2009) argues that social media perform different communication functions for social movement organizations such as providing information about movement identity, views and issues to interested recipients both inside and outside the movement; assisting action and mobilization, organizing of collective action and initiatives; promoting interaction and dialog among subordinated groups; making lateral linkages among movement members; serving as an outlet for creative expression of emotion, imagination, and aesthetics; and promoting fundraising and resource generation through requests for donations or the sale of merchandise. Similarly, Lynch (2011) claims that social media contributes to collective action in four ways: organizing and coordinating disaffected citizens to act publicly; creating information flows to make protesters believe the likelihood of success; fighting against repression by the ruling regimes; and accomplishing publicity to regional and global publics. As such, for example, online blogs and social networking sites were extremely important sources of information for the public in terms of gathering support against governments in the Arab nations. Facebook was the most popular social networking site for information spreading during the revolt in Egypt. Even the Egyptian government's severe punishments of social media activists did not stop Egyptians from expressing their ideas on social networks (Maurushat, Chawki, Al-Alosi & el Shazly, 2014).

Although much research highlights the impact of social media on diffusion of information about and communication of offline social movements, some social movements start online, organize online and then are carried offline. Thus, social media can also initiate social movements, especially political social movements (e.g., Maurushat, Chawki, Al-Alosi & el Shazly, 2014; Lee, So & Leung, 2015). As such, the revolutionary actions in Tunisia and Egypt are considered as the first digital revolutions in the Arab world. The virtual space provides public space to people especially when freedom is suppressed. If the people do not have any other channel to express their ideas freely, virtual space offers them this opportunity. The power of social media in such political activities was confirmed with the limiting of access to such technologies, i.e. blocking the Internet by Egyptian and Tunisian governments. For example, the "6 April 2008 Youth Movement" was organized by a young Egyptian girl through Facebook. This movement was established with the purpose of encouraging workers to strike against immoral working conditions like low wages and high food prices. This activist group used online networking sites also to mobilize people to unite and rise against the existing regime. The scenes from this demonstration were shared heavily at social networking sites like Twitter and Facebook. Then the Egyptian government blocked the Internet sites that include any material regarding the April 6 Youth Movement. "We are all Khaled Said" was also a Facebook group formed in order to inform people about the death of Khaled Said who was taken out from an internet café in Alexandria and beaten to death by Egyptian police in June 2010. The mission of this online community was to organize demonstration events against torture, corruption and any act of human rights violations. This group gained huge support from citizens (Maurushat, Chawki, Al-Alosi & el Shazly, 2014). These protests accumulated and again in early 2011 social media in general, Twitter and Facebook in particular employed a critical role in mobilizing people to protest in Tahrir Square which eventually lead to the downfall of President Mubarak (Tufekci & Wilson, 2012). The situation was similar in Tunisia. The revolution in Tunisia was catalyzed with the help of the Internet and social networking channels. Facebook, YouTube and Twitter were the most common spaces where people could access the latest updates about the revolts. The spread of the revolutions to other Arab countries such as Yemen, Libya and Syria was also progressed with the use on Internet and social networking sites. The events of Arab Spring proved that on the political level, social networks and related technologies were more powerful than expected (Maurushat, Chawki, Al-Alosi & el Shazly, 2014).

The power of social media in initiating and organizing social movements is not limited to the Arab World. The Umbrella Movement, which is also called The Umbrella Revolution, is another "leaderless" movement in which social network sites played a crucial role in the formation and spread of the movement in Hong Kong in 2014. The movement occurred when Chinese central government decided to make some changes in the Hong Kong election system. These changes were considered restrictive and unfair, which triggered the protests. These protests turned into a 79-day movement, which is called as the Umbrella Movement worldwide. The movement is called the umbrella movement because the protestors were using umbrellas to protect themselves from pepper and tear gas that was sprayed by the police. This revolution is also characterized by the new form of mobilization, which is utilized with digital social networks. Through these digital social networks, the movement's momentum is synchronized and sustained. Social media served as an important organizational tool for public to unite, mobilize and rise against the existing political actors (Lee, So & Leung, 2015). Another example for social media and social movement relationship can be the Gezi Park demonstration that had started on 28 May 2013 in order to protest the urban development plan for Istanbul's Taksim Gezi Park. The protests began as an environmental protest however it evolved into a demonstration of human rights, freedom of press and expression. In Gezi Park movement, there was no centralized leadership however social media play a key role in the organization of the protests as the main stream media give a lower profile of the demonstrations. Gezi park protests are found to be similar to Occupy movement and May 1968 events (Wikipedia, 2016)

Social movements may also spring from existing online communities through social media. Social media serve as an outlet for those in search of information that aligns with their own ideas and world view motivating people to join or found an online group (Bode, Vraga, Borah & Shah, 2014; Tang & Lee, 2013). The helpful and agreeable information found on online communities and social networking sites generate both informational and emotional support, two dimensions of social support that some social media users are searching for (Ballantine & Stephenson, 2011; Liang et al. 2011). As such, Wojcieszak's study (2009) of online neo-Nazi and radical environmentalist groups put forward the proposition that online groups corroborated the collective identity. People who belong to online communities are more likely to volunteer in activity because these memberships increase the chance of being asked to volunteer (Musick & Wilson, 2008; Wojcieszak, 2009). Thus, as individuals belong to a network/ online group, their likelihood to be involved in activist movements increase, since they are frequently asked to volunteer by the groups that they belong to or they see other people express their ideas or volunteer for actions and become influenced to do so as well (Vitak et al., 2011). Chances of mobilizing a large number of individuals increase this way. For instance, in Chile the government approved a project that would turn the habitat of Humboldt penguins into a power plant. 118 groups against this project were established on Facebook just within two days of the approval. With the help of these groups, protests were organized and the company could not build the plant. It can be concluded that

Facebook use and online communities stopped this project (Valenzuela, Arriagada & Scherman., 2012).

ANTI-CONSUMPTION AS A SOCIAL MOVEMENT

Anti-consumption, the attitude, and behavior of staying away from consumption of certain goods and services (Cherrier, 2009), is a relevant social movement, opposing the dominating trend of consumerism and overconsumption. Its aim is to change several fundamentals of social order related to consumption and marketing (Kozinets & Handelman, 2004). It advocates an alternative way of living, opposing modernism and its outcome, consumerism, in the society; and is the byproduct of a postmodern way of thinking. Staying away from excessive consumption, caring about the environment and underprivileged people is, for example, an anti-consumption lifestyle alternative. Voluntary simplicity and brand avoidance are different labels for anti-consumption behaviors (Iyer & Muncy, 2009). Anti-consumptionists or voluntary simplifiers are defined as group of individuals, who maintain a 'consumption style' of not consuming (Walther & Sandlin, 2011) or as 'individuals who are searching for a simpler lifestyle for societal reasons like ethical concerns, green consumption, or community development' (Oates et al.,2008: 352). They are trying to consume less, pursue a strong cautious attitude in shopping, do not rely on materialism for supporting their fulfillment, prefer to live committed to environments that are smaller, decentralized, and less complex (McDonald et al., 2006; Elgin & Mitchell, 1977). However, Craig-Lees (2006) argues that anti-consumption as a social movement has never reached a massive magnitude. The reason for this can be that anti-consumption behavior occurs due to varying factors such as political, personal and environmental concerns (Iyer & Muncy, 2009). Therefore, it is nearly impossible to conceptualize one type of anti-consumption. Anti-consumption as a phenomenon ranges from brand avoidance to anti-globalization protests, from green consumption to voluntary simplicity. In short, any activity that goes against consumption is anti-consumption. This wide range of activities complicates the process of anti-consumption becoming a huge and massive social movement.

Impact of Modernity and Postmodernity on Consumption and Anti-Consumption

Although there is no consensus on its definition, modernism is actually a period in Western culture, rooted in the Enlightenment period in 18th century (Burke, 2000). It is characterized by the powers of reason, order and science over ignorance, disorder and superstition. These three powers led to unity, orderliness and adherence to rules, which gave way to the rise of modern nation states with central governments and industrial capitalism (Berner & van Tonder, 2003). They brought about urbanization, growth of cities, and the rise of the middle class as the target of consumption (Yüksel & Mirza, 2010). Modern consumerism, democratization of pleasure, and increasing availability of luxuries to mass populations were end results (McNaughtan, 2012). Consumerism is an idea that ties personal and economic development fundamentally to material possessions and consumption (Friedman, 2008). The dictionary definition of the concept includes (1) protection and promotion of the interests of the consumers, (2) preoccupation of the society with the acquisition of consumer goods (Oxford Dictionary, 2015). Consumerism creates the feeling that consumption of goods and services is the only means to serving consumer interest. A culture that is predominated by consumerism is described as the consumer culture (Friedman, 2008). Towards the end of 1970s, postmodernism emerged as a reaction to modernism. Modernism had brought reason and scientific thinking, yet it also led to racism, threat of nuclear wars and the Third World hunger (Burke, 2000). The postmodern era is characterized as a movement away from the values of modern era towards intuition, differentiation and decentralization. Whereas the early 20th century consumer was a mass-market consumer, the postmodern consumer puts a general emphasis on individual style, paralleling customization and personalization (Sassatelli 2007).

As it was with modern era and consumers, postmodernism created its own consumption habits and consumers. In the postmodern era, consumption is no longer secondary to production. Actually it is perceived as a mean of developing self-identity in a fragmented and dynamic society (Podesta & Addis, 2005; Berner & van Tonder, 2003). Postmodern individuals are aware of what is going on due to availability of information, assertive due to the increasing power of the individual, and exposed to various consumption options (Firat & Venkatesh, 1995; Berner & van Tonder, 2003). Thus, they have unpredictable behavior patterns and lead multiple lifestyles, having contradictory value systems, which is a reflection of their self-identity and perception. Anti-consumption is one method of revealing personal identity in the post-modern world (Yüksel & Mirza, 2010).

Some consumers, fearing to become objects of consumer culture, have responded rebelliously to consumerism and the modern way of living. They fear and rebel against the idea of affluenza (de Graaf *et al.*, 2005), believing it to be painful, contagious, and a socially transmitted condition of overload, debt, anxiety, and waste resulting from the dogged pursuit of more. These rebels form the anti-consumption movement, questioning the rationalized pleasurable enslavement of the human race by brands, technology, organized consumption and outlined satisfaction. They hold that overconsumption is usually driven by hedonism, and is linked to unhealthy, energy-dense food, alcoholic beverages, tobacco, and usage of nonrenewable resources. The end result is harm to the society, the world, and the self. The value system of the society, ecological environment, nonrenewable resources, physical and psychological health of the individual are all adversely effected from consuming too much (Hakansson, 2014). In summary, the dominating trend of consumerism and overconsumption created its own opposing social movement; anti-consumerism, anti-consumption.

Historically, the anti-consumption or voluntary simplicity concept is not new. It is supported by many religions and practiced by important figures such as Jesus, Buddha, Lao Tse, Moses and Mohammed, and also by leaders such as Lenin and Gandhi (Gregg, 1936; Elgin & Mitchell, 1977). It was Gregg (1936), a student of Gandhi, who first talked about the concept and defined it. However, the concept did not attract a lot of attention until the hippie movement of the 1960s. Life in the hippie movement was simple and meaningful and hippies were against consumption as a way of living (Bekin et al., 2005). By the 1970s, anti-consumption became a valuable concept and was analyzed by many researchers. The concept peaked attention with Duane Elgin's book "Voluntary Simplicity", which was published in the USA in 1981. After that, it remained silent again until the middle of 1990s (Chieh-Wen et al., 2007). It was because of the crises in mid 1990s that people were motivated to seek meaning in their lives without materialism, once again leading the path for not consuming (Zavestoski, 2002).

According to Rao (1998), the anti-consumption movement in the United States (US) reignited with "the rise of nonprofit consumer watchdog organizations" which led to a period of legal and more organized activism. "Buy Nothing Day" in the United States and "In Town without My Car" in the United Kingdom are some well-known activities that are organized by the followers of anti-consumption movement. Although started in the US and other developed countries, currently this movement is widespread around the world as anti-consumption does not have geographic and/or cultural limits. Choi (2011) argues that,

The consumption fatigue and preference for a simple life first appeared among high-income earners in developed markets. Now, however, they are spreading to the consumers in emerging markets. This trend is also evident in Korea (p. 117).

Therefore, the movement can be said to have become diffused and accepted worldwide.

Anti-Consumption on Social Media

The anti-consumption social movement benefits from the Internet in general, and social media tools in particular (Dahl, 2014; Hollenback & Zinkhan, 2006). Today online communities against the consumption of some brands are created by consumers who are dissatisfied or by people who simply hate a brand just like brand loyal consumers who establish online brand communities to promote a brand (Cromie & Ewing, 2009; Kozinets & Handelman, 2004). These virtual anti-consumption communities are effective in affecting purchasing decisions of potential consumers (Veloutsou & Moutinho, 2009). They are built upon virtual social interactions and possess characteristics of what is described as community since they rely upon one another, make joint decisions, have standard rules and procedures for socializing and communication, and are committed to each other. These virtual groups help members with social identification as well (Hollenback & Zinkhan, 2006). Furthermore, compared to offline communities, these virtual communities are more durable because there is continuous communication, linking conversations across Websites, and archiving of communication and information (Renninger & Shumar, 2002).

Anti-Consumption in Emerging Markets

Emerging markets (Ems) have attained great attention in the last decades due to the importance attached to them as drivers of the world economy. Given the aging and saturated population in developed countries, emerging markets appeared as ideal places to create a consumer culture, which is believed to be beneficial for the interest of the existing economic system. Most of the multinational companies (MNCs) directed their efforts to these markets to grow and gain market share because the consumers in these markets are very attractive with rising incomes and a high number of young consuming individuals (Slocum et al. 2006; Özsomer, 2012). Especially the populous, young adult cohort in these markets is characterized as innovative and open to new ideas and brands. They are also considered to be homogenous and globally oriented, which makes them good targets for both global and local brands (Askegaard, 2006; Burgess & Steenkamp, 2006).

The consumer culture dominant in the West was imported to EMs through music, movies, the Internet and lifestyle images (McNaughtan, 2012) and was seen as heavily foreign, a clear import, even if it appealed to both new and traditional interests in those countries. Because of the differences between consumers in EMs and consumers in developed countries in terms of culture and lifestyle, this foreignness generated reactions. The first reaction was the appeal of the strange and modern way of consuming to some consumers. For some consumers, consumerism even became as 'natural' as it was in the West (Stearns, 2006). Strizhakova et al. (2011) identified the different groups of consumer culture in the emerging markets as global, glocal, national, and unengaged. Global consumers relate and compare themselves to other cultures such as "economic center" of North America or Europe and position themselves accordingly (Holt et al., 2004). Glocal consumers, on the other hand, often blend all available global and local objects to position themselves in the local society (Ger and Belk, 1996). Thus, both consumers of the global and glocal culture preferred to use global brands to define themselves, whereas the national culture consumers preferred to identify themselves only with local brands. The unengaged consumers, on the other hand, remained indifferent to global vs. local dichotomy, and purchased based on convenience rather than preference. This group may also be characterized as uninterested in consumption and cynical of globalization (Steenkamp & de Jong, 2010). Thus, they may have formed the basis of anti-consumption groups in emerging markets.

Arnould (2010) classified this anti-globalization and anti-consumerism activism in emerging markets as anti-consumption, resistance to sweatshop labor in developing countries, producing alternative fair-trade brands, and promoting local, regional brands. As Choi (2011) argues, "The Consumption fatigue and preference for a simple life first appeared among high-income earners in advanced markets. Now, however, they are spreading to the consumers in emerging markets" (p. 117). Therefore, it is timely and necessary to understand the situation of the anti-consumption movement in developed versus emerging countries. The understanding of the spread of the movement in emerging markets may yield interesting results for future strategy building since emerging markets are identified as the prospering targets of consumerism by the MNCs. Since social media usage is very appealing in emerging markets, exploring the anti-consumption movement on social media is a wise method to follow. Comparison of developed versus emerging markets will also add to the findings since the movement began in developed markets, which can be taken as a reference point to understand its development in emerging markets.

METHODOLOGY

The aim of this study is to illustrate how online communities and social media support social movements, using the example of anti-consumption. The comparison between developed and emerging markets is a secondary objective Content analysis was identified as the method of data analysis. First, the countries to be included in the study were selected; and then the Facebook accounts of online communities on anti-consumption were identified and selected.

Selection of Countries

The USA (developed) and Turkey (emerging) were selected as the countries to be compared and contrasted in this study. The selection criteria were based on social media usage and convenience. The countries showed similarities in terms of the social media preferences (Facebook, Twitter, and Google plus) and demographic distribution of social media users (with young people leading the way) (Chaffey, 2016). Even though the countries do not resemble each other in terms of culture or economic development, some form of similarity is observed on social media usage which makes comparison between them viable.

According to Digital Yearbook that is developed by Global Web Index (We Are Social 2016), Turkey has a population of 79.14 million with an urbanization rate of 74%. There are 46.3 million active Internet users with 58% penetration in the country. 77% of the Internet users become online daily and 16% use the Internet at least once a week. 42 million of the Internet users actively participate in social media platforms with 53% penetration. The social media usage is dominated by Facebook with 32%, as in any other country. Facebook is followed by WhatsApp with 24%. The third most popular social media channel is Facebook Messenger with 20%, which is followed by Twitter and Instagram with 17% and 16% respectively. In Turkey, 51% of people use laptops or PCs; 46% use mobile devices; and 4% use tablets to access the Internet. According to the analytics of Statista (2016), Turkey ranks the 10th country in terms of Facebook usage (33.09 million users), whereas the USA is ranked the 2nd (191.3 million users).

As stated by Digital Yearbook that is developed by Global Web Index (We Are Social 2016), the USA has a population of 322.9 million, with 82% urbanization rate. There are 282.1 million active Internet users with 87% penetration in the country. 79% of the Internet users becomes online daily and 14% uses the Internet at least once a week. 192 million of the Internet users actively participate in social media platforms with 59% penetration. In the USA, the social media usage is again dominated by Facebook. Facebook is followed by Facebook messenger with 26%. The third most popular social media channel is Twitter with 17%, which is followed by Pinterest and Instagram with 15%. In the USA, 64% of people use laptop or PCs, 29% uses mobile devices and 7% uses tablets to access the Internet.

Selection of the Cases

To most effectively identify and understand the spread and diffusion of anti-consumption social movement on social media, a multiple case study approach was used. Facebook was identified as the social medium to be studied since it was the most commonly used tool and most popular social media channel in every country (Bullas, 2004; Akçay, 2011). Twitter and Google were also searched to triangulate results of the Facebook search in order not to miss any online community that could not be found because of using the wrong key word on Facebook. "Anti-consumption", "Anti-consumption online community", "anti-consumerism" were selected as the keywords for searching online communities. The cases of online communities were selected based on the criteria listed below:

1. Publicizing the idea of anti-consumption philosophy in the description of the aim of the online community
2. At least three years' online presence of the community in order to ensure enough data for content analysis
3. Activeness of the online community (regular posting and interaction among the participants at least twice a week) in order to ensure information-rich cases.

The Facebook and Google search provided the following results. In Turkey, there is only one open anti-consumption group, which is called "Tüketim Karşıtlığı" ("Anti-consumption" in English) and there are several commercial swapping and buying groups. In the USA, on the other hand, there are several anti-consumption related groups such as "anti-branding", "freegan", "sustainable living", "environmentalism" etc. Freegan community on Facebook (USA) fulfilled the criteria above and had 4522 members. The Freegan online communities could have been included in this study because Freeganism is mainly developed around anti-consumption principles and promotes an anti-consumerist lifestyle. Freegan people are encouraged to find alternative ways of living, which is based on "limited participation in the conventional economy and minimal consumption of resources" as stated in Freegan community's Facebook page. However, Freegan online communities are excluded from this study because the Turkish freegan group called Freegan İstanbul is a closed group and has only 33 members. Therefore, only two other cases (one from USA- Buy Nothing Project-, and one from Turkey-Tüketim Karşıtları (Anti-Consumption) were identified that fit with the online community criteria described above and selected as the cases to be explored.

*   **Buy Nothing Project (USA):** The Buy Nothing Project began when two friends, Rebecca Rockefeller and Liesl Clark, created an experimental hyper-local gift economy in the USA. It is a grass-roots volunteer-driven project with no funding. In just two and a half years, it grew over 280,000 members in 18 nations with 1300 groups. The aim of the group is giving away, lending, or sharing among neighbors. Members post news and interesting stuff from buy nothing project websites around the world. The members need to be 21 or older. The group rethinks consumption and refuses to buy new in favor of asking for an item from neighbors. Individuals and communities reduce their own dependence on single-use and virgin materials by extending the life of existing items through gifting and sharing among group members. This way, it is believed that overconsumption of unnecessary products would decrease.

The first post was posted 8 July 2011 on the Facebook group. The first posts are mainly about weekly meetings in order to make exchanges with the motto "bring a basketful, leave a basketful". In July 2013, they decided to expand the project, "to connect people on a daily basis, around a much wider variety of goods." The posts after July 2013 starts to include information about gift economy, gratitude and sustainable living. In August 2014, the Facebook group reached 5000 likes. Currently, the group consists of 35,630 members.

- **Tüketim Karşıtlığı:** Although the exact date of the establishment of the group is not clear, the first post on the Facebook group dates back to December 19, 2010. The group was founded to display the truth about entities that turn people into consumerist beings with the help of a fictionalized system of advertisements and subconscious messages. The aim is to increase environmental consciousness and form consumption awareness for a viable world. The group defines itself as environmentalist and anti-capitalist. Currently, the group consists of 708 people.

FINDINGS

Data analysis yielded similarities and differences between the sharing, interactions, and activeness of online anti-consumption groups in developed and emerging markets. The similarities may be listed as publicizing (1) anti-consumption, (2) reusing, sharing or swapping, (3) environmentalism, (4) human size living, and (5) personal growth. The differences, on the other hand can be enumerated as (1) concentration of the posts, (2) institutionalization of the community, (3) spread of movement, and (4) organization of events. Social media definitely helped with the spread and diffusion of the anti-consumption in general. As shared in one of the posts of Buy Nothing Project, "So far, Facebook as a free social platform has worked for us.... One thing, nonetheless, is for sure: The real-world interconnectedness we experience in our Buy Nothing groups has been facilitated by social media".

What Is Shared Similarly as Posts

Anti-Consumption, Sharing and Reusing

Both of these groups express their ideas and share stories on anti-consumption, sharing, and reusing. Both of the groups have visionary ideals for a life with no or minimized consumption. The Buy Nothing project frequently talks about the merits of anti-consumption as such one member posts "Earth provides us with all that we need, we have created a consumption-driven economy that asks, "What more can we take from the Earth?" The merits of sharing are expressed with posts such as "think about sharing before throwing it away". Overconsumption is also one of the main concentrations of the Tüketim Karşıtlığı group. They share various posts that claim overconsumption and capitalism as the main problem of the world today and as the reason of unhappiness of the human race in cities. One of their posts also liken using credit cards to slavery period of the 19th Century, promote the idea of self-determination and knock reliance on money that is non-existent. Unnecessary property ownership is also critiqued. Modern way of living, consumption, and capitalism are expostulated in their posts with negative words or with caricatures.

Ideas of sharing and reusing are encouraged within the Buy Nothing project as an alternative to consumption with posts or projects such as sharing your clothing as gifts with your neighbors, sharing excess food, or creating lending libraries. The thank you posts of members who received gifts of cloths or other items are also shared to hearten others. Sharing and community building is ultimate aim of the group as they say in one of their posts,

The Buy Nothing Project has not raised a single penny, yet the social capital we've raised is priceless. With nearly 2,000 volunteers and 285,000 members worldwide we are proving that a new era is upon us: Sharing and community can happen without money being a part of the equation.

Even though sharing is not a strong aim of the Tüketim Karşıtlığı group when compared to Buy Nothing Project, their news covers individual stories of those who establish systems for sharing and reusing. Some posts also publicize the idea of mending, swapping, reusing rather than buying new items. For example, one of these posts covers a Turkish woman's successful experiment to wear a single dress in her daily life for 30 days. Another example post from South Africa tells of how they produced biogas from garbage.

Environmentalism

Environmentalism is the main theme in the Tüketim Karşıtlığı group's posts. Preserving the environment and animals is utmost importance. Some of their posts are quite romantic as they play music for the plants or they ask members to grow plants to keep bees fed or they inspire members to ride bicycles rather than drive cars. On the other hand, some of their posts give the feeling of fear to the readers displaying facts about extinct animals or future of the Earth. Ecological agriculture in small villages is also encouraged. Some of the posts include advertisements of ecological producers as well as stories of successful examples of ecological living. News and supportive views about collective environmental protests against the attempted hydroelectrical power plants in Turkey (e.g., Alakır, Ayancık) or cutting down forests to build residential areas are posted as well. During the Gezi Park protests in Turkey, the group lent their support with their posts. They rarely post news about global protests against environmental vandalism such as the opposition of Mapuches against Chilean forestry industry. The group also has close linkage to yesilgazete.org (greennewspaper.org) as most of the news from that newspaper are shared on their Facebook account.

Preserving the environment is also an aim of the Buy Nothing project. Their belief is that by buying nothing, they are going to do the right thing for the environment as well. The project encourages members to buy from environmentally and ecologically friendly organizations if they have to buy anything. However, comparably their posts related to environmentalism are fewer compared to Tüketim Karşıtlığı group's posts.

Human Size Living

Human size living, which is commitment to environments that are smaller, decentralized, and less complex (McDonald et al., 2006), is an emphasis of both groups, even though it is more evident in the Buy Nothing project's posts and stance to community forming. The Buy Nothing project is quite local in its attempts to bring people together to share. One can only become a member of only one Buy Nothing group, which is closest to where s/he lives. The project believes in the community spirit and small city concept. As told in one of the posts, "One of our founders is doing just that. Using her local Buy Nothing group is one of the best steps she's taken in ... re-connect with her neighbors at the same time". The Buy Nothing group Facebook page also talks about buy nothing project organizations that were done in various places of the USA and promote the ideas of the project in most of its posts. Praising the local producers is also evident in the posts of Tüketim Karşıtlığı group. They post messages to encourage members to buy from environmentally conscious local producers and even grow food themselves.

Personal Growth

The Buy Nothing project is mostly positive for the future and believes that their efforts will eventually make the world a better place. They believe in the power of positivity and every once in a while posts about being positive. In the group gratitude is also an important concept that is emphasized frequently. In their own words, "The Buy Nothing Project is an opportunity to practice kindness, build empathy, and strengthen community." In Tüketim Karşıtlığı group cartoons, music, movies and film festivals about environmentalism, activism and sustainable living posts are shared. There are also some articles about capitalism and its damage to humanity.

These posts are informative, highly philosophical and intellectual. However, they all point out to a negative future if we continue the way we are living at the moment.

What Is Different Between Groups

When the two online communities are compared, the Buy Nothing project is a very well organized online community, which enables systematic and regular interaction between its members. Although it started as a social experiment, it quickly grew into a more organized movement. Currently, there are 1300 Buy Nothing groups in 18 different countries. The groups are decentralized, local and organized. The Buy Nothing project, the starting point of the online community, basically publicizes anti-consumption philosophy to its members. The localized Buy Nothing groups, on the other hand, organizes their own offline events in their areas. On the other hand, although established before the Buy Nothing Project group, the Tüketim Karşıtlığı group did not evolve into an organized community yet. The online community did not find enough supporters in Turkish online society, and has only 708 members. The group does not organize any offline events. In Buy Nothing Project group the posts were regularly shared since the foundation. However, in the Tüketim Karşıtlığı group, posts are shared on irregular intervals, and sometimes large time gaps exist between posts. Furthermore, the posts of the Tüketim Karşıtlığı group are usually focused on environmentalism and ecological awareness.

SOLUTIONS AND RECOMMENDATIONS

The findings of our research show that social media can be the right medium to increase coverage of social movements in the society. Buy Nothing Project can be a seminal online community example of the support of social media on social movement objectives. The project had started as a social experiment in 2011; and reached more than 35000 members as of 2016, with a spread of 16 nations worldwide. In order to understand the reasons of this online and offline circulation of the movement needs more probing and data analysis. However, it can be inferred from the Facebook page of the group that some of this progress can be entwined to the institutionalization and decentralized organization of the online community as well as stable social media sharing. Some of the success can be attributed to the local online subgroups and their offline anti-consumption organizations such as swapping days in local districts. Thus, the group uses a decentralized structure and leadership under the guidance and philosophy of the main Buy Nothing Project group. There is probably offline organization, leadership, and strong commitment beneath the whole online movement. The organization shares anti-consumption posts in short intervals, informs individuals, and also encourage them to join various offline anti-consumption events. The Turkish Tüketim Karşıtlığı group, on the other hand, was established one year earlier than the Buy Nothing Project, but evolved much less in time. There are only 708 members, and the group mostly shares information or publicizes individual anti-consumption experiences on irregular basis, and has not organized any offline activities yet as it can be inferred from their Facebook account. However, we have to note that we did not have knowledge of or trace offline anti-consumption activities of the group.

Anti-consumption is a redemptive social movement attempting to change individuals at a radical level by cutting down buying and consuming. However, the movement does not go after radical societal ends or changes. Given the information provided above, it can be deduced that online presence and social media can help a social movement to gain supporters and move behind where it was first established, if there is decentralized centralization of the movement. In other words, an integration of aims of the organization is a must, and standardization of the movement in terms of what is shared as an ideology is necessary. On the other hand, the movement needs to be organized offline in a decentralized way because of time and place constraints. Thus, an organizational structure that lets local groups to be formed to run offline events is also necessary. Online presence and publicizing should be blended with offline local events to exert positive influence on redemptive social movements like anti-consumption. Unlike reformative and radical movements that catch fire in a short time, in a leaderless fashion, redemptive movements may require more organization and leadership both online and offline in order to be successful. More time might also be needed for the results to flourish. From the Turkish Tüketim Karşıtlığı group example, it is understood that mere irregular information sharing and publicizing in online platforms does not help much with the progress of the movement since the online standpoint of the movement in Turkey is rather behind the movement in the USA in terms of scope, reach, and support. Similar to what Vitak et al. (2011) argues, social media groups enhance the collective identity, but activism would not happen unless there is call for action, online or offline. In the Turkish example, the call for voluntary action is missing out of the picture on Facebook accounts, what might probably limit the scope and effectiveness of the movement.

Findings of this research may imply that that anti-consumption idea is still at its infancy stage in the emerging market, Turkey. The movement's progress looks disorganized, mostly based on environmental and ecological publicity related to anti-consumption. However, social media is dynamic and change can happen quickly (Hoffman & Fodor, 2010). Therefore, there is chance that movement can become organized and catch up with the USA based Buy Nothing Project in short time. Currently, the Tüketim Karşıtlığı group publicizes individual experiences, what might mean that there are scattered, individual attempts of anti-consumption in Turkey. They are independent and disconnected to each other. What is needed is institutionalization and active leadership so that legitimacy is gained and attempts are organized under one roof with local decentralization. Then the direction of the current may turn in favor of the social movement in Turkey as well. In addition, just because the investigated online community is small may not mean that the anti-consumption movement is any less developed than in the USA. It might be that Turkish citizens prefer to organize offline to participate in such movements and prefer to keep it to themselves rather than sharing their experiences on social media. Therefore, business organizations should not underrate the potential of anti-consumption in their future strategic decision-making.

The main aim of marketing is to "satisfy the needs of the customers". The question that the organizations have to consider is that what happens if the customers are not willing to consume. Therefore, the business organizations have to understand the needs, motives and characteristics of anti-consumerists. As anti-consumption is a spreading movement, if the organizations underestimate "anti-consumption" segments, they would probably misjudge future generations' needs, wants and desires for alternative life-styles. Eventually, the organizations, which undervalue these movements will lose their competitive advantage. In today's world with the help of technology and social media, successful online social movements organizations can become global if they are well organized. Therefore, today the business organizations have to be aware of online movements, their establishment and growth processes in order to learn from them. In addition to the business organizations, the governments and governmental instructions also have to develop policies that would fulfill the needs and demands of anti-consumerist groups. For example, social responsibility projects of business organizations can be organized jointly with the anti-consumption groups especially around the ideas of sharing, reusing or swapping among consumers. In this way, a linear relationship and collaboration may be built between business organizations and anti-consumption groups, what might become a competitive advantage for the business organizations in the long run.

FUTURE RESEARCH DIRECTIONS

This study's ultimate aim is to offer new insights considering the impact of social media on social movements, in this case anti-consumerism. The study took a case study approach and studied two countries, and one case in each country. Further research is needed for generalization of the results. Different developed and emerging market contexts may be compared and contrasted. As stated in literature review, anti-consumption is an infrequently researched area. Therefore, further research is also strongly needed on antecedents and consequences of the topic.

243

More qualitative and quantitative research with the members of the organization can be necessary to understand the whys and how of choice of anti-consumption among individuals. In addition to that, because anti-consumerism is a complex phenomenon more studies are needed from different perspectives such as political, cultural, psychological, sociological, ecological, organizational, technological and economical. Interdisciplinary research is also required.

Further research on the relationship between social media and social movements are also essential in order to understand the mechanisms and processes of information diffusion and its impact. There is a need for both quantitative and qualitative research methods. Case studies of social movements that became global would be helpful for creating guidelines to social movements that are at early stages of their evolvement. Longitudinal studies would be beneficial in order to understand the processes of formation, expansion or termination of social movements in general and the impact of social media on these processes in specific. Moreover, failed social movements and the social media interaction can be another interesting topic of research.

CONCLUSION

The aim of this research was to shed a light on the impact of social media on the spread and diffusion of social movements in the society. Anti-consumption, an outcome of postmodern society was taken as the subject of this research since it is a new way of self-identification and a possible threat to today's economic system; and thus worth research. The results put forward that although regarded as a collective culture, a tightly-knit framework in society, in which there is loyalty and group acting (Hofstede, 1983), in Turkey, anti-consumption movement stayed mostly at the individual level, with collective organization of the movement either online or offline staying pretty limited. Even though there is a huge population of social media users in the country, the movement remained silent, passive (mostly at the level of publicizing and sharing), and small scale even at the online level. One reason can be that the country has a quite young population, who are at the building stage of their lives, just starting to earn money and willing to consume and spend rather than not to consume. Time is needed to see where the movement will lead to in the future, and whether it will become a more organized alternative way of living just like its counterpart in the USA.

Although considered as an individualistic culture, a loosely-knit social framework in which individual is more important than the group, in the USA, anti-consumption group organized itself very well centrally, developed into subgroups, which are very active and tied closely to the main group. Therefore, it can be regarded as successful in becoming an online social movement organization. The reason can be that there is more saturation with modernism and its outcome, consumerism in the USA, since it is where branding, marketing, and consumerism were first born, and some people may feel they experienced enough of it. Thus, they became organized more quickly, and took action. Social media and online environments helped with the spread and diffusion of the movement. Offline activities also supported the cause and helped people come together.

Today, we live in a very dynamic world; and things may change direction very quickly. In a short while, the anti-consumption social movement may find supporters in the emerging markets as well and be organized quickly with the help of social media. It is true that the young population in these markets is mostly consumerists and good targets of business organizations; however, they are also good users of social media. Thus, if anti-consumption idea becomes popular for one reason (such as it is becoming popular in the USA), there is a good chance that it might spread very quickly among people with the help of social media. Therefore, it is not wise to assume that anti-consumption is not a threat in emerging markets. The nature of anti-consumption as a social movement should also be taken into consideration. Anti-consumption is happening but it has various forms, thus anti-consumption would be unlikely to become a social movement like Occupy movement. However, it can still be considered as a social movement because many people are employing practices, which go against consumption. Business organizations should start to think of strategies either to fence off these groups or collaborate with them and gain at least some of their support through social responsibility projects. How to do this is another swath of research. Further research is encouraged on the impact of social media on social movements, and detailed understanding of the anti-consumption ideology.

REFERENCES

Aberle, D. (1966). *The Peyote Religion among the Navaho*. Chicago: Aldine.

Akçay, H. (2011). Kullanımlar ve Doyumlar Yaklaşımı Bağlamında Sosyal Medya Kullanımı. *Gümüşhane Üniversitesi Üzerine Bir Araştırma İletişim Kuram ve Araştırma Dergisi.*, *33*, 137–162.

Arnould, J. (2010). Global Consumer Culture. In J. Sheth & N. Maholtra (Eds.), *Encyclopedia of International Marketing*. Retrieved from http://www.uwyo.edu/sustainable/recent-research/docs/global%20consumer%20culture%20arnould.pdf

Askegaard, S. (2006). Brands as a global ideoscape. In J. E. Schroeder & M. Salzer-Mörling (Eds.), *Brand culture* (pp. 91–101). London: Routledge Press.

Ballantine, P. W., & Stephenson, R. J. (2011). Help me, I'm fat! Social support in online weight loss networks. *Journal of Consumer Behaviour*, *10*(6), 332–337. doi:10.1002/cb.374

Bauermeister, M. R. (2014). *Social movement organizations in the local food movement: Linking social capital and movement support* [Unpublished doctoral dissertation]. Iowa State University.

Bekin, C., Carrigan, M., & Szmigin, I. (2005). Defying Marketing Sovereignty: Voluntary Simplicity at New Consumption Communities. *Qualitative Market Research: An International Journal*, *8*(4), 413–429. doi:10.1108/13522750510619779

Berner, A., & van Tonder, C. L. (2003). The postmodern consumer: Implications of changing customer expectations for organization development in service organizations. *SA Journal of Industrial Psychology*, *29*(3), 1–10.

Bode, L., Vraga, E. K., Borah, P., & Shah, D. V. (2014). A new space for political behavior: Political social networking and its democratic consequences. *Journal of Computer-Mediated Communication*, *19*(3), 414–429. doi:10.1111/jcc4.12048

Boulianne, S. (2015). Social media use and participation: A meta-analysis of current research. *Information Communication and Society*, *18*(5), 524–538. doi:10.1080/1369118X.2015.1008542

Boundless Sociology. (2016, September 20). Types of Social Movements. Retrieved from https://www.boundless.com/sociology/textbooks/boundless-sociology-textbook/social-change-21/social-movements-140/types-of-social-movements-768-4965/

Brodock, K., Joyce, M., & Zaeck, T. (2009). Digital Activism Survey Report 2009. *DigiActive*. Retrieved from http://www.digiactive.org/wpcontent/uploads/Research4_SurveyReport2009.pdf

Bullas, J. (2014). 22 Social media facts and statistics you should know in 2014. *Jeffbullas.com*. Retrieved from http://www.jeffbullas.com/2014/01/17/20-social-media-facts-and-statistics-you-should-know-in-2014/

Burgess, S. M., & Steenkamp, J.-B. E. M. (2006). Marketing Renaissance: How Research in Emerging Markets Advances Marketing Science and Practice. *International Journal of Research in Marketing*, *23*(4), 337–356. doi:10.1016/j.ijresmar.2006.08.001

Burke, B. (2000). *Post-modernism and post-modernity*. The Encyclopedia of Informal Education. Retrieved from www.infed.org/biblio/b-postmd.htm

Castells, M. (2001). *The Internet Galaxy: Reflections on the Internet, Business and Society*. Oxford: Oxford University Press. doi:10.1007/978-3-322-89613-1

Chaffey, D. (2016). Global social media research summary. Retrieved from http://www.smartinsights.com/social-media-marketing/social-media-strategy/new-global-social-media-research/

Cherrier, H. (2009). Anti-consumption discourses and consumer resistance identities. *Journal of Business Research*, *62*(2), 181–190. doi:10.1016/j.jbusres.2008.01.025

Chieh-Wen, S., Shen, M., & Chen, M. (2007). Special Interest Tour Preferences and Voluntary Simplicity Lifestyle. *International Journal of Culture*, *2*(4), 389–409.

Choi, S. (2011). Anti-consumption becomes a trend. *SERI Quarterly*, *4*(3), 117–121.

Ciszek, E. L. (2016). Digital activism: How social media and dissensus inform theory and practice. *Public Relations Review*, *42*(2), 314–321. doi:10.1016/j.pubrev.2016.02.002

Craig-Lees, M. (2006, June 20–21). Anti-consumption: concept clarification and changing consumption behavior. *Paper presented at the Anti-consumption Seminar*, International Centre for Anti-Consumption Research, Auckland, New Zealand

Cromie, J. G., & Ewing, M. T. (2009). The rejection of brand hegemony. *Journal of Business Research*, *62*(2), 218–230. doi:10.1016/j.jbusres.2008.01.029

Dahl, S. (2014). Social Media Marketing: Theories and Applications. *Atlanta, GA: Sage*.

De Graaf, J., Wann, D., & Naylor, T. L. (2005). *Affluenza: The All-Consuming Epidemic* (2nd ed.). USA: Berrett-Koehler Publishers.

Delia, P. D., & Diani, M. (2006). *Social Movements: An introduction* (2nd ed.). Maiden, MA: Blackwell.

Elgin, D., & Mitchell, A. (1977). Voluntary Simplicity. *The Coevolution Quarterly*, (Summer), 4–18.

Firat, A. F., & Venkatesh, A. (1995). Liberatory postmodernism and the enchantment of consumption. *The Journal of Consumer Research*, *22*(3), 239–267. doi:10.1086/209448

Friedman, T. L. (2008, November 16). Gonna need a bigger boat. *New York Times*. Retrieved from http://www.nytimes.com/2008/11/16/opinion/16friedman.html?_r=1&h

Ger, G., & Belk, R. W. (1996). Cross-cultural differences in materialism. *Journal of Economic Psychology*, *17*(1), 55–77. doi:10.1016/0167-4870(95)00035-6

Gerbaudo, P. (2012). *Tweets and the streets: Social media and contemporary activism*. Pluto Press.

Gregg, R. (1936). *"Voluntary Simplicity" reprinted in*. Manas. (reprinted in 1974)

Hakansson, A. (2014). 'What is overconsumption? A step towards common understanding. *International Journal of Consumer Studies*, *38*(6), 692–700. doi:10.1111/ijcs.12142

Hoffman, D. L., & Fodor, M. (2010). Can you measure the ROI of your social media marketing? *MIT Sloan Management Review*, *52*(1), 41.

Hofstede, G. (1983). National cultures in four dimensions: A research-based theory of cultural differences among nations. *International Studies of Management & Organization*, *13*(1-2), 46–74. doi:10.1080/00208825.1983.11656358

Holt, D. B., Quelch, J. A., & Taylor, E. L. (2004). How global brands compete. *Harvard Business Review*, *82*(9), 68–75. PMID:15449856

Iyer, R., & Muncy, J. A. (2009). Purpose and object of anti-consumption. *Journal of Business Research*, *62*(2), 160–168. doi:10.1016/j.jbusres.2008.01.023

Juris, J. S. (2005). The new digital media and activist networking within anti-corporate globalization movements. *The Annals of the American Academy of Political and Social Science*, *597*(1), 189–208. doi:10.1177/0002716204270338

Kozinets, R. V., & Handelman, J. M. (2004). Adversaries of Consumption: Consumer Movements, Activism, and Ideology. *The Journal of Consumer Research*, *31*(3), 691–704. doi:10.1086/425104

Lau, K. M., Hou, W. K., Hall, B. J., Canetti, D., Ng, S. M., Lam, A. I. F., & Hobfoll, S. E. (2016). Social media and mental health in democracy movement in Hong Kong: A population-based study. *Computers in Human Behavior*, *64*, 656–662. doi:10.1016/j.chb.2016.07.028

Lee, P. S., So, C. Y., & Leung, L. (2015). Social media and Umbrella Movement: Insurgent public sphere in formation. *Chinese Journal of Communication*, *8*(4), 356–375. doi:10.1080/17544750.2015.1088874

Liang, T. P., Ho, Y. T., Li, Y. W., & Turban, E. (2011). What drives social commerce: The role of social support and relationship quality. *International Journal of Electronic Commerce*, *16*(2), 69–90. doi:10.2753/JEC1086-4415160204

Lopes, A. R. (2014). The Impact of Social Media on Social Movements: The New Opportunity and Mobilizing Structure. *Journal of Political Science Research.*

Lynch, M. (2011). After Egypt: The limits and promise of online challenges to the authoritarian Arab state. *Perspectives on Politics, 9*(2), 301–310. doi:10.1017/S1537592711000910

Maurushat, A., Chawki, M., Al-Alosi, H., & el Shazly, Y. (2014). The Impact of Social Networks and Mobile Technologies on the Revolutions in the Arab World—A Study of Egypt and Tunisia. *Laws, 3*(4), 674–692. doi:10.3390/laws3040674

McAdam, D., & Snow, D. (Eds.). (2010). *Readings on Social Movements: Origins, Dynamics and Outcomes* (2nd ed.). Oxford: Oxford University Press.

McCarthy, J. D., & Zald, M. N. (1987). *Social movements in an organizational society: Collected essays.* New Brunswick, NJ: Transaction.

McDonald, S., Oates, C., Young, C. W., & Hwang, K. (2006). Toward Sustainable Consumption: Researching Voluntary Simplifiers. *Psychology and Marketing, 23*(6), 515–534. doi:10.1002/mar.20132

McNaughtan, H. (2012). Distinctive consumption and popular anti-consumerism: The case of Wall*E. *Journal of Media & Cultural Studies, 26*(5), 753–766. doi:10.1080/10304312.2012.664116

Musick, M. A., & Wilson, J. (2008). *Volunteering: A social profile.* Bloomington, IN: Indiana University.

Oates, C., McDonald, S., Alevizou, P., Hwang, K., Young, W., & McMorland, L. (2008). Marketing Sustainability: Use of Information Sources and Degrees of Voluntary Simplicity. *Journal of Marketing Communications, 14*(5), 351–365. doi:10.1080/13527260701869148

Özsomer, A. (2012). The interplay between global and local brands: A closer look at perceived brand globalness and local iconness. *Journal of International Marketing, 20*(2), 72–95. doi:10.1509/jim.11.0105

Peattie, K., & Peattie, S. (2009). Social marketing: A pathway to consumption reduction? *Journal of Business Research, 62*(2), 260–268. doi:10.1016/j.jbusres.2008.01.033

Podesta, S., & Addis, M. (2005). Long life to marketing research: A Postmodern view. *European Journal of Marketing, 39*(3/4), 386–412. doi:10.1108/03090560510581836

Rao, H. (1998). Caveat Emptor: The Construction of Nonprofit Consumer Watchdog Organizations. *American Journal of Sociology*, *103*(January), 912–961. doi:10.1086/231293

Renninger, K. A., & Shumar, W. (2002). *Building virtual communities: Learning and change in cyberspace.* Cambridge University Press. doi:10.1017/CBO9780511606373

Rolfe, B. (2005). Building an electronic repertoire of contention. *Social Movement Studies*, *4*(1), 65–74. doi:10.1080/14742830500051945

Rosenau, J. N. (1995). Governance in the Twenty-first Century. *Global Governance*, *1*(1), 13–43.

Safko, L., & Brake, D. K. (2009). *The Social Media Bible*. New Jersey: John Wiley & Sons, Inc.

Sassatelli, R. (2007). Consumer culture: History, theory and politics. *Sage (Atlanta, Ga.)*.

Shelley, B. (2015). Social media use and participation: A meta- analysis of current research. *Information Communication and Society*, *18*(5), 524–538. doi:10.1080/1 369118X.2015.1008542

Slocum, J. W. Jr, Conder, W., Corradini, E., Foster, R., Frazer, R., Lei, D., & Scott, S. et al. (2006). Fermentation in the China Beer Industry. *Organizational Dynamics*, *35*(1), 32–48. doi:10.1016/j.orgdyn.2005.12.002

Snow, D. A., Soule, S. A., & Kriesi, H. (2007). Mapping the Terrain. In D. A. Snow, S. A. Soule, & H. Kriesi (Eds.), *The Blackwell Companion to Social Movements* (pp. 3–16). Malden, MA: Blackwell Publishing. doi:10.1002/9780470999103.ch1

Statista. (2016). Leading countries based on number of Facebook users as of May 2016 (in millions), Retrieved from http://www.statista.com/statistics/268136/top-15-countries-based-on-number-of-facebook-users/

Stearns, P. (2006). *Consumerism in World History: The Global Transformation of Consumer Desire* (2nd ed.). London, New York: Routledge.

Steenkamp, J.-B. E. M., & de Jong, M. G. (2010). A global investigation into the constellation of consumer attitudes toward global and local products. *Journal of Marketing*, *74*(4), 18–40. doi:10.1509/jmkg.74.6.18

Stein, L. (2009). Social Movement Web Use in Theory and Practice: A Content Analysis of US Movement Websites. *New Media & Society*, *11*(5), 749–771. doi:10.1177/1461444809105350

Strizhakova, Y., Coulter, R. A., & Price, L. L. (2011). Branding in a global marketplace: The mediating effects of quality and self-identity brand signals. *International Journal of Research in Marketing*, *28*(4), 342–351. doi:10.1016/j.ijresmar.2011.05.007

Tang, G., & Lee, F. L. F. (2013). Facebook use and political participation: The impact of exposure to shared political information, connections with public political actors, and network structural heterogeneity. *Social Science Computer Review*, *31*(6), 763–773. doi:10.1177/0894439313490625

Tilly, C. (2004). *Social movements: 1768-2004*. Boulder, CO: Paradigm.

Tufekci, Z., & Wilson, C. (2012). Social media and the decision to participate in political protest: Observations from Tahrir Square. *Journal of Communication*, *62*(2), 363–379. doi:10.1111/j.1460-2466.2012.01629.x

Valenzuela, S., Arriagada, A., & Scherman, A. (2012). The social media basis of youth protest behavior: The case of Chile. *Journal of Communication*, *62*(2), 299–314. doi:10.1111/j.1460-2466.2012.01635.x

Veloutsou, C., & Moutinho, L. (2009). Brand relationships through brand reputation and brand tribalism. *Journal of Business Research*, *62*(3), 314–322. doi:10.1016/j.jbusres.2008.05.010

Vitak, J., Zube, P., Smock, A., Carr, C. T., Ellison, N., & Lampe, C. (2011). Its complicated: Facebook users political participation in the 2008 election. *Cyberpsychology, Behavior, and Social Networking*, *14*(3), 107–114. doi:10.1089/cyber.2009.0226 PMID:20649449

We are Social. (2016). 2016 Digital Yearbook. Retrieved from http://wearesocial.com/uk/special-reports/digital-in-2016

Wikipedia. (n. d.). Gezi Park Protests. Retrieved from https://en.wikipedia.org/wiki/Gezi_Park_protests

Wojcieszak, M. (2009). Carrying online participation offline: Mobilization by radical online groups and politically dissimilar offline ties. *Journal of Communication*, *59*(3), 564–586. doi:10.1111/j.1460-2466.2009.01436.x

Yüksel, Ü., & Mirza, M. (2010). Consumers of the postmodern world: Theories of Anti-consumption and impression management. *Marmara Üniversitesi İİBF Dergisi*, *29*(2), 495–512.

Zavestoski, S. (2002). The Social–Psychological Bases of Anticonsumption Attitudes. *Psychology and Marketing*, *19*(2), 149–165. doi:10.1002/mar.10007

KEY TERMS AND DEFINITIONS

Activism: Activities to publicize, direct, and lead change in social, economic, political, or environmental life.

Consumerism: A byproduct of modernism and modern way of living, in which standardization of culture, media, products, ideas and way of living are praised and encouraged.

Emerging Markets: A group of countries that are believed to be developed markets in the future, but does not carry all the characteristics of developed markets at the time being.

Environmentalism: Ideology that is concerned with the continuance and protection of environment, especially non-human elements.

Freeganism: A community of people that believe in limited participation in the conventional economy and minimal consumption of resources.

Human Size Living: Commitment to live in a decentralized, small, and less complex environments.

Modernism: A period in Western culture characterized by three powers as reason, order and science over ignorance, disorder and superstition.

Online Community: Virtual communities, whose interactions happen online.

Postmodernism: A period that welcomes and celebrates individualism, multiplicity of ideas, products and media.

Social Networking: The creation and sharing of information and ideas in online communities accessed via mobile and web-based technologies.

Chapter 10
Free and Open Source Software Movements as Agents of an Alternative Use of Copyright Law

Pedro Pina
Polytechnic Institute of Coimbra, Portugal

ABSTRACT

Digital technology produced a move from a performative model to a player-as producer paradigm since it has potentiated user-generated transformative uses of intellectual works. In fact, sharing, sampling, remixing and creating new derivative content through digital network collaboration platforms are today pillars of the so-called "age of remix". However, when unauthorized, such activities may constitute copyright infringement since the making available right and the right to make new derivative works are exclusive rights granted by copyright law. A restrictive exercise of exclusive rights may hinder the implementation of online platforms envisioned to facilitate access to knowledge and to potentiate the creation of new works. The present chapter analyzes the creation the importance of online communities of practice using free/open source software licenses like GNU GPL or Creative Commons Licenses as agents of an alternative and less rigid exercise of the powers granted by copyright law in favor of a freer system of creation and dissemination of creative works in the digital world.

DOI: 10.4018/978-1-5225-2495-3.ch010

INTRODUCTION

In recent years, online creative communities have been reaching a high level of economic and cultural significance. Copyrightable, content-oriented, peer and mass collaboration initiatives have proliferated as free and open source software (FOSS) online projects. Examples of such projects are Wikipedia, WordPress, Android, Mozilla Firefox, LibreOffice, MySQL, Linux, Suncloud and Flickr. Projects such as these incorporate online organized communities of people sharing the different movements' objectives of freely creating, remixing and disseminating cultural information. With the advent of digital technology, activities like sharing, sampling, mashing-up or creating new derivative content through digital network collaboration platforms became possible, forming the pillars of the so-called "age of remix" (Derecho, 2008; Rostama, 2015). If, in the analog world creating, printing, recording and distributing cultural goods was expensive, consumers of copyrighted works could now abandon a merely passive and consumptive role to effortlessly become content creators, individually or working within an online community seeking free dissemination of knowledge and culture. Digital technology thus facilitated the making of user-generated transformative uses, that is to say "the use of existing expression as an input into the creative process, resulting in the creation of new expression that, while still embodying elements of the original work, is original in its own right" (Suzor, 2006, p. 1). This new Read/Write culture based on acts of producing and recreating previously experienced digital cultural goods (Lessig, 2008, 28) reflects the move from a performative model to a player-as-producer paradigm (Salen and Zimerman, 2004), where the creation and the diversity of cultural goods are promoted and access to knowledge and to information is democratized.

However, when unauthorized, such activities may constitute copyright infringement. In fact, the rights to make new derivative works and to make them available in the internet are exclusive rights granted by copyright law to rightholders, excluding others from it without proper authorization and, normally, remuneration, whether the use is mere consumptive or creative. A restrictive exercise of exclusive rights may hinder the implementation of online platforms envisioned to facilitate access to knowledge and to potentiate the creation of new works.

Projects like the ones mentioned above are based on the openness for the collaboration of members of the online community who wish to contribute with their knowledge, effort and creative expression over preexistent digital works without copyright restrictions. Because copyright may work as an instrument to lock-up creative information, lawful licensing schemes had to be created so that FOSS movements could keep their *ethos* of openness.

The present chapter analyses the traditional exercise of the powers traditionally granted by copyright law as an instrument to lock-up creative information, the existence of FOSS collaborative projects as online communities of practice, the adoption of specific licensing schemes and their role as agents of an alternative use of the exclusive powers granted by copyright in favor of a freer system of creation and dissemination of works with creative content in the digital world.

COPYRIGHT AS AN INSTRUMENT TO LOCK-UP DIGITAL CREATIVE CONTENT

Without proper authorization from copyright holders, operations like sharing, making available to the public or remixing works may conflict with core powers granted by copyright law, namely the exclusive patrimonial rights to reproduce, to distribute or to communicate their works to the public or to authorize such usages by others. From the rightholders' perspective, an unregulated internet allows a vast amount of digital creative content to escape from their *de facto* control. In the digital environment, copyrighted works may easily be downloaded, uploaded and disseminated throughout the internet without previous authorization and the payment of remuneration to rightholders, thus decreasing the incentive to create. For that reason, in the continuous task of adapting copyright laws to the digital environment, the European Commission, for instance, declared in the Green Paper on Copyright in the Knowledge Economy that

A high level of copyright protection is crucial for intellectual creation. Copyright ensures the maintenance and development of creativity in the interests of authors, producers, consumers and the public at large. A rigorous and effective system for the protection of copyright and related rights is necessary to provide authors and producers with a reward for their creative efforts and to encourage producers and publishers to invest in creative works (Commission of the European Communities, 2008, p. 4).

Despite the differences, legislators around the world tended to adapt copyright laws to the digital environment by importing the core of exclusive rights foreseen that were foreseen for the analog world. Moreover, new forms of exploitation rights were created by granting the novel exclusive right to make the work available to the public by digital means. Specifically, USA law officially recognized that such new right was covered by the exclusive rights of distribution, of public performance and of public display foreseen under Section 106 (3, 4, 6) of the Copyright Act (U.S.C.) (United States Copyright Office, 2016, p. 4). In the European Union, the referred novel right was introduced by article 3 of Directive 2001/29/EC of the European Parliament and of the Council of 22 May 2001 on the harmonization of certain aspects of copyright and related rights in the information society (Infosoc Directive). According to recital 24 of the mentioned Directive, the making-available right covers "all acts of making available such subject-matter to members of the public not present at the place where the act of making available originates, and as not covering any other acts".

Still, the mere legal provision of exclusive rights in the digital world was insufficient for the protection of rightholders' interests. Considering the empirical possibility of massive and global infringement combined with the inefficiency of legal tools for analog copyright enforcement, the reactive nature of courts and the lack of jurisdictional sovereignty in cases of transnational violations, the mere provision of new digital rights seemed insufficient. Following Clark's seminal statement "the answer to the machine is in the machine" (1996, p. 139), rightholders implemented self-help systems based on technological protection measures (TPM) like encryption, steganography, watermarking or the use of electronic agents like web crawlers or spy-bots able to identify or to impede online infringements and economic losses and, at the same time, to provide them to manage digital rights in their contractual relations with intermediaries and consumers. By combining digital rights management (DRM) systems based on TPM with restrictive end-user license agreements, rightholders were now able to potentially control all the utilizations of digital copyrighted works, including, *inter alia*, access to contents or even to some personal data of the users. The idea of a technological perfect control of digital contents was so robust that, according to Lessig (2006, p. 183), it seemed like the protection of rightholders' interests could dismiss or devalue copyright law's protection, since by combining TPM and contracts, they could unilaterally establish the conditions for end users to access and use protected contents.

Even so, since TPM could be circumvented by software and other technological devices, the information and communication technologies (ICT) industry started lobbying for the enactment of new laws internalizing and recognizing self-help digital systems side by side with substantive copyright (Pina, 2015, p. 54).

Several international treaties and digital copyright national laws – from the Agreement on Trade Related Aspects of Intellectual Property Rights (TRIPS) or the World Intellectual Property Organization (WIPO) Copyright Treaty and the WIPO Performances and Phonograms Treaty, at the international level, to the Digital Millennium Copyright Act (DMCA), in the USA, or the InfoSoc Directive in the European Union, followed by subsequent transpositions into member state laws – posited a legal-technological approach for the protection of creative expression. It was now officially recognized that the use of TPM was a lawful means that rightholders could use to manage their digital rights and that circumvention acts and the creation or dissemination of circumvention devices were forbidden and punished as criminal offenses.

The referred provisions on TPM and DRM regard more the enforcement question than the substance of copyright itself. For that reason, it is more correct to denominate them as paracopyright (Jaszi, 1988) or übercopyright (Helberger & Hugenholtz, 2007) provisions. Disregarding the conceptual question, it is safe to conclude that, considering the legal protection of TPM and DRM, rightholders have now more rights than the ones foreseen in the analog world. In fact, in the digital environment rightholders are entitled to three different and cumulative levels of protection: firstly, the legal protection by copyright; secondly, the technical protection of works through measures protection techniques, and, finally, the paracopyright protection against circumvention of TPM (Werra, 2001, p. 77).

Beyond mere consumption of protected works, amongst the uses of a copyrighted work that are reserved to rightholders there is one that specifically contends with the possibility of making transformative uses of a work: the exclusive right to create derivative works. A derivative work is a secondary work, *i.e.*, a work based upon a preexisting one. Nevertheless, it has to differ from the first work, since it must contain a substantial amount of innovative and creative material. Only with such characteristics can the derivative work be considered original and not a mere reproduction with minor changes. Translations, sequels, prequels, spin-off, adaptations of literary works to cinema and upgraded or updated versions of software are good examples of derivative works.

Article 2, no. 3, of the Berne Convention, protects derivative works as original works without prejudice to the copyright in the original work. Despite of the fact that a derivative work has an original content, the preexistent base is reserved for its author's future exploitation as the holder has the moral right to claim authorship of the work and to object to any distortion, mutilation or other modification of, or other derogatory action in relation to, the said work, which would be prejudicial to his honor or reputation (article 6bis (1) of the Berne Convention).

Article 12 of the Berne Convention states that "authors of literary or artistic works shall enjoy the exclusive right of authorizing adaptations, arrangements and other alterations of their works." This means that third parties are excluded from the possibility of creating derivative works without the rightholders' permission.

Before the digital era, copyright laws foresaw rules internalizing a reasonable balance between holders' and users' interests as some relevant limitations to the powers granted to the formers were recognized. After adaptation to the digital realm, limitations continued to be foreseen, but in narrower terms.

Respecting the Berne Convention, copyright laws usually foresee objective limitations, defining copyright itself, as protection is only granted to the original exteriorization of one idea, not to the idea itself – the idea-expression dichotomy.

Temporal limitations are also normally predicted, as copyright laws consider that copyright protection is time-bounded and that, exceeding its term, the work enters into the public domain. Moreover, habitually, copyright acts also preview exemptions or limitations on exclusive rights, allowing free usages of copyrighted works. That is the case of fair use or fair dealing in common law copyright systems or, in the continental European systems, the statutory exemptions expressly listed in legal instruments, combined with the *infra* described three-step test rule for states to create exemptions foreseen in the Berne Convention for the Protection of Literary and Artistic Works (BC).

The fair use doctrine is foreseen at 17 U.S.C. § 107 as a general clause previewing limitations on holders' rights for purposes such as criticism, comment, news reporting, teaching (including multiple copies for classroom use), scholarship, or research. When determining if a use is fair, some factors must be considered, such as the purpose and character of the use, namely if such use is of a commercial nature or is for nonprofit educational purposes; the nature of the copyrighted work; the amount and substantiality of the portion used in relation to the copyrighted work as a whole; and the effect of the use upon the potential market for or value of the copyrighted work. Considering that the rationale of both the fair use general clause and copyright law itself is to promote creation, diversity and culture, the US Supreme Court, following a seminal article of Judge Leval (1990), when deciding the Campbell v. Acuff-Rose Music case, has considered that transformative uses may, in some cases, not infringe copyright law. To conclude that a transformative use does not infringe copyright on the previous work,

[T]he use must be productive and must employ the quoted matter in a different manner or for a different purpose from the original. A quotation of copyrighted material that merely repackages or republishes the original is unlikely to pass the test. [...] If, on the other hand, the secondary use adds value to the original -if the quoted matter is used as raw material, transformed in the creation of new information, new aesthetics, new insights and understandings - this is the very type of activity that the fair use doctrine intends to protect for the enrichment of society. Transformative uses may include criticizing the quoted work, exposing the character of the original author, proving a fact, or summarizing an idea argued in the original in order to defend or rebut it. They also may include parody, symbolism, aesthetic declarations, and innumerable other uses (Leval, 1990, p. 1111).

The fair use defense, although elastic, is, therefore, appreciated after the alleged infringement, as the judgment on the extension and the substantiality of the original work's portion that is used can only be made on casuistic terms. As a result, "the economic risk inherent in relying on the doctrine — not to mention the up-front costs of defending a lawsuit or seeking a declaratory judgment" (Hayes, 2008, p. 569), is increased, reducing certainty and security over the legality of the transformative use.

In contrast, the European Union, article 5, no. 2, of the Directive 2001/29/EC of the European Parliament and of the Council of 22 May 2001 on the harmonization of certain aspects of copyright and related rights in the information society (InfoSoc Directive), prescribes a list of mandatory exceptions to the exclusive rights of reproduction, of communication to the public of works and of making the work available to the public that are basically regarded to educational or scientific purposes, but that also includes "reproductions on any medium made by a natural person for private use and for ends that are neither directly nor indirectly commercial, on condition that the rightholders receive fair compensation".

Subsequently, the InfoSoc Directive lists in Article 5, no. 3, some facultative exceptions including the "use for the purpose of caricature, parody or pastiche". However, after setting the above mentioned exhaustive list of exceptions and narrowing the field of their application, the InfoSoc Directive foresees the existence of limits on the recognition of limitations, since the latter shall only be applied in certain special cases which do not conflict with a normal exploitation of the work or other subject-matter and do not unreasonably harm the legitimate interests of the right´s holder. In other words, the InfoSoc Directive enacts that limitations must respect this three-step test, when, in its original sense, predicted in the Berne Convention, it was only a sort of general clause for member States to respect when foreseeing internal limitations on exclusive rights. The European Union's two-levelled filter of copyright's internal limitations on exclusive rights leaves short space for users to create transformative works without the holder's authorization.

Exclusive rights granted by copyright laws, strengthened and combined with TPM and contractual arrangements, have thus legally become an instrument to lock-up creative, cultural and scientific digital information. The internal balance that traditionally characterized copyright provisions was lost to the detriment of the public interest in accessing and in disseminating creative information. The referred proprietary mechanism ineluctably affects the practice of sharing knowledge online as, without the authorization of rightholders, almost every activity may be considered copyright infringement.

A COUNTER-HEGEMONIC USE OF THE EXCLUSIVE RIGHTS GRANTED BY COPYRIGHT LAW

The most relevant opposition movement to the proprietary model established by the combination of copyright law and contractual restrictive arrangements related to intellectual creations has emerged from the software developers' community.

There is a strong international tendency to recognize that software may be protected under copyright law or under a *sui generis* right that lies between copyright and patent law protection. The reason for such kind of legal protection relied in the fact that software could be compared to literary works, since the developer expressed its ideas through a specific code or language. However, unlike traditional literary works, such as novels or articles, where the code/language is immediately perceived by the reader, software has an own specific code, the source code, written in a program language, that the author may choose not to provide to the user. Algorithms, principles and concepts behind software are usually not disclosed to the end-users of the software, since the source code for closed source software is almost never provided to the end-users without heavy confidentiality protection.

However, in the early days of software development, a culture of sharing was embraced by almost all programmers. The idea was to make a program's source code available for others to improve it, fix it or adapt it. Prior to the advent of the personal computer in the 1980's, the market was hardware-driven. Only after software started to be commercialized separately, gaining autonomous importance and value, did companies impose non-disclosure agreements to programmers, restricting the possibilities of revealing source code. As Chang points out, "commercial remunerations tempted programmers to sell their software to companies who in turn guarded their intellectual property jealously" (2005, p. 22). More than a matter of ownership, proprietary software is, therefore, software for which access to the source code is not provided. Such action precludes the possibilities of transforming or improving the software in benefit of the community since, without rightholders' agreement, such acts may constitute copyright infringement even in the cases where, beyond the use of the copyrighted preexisting work basis, a strong creative content addition can be found.

As a reaction to the growing trend of non-disclosure of source code, some software developers decided that a new software sharing community had to be created so that everyone interested could cooperate with others to freely write, re-write, adapt or improve software. The term "freely" here does not mean free of charge but rather that everyone should be able to access to the source code and that no authorization should be needed to make new transformative uses.

The Free software (FS) movement, supported by the Free Software Foundation FSF, founded by Richard Stallman, supports the objective that the user must have the freedom to run, copy, distribute, study, change and improve the software. Stallman and the FSF developed the GNU Project, an operating system with open code, as a response to AT&T's restrictive Unix software licensing terms. Actually, GNU is the recursive acronym for GNU is Not Unix. Subsequently, Stallman and the FSF created a special license, the GNU General Public License (GNU GPL) which intends to guarantee the program's users freedoms to run the program, for any purpose (freedom 0); to study how the program works, and change it to make it do what the users wish (freedom 1); to redistribute copies (freedom 2); and to distribute copies of modified versions to others (freedom 3).

After announcing the software users' essential freedoms, the GNU GPL imposes on ulterior developers a moment of freedom restraint, which is considered absolutely necessary to safeguard the referred freedoms. Specifically, it prohibits the user/new creator, when modifying and distributing previously-licensed FS works, to license its derivative work in proprietary terms, obliging him/her to license it in FS terms. For that reason, this licensing scheme is foreseen to be viral in effect and to expand through derivative creation and dissemination of new works. According to the GNU GPL, commercial uses are not forbidden, since "free" is a matter of liberty and not a question of pecuniary cost.

Although GNU GPL withdraws several exclusive powers granted by copyright law, it is not correct to say that free software is not copyrighted or that it has entered the public domain. In fact, the terms of the GNU GPL license remain within copyright law and need to be enforceable, as the exclusive power to control the uses of copyrights works is still exercised by their holders. The originality of the GNU GPL is that the FS licensors don't exercise the powers granted by copyright law in the traditional proprietary way, making a "counter-hegemonic use of law" (Santos, 2005). The GNU GPL doesn't enclose the creative information: on the contrary, it uses its legal powers to authorize third parties' usage of works in terms that protect and ensure freedom of adaptation, distribution and transformative creation. The expression "copyleft", commonly used to identify FS, must be interpreted in the referred way as it classifies a reality that lies halfway between the traditional exercise of powers granted by copyright and the public domain.

One other major movement that fights against the restrictions that traditional exercise of copyright brings to creative expression is the open source software (OSS) movement, led, among others, by Creative Commons (CC). This non-profit organization created and released several OSS licenses, known as CC licenses, that cover a wide range of possible uses of the protected work and may be combined with others. The less restrictive license is the Attribution license, since it allows licensees to copy, distribute, display and perform the work and make derivative works and remixes based on it if they give the author or licensor the credits in the manner specified by the license. According to the Share-alike CC License, which presents great similitudes with GNU GPL, licensees may distribute derivative works only under a license identical to the license that governs the original work.

In the case of CC Non-commercial license, licensees may copy, distribute, display, and perform the work and make derivative works and remixes based on it only for non-commercial purposes. The licensor may prohibit transformative uses of works if he/she opts for the CC No derivative works license, according to which licensees may copy, distribute, display and perform only verbatim copies of the work, not derivative works and remixes based on it.

The combination of the Attribution, the Non-commercial and the No derivative license creates the more restrictive license, which is not considered copyleft by the FSF not only because derivative works are forbidden but also because they do not obligate the licensee to distribute derivative works under the same license.

Exclusively from a transformative use point of view, the most restrictive CC licenses are very similar to the traditional exercise of copyright law, as they don't allow the user to modify the work. For that reason, as some CC licenses don't respect social norms of the remix culture, the FSF doesn´t recognize all of them as copyleft. Contrarily, the most permissive licenses promote and impose freedom of use and of re-use as they pass it along to successive users with the faculty of making transformative uses.

As exposed supra, FS and OSS are still in copyright's orbit since they correspond to a certain kind of exercise of the exclusive powers granted by copyright law and need it to be in its orbit to be enforceable. The way software developers license, *i.e.,* in a more permissive or in a more restrictive way, is consistent to the alienable exclusive powers copyright law grants them. Nevertheless, from a potential creator of derivative works point of view, FS and OSS licenses like the ones mentioned give the developer a degree of certainty: if he/she has modified a copyleft licensed work, whether it is licensed under GNU GPL, under CC attribution license or another compatible one, he/she knows that, beyond distribution, transformative use is allowed. On the contrary, if a developer reverse engineers, decompiles the code, changes and adapts proprietary software without proper authorization, he/she will be most certainly committing copyright infringement even if, beyond the use of the copyrighted preexisting work basis there is still a strong creative content addition.

FS and OSS, like GNU GPL and CC licenses, may be considered legal instruments to ensure the creation and dissemination of intellectual works through free remixtures and transformative uses. However, by itself, the mere provision of the licenses does not assure the existence of online communities of sharing and remixing. The proliferation of online communities is at the core of every FOSS project and is vital for the success of the FOSS movement towards a more flexible copyright law that promotes remixture culture. However, FS and OSS licenses will only have a significant role in the copyright field if effectively adopted by online communities of practice stressing the traditional exercise of exclusive rights.

FOSS ONLINE COMMUNITIES OF PRACTICE

Virtual communities may be defined as "social aggregations that emerge from the Net when enough people carry on those public discussions long enough, with sufficient human feeling, to form webs of personal relationships in cyberspace" (Rheingold, 1993) or as "a group of people to whom interactions and communications via computer play an important role in creating and maintaining significant social relations" (Tardini & Cantoni, 2005, p. 373). Such broad definitions cover the heterogeneity of members' interests and qualities that are essential to building a community. Two major types of communities may be differentiated: cultural communities and communities of practice. Cultural communities "originate from the communal common ground of their members, i.e. on the encyclopedic knowledge of the communities [that] members belong to" (Tardini & Cantoni, 2005, p. 372). Communities of practice may be defined as "groups of people who share a concern, a set of problems, or a passion about a topic, and who deepen their knowledge and expertise in this area by interacting on an ongoing basis" (Wenger et al., 2002, p. 4). Since communities of practice are based on collaboration and sharing between newcomers and senior actors, they are characterized by three essential features: a mutual engagement, a joint enterprise, and a shared repertoire (Wenger, 1998, pp. 73-82). In fact, communities of practice are related to a process of social learning that occurs when people with common interests in some subject or problem collaborate over an extended period to share ideas, find solutions, and build innovations (Toral, Barrero & Martinez-Torres, 2009). Communities of practice do not have to be formal structures, although they me be potentiated by existing ones. In fact, according to Wenger & Snyder (2000), such a community works informally, as it "may or may not have an explicit agenda on a given week, and even if it does, it may not follow the agenda closely. Inevitably, however, people in communities of practice share their experiences and knowledge in free-flowing, creative ways that foster new approaches to problems".

FOSS communities may be characterized as virtual communities of practice. In fact, their members jointly collaborate for the creation and the dissemination of new creative works in a way that appoints to a less restrictive and more flexible copyright law. Works licensed under FOSS licenses are, therefore, freely shared by the members of the communities for purposes of mere consumption or for future development by other members. Within the community and under FOSS licenses, creation is meant or open to be collective and works are made to be shared and freely transformed.

The use of open and collaborative community-based knowledge development structures under FOSS licenses goes beyond the confines of a single firm or an individual labor. As in other virtual communities, the network form of organization

(Powell, 1990) and the collaborative innovation model followed by FOSS communities are in opposition to a centralized model of knowledge production which "needed to be built like cathedrals, carefully crafted by individual wizards or small bands of mages working in splendid isolation, with no beta to be released before its time" (Raymond, 2001, p. 21).

From hobbyists seeking fun and enjoyment to need-driven individuals or even firms motivated by the need for software-related changes, alterations or assistance (Shah, 2006), online FOSS communities integrate a heterogeneous group of participants. Whether motivated by future commercial advantages or by mere recognition for the altruistic contribution (Lerner & Tirole, 2002), participants share common ethics related to freedom of information, creation and dissemination of knowledge without the restrictions of proprietary exercise of exclusive rights granted by copyright law. The recognition of the freedom to share, to remix or to sample necessarily involved a collective consciousness of the limits of (the classical exercise of) copyright law by individuals with the referred common goals (like the community of software programmers) and the need for a growing common response.

Such communities were, in their origins, formed only or mainly by software programmers using online platforms to share and to improve their works. Software programmers collectively created a social online network which is at the same time a product and a facilitator of the collective action regarding the dissemination of works and the freedom to create. Furthermore, as facilitators, social and digital media allowed the collectivization of actions by many individuals who shared the objectives of the online communities to which they belonged and the open source movement in general.

One of the best examples of a FOSS online community is the Linux community. Linux is one of the most disseminated computer operating systems in the world. Linux was created by the original effort and labor of Linus Torvalds. Its kernel is licensed under the GNU GPL, version 2, which foresees that anyone who commercially or non-commercially distributes software based on source code under the referred license must make the source code and eventual modifications available to the recipient under the same terms. Because of the terms of the license, programmers started developing Linux distributions, like Ubuntu, Suse, Debian or Fedora for computers and for Android and Firefox OS for smart devices. All the referred Linux-based distributions are developed from the original source code and, as FOSS projects, are a result of the collaboration of the members of the community who are able to freely download the source code when interested in improving the program.

The success of the referred projects is manifest. For example, according to data from the International Data Corporation (2016), in 2015 Android dominated the market with an 82.8% share of mobile devices, and proprietary software like iOS and Windows Phone had only 13.9% and 2.6%, respectively.

Going beyond the software field, the elasticity of open source licenses permitted their exportation to other kinds of intellectual creation in the field of music, literature, films, etc. Wikipedia, for instance, is, according to the information given in its own website "a multilingual, web-based, free-content encyclopedia project supported by the Wikimedia Foundation and based on a model of openly editable content" (2016a) with more than 38 million articles written by about 70,000 editors. Wikipedia "is free content that anyone can use, edit, and distribute: Since all editors freely license their work to the public, no editor owns an article and any contributions can and will be mercilessly edited and redistributed. Respect copyright laws, and never plagiarize from sources. Borrowing non-free media is sometimes allowed as fair use, but strive to find free alternatives first" (2016b).

In the field of photographic creations, Flickr, a popular photo hosting and sharing website, has a prominent role. It offers several licensing possibilities, from traditional copyright "all rights reserved" to differentiated CC licenses, from the more to the less restrictive. According to data provided by Flickr (2016), in December 2016, 67,120,562 photos were shared under a CC attribution license, 50,648,373 photos under a CC Attribution + Noncommercial license, and 98,881,671 photos under a CC Attribution + Noncommercial + Share-alike license.

Record labels and websites distributing free music under FOSS licenses like Jamendo, Audition Records, Dogmazic and Soundcloud have proliferated. Video hosting and sharing online platforms like Vimeo and YouTube encourage people to contribute to the community with their personal creations and to share it, allowing users to mark the videos with CC licenses in order to facilitate the proliferation of art and culture through sharing.

In brief, FOSS online communities are now widespread, demonstrating how the production of knowledge and culture has become democratized and is no longer dependent on firms or state subventions.

CONCLUSION

Copyright law is an heir of an analog era. Nevertheless, the tension between copyright and technology is a constant in history since technology has always been an essential element for copyright regulation. In fact, considering that copyright regards the protection of intellectual aesthetic creations, *i.e.*, immaterial goods, their externalization needs the mediation of a physical support which is the element that may transform and evolve according to the available technology. The referred considerations are the basis for the well-known Kantian dichotomy between *corpus mysticum* and *corpus mechanicum* (Kant, 1996, pp. 437-438), regarding the copyrighted creative and immaterial expression that is revealed by the *corpus mechanicum* that technology permits, like printed books, audio or video cassette, cd's, DVDs, etc. Although intellectual creation derives from being human, in the pre-digital era its externalization in a physical support and ulterior distribution was expensive and needed huge resources only available to industry. Copyright was, amongst other purposes, an instrument of protection again free-riders who commercialized copies of works without having to make expensive investments. For that reason, the consumer was practically absent from copyright law.

Digital technology brought the possibility of experiencing works without a corporeal fixation, reduced the need of physical objects to experience copyrighted works, and has favored an enormous flow of intangible information, including copyrighted content. It has become very cheap to create, to remix and to distribute digital works. Business models created for the analog world and legal instruments for its protection, like copyright law, were stressed by the brave new decentralized world brought by digital technology. Knowledge and culture production dispersed worldwide and became democratized. Law didn´t keep pace, as it merely adapted old concepts of the analog world related to strong exclusive rights in favor of industry, which flourished within the old business model and was able to restrict disclosure of source code so as to hinder interoperability and avoid competition from traditional industrial competitors and creative users. Restricting creative transformation permitted by digital technology, copyright law treated consumers like potential infringers, allowing rightholders to slow down the process of a broader access to knowledge and cultural creations. FOSS movements, operating with FOSS licenses, constitute community-based forms of reaction to the rigidity of the exercise of copyright law by the copyright industries. The proliferation of FOSS community-based projects exposed how the traditional exercise of exclusive powers granted by copyright law were maladjusted to the needs of collaborating collective creators searching for free access and sharing of knowledge and culture. From communities to market, several agents opted to support FOSS projects even for commercial purposes. IBM, for instance, has committed to FOSS with contributions to more than 120 projects, including more than 1 billion USD in Linux development; Google leads the Android project; even Microsoft opened itself to FOSS collaboration, promoting the building of communities for projects like Azure, an Open Cloud service, and Chakra JavaScript. Such behaviors reveal that a move toward a freer access to culture and knowledge is compatible with commercial exploitation and not necessarily copyright infringement. Curiously, as exposed above, the instruments to combat the excessive rigidity of copyright law by FOSS communities were licenses that constitute an alternative exercise of the exclusive powers prescribed by the same copyright law.

REFERENCES

Chang, S. S. (2005). Copyright and Open Source Software Licensing. Bepress Legal Series. Working Paper 773. Retrieved from http://law.bepress.com/expresso/eps/773

Commission of the European Communities. (2008). *Green Paper. Copyright in the Knowledge Economy.* Retrieved from http://ec.europa.eu/internal_market/copyright/docs/copyright--infso/greenpaper_en.pdf

Derecho, A. (2008). *Illegitimate Media: Race, Gender and Censorship in Digital Remix Culture. Northwestern University. Comparative Literary Studies.* Evanston: ProQuest.

Flickr (2016). Creative Commons. Retrieved from https://www.flickr.com/creativecommons/

Helberger, N., & Hugenholtz, P. B. (2007). No place like home for making a copy: Private copying in European copyright law and consumer law. *Berkeley Technology Law Journal, 22,* 1061–1098.

International Data Corporation. (2016). Smartphone OS Market Share, 2015 Q2. Retrieved from http://www.idc.com/prodserv/smartphone-os-market-share.jsp

Jaszi, P. (1998). Intellectual property legislative update: Copyright, paracopyright, and pseudocopyright. *Paper presented at the Association of Research Libraries Conference: The Future Network: Transforming Learning and Scholarship,* Eugene, OR. Retrieved from http://old.arl.org/resources/pubs/mmproceedings/132mmjaszi~print.shtml

Kant, I. (1996). The Metaphysics of Morals. In *Practical Philosophy* (M.J. Gregor, Trans.). Cambridge University Press.

Lerner, J., & Tirole, J. (2002). Some simple economics of open source. *Journal of Industrial Economics, 50*(2), 197.

Lessig, L. (2006). *Code 2.0.* New York: Basic Books.

Lessig, L. (2008). *Remix: making art and commerce thrive in the hybrid economy.* New York: Penguin Press. doi:10.5040/9781849662505

Pina, P. (2015). File-Sharing of Copyrighted Works, P2P, and the Cloud: Reconciling Copyright and Privacy Rights. In M. Gupta (Ed.), Handbook of Research on Emerging Developments in Data Privacy (pp. 52-69). Hershey, PA: IGI Global.

Powell, W. W. (1990). Neither market nor hierarchy: Network forms of organization. *Research in Organizational Behavior, 12,* 295–336.

Raymond, E. S. (2001). *The cathedral and the bazaar: Musings on Linux and Open Source by an accidental revolutionary*. Sebastopol, CA: O'Reilly.

Rheingold, H. (2000). *The Virtual Community*. Retrieved from http://www.rheingold.com/vc/book/intro.html

Rostama, G. (2015). Remix Culture and Amateur Creativity: A Copyright Dilemma. *WIPO*. Retrieved from http://www.wipo.int/wipo_magazine/en/2015/03/article_0006.html

Salen, K., & Zimmerman, E. (2004). *Rules of Play – Game Design Fundamentals*. Massachusetts Institute of Technology.

Santos, B. S. (2005). The counter-hegemonic use of law in the struggle for a globalization from below. *Anales de la Cátedra Francisco Suarez, Revista de Filosofía Jurídica y Política*, *39*, 363-474. Retrieved from http://revistaseug.ugr.es/index.php/acfs/article/viewFile/1035/1225

Shah, S. K. (2006). Motivation, governance, and the viability of hybrid forms in open source software development. *Management Science*, *52*(7), 1000–1014. doi:10.1287/mnsc.1060.0553

Suzor, N. (2006). *Transformative Use of Copyright Material* [LLM Thesis]. QUT School of Law. Retrieved from http://nic.suzor.com/articles/TransformativeUse.pdf

Tardini, S., & Cantoni, L. (2005). A semiotic approach to online communities: belonging, interest and identity in websites' and videogames' communities. In P. Isaías, P. Commers, & M. McPherson (Eds.), *e-Society 2005, Proceedings of the IADIS International Conference, Qawra, Malta, International association for development of the information society* (pp. 371-378).

United States Copyright Office. (2016). *The Making Available Right in the United States*. Retrieved from http://copyright.gov/docs/making_available/making-available-right.pdf

Wenger, E. (1998). *Communities of practice. Learning, meaning and identity*. Cambridge: Cambridge University Press. doi:10.1017/CBO9780511803932

Wenger, E., McDermott, R. A., & Snyder, W. (2002). Cultivating communities of practice. Boston, MA: Harvard Business School Press.

Wenger, E., & Snyder, W. (2000). Communities of practice: The organizational frontier. *Harvard Business Review*, *78*(1), 139–144. PMID:11184968

Werra, J. (2001). Le régime juridique des mesures techniques de protection des oeuvres selon les Traités de l'OMPI, le Digital Millennium Copyright Act, les Directives Européennes et d'autres legislations (Japon, Australie). *Revue Internationale du Droit d'Auteur, 189*, 66–213.

Wikipedia. (2016a). *About.* Retrieved from https://en.wikipedia.org/wiki/Wikipedia:About

Wikipedia. (2016b). *Five pillars.* Retrieved from https://en.wikipedia.org/wiki/Wikipedia:Five_pillars

KEY TERMS AND DEFINITIONS

Community of Practice: Groups of active practitioners who share common concerns, sets of problems, or a passion about a topic, and who deepen their knowledge and expertise in this area by interacting on an ongoing basis.

Copyleft: A non-proprietary way of exercising copyright law's exclusive rights safeguarding the right to freely use, modify, copy, and share copyrighted works on the condition that the referred rights shall be granted to all subsequent users or owners.

Derivative Work: A secondary work, in the sense that it is based upon a preexisting original work, but differing from it, in view of the fact that it must contain a substantial amount of innovative and original material so that it can be considered original and not a mere reproduction with minor changes.

Distribution (Right of): The exclusive right of a copyright owner to distribute copies of the original work to the public by sale, lease, or rental, physically or by wire or wireless means.

Free/Open Source Software (FOSS): A software for which access to the source code is provided and, in principle, users are allowed to freely run the program for any purpose, modify the program as they want, and also to freely distribute copies of either the original version or their own modified version.

Limitations on Copyright: A set of free uses of copyrighted works that escape rightholder's control, mainly because of public interests related to research, study, freedom of speech or the respect for privacy rights.

Proprietary Software: A software for which access to the source code is not provided, precluding the possibilities of transforming or improving it without rightholder's authorization.

Remix: An intellectual work which results from the alteration of a previous original work by adding, removing or changing elements of the item.

Reproduction (Right of): The exclusive right of a copyright owner to make copies of the original work.

Transformative Use: The use of existing expression as an input into the creative process, resulting in the creation of new expression that, while still embodying elements of the original work, is original in its own right.

Chapter 11
A Social Influence Perspective on Uses of Online Football Forums:
The Case with Turkish Football Fans

Anıl Sayan
Istanbul Bilgi University, Turkey

Itır Erhart
Istanbul Bilgi University, Turkey

Vehbi Gorgulu
Istanbul Bilgi University, Turkey

Yonca Aslanbay
Istanbul Bilgi University, Turkey

ABSTRACT

This study aims to shed light on Turkish football forum users on the Internet from a social identity and uses and gratifications (U&G) perspective in order to reveal joint intentions among football fans online. The research model of the current study applies a uses and gratifications approach to examine whether fan motivations while using online football forums determine we-intentions among forum members. Social influence processes are also essential in the context of research on online forums, since they determine changes in attitudes and actions produced by the virtual social influence that may occur at different levels. Findings reveal uses and gratifications of football forum participation as maintaining interpersonal interconnectivity, generating entertainment and purposive value along with affective social identity construct determined we-intention among forum users.

DOI: 10.4018/978-1-5225-2495-3.ch011

INTRODUCTION

New media technologies extend the limits of cultural fluidity and groupings by providing multifaceted digital platforms, such as online petitions, blogs, forums and other social media, that enable civic participation and engagement. Communities of interest, whether they exist online or offline, can use these platforms to engage in civic issues (Smith, 2013). Online sports fan groups are examples of communities that employ new media technologies increasingly for civic participation. As Yang (2009) reveals, online communities utilize different digital spaces for various civic aims in contemporary societies. Hence, online communities and the online spheres in which they exist, are critical factors to consider when analyzing civic engagement and participation in an era marked by intense uses of new information and communication technologies (ICTs).

Sports fans are social agents who exist in various social networks and contribute to the online social world with their unique individual and collective practices. For instance, politically oriented football fan groups in Turkey, such as çArşı, have used technological means to affect Turkey's mainstream political agenda with their social actions (McManus, 2013). From a similar perspective, Erhart (2014) shows how football fans in Turkey were politicized in protests at Istanbul's Gezi Park and organized using various digital tools such as Twitter. These examples show that online fan groups are important not only for their commitment to sports clubs, but also because they can act as agents of social change. This situation is consistent with the fundamental aim of this study, which is to explore the underlying motivations of Turkish football fans for utilizing online forums as means of social change and civic participation.

This study aims to shed light on Turkish football forum users on the Internet from the perspectives of social identity and uses and gratifications (U&G) to reveal joint intentions among football fans online. In the context of forum use, previous research has explored motivations triggering football fans to get involved in joint interactions for various team-specific and football-related purposes. These studies reveal that forums are useful platforms for gathering fans to discuss issues related to the football teams they support (Natelli, 2008; Cook & Hynes, 2013). Previous research also revealed that the construct of "uses and gratifications" is necessary to understand the motivations that drive football fans to get involved in joint interactions through online football discussion forums (Reysen & Branscombe, 2010). Thus, the research model of the current study applies the uses and gratifications construct to explain and examine whether fan motivations while using online football forums determine individual commitment to joint intentions among forum members. Social influence processes are also essential in the context of research on online forums, since they determine changes in attitudes and actions produced by the virtual social influence.

The intensity of Turkey's youth population, nationwide use of social media, and the strong presence of football fanship make Turkey-based online football forums an attractive arena for studying collective actions. Results indicate that football forums are useful platforms to create joint intentions (we-intention) among forum user fans by establishing emotional bonds.

The following section addresses the constructs used to understand online football forums as platforms for collective action. Next, the research methods used for this study are described followed by the results, conclusions, and finally, directions for future study.

ONLINE FOOTBALL FORUMS AS PLATFORMS OF COLLECTIVE ACTION

Online discussion forums can be considered as "web-based software applications used for groups to communicate online" (Wang, 2008). Although online social networks such as Twitter and Facebook challenge online forums in terms of popularity, they are still effective in capturing the attention of football fans. For instance, RedCafe. net, the most popular unofficial Manchester United Football Club Football Fan Forum, has 27,418 members and 16,890,118 forum posts. Bluemoon, another unofficial football forum, established by Manchester City Fans, has 56,334 members and 7,092,835 forum posts. Additionally, 70% of Danish football supporters have accounts on online football discussion forums and Swedish fans send a new post on online football discussion forums every five minutes during a major football tournament (The Social Issues Research Centre, 2008). Furthermore, according to a Pew Research study (Smith, 2013), young American adults perceive discussing issues in online forums as more important than discussions held in offline forums. From a fanship perspective, End (2001) states that fans express their affiliations with sports teams in several ways, including public displays of their fanship on forums or blogs. In the light of the above, online forums should be considered as important spheres of digital communication.

In general, fans use online discussion forums to get involved in football or fan related issues to perform a joint action in practical and virtual manners (Numerato, 2016). Pegoraro (2013) asserts that sports fans use social media to join with other fans and engage in typical sports fanship behavior by taking some traditional sports fan strategies, such as rallies or protests, directly into the digital world. Several Turkish instances exemplify this situation. For instance, Fenerbahce fans organized several street rallies in 2011 and 2012 when the club's five officials, including president Aziz Yıldırım, were jailed on charges of match fixing and setting up an organized crime gang. These rallies and the gatherings outside the court where Yildirim was tried were attended by thousands of fans in their yellow and blue Fenerbahce jerseys who were informed about the details of the trial through online forums like Antu. com. Similarly, on January 15, 2011, a large group of Galatasaray fans protested before the Turkish Prime Minister during the opening ceremony of the new Turk Telekom Arena. After this incident, the outcry caught public interest and remained on the Turkish agenda as the first massive protest against the Prime Minister's state policies. As a continuation of the protests, Alisamiyen.net members also made a public announcement in a popular Turkish daily called *Posta Gazetesi*, regarding reactions of the PM to raise the awareness about the protest. In that sense, football fanship in Turkey remains a unique case worth exploring in the context of social change and civic participation.

The following subsections define each construct of the current study.

Fanship

Anderson (1979) points out the Latin origin of the term "fan" and explains that a fan should be defined as an ardent devotee of sport or an individual with intense enthusiasm for sport. More broadly, the term "fan" is generally linked with those who follow sports (Gantz et al., 2006). Referring to a keen and regular spectator of a professional sport as stated in its first meaning, Reysen and Branscombe (2010) explain it as "as any individual who is an enthusiastic, ardent and loyal admirer of an interest" (p. 117). The concept has attracted considerable scholarly attention (Ghantz et al., 2006), as a majority of research on empirical fan studies investigated motivations, concomitant and post-viewing behaviors for sport viewing self-representation, political participation and activism (Bennet, 2013; Dietz-Uhler, Harrick, End, & Jacquemotte, 2000; Eastman & Land, 1997; Gantz, Wang, Paul, & Potter, 2006; Jenkins & Shretshova, 2012; Kaplan and Langdon, 2012; Numerato, 2015; Reysen & Branscombe, 2010; Click, Lee & Holloway, 2013).

In sports literature, fanship is explained as a key motivation behind the empowerment and generation of passion among sports fans (Grossberg, 1992). Such conceptualizations imply the perceived interests of individuals towards sports emphasizing the multidimensionality of the term on psychological bases. Gantz and Wenner (1995) explain that multidimensional operations of sports fanship indicates the need to go "beyond emotional involvement or identification, carving the concept along a continuum that is made up of cognitive, affective and behavioural components ... as a composite of knowledge, affect and viewership" (p. 59). Reysen and Branscombe (2010) suggest that social identity (Tajfel, 1978) and self-categorization (Turner et al., 1987) can be applied to fan cognition and behavior, as both theories argue that different psychological and social behaviors occur when individuals define themselves as members of a particular group.

Recent studies show that new dimensions, such as political participation, activism and social interests are impinging on the fanship concept. As Jenkins (2012) underlines, fan activism is a sort of politically civic engagement that appears through the fan culture's inner dynamics and exists through the metaphors of popular or participatory culture. For Jenkins and Shresthova (2012), civic engagement and political participation are not independent of the fan culture; on the contrary, they are naturally within the core of fan culture itself. Similarly, Brough and Shresthova (2012) explain that contemporary fans can be understood as the critical actors of civic or political issues. Monaghan (2014) also states that social media tools can enable football fans to politicize around a social issue or shared interest.

We-Intention

The Internet and Internet-based services have potential as alternative venues for collective action Brunsting and Postmes (2002). In this study, our aim is to understand the nature of collective actions in online football discussion forums. Thus, we-intention, underlining the individual commitment in joint intention (Tuomela & Miller, 1988), is taken as the main construct explaining the motivation for football fans to use online forums as a tool of social change. Joint intention, which is conceptualized as we-intention in previous literature, refers to a group of individuals jointly and intentionally sharing a common intended goal (Tuomela & Miller, 1985), invoking commitment to 'imagined communities', through the internalization of the group notion among group members (Tuomela & Miller, 1988). According to Tuomela (1995), joint intention is performing a particular social action jointly or as a group. Hence, "You and I intend to write an article" refers to the case that includes at least two individuals' shared intention and implicit or explicit agreement as a consequence of the social engagement between them. In the context of this study, what is meant by social action is the activities performed together by more than a single forum member. Thus, we-intention can be employed to understand the dynamics of collective activity whose purpose is to mobilize, to act or to communicate ways of reaching an intended goal (Cheung, Chiu, & Lee, 2010).

According to Tuomela (1995), we-intention is defined as performing a particular social action based on shared intention and implicit or explicit agreement as a consequence of the social engagement among the members. Due to the collective nature of user-based Internet services, we-intention is increasingly used to examine dynamics and levels of collective attachments on online social networks. Dholakia, Bagozzi and Pearo (2004) use we-intention, as a mediating factor, to analyze whether group and social identity determine the level of participation in online communities. Cheung, Chiu and Lee (2010) also employ we-intention to explore whether joint intentions in online social networks are determined by uses and gratifications and social influence processes among students. As can be inferred from previous research, adopting the we-intention construct to online social network research does not only supply insights into the nature of online communities, but also proposes a framework to explore patterns of collective action in online environments.

Although both models (Dholakia et al, 2004; Cheung et al, 2010) are conceptually and empirically comprehensive, this study is based on Cheung et al.'s model (2010). While the study of Dholakia et al. (2004) explores consumer communities in general, Cheung et al., (2010) specifically focus on goal-oriented online communities and students as social network users. Findings of Cheung et al. (2010) indicate that factors determining we-intention could be adapted also for other virtual communities including football fans, their collective actions, activities in chat rooms, forums and social networking sites. Thus, online football fanship is assumed to be a group-oriented phenomenon, determined by social influence processes, and uses and gratifications factors.

The following sections aim to define these two groups of constructs as potential variables determining we-intention.

Uses and Gratifications

Uses and gratifications, as a media paradigm, seeks to understand reasons behind the selection process of a medium and why a person uses it (Katz, Blumler & Gurevitch, 1974). The main assumption of the uses and gratifications paradigm is that individuals are goal-oriented in their social practices and aware of their needs in contrast to the classic media approaches in which the audience is considered to be passively exposed to the message. The uses and gratifications paradigm proposes that the audience has a semi-active role in communication and the selection process of a specific medium over alternatives with the purpose of satisfying personal needs (Katz, Blumler & Gurevitch, 1974). Katz, Blumler and Gurevitch (1974) introduced the theory with a comprehensive list of social and psychological needs satisfied through exposure to the mass media.

Several studies have increasingly applied uses and gratifications theory to understand the influence of new media technologies over individuals (Kaye, 1998; Papacharissi & Rubin, 2000; LaRose, Mastro & Eastin, 2004; Chang, Lee, & Kim, 2006). Ruggerio (2000) points out the widespread use of the Internet and explains that its services lie at the locus of new media ecology where the content is easily 'observable, recorded and copied'. The new media technologies, thus, are relevant with the uses and gratifications paradigm since the new media characterize individuals as active and participative on collective bases and pluralist structures (Cheung, Chiu, & Lee, 2011; Dholakia, Bagozzi, & Pearo, 2004; Stafford, Stafford, & Schkade, 2004).

Growing bodies of research also apply the uses and gratification theory to online social network, political participation and civic engagement research (Shah et al. 2001; Kaye & Johnson, 2002; Lin, Salwen & Abdulla, 2005; Tian, 2006; Yu, 2016). For instance; Kaye and Johnson (2002) apply the theory in their study to explore the usage of political information at online platforms. More specifically; Tian (2006) utilizes the uses and gratification theory for analyzing the effects of political use of the Internet at the individual-level and its perceived effects on political life.

Previous research indicates that purposive value, maintaining interpersonal interconnectivity and entertainment value are among key uses and gratification constructs within the context of online communities (Cheung et al., 2010). Purposive value refers to the value "derived from accomplishing some pre-determined informational and instrumental purpose", maintaining interpersonal interconnectivity refers to the social benefits "derived from establishing and maintaining contact with other people such as social support, friendship and intimacy"; while entertainment value refers to "fun and relaxation through playing or otherwise interacting with others" (Cheung et al., 2010, p. 1338).

RQ1: How are different uses and gratifications associated with we-intention in online football team forums?

The Social Influence Processes

Social influence processes are relevant to joint intentions among online communities and can be employed to understand the impact of the "feeling of acceptance" among individuals, while getting involved in collective action (Dholakia et al, 2004; Cheung et al, 2010). Social influence theory mainly raises the question of how social processes affect decision-making. Kelman asserts (1958) that the three social influence processes are composed of subjective norm (compliance), social identity (identification), and group norm (internalization). Each process is associated with one's self-social orientation and shapes the habits of individuals through daily life practices (Kelman, 1958).

The subjective norm as a social influence process refers to the decision making process of an individual, in accordance with the expectations of "significant others". The case of an individual tending to be a part of a community or participating in a collective action through the recommendation of a significant other shows us the importance of significant others' opinions during the decision making process of the individual. In the context of online communities and participation, Cheung et al. (2010) reveal that the subjective norm determined the user's decision to use a particular online social networking site. In a parallel manner, Zhou (2011) shows that the subjective norm has significant effects on Chinese students' participation in online settings. In this study's context, significant others may refer to leading figures of collective action, such as the terrace leaders and/or iconic individuals of the football clubs, who can easily mobilize fans over shared interests via protests, online petitions, etc. (Sayan, 2013).

Social identity refers to the identification process of an individual with a group or another individual through a self-satisfied relationship. Fink, Trail and Anderson (2002) explain that social identity theory can be applied to fan cognitions to examine the team and fan identification of individuals, as it is relevant to the identification of one's self as a group member or an individual (Tajfel, 1978). Social identity has three sub-components, which entail cognitive (an awareness of the self's membership to a particular social group), evaluative (the assessment of self-esteem to a particular social group on the degree of relation) and affective (a sense of emotional attachment to the group with an affective commitment) components (Cheung et al., 2010). Identification requires individual group members to facilitate a progressive relationship with other members. Previous researches also reveal the significance of identification in-group dynamics to form a collective spirit (Shen et al., 2010; Varnali & Gorgulu, 2015). Therefore, components of social identity are essential to take into consideration while analyzing patterns of engagement in collective actions among online fan communities.

Group norm refers to the internalization process of reasonable collective standards. Group norm occurs when the influence of significant others is accepted by one's own value system. Dholakia et al. (2004) explain that group norms are relevant to online community research and add that the surveillance of activity (Toder-Alon, Brunel & Schneier Siegal, 2004) and availability of community interactions (i.e. online forum archives) make it possible for researchers to measure this construct. Cheung et al. (2010) also reveal that internalized group norms by an individual lead to higher level of we-intention in online participation. Within the context of this study, it is assumed that the collective spirit of football fans will lead football fans to higher level of internalization in online collective actions. As underlined by Kelman (1974), individuals who have common or shared goals have more tendency to take action collectively through utilizing group norms.

RQ2: How are different components of social influence processes as subjective norm (compliance), social identity (identification), and group norm (internalization) associated with we-intention on online football team forums?

METHOD

Measures

The model of Cheung et al. (2010) is adapted to the current research to measure the impact of uses and gratifications and social influence processes on we-intention among online football forum members' collective actions. The main contribution of the current study is the adaption of the model to football fans, which is essential to understanding joint intentions among online football fan communities. The structured scales are built on construct items of we-intention, uses and gratifications, subjective norm, group norm, affective social identity, evaluative social identity and cognitive social identity, as used in the original model examining joint intentions among online communities (Cheung et al, 2010). We-intention is measured by a 2-item scale (Cheung et al, 2010), which include items "I intend that (our supporter group) will interact in our online football forum together in the next two weeks" and "We (our supporter group) intend to interact in the online football forum in the next two weeks." Based upon the results of confirmatory factor analysis, 9 items on "purposive value", 3 items on "entertainment value" and 2 items on "maintaining interpersonal interconnectivity" are loaded as in line with the original research model (Cheung et al, 2010). Items that are not loaded on any of the major components in the original model with sufficiently large factor loadings were removed during pre-test, which included 2 items on "self-discovery" and 5 items on "social presence" (Cheung et al, 2010). Items on social influence processes included subjective norm (i.e. "Most people who are important to my life think I will use the online forum of the football team that I support sometime during the next two weeks", group norm (i.e. "I aim to interact together with members of the online football forum I am a member of within the next two weeks" and (affective, evaluative and cognitive) social identity (i.e. "I am a valuable member of the online football forum"). The fanship scale was adapted from the study of Reysen and Branscombe (2010) and included 11 items (i.e. "I would devote all my time to my football team if I could"). All scaled questions were asked through the use of the 6-point Likert scale (1: Totally Disagree, 6: Totally Agree) except for questions on demographics. A cross-sectional design was employed that contains several self-report measures. Reliability estimates were obtained for each of the construct domains. Cronbach's α values range from 0.76 to 0.9 for each construct. The high μ-value of we-intention ($\mu=5.15$) underlines the significance of the construct in explaining online football team forum use.

Procedures and Participants

As a populous country at the crossroads of Europe and Asia, Turkey stands as a unique case where football games offer a characteristic opportunity of engagement over shared values (Talimciler, 2012, Battini, 2012). Therefore, the physical or metaphorical effects of football culture on Turkish society can be observed in most of daily life practices, from daily talks to media consumption and productions habits. For instance, the total number of Galatasaray (GS), Beşiktaş (BJK) and Fenerbahçe (FB) fans composes 82% of the country's population, which exceeds 74 million (TUIK, 2013).

The Turkish football culture, which is deeply diffused into social life, also has phenomenal influence on the traditional media ecology. Sport television programs where former referees, journalists, football players discuss the football issues for hours receive considerable attention from spectators. These programs also compose an important part of the national (and local) channels' weekly line-up. The shows are mostly curated in a belligerent manner, including aggressive and intense discussions before and after the football matches, confronting representatives of rival teams or covering football related scandals (Gorgulu et al., 2015). As opposed to football entertainment and football news shows, belligerent football shows are mostly marked with the high tension felt between hosts through expressions of belligerence and with loud and angry voices. The sport dailies are also mostly based on football or football related occasions.

Football fans also utilize digital tools for experiencing their culture in different virtual spheres. According to the Twitter's yearly statistics of 2015, #fener, #galatasaray, #besiktas and #fenerinmacivar constitute the first five hashtags on Turkey's sports related topics. On match days, the football match related hashtags generally appear on the Twitter's worldwide trending topics. The official Twitter accounts of Galatasaray and Fenerbahçe are ranked as the third and seventh most followed football clubs respectively on Twitter. These sorts of statistics give us some important quantitative insights and they also indicate how the Turkish football fans establish their identity as an absolute majority in digital spaces and how the fan sphere in Turkey offers a unique and dynamic context for various sports studies.

As Facebook and Twitter have globally become the most populated social network sites for anyone's use, online forums are still critical digital tools for online communities in terms of their collective action. Since the early 2000s, the Turkish football fans have been massively using online forums for sharing their ideas, reproducing their ritualistic behaviors, being virtually together or realizing online or offline goal-oriented collective actions[1] (Sayan, 2013).

In the current study, the unofficial football fan forums, which were established by fans, namely, Alisamiyen.net (forum of the football team, Galatasaray), Carsiforum.

Figure 1. A screenshot retrieved from Alisamiyen.net's Home Page

net (forum of the football team, Beşiktaş), and Antu.com (forum of the football team, Fenerbahçe), are analyzed. These forums are solely composed of the leading three's fans and are the most populated unofficial football fan forums of these three clubs. These three forums are semi-closed online spaces, which have their own collective rules and 'traditions', and have administrators that oversee the communication activities within the forums. For instance, there are some basic requirements for being official members of these forums, such as, sharing one's Turkish identity number with the administrator group and getting an invitation from a forum member. Furthermore, forum members are expected to comply with the written rules of these three forums. If a forum member uses slang words or phrases in his/her forum posts, he/she can be temporarily suspended or completely banned by the administrator group of the forum.

An Internet-based survey instrument was pilot tested before the actual fieldwork. The pilot test revealed the survey took approximately 15 minutes to complete. Contacting a significant number of forum administrators publicized the survey. Administrators informed forum members about the survey with the creation of a new permanent forum topic and encouraged their members to participate by visiting the website where the Internet-based survey was made available. The study was introduced to participants as an opinion survey on football fans in Turkey. A total of 257 respondents took part in the survey among three forums selected between 14 and 21 December 2015. The language of the survey was Turkish. Multiple survey submissions from same respondents were prevented by the IP address tracking option offered by the online survey service employed. Following the removal of

Figure 2. A screenshot retrieved from Antu.com's Homepage

submissions with missing data, 240 participants (12.1% females) remained in the main analysis. All participants were aged 18 and older and the average age of the participants was 26. Fanship level is considerably high among participants (μ=4.56; SD=1.18; α=.845).

RESULTS

To assess the relative predictive value of independent variables, independent variables of uses and gratifications (U&G) and social identity process components (purposive value, entertainment value, maintaining interpersonal interconnectivity, subjective norm, group norm, affective social identity, evaluative social identity and cognitive social identity) were entered into a multiple regression analysis with the dependent variable, we-intention. Findings revealed uses and gratifications of football forum use as maintaining interpersonal interconnectivity, generating entertainment and purposive value along with affective social identity construct determined we-intention among forum users. Multicollinearity checks were done over the variance inflation factor (VIF). Inspection of the correlation matrix revealed generally moderate correlations between the nine constructs (Table 1).

The results indicate that the relative ability of the model to explain variation in we-intention is 43.4%. The variance in the level of we-intention is explained by "affective social identity" along with uses and gratifications factors as "maintaining interpersonal interconnectivity", "entertainment value" and "purposive value" (F

Figure 3. A screenshot retrieved from ForzaBesiktas.com's Home Page

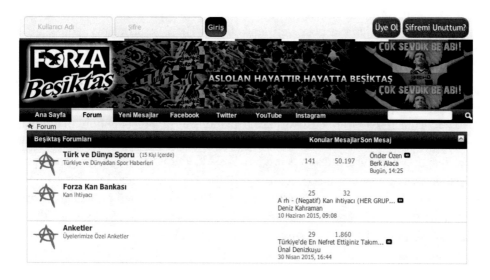

Table 1. Correlation matrix (N=240)

	U&G Purposive value	U&G Entertainment value	U&G Maintaining interpersonal interconnectivity	Subjective norm	Group norm	Affective social identity	Evaluative social identity	Cognitive social identity	We intention
U&G Purposive value	1								
U&G Entertainment value	.408**	1							
U&G Maintaining interpersonal inter-connectivity	.749**	.285**	1						
Subjective norm	.277**	.059	.244**	1					
Group norm	.025	-.198**	.005	.149*	1				
Affective social identity	.493**	.235**	.433**	.343**	-.064	1			
Evaluative social identity	.428**	.129*	.409**	.347**	.111	.480**	1		
Cognitive social identity	.392**	.104	.426**	.318**	.087	.657**	.369**	1	
We intention	.573**	.376**	.571**	.251**	.034	.467**	.268**	.390**	1

Standardized beta-coefficients

*p <.05; **p<.01; ***p<.001

= 44.989, *df* = 235, *p* < 0.001). Pearson Product-moment correlations (with pair-wise exclusion of missing cases) revealed that the dependent variable and the all independent variables are positively correlated. The ß coefficients indicate the highest relationship to we-intention is maintaining interpersonal connectivity (ß = .299, t = 4.011, p<.001), followed by affective social identity (ß = .211, t = 3.719, p<.001). Purposive value (ß = .176, t = 2.182, p < .05) and entertainment value (ß = .169, t = 3.131, p < .05) are also found to moderately explain we-intention.

The current research aimed to reveal the relationship of joint intentions of football fans with social influence processes and uses and gratifications obtained from forum use. In sports literature, fanship is rendered as a key motivation for the generation of passion among sports fans (Grossberg, 1992). User-generated Internet services expand the limits of cultural fluidity and stand as multifaceted digital platforms that generate neo tribal online identities and social formations (Hodkinson, 2003). This allows football fans, as a subcultural group marked by group belongings, to reproduce their ritualistic behaviors and create new cultural practices through neo tribal formations (Herring, Scheidt, Bonus & Wright, 2005; Millward, 2008; Norman, 2012). These findings are consistent with previous research which show that fans who are strongly attached to the football teams they support are more likely to anonymously engage in collective activities (Wann, Hunter, Ryan, & Wright, 2001).

Although Wertsch (2002), who coined the term "imagined collective" to refer to members of a group sharing a common ground, argues that imagined collectives do not necessarily need to interact with each other synchronously, sports fans are aware of the individual and mutual advantages of social cohesion created over sport teams. Moreover, they strive for a positive social identity (Boen, Vanbeselaere and Feys, 2002). This results with the development of reciprocity, the building of relationships and friendships and the development of personal and social skills (Dorokhina, Hosta & Sterkenburg, 2011). The results show that football fan forums, offering certain uses and gratifications for their users, stand out as useful platforms for collective actions. In parallel with the argument that fanship encompasses affective traits (Dietz-Uhler & Lanter, 2008), having sentimentally attached and emotionally committed self-identities, football fans are more likely to take part in joined actions.

Overall, subjective and group norms along with the evaluative and cognitive social identity process components, as used in Cheung et al.'s model (2010) to explain we-intention through Facebook uses among students, do not explain we-intention of football fans when using team forums. It can be inferred that social identity processes and norms are more established in online football discussion forums, for having a longer history in comparison with the online social networks such as Facebook. This is an important finding for further studies exploring dynamics of group identities in various social contexts.

CONCLUSION

While the conclusion section was being written, Kocaelispor[2] fans organized a Twitter hashtag campaign to take attention to the deep financial crisis of their club. Their hashtag #Kocaelisporyaşasın (#*LongLiveKocaelispor* in English) topped the trending topic list of Twitter. Such fan-based collective actions clearly illustrate the focus of our study. Especially, after the massive penetration of social networks into the daily life, new dimensions have been articulated into civic engagement and political participation processes. In this sense, blogs, micro-blogging sites, crowdfunding sites, online forums and online petitions have gradually been major digital tools to acquire the attention of public opinion about a social issue. As a result, it is hard to imagine a fan activism process without considering its online and offline dimensions today.

As Hughson (2000) indicates, football fans can be considered to be neo-tribal emotional communities. Hence, the neo-tribal structure of online forums can offer football fans sentimental bonds for taking joint actions. In that sense, football fans that visit and participate in online football forums do not simply relax or pass time, but also enrich and set purposive conventions and goals with emotional attachment to the team and supporters of the team.

This study lends a comprehensive insight into the effects of social influence processes, association level with the football team and uses and gratifications obtained from forum use on understanding we-intentions among online football forum members. In the context of Turkey, our analysis reveals that Turkish football fans visit football forums to get together with other members of the community and to take joint actions based on interpersonal connectivity, affective social identity, purposive value and entertainment value. Based on our findings, it can be inferred that interpersonal connectivity matters for football fans. Moreover, online football forums represent one of the important platforms for football fans to connect with their peers.

Our findings reveal that affective social identity prevails over cognitive and evaluative dimensions of social identity for having a significant relationship with we-intention. In other words, our findings reveal that emotional feeling of belonging within the group is an essential component to take joint action among football fans. This finding indicates that emotional belonging is more important for football fans over evaluative and cognitive dimensions of social identity, while taking and organizing collective action in online football discussion forums.

Our analysis also confirms that Turkish football fans visit online forums to get together with other members of their community to perform a joint action. In line, purposive value and entertainment value significantly explain we-intention in online football forums. This explanation indicates that football fans join and use online football forums, not solely for entertainment purposes but also to actualize certain social and even political goals with other fans. For instance during the Gezi Demonstrations, "football fandom" and what it represents presumed as political actors in the society. çArşı fan collective, have used various technological means to affect Turkey's mainstream political agenda with their social actions during and after the demonstrations. Thus, although "fan activism" is relatively a new term in the realm of Turkish football fandom, football fans have increasingly brought their political or social agenda to the terraces or their digital spaces after the demonstrations. Accordingly, it is possible to see more proactive football fan reactions with the convergence of various social networks in everyday life practices.

REFERENCES

Anderson, D. F. (1979). Sport Spectatorship: Application of an Identity or Appraisal of Self. *Review of Sport and Leisure*, *4*(2), 115–127.

Battini, A. (2012). Reshaping the national bounds through fandom: The UltrAslan of Galatasaray. *Soccer & Society*, *13*(5-6), 701–719. doi:10.1080/14660970.2012.730771

Bennett, L. (2013). Researching online fandom. *Cinema Journal*, *52*(4), 129–134. doi:10.1353/cj.2013.0033

Bennett, W. L. (2008). *Civic life online: Learning how digital media can engage youth*. Mit Press.

Boen, F., Vanbeselaere, N., & Feys, J. (2002). Behavioral consequences of fluctuating group success: An internet study on soccer teams. *The Journal of Social Psychology*, *142*(6), 769–781. doi:10.1080/00224540209603935 PMID:12450350

Boyle, R., & Haynes, R. (2004). *Football in the new media age*. London: Routledge.

Brough, M. M., & Shresthova, S. (2011). Fandom meets activism: Rethinking civic and political participation. *Transformative Works and Cultures, 10*.

Brunsting, S., & Postmes, T. (2002). Social movement participation in the digital age predicting offline and online collective action. *Small Group Research*, *33*(5), 525–554. doi:10.1177/104649602237169

Chang, B., Lee, S., & Kim, B. (2006). Exploring factors affecting the adoption and continuance of online games among college students in South Korea. *New Media & Society*, *8*(2), 295–319. doi:10.1177/1461444806059888

Cheung, C. M. K., Chiu, P. Y., & Lee, M. K. O. (2010). Online social networks: Why do we use Facebook? *Computers in Human Behavior*, *27*(4), 1337–1343. doi:10.1016/j.chb.2010.07.028

Click, M. A., Lee, H., & Holladay, H. W. (2013). Making monsters: Lady Gaga, fan identification, and social media. *Popular Music and Society*, *36*(3), 360–379. doi:10.1080/03007766.2013.798546

Cook, A., & Hynes, D. (2013). From the football terraces to the television screen: Gender, sexuality and the challenges of online fan communities. *Proceedings of the Global Research Project on Fan Communities and Fanship Conference*, Oxford, UK.

Dahlgren, P. (2013). *Young citizens and new media: Learning for democratic participation*. Routledge.

Dholakia, U. M., Bagozzi, R. P., & Pearo, L. K. (2004). A social influence model of consumer participation in network-and small-group-based virtual communities. *International Journal of Research in Marketing*, *21*(3), 241–263. doi:10.1016/j.ijresmar.2003.12.004

Dietz-Uhler, B., Harrikc, E. A., End, C., & Jacquemotte, L. (2000). Sex differences in sport fan behavior and reasons for being a sport fan. *Journal of Sport Behavior*, *23*, 219–231.

Dietz-Uhler, B., & Lanter, J. R. (2008). The consequences of sport fan identification. In L. Hugenberg, P. Haridakis, & A. Earnheardt (Eds.), *Media and mediate sports fanship* (pp. 103–113). McFarland & Company, Inc.

Dorokhina, O., Hosta, M., & van Sterkenburg, J. (2012). *Targeting Social Cohesion in Post-Conflict Societies through Sport. EPAS Handbook on Good Practices, 1*. Council of Europe.

Eastman, S.T. & Land, A.M. (1997). The best of both worlds: Sports fans find good seats at the bar. *Journal of Sport and Social Issues, 21*(2), 156,178.

End, C. M. (2001). An examination of NFL fans' computer mediated BIRGing. *Journal of Sport Behavior*, *24*(2), 162.

Erhart, I. (2014). United in protest: From Living and dying with our colours to Let all the colours of the world unite. *The International Journal of the History of Sport*, *31*(14), 1724–1738. doi:10.1080/09523367.2014.929116

Fink, J. S., Trail, G. T., & Anderson, D. F. (2002). An Examination of Team Identification: Which Motives are Most Salient to its Existence? *International Sports Journal*, *6*(2), 195–207.

Gantz, W., Wang, Z., Paul, B., & Potter, R. F. (2006). Sports versus All Comers: Comparing TV sports fans with fans of other programming genres. *Journal of Broadcasting & Electronic Media, 50*(1), 95–118. doi:10.1207/s15506878jobem5001_6

Gantz, W., & Wenner, L. A. (1995). Fanship and the television sports viewing experience. *Sociology of Sport Journal, 12*(1), 56–74. doi:10.1123/ssj.12.1.56

Gorgulu, V., Aslanbay, Y., Bursa, G., & Yucel, A. G. (2015). Television program format preferences and aggression of football fans. *International Journal of Humanities and Social Science, 1*(1), 38–46.

Grossberg, L. (1992). Is there a fan in the house? The affective sensibility of fanship. In L. A. Lewis (Ed.), *The adoring audience: Fan culture and the popular media* (pp. 50–56). London: Routledge.

Herring, S. C., Scheidt, L. A., Bonus, S., & Wright, E. (2005). Weblogs as a bridging genre. *Information Technology & People, 18*(2), 142–171. doi:10.1108/09593840510601513

Hodkinson, P. (2003). 'Net.Goth': Internet communication and (sub) cultural boundaries. In K. Gelder (Ed.), *The Subcultures Reader* (pp. 564–574). London: Sage.

Hofstede, G. (2003). Turkey - Geert Hofstede. Retrieved from http://geerthofstede.com/turkey.html

Ito, M., Horst, H. A., Bittanti, M., Stephenson, B. H., Lange, P. G., Pascoe, C. J., & Martínez, K. Z. (2009). *Living and learning with new media: Summary of findings from the Digital Youth Project*. MIT Press.

Jenkins, H. (2015). "Cultural acupuncture": Fan activism and the Harry Potter alliance. In Popular Media Cultures (pp. 206-229). UK: Palgrave Macmillan.

Jenkins, H., Clinton, K., Purushotma, R., Robinson, A. J., & Weigel, M. (2006). *Confronting the challenges of participatory culture: Media education for the 21st century*. Chicago: IL The John D. and Catherine T. MacArthur Foundation.

Jenkins, H., & Shresthova, S. (2012). Up, up, and away! The power and potential of fan activism. *Transformative Works and Cultures, 10.*

Kaplan, S., & Langdon, S. (2012). Chinese fanship and potential marketing strategies for expanding the market for American Professional sports into China. *International Journal of Sports Marketing & Sponsorship, 14*(1), 7–21. doi:10.1108/IJSMS-14-01-2012-B002

Katz, E., Blumler, J. G., & Gurevitch, M. (1974). Utilization of mass communication by the individual. In J. G. Blumler & E. Katz (Eds.), *The uses of mass communications: Current perspectives on gratifications research* (pp. 19–32). Beverly Hills: Sage.

Kaye, B. K. (1998). Uses and gratifications of the World Wide Web: From couch potato to web potato. *The New Jersey Journal of Communication*, 6(1), 21–40. doi:10.1080/15456879809367333

Kaye, B. K., & Johnson, T. J. (2002). Online and in the know: Uses and gratifications of the web for political information. *Journal of Broadcasting & Electronic Media*, 46(1), 54–71. doi:10.1207/s15506878jobem4601_4

Kelman, H. C. (1958). Compliance, Identification, and Internalization: Three processes of attitude change. *The Journal of Conflict Resolution*, 2(1), 51–60. doi:10.1177/002200275800200106

Kelman, H. C. (1974). Further thoughts on the processes of compliance, identification, and internalization. In *Perspectives on social power* (pp. 125-171).

LaRose, R., & Eastin, M. S. (2004). A social cognitive theory of Internet uses and gratifications: Toward a new model of media attendance. *Journal of Broadcasting & Electronic Media*, 48(3), 358–377. doi:10.1207/s15506878jobem4803_2

Lin, C., Salwen, M. B., & Abdulla, R. A. (2005). Uses and gratifications of online and offline news: New wine in an old bottle. In *Online news and the public* (pp. 221-236).

McManus, J. (2013). Been there, done that, bought the t-shirt: Beşiktaş fans and the commodification of football in Turkey. *International Journal of Middle East Studies*, 45(01), 3–24. doi:10.1017/S0020743812001237

Millward, P. (2008). The rebirth of football fanzine: Using e-zines as data source. *Journal of Sport and Social Issues*, 32(3), 299–310. doi:10.1177/0193723508319718

Monaghan, F. (2014). Seeing Red: social media and football fan activism. In The Language of Social Media (pp. 228-254). Palgrave Macmillan UK. doi:10.1057/9781137029317_11

Natelli, A. (2008). *Online discussion forum influence on professional sport fan support: An exploratory study* [unpublished doctoral dissertation]. Victoria University of Wellington, Wellington, New Zealand.

Norman, M. (2012). Online community or electronic tribe? Exploring the social characteristics and spatial production of an Internet hockey fan culture. *Journal of Sport and Social Issues.* doi:10.1177/0193723512467191

Numerato, D. (2016, July 10-14). Unanticipated Outcomes of Social Movements: The Case of Football Fan Activism. *Proceedings of the Third ISA Forum of Sociology.*

Papacharissi, Z., & Rubin, A. M. (2000). Predictors of Internet use. *Journal of Broadcasting & Electronic Media, 44*(2), 175–196. doi:10.1207/s15506878jobem4402_2

Pegoraro, A. (2013). Sport fanship in the digital world. In P. Pedersen (Ed.), *The Routledge Handbook of Sport Communication* (pp. 248–258). New York: Routledge.

Reysen, S., & Branscombe, N. R. (2010). Fanship and Fanship: Comparisons between sport fans and non-sport fans. *Journal of Sport Behavior, 33*, 176–193.

Ruggerio, T. E. (2000). Uses and Gratification Theory in the 21st Century. *Mass Communication & Society, 3*(1), 3–37. doi:10.1207/S15327825MCS0301_02

Sayan, A. (2013). *Futbol tribünlerinin izinde forumlar: Alisamiyen.net analizi* [Online forums as football terraces: Analysis of Alisamiyen.net] [Unpublished doctoral dissertation]. İstanbul Bilgi University.

Shah, V., Nojin Kwak, R., & Lance Holbert, D. (2001). Connecting" and" disconnecting" with civic life: Patterns of Internet use and the production of social capital. *Political Communication, 18*(2), 141–162. doi:10.1080/105846001750322952

Shen, A. X., Cheung, C. M., Lee, M. K., & Chen, H. (2011). How social influence affects we-intention to use instant messaging: The moderating effect of usage experience. *Information Systems Frontiers, 13*(2), 157–169. doi:10.1007/s10796-009-9193-9

Smith, A. (2013). Civic engagement in the digital age. Pew Research Center.

Social Issues Research Centre. (2008). Football Passions (Research Report). Retrieved from http://www.sirc.org/football/football_passions.pdf

Stafford, T. F., Stafford, M. R., & Schkade, L. L. (2004). Determining uses and gratifications for the Internet. *Decision Sciences, 35*(2), 259–288. doi:10.1111/j.00117315.2004.02524.x

Tajfel, H. (1978). *Differentiation between social groups: Studies in the social psychology of intergroup relations.* London: Academic Press.

Talimciler, A. (2012). *1920'den günümüze Türkiye'de toplumsal yapı ve değişim.* İstanbul: Phoenix Yayınları.

Tian, Y. (2006). Political use and perceived effects of the Internet: A case study of the 2004 election. *Communication Research Reports*, *23*(2), 129–137. doi:10.1080/08824090600669103

Toder-Alon, A., Brunel, F. F., & Schneier Siegal, W. L. (2005). Ritual behavior and community change: Exploring the social-psychological roles of net rituals in the developmental processes of online consumption communities. In *Online consumer psychology: Understanding and influencing consumer behavior in the virtual world* (pp. 7-33).

Totten, M. (2015). Sport activism and political praxis within the FC Sankt Pauli fan subculture. *Soccer & Society*, *16*(4), 453–468. doi:10.1080/14660970.2014.882828

TUIK. (2013). Spor istatistikleri (data). Retrieved from http://www.tuik.gov.tr/VeriBilgi.do?alt_id=1087

Tuomela, R. (1995). *The importance of us: A philosophical study of basic social notions*. Stanford, CA: Stanford University Press.

Tuomela, R., & Miller, K. (1985). We-Intentions and social action. *Analyse & Kritik*, *7*(1), 26–43. doi:10.1515/auk-1985-0102

Tuomela, R., & Miller, K. (1988). We-intentions. *Philosophical Studies*, *53*(3), 367–389. doi:10.1007/BF00353512

Turkish Statistical Institute. (2013). Demographic statistics of Turkey. Retrieved from http://www.turkstat.gov.tr

Turner, J. C., Hogg, M. A., Oakes, P. J., Reicher, S. D., & Wetherell, M. S. (1987). *Rediscovering the social group*. Oxford, England: Basil Blackwell.

Varnali, K., & Gorgulu, V. (2015). A social influence perspective on expressive political participation in Twitter: The case of #OccupyGezi. *Information Communication and Society*, *18*(1), 1–16. doi:10.1080/1369118X.2014.923480

Wang, K. Y. (2008). Online Forums as an Arena for Political Discussions: What Politicians and Activists can Learn from Teachers. *American Communication Journal, 10*(3).

Wann, D. L., Grieve, F. G., End, C., Zapalac, R. K., Lanter, J., Pease, D. G., & Wallace, A. et al. (2013). Examining the superstitions of sport fans: Types of superstitions, perceptions of impact, and relationship with team identification. *Athletic Insight, 5*, 21–44.

Wann, D. L., Hunter, J. L., Ryan, J. A., & Wright, L. A. (2001). The relationship between team identification and willingness of sport fans to consider illegally assisting their team. *Social Behavior and Personality*, *29*(6), 531–536. doi:10.2224/sbp.2001.29.6.531

Wertsch, J. V. (2002). *Voices of collective remembering*. Cambridge, UK: Cambridge University. doi:10.1017/CBO9780511613715

Whiting, A., & Williams, D. (2013). Why people use social media: A uses and gratifications approach. *Qualitative Market Research: An International Journal*, *16*(4), 362–369. doi:10.1108/QMR-06-2013-0041

Yang, G. (2009). Online activism. *Journal of Democracy*, *20*(3), 33–36. doi:10.1353/jod.0.0094

Yu, R. P. (2016). The relationship between passive and active non-political social media use and political expression on Facebook and Twitter. *Computers in Human Behavior*, *58*, 413–420. doi:10.1016/j.chb.2016.01.019

Zhou, T. (2011). Understanding online community user participation: A social influence perspective. *Internet Research*, *21*(1), 67–81. doi:10.1108/10662241111104884

ENDNOTES

[1]   While working on the theoretical basis of the current study, we have consulted with a group of key forum users to gain more insights. An interviewee portrays how football fans utilize online forums for collective actions as follows: "First of all, Alisamiyen.net is closed to the outsiders. We are all intimate with each other. Therefore, it is quite easy to take action in our forum. When Galatasaray was in a deep financial crisis, we had a whip-round for the team's flight fee in 2006. In short, the collectiveness is the key in our actions. Alisamiyen.net technically provides what we need for our actions".

[2]   A legendary football club in the history of Turkish football league.

Compilation of References

Abadie, A. (2006). Poverty, political freedom, and the roots of terrorism. *The American Economic Review*, *96*(2), 50–56. doi:10.1257/000282806777211847

Abadpour, A., & Anderson, C. (2013). *Fights, adapts, accepts: Archetypes of Iranian Internet use*. Iran Media Program.

Abdel Fattah, E. (2011). Personal Communication.

Abdel Nasser, Gehad. (2011). *The Silent Speak Up* (documentary). Aljazeera.

Aberle, D. (1966). *The Peyote Religion among the Navaho*. Chicago: Aldine.

Aday, S., Farrell, H., Lynch, M., Sides, J., Kelly, J., & Zuckerman, E. (2010). *Blogs and bullets: New media in contentious politics*. Washington, DC: United States Institute of Peace.

ADHA. (2011) Older Australians and the Internet: bridging the digital divide. *National Seniors Productive Ageing Centre* (NSPAC). Retrieved from http://nationalseniors.com.au/be-informed/research/productive-ageing-centre

Akçay, H. (2011). Kullanımlar ve Doyumlar Yaklaşımı Bağlamında Sosyal Medya Kullanımı. *Gümüşhane Üniversitesi Üzerine Bir Araştırma İletişim Kuram ve Araştırma Dergisi.*, *33*, 137–162.

Akhavan, N. (2013). *Electronic Iran: The cultural politics of an online revolution*. New Brunswick, NJ: Rutgers University Press.

Akipress. (2016). *В Интернете и соцсетях издеваются над чиновниками, — завотделом Аппарата правительства А.Исаев*. Retrieved from http://kg.akipress.org/news:1194600?from=portal&place=last

Alesina, A., & Perotti, R. (1996). Income distribution, political instability, and investment. *European Economic Review*, *40*(6), 1203–1228. doi:10.1016/0014-2921(95)00030-5

Alfaro, A. (2012). En otras 12 ciudades se realizaron manifestaciones contra *Televisa*. Retrieved from http://www.jornada.unam.mx/2012/07/28/politica/004n1pol

Almond, G., & Verba, S. (1963). *The Civic Culture: Political Attitudes and Democracy in Five Nations* (S. Publications, Ed.). doi:10.1515/9781400874569

Al-Rawi, A. (2014). Framing the online women's movements in the Arab world. *Information Communication and Society, 17*(9), 1147–1161. doi:10.1080/1369118X.2014.889190

Álvarez, C. (2014, March 31). EPN, ¿su iniciativa viola la Constitución? Diario El Financiero.

AMICPI. (2016). *Hábitos de los usuarios de Internet 2016.* México: Amipci.

Anderson B. (2006). *Imagined Communities.*

Anderson, D. F. (1979). Sport Spectatorship: Application of an Identity or Appraisal of Self. *Review of Sport and Leisure, 4*(2), 115–127.

Anderson, J. (1999). *Kyrgyzstan: Central Asia's island of democracy.* Amsterdam: Harwood Academic Publisher.

Andión, M. (2013). Las redes sociales virtuales como medios alternativos al poder de la telecracia en México. *Revista Versión, 31,* 114-139.

Anpuh - Associação Nacional de História. (2015). Apoie uma escola ocupada: doe uma aula. Retrieved from http://site.anpuh.org/index.php/2015-01-20-00-01-55/noticias2/diversas/item/3106-apoie-uma-escola-ocupada-doe-uma-aula

Arnould, J. (2010). Global Consumer Culture. In J. Sheth & N. Maholtra (Eds.), *Encyclopedia of International Marketing.* Retrieved from http://www.uwyo.edu/sustainable/recent-research/docs/global%20consumer%20culture%20arnould.pdf

Askegaard, S. (2006). Brands as a global ideoscape. In J. E. Schroeder & M. Salzer-Mörling (Eds.), *Brand culture* (pp. 91–101). London: Routledge Press.

Aus Govt. (2010) *Australia to 2050: future challenges* Retrieved from http://archive.treasury.gov.au/igr/igr2010/report/pdf/IGR_2010.pdf

Auyero, J. (2003). Relational riot: Austerity and corruption protest in the neoliberal era. *Social Movement Studies, 2*(2), 117–145. doi:10.1080/1474283032000139742

Azattyk. (2015). *Налогоплательщики учат чиновников экономии бюджетных средств.* Retrieved from http://rus.azattyk.org/a/27434902.html

Azattyk. (2016). *Сариев: Все школы в 2016 году будут подключены к Интернету.* Retrieved on March 21, 2016, from http://rus.azattyk.org/archive/ky_News_in_Russian_ru/20160304/4795/4795.html?id=27588847

Azuela, M., & Tapia, M. (2013). *Construyendo ciudadanía desde el activismo digital.* México: Alternativas y Capacidades.

Baldino, D., & Goold, J. (2014). Iran and the emergence of information and communication technology: The evolution of revolution? *Australian Journal of International Affairs, 68*(1), 17–35. doi:10.1080/10357718.2013.840263

Ballantine, P. W., & Stephenson, R. J. (2011). Help me, I'm fat! Social support in online weight loss networks. *Journal of Consumer Behaviour, 10*(6), 332–337. doi:10.1002/cb.374

Barber, B. (1996). *Jihad vs. McWorld: How globalism and tribalism are reshaping the world*. New York, NY: Ballantine Books.

Bardin, L. (2006). Análise de Conteúdo. Edições 70. Lisboa.

Barlow, A. (2008). *The blogging America: the new public sphere*. Westport, CT: Praeger.

Baron, L. F., Abokhodair, N., & Garrido, M. (2013, May). Human and Political Grievances for Mobilization: Different roles of Facebook during the Egyptian Arab Spring. *Proceedings of the 12th International Conference on Social Implications of Computers in Developing Countries*, Montego Bay, Jamaica.

Battini, A. (2012). Reshaping the national bounds through fandom: The UltrAslan of Galatasaray. *Soccer & Society, 13*(5-6), 701–719. doi:10.1080/14660970.2012.730771

Bauermeister, M. R. (2014). *Social movement organizations in the local food movement: Linking social capital and movement support* [Unpublished doctoral dissertation]. Iowa State University.

BBC. (2005). *Profile: Askar Akayev*. Retrieved on June 29, 2016, from http://www.news.bbc.co.uk/2/hi/asia-pacific/4371819.stm

BBC. (2015). *Kyrgyzstan: Online protests over new chairs for MPs*. Retrieved on March 5, 2016, from http://www.bbc.com/news/blogs-news-from-elsewhere-34527694

Bekin, C., Carrigan, M., & Szmigin, I. (2005). Defying Marketing Sovereignty: Voluntary Simplicity at New Consumption Communities. *Qualitative Market Research: An International Journal, 8*(4), 413–429. doi:10.1108/13522750510619779

Bengard, A. (2015). *Минфин передумал закупать кожаные кресла и планшеты*. Retrieved on March 5, 2016, from http://24.kg/obschestvo/25025_minfin_peredumal_zakupat_kojanyie_kresla_i_planshetyi_/

Bengard, A. (2016). *Депутаты считают, что Кыргызстан остро нуждается в получении гуманитарной помощи*. Retrieved on June 29, 2016, from http://24.kg/vlast/30204_deputatyi_schitayut_chto_kyirgyizstan_ostro_nujdaetsya_v_poluchenii_gumanitarnoy_pomoschi/

Bennett, L. (2013). Researching online fandom. *Cinema Journal, 52*(4), 129–134. doi:10.1353/cj.2013.0033

Bennett, W. L., & Segerberg, A. (2012). The logic of connective action: Digital media and the personalization of contentious politics. *Information Communication and Society, 15*(5), 739–768. doi:10.1080/1369118X.2012.670661

Bennett, W. L. (2008). *Civic life online: Learning how digital media can engage youth*. Mit Press.

Bennett, W. L., & Segerberg, A. (2011). Digital Media and the Personalization of Collective Action. *Information Communication and Society, 14*(6), 770–799. doi:10.1080/1369118X.2011.579141

Berkowitz, L. (1978). *Group processes*. New York: Academic Press.

Berner, A., & van Tonder, C. L. (2003). The postmodern consumer: Implications of changing customer expectations for organization development in service organizations. *SA Journal of Industrial Psychology, 29*(3), 1–10.

Bimber, B. (2003). *Information and American Democracy: Technology in the Evolution of Political Power*. Cambridge University Press. doi:10.1017/CBO9780511615573

Blurton, C. (1999). New directions of ICT-use in education. Retrieved from https://goo.gl/6SgGxV

Bode, L., Vraga, E. K., Borah, P., & Shah, D. V. (2014). A new space for political behavior: Political social networking and its democratic consequences. *Journal of Computer-Mediated Communication, 19*(3), 414–429. doi:10.1111/jcc4.12048

Boen, F., Vanbeselaere, N., & Feys, J. (2002). Behavioral consequences of fluctuating group success: An internet study on soccer teams. *The Journal of Social Psychology, 142*(6), 769–781. doi:10.1080/00224540209603935 PMID:12450350

Bogad, L. M. (2005). Tactical carnival: Social movements, demonstrations, and dialogical performance. In J. Cohen-Cruz & M. Schutzman (Eds.), *A Boal companion* (pp. 46–58). New York, NY: Routledge.

Bohlken, A. T., & Sergenti, E. J. (2010). Economic growth and ethnic violence: An empirical investigation of Hindu-Muslim riots in India. *Journal of Peace Research, 47*(5), 589–600. doi:10.1177/0022343310373032

Boulianne, S. (2015). Social media use and participation: A meta-analysis of current research. *Information Communication and Society, 18*(5), 524–538. doi:10.1080/1369118X.2015.1008542

Boulianne, S. (2009). Does Internet use affect engagement? A meta-analysis of research. *Political Communication, 26*(2), 193–211. doi:10.1080/10584600902854363

Boundless Sociology. (2016, September 20). Types of Social Movements. Retrieved from https://www.boundless.com/sociology/textbooks/boundless-sociology-textbook/social-change-21/social-movements-140/types-of-social-movements-768-4965/

Bowe, B., Freedman, E., & Blom, R. (2012). Social Media, Cyber-Dissent, and Constraints on Online Political Communication in Central Asia. *Central Asia and Caucasus, 13*(1), 144–152.

Boyle, R., & Haynes, R. (2004). *Football in the new media age*. London: Routledge.

Brandt, P. T., & Ulfelder, J. (2011). Economic growth and political instability.

Breuer, A., Landman, T., & Farguhar, D. (2014). Social media and protest mobilization: Evidence from the Tunisian revolution. *Democratization, 22*(4), 764–792. doi:10.1080/13510347.2014.885505

Brodock, K., Joyce, M., & Zaeck, T. (2009). Digital Activism Survey Report 2009. *DigiActive*. Retrieved from http://www.digiactive.org/wpcontent/uploads/Research4_SurveyReport2009.pdf

Brough, M. M., & Shresthova, S. (2011). Fandom meets activism: Rethinking civic and political participation. *Transformative Works and Cultures, 10.*

Brundidge, J., & Rice, R. (2009). Political engagement online: Do the information rich get richer and the like-minded more similar? In A. Chadwick & P. N. Howard (Eds.), Routledge Handbook of Internet Politics (pp. 145-156). New York: Routledge.

Bruns, A., & Burgess, J. (2011). The use of Twitter hashtags in the formation of ad hoc publics. *Proceedings of the 6th European Consortium for Political Research (ECPR) General Conference 2011*, University of Iceland, Reykjavik.

Bruns, A., & Stieglitz, S. (2012). Quantitative approaches to comparing communication patterns on Twitter. *Journal of Technology in Human Services*, *30*(34), 160–185. doi:10.1080/1522883 5.2012.744249

Brunsting, S., & Postmes, T. (2002). Social movement participation in the digital age predicting offline and online collective action. *Small Group Research*, *33*(5), 525–554. doi:10.1177/104649602237169

Bucar, E. M., & Fazaeli, R. (2008). Free speech in Weblogistan? The offline consequences of online communication. *International Journal of Middle East Studies*, *40*(3), 403–419. doi:10.1017/S0020743808080999

Buechler, S. M. (2000). *Social movements in advanced capitalism: The political economy and cultural construction of social activism*. Oxford: Oxford University Press.

Bullas, J. (2014). 22 Social media facts and statistics you should know in 2014. *Jeffbullas.com.* Retrieved from http://www.jeffbullas.com/2014/01/17/20-social-media-facts-and-statistics-you-should-know-in-2014/

Burgess, L., Hasan, H., & Alcock, C. (2012) Information Systems for the Social Wellbeing of Senior Australians, *Proceedings of ISD2012*, Prato, Italy

Burgess, S. M., & Steenkamp, J.-B. E. M. (2006). Marketing Renaissance: How Research in Emerging Markets Advances Marketing Science and Practice. *International Journal of Research in Marketing*, *23*(4), 337–356. doi:10.1016/j.ijresmar.2006.08.001

Burke, B. (2000). *Post-modernism and post-modernity*. The Encyclopedia of Informal Education. Retrieved from www.infed.org/biblio/b-postmd.htm

Cabrera, R. (2014, April 7). La iniciativa Telecom es la más regresiva desde que Internet existe en México. Animalpolitico.com. Retrieved from http://www.animalpolitico.com/2014/04/la-iniciativa-de-telecom-es-la-mas-regresiva-desde-que-internet-existe-en-mexico/#ixzz2zXy9GsmF

Calingaert, D. (2010). Autoritarianism vs. the Internet. *Policy Review*, *160*, 63–75.

Camacho, F. (2011). Las nuevas tecnologías de la información hacen más vulnerables a ciudadanos. Retrieved from http://www.jornada.unam.mx/2011/10/19/politica/012n2pol

Camacho, F. (2013). Presenta #YoSoy132 iniciativa para la reforma de los medios. Retrieved from http://www.jornada.unam.mx/2013/02/27/politica/022n1pol

Carr, A., & Higginson, I. (2001). Are quality of life measures patient centred? *BMJ (Clinical Research Ed.)*, *322*(7298), 1357–1360. doi:10.1136/bmj.322.7298.1357 PMID:11387189

CartaCapital. (2015). Em vídeos e fotos, a repressão da PM aos estudantes secundaristas. Retrieved from http://www.cartacapital.com.br/blogs/parlatorio/em-videos-e-fotos-a-repressao-da-pm-aos-estudantes-secundaristas-8726.html

Castells, M. (2001). *The Internet Galaxy: Reflections on the Internet, Business and Society*. Oxford: Oxford University Press. doi:10.1007/978-3-322-89613-1

Castells, M. (2000). Materials for an exploratory theory of the networked society. *The British Journal of Sociology*, *51*(1), 5–24. doi:10.1080/000713100358408

Castells, M. (2000). *The Rise of The Network Society: The Information Age: Economy, Society and Culture* (Vol. 1). Chichester, UK: Wiley.

Castells, M. (2007). Communication, power, and counter-power in the network society. *International Journal of Communication*, *1*(1), 238–266.

Castells, M. (2009). *Communication Power*. Oxford, New York: Oxford University Press.

Castells, M. (2011). A Network Theory of Power. *International Journal of Communication*, *5*, 773–787.

Castells, M. (2012). *Networks of outrage and hope – social movements in the Internet age*. Chichester, UK: Wiley.

Castells, M. (2012). *Networks of Outrage and Hope: Social Movements in the Internet Age*. Cambridge, UK: Polity Press.

Castells, M. (2013). *Networks of outrage and hope: Social movements in the internet age*. John Wiley & Sons.

Castillo, M. (2012, May 9). Mesa de debate Tecnología y lucha social. *Proceedings of the Tercer Congreso Nacional Multidisciplinario*, CUCSH-UDG.

Chadwick, A. (2011). Explaining the Failure of an Online Citizen Engagement Initiative: The Role of Internal Institutional Variables. *Journal of IT & Politics, 8*, 21–40.

Chaffey, D. (2016). Global social media research summary. Retrieved from http://www.smartinsights.com/social-media-marketing/social-media-strategy/new-global-social-media-research/

Cha, M., Benevenuto, F., Haddadi, H., & Gummadi, K. (2012). The World of Connections and Information Flow in Twitter. *IEEE Transactions on Systems, Man, and Cybernetics. Part A, Systems and Humans, 2*(4), 991–998.

Chang, B., Lee, S., & Kim, B. (2006). Exploring factors affecting the adoption and continuance of online games among college students in South Korea. *New Media & Society*, 8(2), 295–319. doi:10.1177/1461444806059888

Chang, S. S. (2005). Copyright and Open Source Software Licensing. Bepress Legal Series. Working Paper 773. Retrieved from http://law.bepress.com/expresso/eps/773

Chen, K., & Chan, A. (2011). A review of technology acceptance by older adults. *Gerontechnology (Valkenswaard)*, 10(1), 1–12. doi:10.4017/gt.2011.10.01.006.00

Chen, F. (2000). Subsistence crises, managerial corruption and labour protests in china. *China Journal (Canberra, A.C.T.)*, 44(44), 41–63. doi:10.2307/2667476

Cherrier, H. (2009). Anti-consumption discourses and consumer resistance identities. *Journal of Business Research*, 62(2), 181–190. doi:10.1016/j.jbusres.2008.01.025

Cheung, C. M. K., Chiu, P. Y., & Lee, M. K. O. (2010). Online social networks: Why do we use Facebook? *Computers in Human Behavior*, 27(4), 1337–1343. doi:10.1016/j.chb.2010.07.028

Chieh-Wen, S., Shen, M., & Chen, M. (2007). Special Interest Tour Preferences and Voluntary Simplicity Lifestyle. *International Journal of Culture*, 2(4), 389–409.

Choi, S. (2011). Anti-consumption becomes a trend. *SERI Quarterly*, 4(3), 117–121.

Choudrie, J., Ghinea, G., & Songonuga, V. N. (2013). Silver surfers, e-government and the digital divide: An exploratory study of UK local authority websites and older citizens. *Interacting with Computers*. Retrieved from http://iwc.oxfordjournals.org/content/early/2013/02/06/iwc.iws020.ful

Christensen, K., Doblhammer, G., Rau, R., & Vaupel, J. W. (2009). Ageing populations: The challenges ahead. *Lancet*, 374(9696), 1196–1208. doi:10.1016/S0140-6736(09)61460-4 PMID:19801098

Ciszek, E. L. (2016). Digital activism: How social media and dissensus inform theory and practice. *Public Relations Review*, 42(2), 314–321. doi:10.1016/j.pubrev.2016.02.002

Click, M. A., Lee, H., & Holladay, H. W. (2013). Making monsters: Lady Gaga, fan identification, and social media. *Popular Music and Society*, 36(3), 360–379. doi:10.1080/03007766.2013.798546

Cline Center for Democracy. (2016). Civil unrest monitoring - dataset. Retrieved from http://www.clinecenter.illinois.edu/data/speed/

Cohen, R. (2011, January 24). Facebook and Arab dignity. *New York Times*. Retrieved from www.nytimes.com/2011/01/25/opinion/25iht-edcohen25.html

Cohen-Mansfield, J., Hazan, H., Lerman, Y., & Shalom, V. (2016). Correlates and predictors of loneliness in older-adults: A review of quantitative results informed by qualitative insights. *International Psychogeriatrics*, 28(04), 557–576. doi:10.1017/S1041610215001532 PMID:26424033

Coillie, C. V., Santamaria, L., Redmond, S., & Torres, A. (2013). *Online Activism. The transformation of the 'Public Sphere', and the creation of collective political identities around activism in the digital age – the case of the 'Occupy' movement. Project work.* Roskilde: Roskilde University.

Commission of the European Communities. (2008). *Green Paper. Copyright in the Knowledge Economy.* Retrieved from http://ec.europa.eu/internal_market/copyright/docs/copyright--infso/greenpaper_en.pdf

Cook, A., & Hynes, D. (2013). From the football terraces to the television screen: Gender, sexuality and the challenges of online fan communities. *Proceedings of the Global Research Project on Fan Communities and Fanship Conference*, Oxford, UK.

Cornwell, E., & Waite, L. (2009). Social Disconnectedness, Perceived Isolation, and Health among Older Adults. *Journal of Health and Social Behavior, 50*(1), 31–48. doi:10.1177/002214650905000103 PMID:19413133

Cottle, S. (2011). Media and the Arab uprisings of 2011. *Journalism, 12*(5), 647–659. doi:10.1177/1464884911410017

Craig-Lees, M. (2006, June 20–21). Anti-consumption: concept clarification and changing consumption behavior. *Paper presented at the Anti-consumption Seminar*, International Centre for Anti-Consumption Research, Auckland, New Zealand

Cromie, J. G., & Ewing, M. T. (2009). The rejection of brand hegemony. *Journal of Business Research, 62*(2), 218–230. doi:10.1016/j.jbusres.2008.01.029

Cummings, S. (2008). Introduction: Revolution not revolution. *Central Asian Survey, 27*(3-4), 223–228. doi:10.1080/02634930802536811

Dahl, S. (2014). Social Media Marketing: Theories and Applications. *Atlanta, GA: Sage.*

Dahlgren, P. (2013). *Young citizens and new media: Learning for democratic participation.* Routledge.

David, R. (1996). The Pyramid Builders of Ancient Egypt: A modern investigation of Pharaoh's workforce (2nd ed.). London: Routledge.

Davison, R. M., Martinsons, M. G., & Kock, N. (2004). Principles of Canonical Action Research. *Information Systems Journal, 14*(1), 65–86. doi:10.1111/j.1365-2575.2004.00162.x

De Graaf, J., Wann, D., & Naylor, T. L. (2005). *Affluenza: The All-Consuming Epidemic* (2nd ed.). USA: Berrett-Koehler Publishers.

De Swaan, M. (2014). Telecomunicaciones, el sector de las promesas incumplidas. *En Voces de Alerta: la contrarreforma de Peña Nieto en telecomunicaciones y radiodifusión.*

Delia, P. D., & Diani, M. (2006). *Social Movements: An introduction* (2nd ed.). Maiden, MA: Blackwell.

della Porta, D., & Diani, M. (2006). Social Movements: An Introduction (2nd ed.). Wiley-Blackwell

Della Porta, D. (2015). *Social movements in times of austerity: Bringing capitalism back into protest analysis*. Cambridge, UK: John Wiley & Sons.

Democracy, C. C. f. (2016). Civil unrest monitoring - datasets. Retrieved from http://www.clinecenter.illinois.edu/data/speed/

Denvir, C. J., Balmer, N. J., & Pleasence, P. (2014). Portal or pot hole? Exploring how older people use the information superhighway for advice relating to problems with a legal dimension. *Ageing and Society, 34*(04), 670–699. doi:10.1017/S0144686X12001213

Derecho, A. (2008). *Illegitimate Media: Race, Gender and Censorship in Digital Remix Culture. Northwestern University. Comparative Literary Studies*. Evanston: ProQuest.

Dewey, T., Kaden, J., Marks, M., Matsushima, S., & Zhu, B. (2012). The impact of social media on social unrest in the arab spring. *Final report prepared for Defense Intelligence Agency* Retrieved from https://goo.gl/pT0Pgi

DeYoung, A. (2010). *Lost in Transition: redefining students and universities in the contemporary Kyrgyz Republic*. Charlotte, NC: Information Age Publishing.

Dholakia, U. M., Bagozzi, R. P., & Pearo, L. K. (2004). A social influence model of consumer participation in network-and small-group-based virtual communities. *International Journal of Research in Marketing, 21*(3), 241–263. doi:10.1016/j.ijresmar.2003.12.004

Diamond, L., & Marc, F. Plattner (2014). Democratization and Authoritarianism in the Arab World. Johns Hopkins University Press.

Diamond, L., & Marc, F. Plattner. (2012). Liberation Technology: Social Media and the Struggle for Democracy. Johns Hopkins University Press.

Diamond, L., Plattner, M. F., & Costopoulos, P. J. (Eds.). (2010). *Debates on Democratization*. Baltimore, MD: Johns Hopkins University Press.

Diani, M. (1992). The concept of social movement. *The Sociological Review, 40*(1), 1–25. doi:10.1111/j.1467-954X.1992.tb02943.x

Diani, M. (2000). Social Movement Networks Virtual and Real. *Information Communication and Society, 3*(3), 386–401. doi:10.1080/13691180051033333

Diene, E. & Chan, M. (2011) Happy People Live Longer: Subjective Well-Being Contributes to Health and Longevity. In *Applied Psychology: Health and Well-Being*.

Dietz-Uhler, B., Harrikc, E. A., End, C., & Jacquemotte, L. (2000). Sex differences in sport fan behavior and reasons for being a sport fan. *Journal of Sport Behavior, 23*, 219–231.

Dietz-Uhler, B., & Lanter, J. R. (2008). The consequences of sport fan identification. In L. Hugenberg, P. Haridakis, & A. Earnheardt (Eds.), *Media and mediate sports fanship* (pp. 103–113). McFarland & Company, Inc.

Dijck, J. (2013). *The culture of Connectivity: A critical history of social media*. Oxford, UK: Oxford University Press. doi:10.1093/acprof:oso/9780199970773.001.0001

Diniz, E., Birochi, R., & Pozzebon, M. (2012). Triggers and barriers to financial inclusion: The use of ICT-based branchless banking in an Amazon county. *Electronic Commerce Research and Applications*, *11*(5), 484–494. doi:10.1016/j.elerap.2011.07.006

Djanbaev, M. (2011). *Expanding Twitter's Reach in Kyrgyzstan*. Retrieved on June 26, 2016, from https://www.opensocietyfoundations.org/voices/expanding-twitter-s-reach-kyrgyzstan

Dorokhina, O., Hosta, M., & van Sterkenburg, J. (2012). *Targeting Social Cohesion in Post-Conflict Societies through Sport*. *EPAS Handbook on Good Practices, 1*. Council of Europe.

Earl, J., & Kimport, K. (2011). *Digitally enabled social change: Activism in the internet age*. Cambridge, MA: MIT Press. doi:10.7551/mitpress/9780262015103.001.0001

Earl, J. (2013). Studying online activism: The effects of sampling design on findings. *Mobilization: An International Quarterly*, *18*(4), 389–406.

Eastman, S.T. & Land, A.M. (1997). The best of both worlds: Sports fans find good seats at the bar. *Journal of Sport and Social Issues, 21*(2), 156,178.

El Informador. (2014). Hashtag #EPNvsInternet se vuelve tendencia mundial en Twitter. *El Informador*. Retrieved from http://www.informador.com.mx/mexico/2014/524189/6/hashtag-epnvsinternet-se-vuelve-tendencia-mundial-en-twitter.htm

El Kholy, T. (2011). personal communication.

Elgin, D., & Mitchell, A. (1977). Voluntary Simplicity. *The Coevolution Quarterly*, (Summer), 4–18.

El-Hamalawy, H. (2009). Speech in a seminar about youth protest movements (YouTube video). http://www.youtube.com/watch?v=ZHMFPSicBCI

Eltantawy, N., & Wiest, J. B. (2011). Social Media in the Egyptian Revolution: Reconsidering Resource Mobilization Theory. *International Journal of Communication*, *5*, 1207–1224.

Encuesta Nacional Sobre Cultura Política y Prácticas Ciudadanas-ENCUP. (2016). Bases de Datos. Retrieved from http://www.encup.gob.mx/en/Encup/Bases_de_datos

End, C. M. (2001). An examination of NFL fans' computer mediated BIRGing. *Journal of Sport Behavior*, *24*(2), 162.

Erhart, I. (2014). United in protest: From Living and dying with our colours to Let all the colours of the world unite. *The International Journal of the History of Sport*, *31*(14), 1724–1738. doi:10.1080/09523367.2014.929116

Escola de Luta Fernão Dias Paes. Facebook page. Retrieved from https://www.facebook.com/OcupaFernao/?fref=ts

Esteinou, J., & Alva, A. (2009). *La "Ley Televisa" y la lucha por el poder en México*. México: UAM.

Esteinou, J. (2008, May 8). *"Políticas públicas en comunicación", Ponencia, panel: Políticas Públicas en Comunicación. Proceedings of the 20th Encuentro Nacional AMIC '08*. Monterrey, Nuevo León: Universidad Autónoma de Nuevo León.

Fahmy, K. (February 17, 2012). Interview with Mahmoud Saad on Akher Alnahar TV Show (YouTube video). Retrieved from http://www.youtube.com/watch?v=RKNM4XFk-hU

Farrell, H. (2012). The consequences of the Internet for politics. *Annual Review of Political Science*, *15*(1), 35–52. doi:10.1146/annurev-polisci-030810-110815

Ferghana News. (2015). *Кыргызстан: В городе Кара-Суу за «религиозные лайки» в социальной сети задержан молодой человек*. Retrieved on February 21, 2016, from http://www.fergananews.com/news/23897

Ferrara, E., De Meo, P., Fiumara, G., & Baumgartner, R. (2014). Web data extraction, applications and techniques: A survey. *Knowledge-Based Systems*, *70*, 301–323. doi:10.1016/j.knosys.2014.07.007

Fink, J. S., Trail, G. T., & Anderson, D. F. (2002). An Examination of Team Identification: Which Motives are Most Salient to its Existence? *International Sports Journal*, *6*(2), 195–207.

Finnemore, M. (1996). *National Interests in International Society*. Ithaca, NY: CornellUniversity Press.

Firat, A. F., & Venkatesh, A. (1995). Liberatory postmodernism and the enchantment of consumption. *The Journal of Consumer Research*, *22*(3), 239–267. doi:10.1086/209448

Flickr (2016). Creative Commons. Retrieved from https://www.flickr.com/creativecommons/

Fokkema, T., & Knipscheer, K. (2007). Escape loneliness by going digital: A quantitative and qualitative evaluation of a Dutch experiment in using ECT to overcome loneliness among older adults.*Aging & Mental Health*,*11*(5),496–504.doi:10.1080/13607860701366129PMID:17882587

Fox, J. (1996). How does civil society thicken? The political construction of social capital in rural Mexico. *World Development*, *24*(6), 1089–1103. doi:10.1016/0305-750X(96)00025-3

Fox, E. (1994). Communication media in Latin America. *Journal of Communication*, *44*(3), 4–8. doi:10.1111/j.1460-2466.1994.tb00695.x

Freedman, E. (2012). Deepening shadows: The eclipse of press rights in Kyrgyzstan. *Global Media and Communication*, *8*(1), 47–64. doi:10.1177/1742766511434732

Freedman, E., & Shafer, R. (2012). Advancing a comprehensive research agenda for Central Asian mass media. *Media Asia*, *39*(3), 119–126. doi:10.1080/01296612.2012.11689927

Freedom House. (2015). *Kyrgyzstan: Freedom on the Net 2015*. Retrieved on February 22, 2016 from https://freedomhouse.org/report/freedom-net/2015/kyrgyzstan

Freedom House. (2016). Freedom in the world. Retrieved from https://freedomhouse.org/report-types/freedom-press

Freedom House. (2016). *Kazakhstan: Freedom on the Net 2015*. Retrieved on October 30, 2016 from https://freedomhouse.org/report/freedom-net/2015/kazakhstan

Freire, P. (2005). *Pedagogia da Autonomia: saberes necessários à prática educativa*. São Paulo: Paz e Terra.

Friedman, T. L. (2008, November 16). Gonna need a bigger boat. *New York Times*. Retrieved from http://www.nytimes.com/2008/11/16/opinion/16friedman.html?_r=1&h

Galeano, E. (1971). *As veias abertas da América Latina*. RJ: Paz e Terra.

Gamson, W. A. (2004). Bystanders, public opinion, and the media. In D. A. Snow, S. A. Soule, & H. Kriesi (Eds.), *The Blackwell companion to social movements* (pp. 242–261). Malden, MA: Blackwell.

Gantz, W., Wang, Z., Paul, B., & Potter, R. F. (2006). Sports versus All Comers: Comparing TV sports fans with fans of other programming genres. *Journal of Broadcasting & Electronic Media*, *50*(1), 95–118. doi:10.1207/s15506878jobem5001_6

Gantz, W., & Wenner, L. A. (1995). Fanship and the television sports viewing experience. *Sociology of Sport Journal*, *12*(1), 56–74. doi:10.1123/ssj.12.1.56

García, F. (2014). Enrique Peña Nieto contra el Internet. *Nexos en línea*. Retrieved from http://www.redaccion.nexos.com.mx/?p=6176#sthash.SviUc2QV.dpuf

Gazeta.kg. (2015). *В Бишкеке открылся информационно-образовательный центр для людей с ограниченными возможностями здоровья*. Retrieved on March 5, 2016,from http://www.gazeta.kg/news/kyrgyzstan/society/32463-v-bishkeke-otkrylsya-informacionno-obrazovatelnyy-centr-dlya-lyudey-s-ogranichennymi-vozmozhnostyami-zdorovya.html

Ger, G., & Belk, R. W. (1996). Cross-cultural differences in materialism. *Journal of Economic Psychology*, *17*(1), 55–77. doi:10.1016/0167-4870(95)00035-6

Gerbaudo, P. (2012). *Tweets and the streets: Social media and contemporary activism*. Pluto Press.

Ghannam, J. (2011). Social media in the Arab world: Leading up to the uprisings of 2011. Retrieved from https://goo.gl/a6KuSC

Gil De Zúñiga, H., Puig-I-Abril, E., & Rojas, H. (2009). Weblogs, traditional sources online and political participation: An assessment of how the Internet is changing the political environment. *New Media & Society*, *11*(4), 553–574. doi:10.1177/1461444809102960

Gladwell, M. (2010, October4). Small change: Why the revolution will not be tweeted. *New Yorker (New York, N.Y.)*.

Gohn, M. da G. (2011). *Teorias dos movimentos sociais. Paradigmas clássicos e contemporâneos*. São Paulo: Loyola.

Golder, S. A., & Macy, M. W. (2014). Digital footprints: Opportunities and challenges for online social research. *Annual Review of Sociology*, *40*(1), 129–152. doi:10.1146/annurev-soc-071913-043145

Gomaa, M. (2010). Extracting the body of the Martyr of Emergency in Egypt. *Aljazeera. net*. Retrieved from http://www.aljazeera.net/humanrights/pages/a6fcf209-0e10-499e-ab4f-1c7454f5b05d

Gonzalez-Bailon, S., Borge-Holthoefer, J., Rivero, A., & Moreno, Y. (2011). The Dynamics of Protest Recruitment Through an Online Network. *Scientific Reports*, *1*(197). PMID:22355712

Gorgulu, V., Aslanbay, Y., Bursa, G., & Yucel, A. G. (2015). Television program format preferences and aggression of football fans. *International Journal of Humanities and Social Science*, *1*(1), 38–46.

Granovetter, M. S. (1973). The strength of weak ties. *American Journal of Sociology*, *78*(6), 1360–1380. doi:10.1086/225469

Gregg, R. (1936). *"Voluntary Simplicity" reprinted in*. Manas. (reprinted in 1974)

Grenade, L., & Boldy, D. (2008). Social isolation and loneliness among older people: Issues and future challenges in community and residential settings. *Australian Health Review*, *32*(3), 468–478. doi:10.1071/AH080468 PMID:18666874

Grossberg, L. (1992). Is there a fan in the house? The affective sensibility of fanship. In L. A. Lewis (Ed.), *The adoring audience: Fan culture and the popular media* (pp. 50–56). London: Routledge.

Guardian. (2016). *Kyrgyzstan detains Briton for 'horse penis' delicacy comparison*. Retrieved from https://www.theguardian.com/world/2016/jan/03/british-worker-kyrgyzstan-gold-mine-held-horse-penis-delicacy-comparison

Gurr, T. R. (1970). *Why men rebel*. Princeton, NJ: Princeton University Press.

Gutstein, D. (1999). *How the Internet undermines democracy*. Toronto, Canada: Sodart.

Hagan, R., Manktelow, R., Taylor, B., & Mallett, J. (2014). Reducing loneliness amongst older people: A systematic search and narrative review. *Aging & Mental Health*, *18*(6), 683–693. doi:10.1080/13607863.2013.875122 PMID:24437736

Hague, B., & Loader, B. (Eds.). (1999). *Digital democracy: Discourse and decision making in the information age*. London, England: Routledge.

Hakansson, A. (2014). 'What is overconsumption? A step towards common understanding. *International Journal of Consumer Studies*, *38*(6), 692–700. doi:10.1111/ijcs.12142

Hakkarainen, P. (2012). No good for shoveling snow and carrying firewood: Social representations of computers and the internet by elderly Finnish non-users. *New Media & Society*, *14*(7), 1198–1215. doi:10.1177/1461444812442663

Hamdy, N., & Gomaa, E. H. (2012). Framing the Egyptian Uprising in Arabic Language Newspapers and Social Media. *Journal of Communication, 62*(2), 195–211. doi:10.1111/j.1460-2466.2012.01637.x

Harlow, S., & Guo, L. (2014). Will the revolution be Tweeted or Facebooked? Using digital communication tools in immigrant activism. *Journal of Computer-Mediated Communication, 19*(3), 463–478. doi:10.1111/jcc4.12062

Harlow, S. (2012). Social media and social movements: Facebook and an online Guatemalan justice movement that moved offline. *New Media & Society, 14*(2), 225–243. doi:10.1177/1461444811410408

Harvey, P., & Thurnwald, I. (2009). Ageing well, ageing productively: The essential contribution of Australias ageing population to the social and economic prosperity of the nation. *Health Sociology Review, 8*(4), 379–386. doi:10.5172/hesr.2009.18.4.379

Hasan, H., & Linger, H. (2016) How Social use of Digital Technologies by the Elderly Enhances their Wellbeing. *Journal of Educational Gerontology.* Retrieved from http://www.tandfonline.com/doi/full/10.1080/03601277.2016.1205425

Haug, C. (2013). Organizing spaces: Meeting arenas as a social movement infrastructure between organization, network, and institution. *Organization Studies, 34*(5-6), 705–732. doi:10.1177/0170840613479232

Heart, T., & Kalderon, E. (2013). Older adults: Are they ready to adopt health-related ICT? *International Journal of Medical Informatics, 82*(11), e209–e231. doi:10.1016/j.ijmedinf.2011.03.002 PMID:21481631

Helberger, N., & Hugenholtz, P. B. (2007). No place like home for making a copy: Private copying in European copyright law and consumer law. *Berkeley Technology Law Journal, 22*, 1061–1098.

Heritage. (2016). *2016 Index of Economic Freedom: Kyrgyzstan.* Retrieved on June 29, 2016, from http://www.heritage.org/index/country/kyrgyzrepublic

Herring, S. C., Scheidt, L. A., Bonus, S., & Wright, E. (2005). Weblogs as a bridging genre. *Information Technology & People, 18*(2), 142–171. doi:10.1108/09593840510601513

Hilty, D. M., Ferrer, D. C., Parish, M. B., Johnston, B., Callahan, E. J., & Yellowlees, P. M. (2013). The effectiveness of telemental health: A 2013 review. *Telemedicine Journal and e-Health, 19*(6), 444–454. doi:10.1089/tmj.2013.0075 PMID:23697504

Hiro, D. (2009). *Inside Central Asia: A Political and Cultural History of Uzbekistan, Turkmenistan, Kazakhstan, Kyrgyzstan, Tajikistan, Turkey and Iran.* London: Overlook.

Hodkinson, P. (2003). 'Net.Goth': Internet communication and (sub) cultural boundaries. In K. Gelder (Ed.), *The Subcultures Reader* (pp. 564–574). London: Sage.

Hoffman, D. L., & Fodor, M. (2010). Can you measure the ROI of your social media marketing? *MIT Sloan Management Review, 52*(1), 41.

Hoffman, L. H., Jones, P. E., & Young, D. G. (2013). Does my comment count? Perceptions of political participation in an online environment. *Computers in Human Behavior, 29*(6), 2248–2256. doi:10.1016/j.chb.2013.05.010

Hofstede, G. (1983). National cultures in four dimensions: A research-based theory of cultural differences among nations. *International Studies of Management & Organization, 13*(1-2), 46–74. doi:10.1080/00208825.1983.11656358

Hofstede, G. (2003). Turkey - Geert Hofstede. Retrieved from http://geerthofstede.com/turkey.html

Holt, D. B., Quelch, J. A., & Taylor, E. L. (2004). How global brands compete. *Harvard Business Review, 82*(9), 68–75. PMID:15449856

Honari, A. (2013). From virtual to tangible social movements in Iran. In P. Aarts & F. Cavatorta (Eds.), *Civil society in Syria and Iran: Activism in authoritarian contexts* (pp. 143–167). Boulder, CO: Lynne Rienner.

Honari, A. (2015). Online social research in Iran: A need to offer a bigger picture. *CyberOrient: The Online Journal of Virtual Middle East, 9*(2).

Honari, A., van Stekelenburg, J., & Klandermans, B. (2014). *Socio-Political Participation in Iran: 2013 Election Data set.* Retrieved from http://IranPolPartResearch.org

Howard, P. N., & Hussain, M. M. (2013). *Democracy's forth wave? Digital media and the Arab Spring.* New York, NY: Oxford University Press. doi:10.1093/acprof:oso/9780199936953.001.0001

Howard, P. N., Duffy, A., Freelon, D., Hussain, M. M., Mari, W., & Maziad, M. *"Opening Closed Regimes: What Was the Role of Social Media During the Arab Spring?"* (2011). SSRN:10.2139/ssrn.2595096

Howard, P. N. (2010). *The digital origins of dictatorship and democracy: Information technology and political Islam.* New York, NY: Oxford University Press. doi:10.1093/acprof:oso/9780199736416.001.0001

Howard, P., & Parks, M. (2012, April). Social Media and Political Change: Capacity, Constraint, and Consequence. *Journal of Communication, 62*(2), 359–362. doi:10.1111/j.1460-2466.2012.01626.x

Ibold, H. (2010). Disjuncture 2.0: Youth, Internet use and cultural identity in Bishkek. *Central Asian Survey, 29*(4), 521–535. doi:10.1080/02634937.2010.537135

Ibragimov, S. (2016). *The Hashtag That Stymied Corruption in Kyrgyzstan.* Retrieved on March 5, 2016, from https://www.opensocietyfoundations.org/voices/hashtag-stymied-corruption-kyrgyzstan

Institute for War and Peace Reporting. (2012). *Kyrgyz Secret Police to Monitor Web.* Retrieved on February 21, 2016, from https://iwpr.net/global-voices/kyrgyz-secret-police-monitor-web

Instituto Nacional Electoral. (2014). Informe País Sobre la Calidad de la Ciudadanía en México.

Instituto Nacional Electoral. (2016). Sistema de Consulta de la Estadística de las Elecciones Federales. Retrieved from http://www.ine.mx/documentos/RESELEC/SICEEF/principal.html

International Data Corporation. (2016). Smartphone OS Market Share, 2015 Q2. Retrieved from http://www.idc.com/prodserv/smartphone-os-market-share.jsp

International Institute for Democracy and Electoral Assistance-IDEA. (2016). Voter Turnout Database. Retrieved from http://www.idea.int/vt/index.cfm

International Research & Exchanges Board. (2013). *Media Sustainability Index: Development of Sustainable Independent Media in Europe and Eurasia*. Washington, DC: IREX.

Internet filtering in Iran . (2009, June 16). Retrieved from Open Net Initiative. Retrieved from https://opennet.net/research/profiles/iran

IRIN News. (2015). *Hope and Fear: Kyrgyz migrants in Russia*. Retrieved from https://www.irinnews.org/report/101398/hope-and-fear-kyrgyz-migrants-russia

Ito, M., Horst, H. A., Bittanti, M., Stephenson, B. H., Lange, P. G., Pascoe, C. J., & Martínez, K. Z. (2009). *Living and learning with new media: Summary of findings from the Digital Youth Project*. MIT Press.

Iyer, R., & Muncy, J. A. (2009). Purpose and object of anti-consumption. *Journal of Business Research*, *62*(2), 160–168. doi:10.1016/j.jbusres.2008.01.023

Jack, G. (2011). Understanding the revolutions of 2011. *Foreign Affairs*, *90*(3), 8.

Jaszi, P. (1998). Intellectual property legislative update: Copyright, paracopyright, and pseudocopyright. *Paper presented at the Association of Research Libraries Conference: The Future Network: Transforming Learning and Scholarship*, Eugene, OR. Retrieved from http://old.arl.org/resources/pubs/mmproceedings/132mmjaszi~print.shtml

Jenkins, H., Clinton, K., Purushotma, R., Robinson, A. J., & Weigel, M. (2006). *Confronting the challenges of participatory culture: Media education for the 21st century*. Chicago: IL The John D. and Catherine T. MacArthur Foundation.

Jenkins, H. (2015). "Cultural acupuncture": Fan activism and the Harry Potter alliance. In Popular Media Cultures (pp. 206-229). UK: Palgrave Macmillan.

Jenkins, H., & Shresthova, S. (2012). Up, up, and away! The power and potential of fan activism. *Transformative Works and Cultures, 10*.

Jovanović, A. S., Renn, O., & Schröter, R. (2012). *Social unrest*. OECD. doi:10.1787/9789264173460-en

Juris, J. S. (2005). The new digital media and activist networking within anti-corporate globalization movements. *The Annals of the American Academy of Political and Social Science*, *597*(1), 189–208. doi:10.1177/0002716204270338

Justino, P. (2005). Redistribution and civil unrest. Retrieved from https://goo.gl/KYkc6c

Kabar. (2016). *We became 6 million, and growth of population of Kyrgyzstan indicates about people's confidence in the future of their country.* Retrieved from https://kabar.kg/eng/society/full/14531

Kalathil, S., & Boas, T. C. (2003). *Open networks, closed regimes: The impact of the internet on authoritarian rule.* Washington, DC: Carnegie Endowment for International Peace.

Kamarck, E., & Nye, J. (1999). *Democracy.com? Governance in a networked world.* Hollis, NH: Hollis Publishing.

Kant, I. (1996). The Metaphysics of Morals. In *Practical Philosophy* (M.J. Gregor, Trans.). Cambridge University Press.

Kaplan, S., & Langdon, S. (2012). Chinese fanship and potential marketing strategies for expanding the market for American Professional sports into China. *International Journal of Sports Marketing & Sponsorship, 14*(1), 7–21. doi:10.1108/IJSMS-14-01-2012-B002

Katz, E., Blumler, J. G., & Gurevitch, M. (1974). Utilization of mass communication by the individual. In J. G. Blumler & E. Katz (Eds.), *The uses of mass communications: Current perspectives on gratifications research* (pp. 19–32). Beverly Hills: Sage.

Kaur, H., & Tao, X. (2014). *Icts and the millennium development goals.* New York: Springer. doi:10.1007/978-1-4899-7439-6

Kaye, B. K., & Johnson, T. J. (2002). Online and in the know: Uses and gratifications of the web for political information. *Journal of Broadcasting & Electronic Media, 46*(1), 54–71. doi:10.1207/s15506878jobem4601_4

Kaye, B. K. (1998). Uses and gratifications of the World Wide Web: From couch potato to web potato. *The New Jersey Journal of Communication, 6*(1), 21–40. doi:10.1080/15456879809367333

Kaye, L., Butler, S., & Webster, N. (2003). Towards a Productive Ageing Paradigm for Geriatric Practice. *Ageing International, 28*(2), 200–213. doi:10.1007/s12126-003-1024-6

Kaye, B., Johnson, T., & Muhlberge, P. (2012). *Blogging in the Global Society: Cultural, Political and Geographical Aspects.* Hershey, PA: IGI Global Publishing.

Kelly, S., Troung, M., Earp, M., Reed, L., Shahbaz, A., & Greco-Stoner, A. (2013). *Freedom on the net 2013: A global assessment of Internet and digital media.* Freedom House.

Kelman, H. C. (1958). Compliance, Identification, and Internalization: Three processes of attitude change. *The Journal of Conflict Resolution, 2*(1), 51–60. doi:10.1177/002200275800200106

Kelman, H. C. (1974). Further thoughts on the processes of compliance, identification, and internalization. In *Perspectives on social power* (pp. 125-171).

Khagram, S., Riker, J. V., & Sikkink, K. (2002). *Restructuring World Politics: transnational social movements, networks, and norms.* Minneapolis: University of Minnesota Press.

Khamis, S., & Vaughn, K. (2011). *Cyberactivism in the Egyptian revolution: How civic engagement and citizen journalism tilted the balance*. Arab Media and Society.

King, G., Pan, J., & Roberts, M. (2013). How Censorship in China Allows Government Criticism but Silences Collective Expression. *The American Political Science Review*, *107*(2), 326–343. doi:10.1017/S0003055413000014

Klandermans, B., & Oegema, D. (1987). Potentials, networks, motivations, and barriers: Steps towards participation in social movements. *American Sociological Review*, *52*(4), 519–531. doi:10.2307/2095297

Klandermans, B. (1988). The formation and mobilization of consensus. *International Social Movement Research*, *1*, 173–196.

Kloop. (2016). *Телеканал «Россия-24» изменил заголовок сюжета о кыргызстанцах в ИГИЛ*. Retrieved on March 5, 2016, from http://kloop.kg/blog/2016/02/26/telekanal-rossiya-24-izmenil-zagolovok-syuzheta-o-kyrgyzstantsah-v-igil/

Kostenko, Y. (2016). *В Кыргызстане чиновников хотят лишить доступа к социальным сетям*. Retrieved from http://24.kg/vlast/37746/

Kozinets, R. V., & Handelman, J. M. (2004). Adversaries of Consumption: Consumer Movements, Activism, and Ideology. *The Journal of Consumer Research*, *31*(3), 691–704. doi:10.1086/425104

Kulikova, S., & Perlmutter, D. (2007). Blogging down the dictator: The Kyrgyz revolution and samizdat websites. *International Communication Gazette*, (69), 29-50.

Kumar, S., Morstatter, F., & Liu, H. (2013). *Twitter data analytics*. Springer.

Kurambayev, B. (2016). Journalism and Democracy in Kyrgyzstan: The impact of victimizations of the media practitioners. *Media Asia*, *43*(2), 102–111. doi:10.1080/01296612.2016.1206248

Kuran, T. (1997). *Private truth, public lies: The social consequences of preference falsification*. Cambridge, MA: Harward University Press.

Kuran, T. (1991). Now out of never: The element of surprise in the east european revolution of 1989. *World Politics*, *44*(1), 7–48. doi:10.2307/2010422

LaRose, R., & Eastin, M. S. (2004). A social cognitive theory of Internet uses and gratifications: Toward a new model of media attendance. *Journal of Broadcasting & Electronic Media*, *48*(3), 358–377. doi:10.1207/s15506878jobem4803_2

Latane, B., & Darley, J. M. (1968). Group inhibition of bystander intervention in emergencies. *Journal of Personality and Social Psychology*, *10*(3), 215–221. doi:10.1037/h0026570 PMID:5704479

Latour, B. (2005). *Reassembling the Social: An Introduction to Actor-Network-Theory*. Oxford: Oxford UP.

Lau, K. M., Hou, W. K., Hall, B. J., Canetti, D., Ng, S. M., Lam, A. I. F., & Hobfoll, S. E. (2016). Social media and mental health in democracy movement in Hong Kong: A population-based study. *Computers in Human Behavior*, *64*, 656–662. doi:10.1016/j.chb.2016.07.028

Lay, T. (2012). *Legislación de medios y poderes fácticos en México 2000-2012*. México: Universidad. de Guadalajara.

Lay, T. (2014). Frentes para la democratización de los medios. Revista Zócalo, 171(14).

Lee, P. S., So, C. Y., & Leung, L. (2015). Social media and Umbrella Movement: Insurgent public sphere in formation. *Chinese Journal of Communication*, *8*(4), 356–375. doi:10.1080/1 7544750.2015.1088874

Lelkes, O. (2013). Happier and less isolated: Internet use in old age. *Journal of Poverty and Social Justice*, *21*(1), 33–46. doi:10.1332/175982713X664047

Lerner, J., & Tirole, J. (2002). Some simple economics of open source. *Journal of Industrial Economics*, *50*(2), 197.

Lessig, L. (2006). *Code 2.0*. New York: Basic Books.

Lessig, L. (2008). *Remix: making art and commerce thrive in the hybrid economy*. New York: Penguin Press. doi:10.5040/9781849662505

Lessig, L. (1999). *Code: And other laws of cyberspace*. New York: Basic Books.

Liang, T. P., Ho, Y. T., Li, Y. W., & Turban, E. (2011). What drives social commerce: The role of social support and relationship quality. *International Journal of Electronic Commerce*, *16*(2), 69–90. doi:10.2753/JEC1086-4415160204

Lim, M. (2006). *Cyber-urban activism and political change in Indonesia*. Eastbound, 1(1), 1–19. Retrieved from http://eastbound.eu/site_media/pdf/060101LIM.pdf

Lim, M. (2003). From real to virtual (and back again). In K. C. Ho & R. Kluver (Eds.), *Asia. Com: Asia encounters the internet* (pp. 113–128).

Lim, M. (2004). Informational terrains of identity and political power: The Internet in Indonesia. *Antropologi Indonesia*, *27*(73), 1–11.

Lim, M. (2012). Clicks, Cabs, and Coffee Houses: Social Media and Oppositional Movements in Egypt 20042001. *Journal of Communication*, *62*(2), 231–248. doi:10.1111/j.1460-2466.2012.01628.x

Lin, C., Salwen, M. B., & Abdulla, R. A. (2005). Uses and gratifications of online and offline news: New wine in an old bottle. In *Online news and the public* (pp. 221-236).

Lippman, P. (2014). Bosnia-herzegovina protests a response to post-war corruption, impoverishment. *The Washington Report on Middle East Affairs*, *33*(3), 29–30.

Liu, J., Hassanpour, N., Tatikonda, S., & Morse, A. S. (2012). Dynamic threshold models of collective action in social networks. *Paper presented at the 2012 IEEE 51st IEEE Conference on Decision and Control (CDC).* doi:10.1109/CDC.2012.6426657

Livingston, S., & Asmolov, G. (2010). Networks and the future of foreign affairs reporting. *Journalism Studies, 11*(5), 745-760. DOI:10.1080/1461670X.2010.503024

Locke, J. L. (1998). *The de-voicing of society: Why we don't talk to each other anymore.* New York, NY: Simon and Schuster.

Lopes, A. R. (2014). The Impact of Social Media on Social Movements: The New Opportunity and Mobilizing Structure. *Journal of Political Science Research.*

Lopes, A. R. (2014). The impact of social media on social movements: The new opportunity and mobilizing structure. Retrieved from https://goo.gl/Jb1OS3

Luo, Y., Hawkley, L. C., Waite, L. J., & Cacioppo, J. T. (2012). Loneliness, health, and mortality in old age: A national longitudinal study. *Social Science & Medicine, 74*(6), 907–914. doi:10.1016/j.socscimed.2011.11.028 PMID:22326307

Lu, X., & Brelsford, C. (2014). Network structure and community evolution on twitter: Human behavior change in response to the 2011 Japanese earthquake and tsunami. *Scientific Reports,* 4. PMID:25346468

Lynch, M. (2011). After Egypt: The limits and promise of online challenges to the authoritarian Arab state. *Perspectives on Politics, 9*(2), 301–310. doi:10.1017/S1537592711000910

MacKinnon, R. (2013). *Consent of the networked: The worldwide struggle for Internet freedom.* New York, NY: Basic Books.

MacKinnon, R. (2009). Book review: The power of the internet in china: Citizen activism online. *Far Eastern Economic Review,* September.

Magee, S. P. (1989). *Black hole tariffs and endogenous policy theory: Political economy in general equilibrium.* Cambridge University Press.

Maher, A. (2012). Interview with author.

Malinen, S. (2015). Understanding user participation in online communities: A systematic literature review of empirical studies. *Computers in Human Behavior, 46,* 228–238. doi:10.1016/j.chb.2015.01.004

Mamdou, V. (2004). Internet, Scale and the Global Grassroots: Geographies of the indymmedia network of independent centers. *Tijschrift voor Economics en Social Geografie, 95*(5), 48297.

Mamytova, A. (2016). *Ирина Карамшукина: Оскорбляя президента, оскорбляете государство.* Retrieved from http://24.kg/vlast/38455_irina_karamshukina_oskorblyaya_prezidenta_oskorblyaete_gosudarstvo/

Mancini, F., & O'Reilly, M. (2013). New technology and the prevention of violence and conflict. *Stability: International Journal of Security and Development*, *2*(3), 1–9.

Margetts, H. (2013). The Internet and Democracy. In W. Dutton (Ed.), The Oxford Handbook of Internet Studies (pp. 421-437). The Oxford University Press.

Maurushat, A., Chawki, M., Al-Alosi, H., & el Shazly, Y. (2014). The Impact of Social Networks and Mobile Technologies on the Revolutions in the Arab World—A Study of Egypt and Tunisia. *Laws*, *3*(4), 674–692. doi:10.3390/laws3040674

Maziad, M. (2011a, January 17). The Egyptian Citizen; The Tunisian Citizen (in Arabic). *Almasry Alyoum Independent Newschapter*. Retrieved from http://www.almasryalyoum.com/node/297381

Maziad, M. (2011b, February 7). Anger and Hope (in Arabic). *Almasry Alyoum Independent Newschapter*. Retrieved from http://www.almasryalyoum.com/node/311401

Maziad, M. (2011c, February 11). Egypt: An idea whose time has come. *Aljazeera*. Retrieved from http://english.aljazeera.net/indepth/opinion/2011/02/20112714401412146.html

McAdam, D., & Snow, D. (Eds.). (2010). *Readings on Social Movements: Origins, Dynamics and Outcomes* (2nd ed.). Oxford: Oxford University Press.

McAdam, D. (1986). Recruitment to high-risk activism: The case of Freedom, Summer. *American Journal of Sociology*, *92*(1), 64–90. doi:10.1086/228463

McCarthy, J. D., & Zald, M. N. (1987). *Social movements in an organizational society: Collected essays*. New Brunswick, NJ: Transaction.

McCaughey, M., & Ayers, M. D. (2003). *Cyberactivism: Online Activism in Theory and Practice*. New York, NY: Routledge.

McDonald, S., Oates, C., Young, C. W., & Hwang, K. (2006). Toward Sustainable Consumption: Researching Voluntary Simplifiers. *Psychology and Marketing*, *23*(6), 515–534. doi:10.1002/mar.20132

McGlinchey, E., & Johnson, E. (2007). Aiding the Internet in Central Asia. *Democratization*, *14*(2), 273–288. doi:10.1080/13510340701245785

McIver, D. J., Hawkins, J. B., Chunara, R., Chatterjee, A. K., Bhandari, A., Fitzgerald, T. P., & Brownstein, J. S. (2015). Characterizing sleep issues using twitter. *Journal of Medical Internet Research*, *17*(6), e140. doi:10.2196/jmir.4476 PMID:26054530

McManus, J. (2013). Been there, done that, bought the t-shirt: Beşiktaş fans and the commodification of football in Turkey. *International Journal of Middle East Studies*, *45*(01), 3–24. doi:10.1017/S0020743812001237

McNaughtan, H. (2012). Distinctive consumption and popular anti-consumerism: The case of Wall*E. *Journal of Media & Cultural Studies*, *26*(5), 753–766. doi:10.1080/10304312.2012.664116

Melucci, A. (1992). Che cosa è "nouvo" nei "nouvi monimenti social"? *Sociologia, 26*(2-3), 271–300.

Melvin, N., & Umaraliev, T. (2011). *New Social Media and Conflict in Kyrgyzstan*. SIRPI Insights on Peace and Security. doi:10.1037/e726612011-001

Millward, P. (2008). The rebirth of football fanzine: Using e-zines as data source. *Journal of Sport and Social Issues, 32*(3), 299–310. doi:10.1177/0193723508319718

Mohamed, A. S. (2012). On the Road to Democracy: Egyptian Bloggers and the Internet. *Journal of Arab & Muslim Media Research, 4*(2), 253–272. doi:10.1386/jammr.4.2-3.253_1

Monaghan, F. (2014). Seeing Red: social media and football fan activism. In The Language of Social Media (pp. 228-254). Palgrave Macmillan UK. doi:10.1057/9781137029317_11

Montalvo, T. (2014). En el Senado, sin votos para acción de inconstitucionalidad contra la Ley Telecom. Retrieved from http://www.animalpolitico.com/2014/07/en-el-senado-sin-votos-para-accion-de-inconstitucionalidad-contra-ley-telecom/

Montalvo, T. (2014b). Hoy vence el plazo para acción de inconstitucionalidad contra la Ley Telecom. Retrieved from http://www.animalpolitico.com/2014/08/vence-el-plazo-para-accion-de-inconstitucionalidad-contra-la-ley-telecom/

Montalvo, T. (2014c). InfoDF interpone acción de inconstitucionalidad contra Ley Telecom; Ifai declina recurso. Retrieved from http://www.animalpolitico.com/2014/08/el-ifai-discute-presentar-accion-de-inconstitucionalidad-contra-ley-telecom/

Moore, R. (1999). Democracy and cyberspace. In B. Hague & B. Loader (Eds.), *Digital democracy: Discourse and decision making in the information age*. London, England: Routledge.

Morales, A., Borondo, J., Losada, J., & Benito, R. (2014). Efficiency of human activity on information spreading on twitter. *Social Networks, 39*, 1–11. doi:10.1016/j.socnet.2014.03.007

Morozov, E. (2010, May/June). 19). Think again: The Internet. *Foreign Policy, 179*, 40–44.

Morozov, E. (2012). *The Net Delusion: The Dark Side of Internet Freedom*. New York: Public Affairs Publishing.

Musick, M. A., & Wilson, J. (2008). *Volunteering: A social profile*. Bloomington, IN: Indiana University.

Nash, V. (2013). Analyzing Freedom of Expression Online: Theoretical, Empirical and Normative Contributions. In W. Dutton (Ed.), The Oxford Handbook of Internet Studies (pp. 441-463). The Oxford University Press.

Nassif, L. (2015). Os estudantes paulistas em uma aula inesquecível de brasilidade. Retrieved from http://jornalggn.com.br/noticia/os-estudantes-paulistas-em-uma-aula-inesquecivel-de-brasilidade

Natelli, A. (2008). *Online discussion forum influence on professional sport fan support: An exploratory study* [unpublished doctoral dissertation]. Victoria University of Wellington, Wellington, New Zealand.

National Bureau of Economic Research. (2015). Data. Retrieved from http://www.nber.org/data/

Naumanen, M., & Tukiainen, M. (2007) Guiding the Elderly into the use of Computers and Internet – lessons taught and learnt IADIS. *Proceedings of theInternational Conference on Cognition and Exploratory Learning in Digital Age(CELDA '07).*

NEF. (2013) *Social Indicators: Individual* Retrieved September 30 2013 from http://www.proveandimprove.org/meaim/individuals.php

Netten, A., Burge, P., Malley, J., & Potoglou, N. (2012). Outcomes of social care for adults: Developing a preference-weighted measure. *Health Technology Assessment Reports, 16*(16), 1366–5278. PMID:22459668

Netten, A., Burge, P., Malley, J., Potoglou, N., Brazier, J., Flynn, T., & Forder, J. (2009) Outcomes of Social Care for Adults (OSCA): Interim Findings. *PSSRU Discussion Paper.* Retrieved from http//:www.PSSRU.ac.uk

Newton, K. (2001). Trust, social capital, civil society, and democracy. *International Political Science Review, 22*(2), 201–2014. doi:10.1177/0192512101222004

Ng, C. (2007). Motivation among older adults in learning computing technologies: A grounded model. *Educational Gerontology, 34*(1), 1–14. doi:10.1080/03601270701763845

Niehaves, B., & Plattfaut, R. (2013). Internet adoption by the elderly: Employing IS technology acceptance theories for understanding the age-related digital divide. *European Journal of Information Systems, 23*(6), 708–726. doi:10.1057/ejis.2013.19

Nikmat, A., Hawthorne, G., & Al-Mashoor, S. (2015). The comparison of quality of life among people with mild dementia in nursing home and home care—a preliminary report. *Dementia (London), 14*(1), 114–125. doi:10.1177/1471301213494509 PMID:24339093

Norman, M. (2012). Online community or electronic tribe? Exploring the social characteristics and spatial production of an Internet hockey fan culture. *Journal of Sport and Social Issues.* doi:10.1177/0193723512467191

Norrie, J. (2012). Loneliness on the rise as our cities atomise. *The Conversation.* Retrieved http://theconversation.edu.au/loneliness-on-the-rise-as-our-cities-atomise-6068

Norris, P. (2002). La Participación Ciudadana: México Desde Una Perspectiva Comparativa. In Avances y Retos en el Desarrollo de la Cultura Democrática en México. Instituto Federal Electoral.

Numerato, D. (2016, July 10-14). Unanticipated Outcomes of Social Movements: The Case of Football Fan Activism. *Proceedings of the Third ISA Forum of Sociology.*

O' Donnell, G. (2004). La Democracia en América Latina. El debate conceptual de la democracia. Hacia una democracia de ciudadanos y ciudadanas. Bases empíricas del informe. Programa de las Naciones Unidas para el desarrollo, Perú.

O'Brian, R., Goetz, A. M., Jan Aart, S. & Williams, M. (2000) Contesting Global Governance: multilateral economic institutions and global social movements, Cambridge: Cambridge University Press.

Oates, C., McDonald, S., Alevizou, P., Hwang, K., Young, W., & McMorland, L. (2008). Marketing Sustainability: Use of Information Sources and Degrees of Voluntary Simplicity. *Journal of Marketing Communications, 14*(5), 351–365. doi:10.1080/13527260701869148

Olson, M. (1965). *The Logic of Collective Action*. Cambridge, MA: Harvard University Press.

Olson, R. S., & Neal, Z. P. (2015). Navigating the massive world of Reddit: Using backbone networks to map user interests in social media. *PeerJ Computer Science, 1*, e4. doi:10.7717/peerj-cs.4

Olsson, T., & Viscovi, D. (2016). Remaining divides: Access to and use of ICTs among elderly citizens. In *Politics, Civil Society and Participation: Media and Communications*. Retrieved from http://www.researchingcommunication.eu

Olvera, A. (2010, October 25-26). *El desarrollo de la sociedad civil en México. Participación en el Coloquio El desarrollo de la sociedad civil en México: un enfoque multidisciplinario.* México: UNAM.

Oprn Net Initiative2013*After the Green Movement: Internet controls in Iran 2009-2012.*

Organized Crime and Corruption Reporting Project. (2016). *Kyrgyzstan: Former Chief Investigator Receives 14 Years for Corruption*. Retrieved from https://www.occrp.org/en/daily/5425-kyrgyzstan-former-chief-investigator-receives-14-years-for-corruption

Oweidat, N., Benard, C., Stahl, D., Kildani, W., O'Connell, E., & Grant, A. K. (2008). *The Kefaya movement: A case study of a grassroots reform initiative*. Retrieved from http://www.rand.org/pubs/monographs/2008/RAND_MG778.pdf

Özsomer, A. (2012). The interplay between global and local brands: A closer look at perceived brand globalness and local iconness. *Journal of International Marketing, 20*(2), 72–95. doi:10.1509/jim.11.0105

Palmer, N. A., & Perkins, D. D. (2012). Technological democratization: The potential role of ict in social and political transformation in china and beyond. *Perspectives on Global Development and Technology, 11*(4), 456–479. doi:10.1163/15691497-12341236

Pannier, B. (2009). *Rethinking Kyrgyzstan's Tulip Revolution*. Retrieved on July 1, 2016, from https://www.rferl.org/content/Rethinking_Kyrgyzstan_Tulip_Revolution/1807335

Papacharissi, Z., & Rubin, A. M. (2000). Predictors of Internet use. *Journal of Broadcasting & Electronic Media, 44*(2), 175–196. doi:10.1207/s15506878jobem4402_2

Pappas, T. S., & OMalley, E. (2014). Civil compliance and political luddism: Explaining variance in social unrest during crisis in Ireland and Greece. *The American Behavioral Scientist*, *58*(12), 1592–1613. doi:10.1177/0002764214534663

Patta, C., & de Valle, V. S. (2015). Ocupações, luta da periferia? Retrieved from http://www. carosamigos.com.br/index.php/artigos-e-debates/5667-ocupacoes-luta-da-periferia

Pearce, E. K., & Kendzior, S. (2012). Networked Authoritarianism and Social Media in Azerbaijan. *Journal of Communication*, *62*(2), 283–298. doi:10.1111/j.1460-2466.2012.01633.x

Pearce, W., Holmberg, K., Hellsten, I., & Nerlich, B. (2014). Climate Change on Twitter: Topics, Communities and Conversations about the 2013 IPCC Working Group 1 Report. *PLoS ONE*, *9*(4), e94785. doi:10.1371/journal.pone.0094785 PMID:24718388

Peattie, K., & Peattie, S. (2009). Social marketing: A pathway to consumption reduction? *Journal of Business Research*, *62*(2), 260–268. doi:10.1016/j.jbusres.2008.01.033

Pegoraro, A. (2013). Sport fanship in the digital world. In P. Pedersen (Ed.), *The Routledge Handbook of Sport Communication* (pp. 248–258). New York: Routledge.

Perland, D. (2004). European and Canadian studies of loneliness among seniors. *Canadian Journal on Aging*, *23*(2), 181–188. doi:10.1353/cja.2004.0025 PMID:15334817

Peschard, J. (2006). *La democracia ayer y hoy. A cuarenta años de La democracia en México de Pablo González Casanova. Ponencia presentada en el homenaje a Pablo González Casanova*. México: Instituto de Investigaciones Sociales, Universidad Nacional Autónoma de México.

Pina, P. (2015). File-Sharing of Copyrighted Works, P2P, and the Cloud: Reconciling Copyright and Privacy Rights. In M. Gupta (Ed.), Handbook of Research on Emerging Developments in Data Privacy (pp. 52-69). Hershey, PA: IGI Global.

Piña-García, C. A., Gershenson, C., & Siqueiros-García, J. M. (2016). Towards a standard sampling methodology on online social networks: Collecting global trends on twitter. *Applied Network Science*, *1*(1), 1–19. doi:10.1007/s41109-016-0004-1

Piña-García, C. A., & Gu, D. (2013). Spiraling Facebook: An alternative metropolis-Hastings random walk using a spiral proposal distribution. *Social Network Analysis and Mining*, *3*(4), 1403–1415. doi:10.1007/s13278-013-0126-8

Pitts, G. (2011). Professionalism Among Journalists in Kyrgyzstan. In E. Freedman & R. Shafer (Eds.), *After the czars and commissars: journalism in authoritarian post-Soviet Central Asia* (pp. 233–243). East Lansing, MI: Michigan State University Press.

Podesta, S., & Addis, M. (2005). Long life to marketing research: A Postmodern view. *European Journal of Marketing*, *39*(3/4), 386–412. doi:10.1108/03090560510581836

Podolskaya, D. (2016). *Глава ОО Психическое здоровье и общество» требует от комиссии по рассмотрению жалоб на СМИ наказать Вести.ru.* Retrieved on July 1, 2016, from http://www.24.kg/obschestvo/28292_glava_oo_psihicheskoe_zdorove_i_obschestvo_trebuet_ot_komissii_po_rassmotreniyu_jalob_na_smi_nakazat_vestiru/

Powell, W. W. (1990). Neither market nor hierarchy: Network forms of organization. *Research in Organizational Behavior, 12*, 295–336.

Radcliffe-Brown, A. (1996). *Estructura y función en la sociedad primitiva.* Barcelona: Península.

Radio Free Europe/Radio Liberty. (2014). *Report: Western Firms Help Central Asian States Spy On Citizens.* Retrieved from http://www.rferl.org/a/26701293.html

Radnitz, S. (2012). *Weapons of the Wealthy: Predatory Regimes and Elite-Led Protests in Central Asia.* Ithaca, NY: Cornell University Press.

Rahimi, B. (2011a). Facebook Iran: The carnivalesque politics of online social networking. *Sociologica, 3.*

Rahimi, B. (2011b). The agonistic social media: Cyberspace in the formation of dissent and consolodation of state power in postelection Iran. *Communication Review, 14*(3), 158–178. doi:10.1080/10714421.2011.597240

Randeree, B. (2011, July 11). The Arab Spring. *Aljazeera.* Retrieved from http://english.aljazeera.net/indepth/features/2011/07/201177101959751184.html

Rao, H. (1998). Caveat Emptor: The Construction of Nonprofit Consumer Watchdog Organizations. *American Journal of Sociology, 103*(January), 912–961. doi:10.1086/231293

Rasouli, M. R., & Moradi, M. (2012, October). Factors affecting the production of contents in Social Networks. *Olum-e Ejtemaei, 55*, 57–66.

Raymond, E. S. (2001). *The cathedral and the bazaar: Musings on Linux and Open Source by an accidental revolutionary.* Sebastopol, CA: O'Reilly.

Renn, O., Jovanovic, A., & Schröter, R. (2011). Social unrest. *OECD.* Retrieved from http://www.oecd.org/governance/risk/46890018.pdf

Renninger, K. A., & Shumar, W. (2002). *Building virtual communities: Learning and change in cyberspace.* Cambridge University Press. doi:10.1017/CBO9780511606373

Reporters without Borders2014World press freedom index 2014.

Reuter, O., & Szakonyi, D. (2015). Online Social Media and Political Awareness in Authoritarian Regimes. *British Journal of Political Science, 45*(1), 29–51. doi:10.1017/S0007123413000203

Reysen, S., & Branscombe, N. R. (2010). Fanship and Fanship: Comparisons between sport fans and non-sport fans. *Journal of Sport Behavior, 33*, 176–193.

Rheingold, H. (2000). *The Virtual Community.* Retrieved from http://www.rheingold.com/vc/book/intro.html

Riaza, J. (1983). La democracia y los poderes fácticos, en *Revista Fomento Social, 152,* 427-434.

Rich, F. (2011, February 5). Wallflowers at the revolution. *New York Times.* Retrieved from http://www.nytimes.com/2011/02/06/opinion/06rich.html

Rieder, B. (2013). Studying Facebook via data extraction: the Netvizz application. *Proceedings of the 5th Annual ACM Web Science Conference* (pp. 346-355).

Risse, T., Ropp, S. C., & Sikkink, K. (1999). *The Power of Human Rights: international norms and domestic change.* Cambridge: Cambridge University Press. doi:10.1017/CBO9780511598777

Roberts, A. (2013). *The end of protest: How free-market capitalism learned to control dissent.* Cornell University Press.

Robles, J. (2014). La guerra abierta de Enrique Peña Nieto Contra Internet. *Vice.com.* Retrieved from http://www.vice.com/es_mx/read/la-guerra-abierta-de-enrique-pena-nieto-contra-internet

Rodrigues, C. (2015). Desinformação sobre reorganização cria boataria e pânico. Retrieved from http://www.cartaeducacao.com.br/reportagens/desinformacao-sobre-reorganizacao-cria-boataria-e-panico/

Rogers, R. (2013). *Digital methods.* Cambridge, MA: MIT Press.

Rogers, R., Weltevrede, E., Niederer, S., & Borra, E. (2012). *National Web Studies: Mapping Iran Online.*

Rojas, M. (2012). Peña no asistirá a debate convocado por #YoSoy132. *Radioformula.com.* Retrieved from http://www.radioformula.com.mx/notas.asp?Idn=248481

Rolfe, B. (2005). Building an electronic repertoire of contention. *Social Movement Studies, 4*(1), 65–74. doi:10.1080/14742830500051945

Rosenau, J. N. (1995). Governance in the Twenty-first Century. *Global Governance, 1*(1), 13–43.

Rosenau, J. (1997). *Along the Domestic Foreign Frontier: exploring governance in a turbulent world.* Cambridge: Cambridge University Press. doi:10.1017/CBO9780511549472

Rosenau, J. (1999). Toward an Ontology for Global Governance. In M. Hewson & J. Sinclair Timothy (Eds.), *Approaches to Global Governance Theory.* Albany: State University of New York.

Rostama, G. (2015). Remix Culture and Amateur Creativity: A Copyright Dilemma. *WIPO.* Retrieved from http://www.wipo.int/wipo_magazine/en/2015/03/article_0006.html

Roubini, N. (2011). The instability of inequality. *Project Syndicate.* Retrieved from https://www.project-syndicate.org/commentary/the-instability-of-inequality

Roy, S. D., & Zeng, W. (2014). *Social multimedia signals.* Springer.

Ruggerio, T. E. (2000). Uses and Gratification Theory in the 21st Century. *Mass Communication & Society, 3*(1), 3–37. doi:10.1207/S15327825MCS0301_02

Ruijgrok, K. (2016). From the web to the streets: Internet and protests under authoritarian regimes. *Democratization.* doi:10.1080/13510347.2016.1223630

Russell, M. A. (2013). *Mining the social web: Data mining Facebook, twitter, LinkedIn, google+, GitHub, and more.* O`Reilly Media Inc.

Safko, L., & Brake, D. K. (2009). *The Social Media Bible.* New Jersey: John Wiley & Sons, Inc.

Salen, K., & Zimmerman, E. (2004). *Rules of Play – Game Design Fundamentals.* Massachusetts Institute of Technology.

Sampedro, V., & Lobera, J. (2014). The Spanish 15-M Movement: A consensual dissent? *Journal of Spanish Cultural Studies, 15*(1-2), 61–80. doi:10.1080/14636204.2014.938466

Sánchez, E. (2009). *Poderes fácticos y gobernabilidad autoritaria. La "Ley Televisa" como estudio de caso, en: Alma Rosa Alva, y Javier Esteinou (Coord), La "Ley Televisa" y la lucha por el poder en México.* México: UAM.

Santos, B. S. (2005). The counter-hegemonic use of law in the struggle for a globalization from below. *Anales de la Cátedra Francisco Suarez, Revista de Filosofía Jurídica y Política, 39,* 363-474. Retrieved from http://revistaseug.ugr.es/index.php/acfs/article/viewFile/1035/1225

Sassatelli, R. (2007). Consumer culture: History, theory and politics. *Sage (Atlanta, Ga.).*

Savchenko, I. (2016). *Kazakhstan: The oppression of journalists and bloggers.* Open Dialogue Foundation. Retrieved from http://en.odfoundation.eu/a/7228,kazakhstan-the-oppression-of-journalists-and-bloggers1

Sayan, A. (2013). *Futbol tribünlerinin izinde forumlar: Alisamiyen.net analizi* [Online forums as football terraces: Analysis of Alisamiyen.net] [Unpublished doctoral dissertation]. İstanbul Bilgi University.

Schattschneider, E. E. (1975). The Semisovereign People: A Realist's View of Democracy in America. Fort Worth, TX: Harcourt Brace Jovanovich College Publishers.

Scheffer, M., Westley, F., & Brock, W. (2003). Slow response of societies to new problems: Causes and costs. *Ecosystems (New York, N.Y.), 6*(5), 493–502. doi:10.1007/s10021-002-0146-0

Segerberg, A., & Bennett, W. L. (2011). Social Media and the Organization of Collective Action: Using Twitter to Explore the Ecologies of Two Climate Change Protests. *Communication Review, 14*(3), 197–215. doi:10.1080/10714421.2011.597250

Seidel, D., Brayne, C., & Jagger, C. (2011). Limitations in physical functioning among older people as a predictor of subsequent disability in instrumental activities of daily living. *Age and Ageing, 40*(4), 463–469. RetrievedOctober102013 doi:10.1093/ageing/afr054 PMID:21609999

Serfass, D. G., & Sherman, R. A. (2015). Situations in 140 characters: Assessing real-world situations on twitter. *PLoS ONE, 10*(11), e0143051. doi:10.1371/journal.pone.0143051 PMID:26566125

Shafiev, A., & Miles, M. (2015). Friends, Foes, and Facebook: Blocking the Internet in Tajikistan. *Demokratizatsiya: The Journal of Post-Soviet Democratization, 23*(3), 297–319.

Shah, S. K. (2006). Motivation, governance, and the viability of hybrid forms in open source software development. *Management Science, 52*(7), 1000–1014. doi:10.1287/mnsc.1060.0553

Shah, V., Nojin Kwak, R., & Lance Holbert, D. (2001). Connecting" and" disconnecting" with civic life: Patterns of Internet use and the production of social capital. *Political Communication, 18*(2), 141–162. doi:10.1080/105846001750322952

Shangapour, I., Hosseini, S., & Hashemnejad, H. (2011). Cyber Social Networks and Social Movements. *Global Journal of Human Social Science, 11*(1), 1–17.

Shaw, M. E. (1964). Communication networks. *Advances in Experimental Social Psychology, 1*, 111–147. doi:10.1016/S0065-2601(08)60050-7

Shen, A. X., Cheung, C. M., Lee, M. K., & Chen, H. (2011). How social influence affects we-intention to use instant messaging: The moderating effect of usage experience. *Information Systems Frontiers, 13*(2), 157–169. doi:10.1007/s10796-009-9193-9

Shirky, C. (2008). *Here comes everybody: How changes happen when people come together*. Penguin Books.

Shirky, C. (2008). *Here Comes Everybody: The Power of Organizing Without Organizations*. Penguin Press.

Siegel, D. A. (2009). Social Networks and Collective Action. *American Journal of Political Science, 53*(1), 12238. doi:10.1111/j.1540-5907.2008.00361.x

Silva, A. M. M. (2002). *Escola pública e a formação da cidadania: possibilidades e limites. 222f. Tese (Doutorado em Educação)*. Universidade de São Paulo, São Paulo: Faculdade de Educação.

Slocum, J. W. Jr, Conder, W., Corradini, E., Foster, R., Frazer, R., Lei, D., & Scott, S. et al. (2006). Fermentation in the China Beer Industry. *Organizational Dynamics, 35*(1), 32–48. doi:10.1016/j.orgdyn.2005.12.002

Smith, A. (2013). Civic engagement in the digital age. Pew Research Center.

Smith, C. (2001). China backs away from initial denial in school explosion. Retrieved from https://goo.gl/AHjpTv

Smith, T. (2013). Food price spikes and social unrest in Africa. *CCAPS Research Brief*(11).

Snow, D. A., Soule, S. A., & Kriesi, H. (2007). Mapping the Terrain. In D. A. Snow, S. A. Soule, & H. Kriesi (Eds.), *The Blackwell Companion to Social Movements* (pp. 3–16). Malden, MA: Blackwell Publishing. doi:10.1002/9780470999103.ch1

Social Issues Research Centre. (2008). Football Passions (Research Report). Retrieved from http://www.sirc.org/football/football_passions.pdf

Sohrabi-Haghighat, M. H., & Mansouri, S. (2010). Where is my Vote? ICT politics in the aftermath of Iran's Presidential Election. *International Journal of Emerging Technologies and Society*, 8(1), 24–41.

Solís Leere, B. (2014) Intervención de Beatriz Solís en reunión con la Amedi. Guadalajara, Jalisco.

Somuano, F. (2011). *Sociedad Civil Organizada y Democracia en México.*

Spósito, M. P. (2002). Educação, gestão democrática e participação popular. In Bastos, J. B. (Ed.), Gestão democrática. Rio de Janeiro: DP&A, SEPE.

Sreberny, A., & Khiabany, G. (2010). *Blogistan: The Internet and politics in Iran.* London: I.B. Tauris.

Srinivasan, R., & Fish, A. (2009). Internet Authorship: Social and Political Implications Within Kyrgyzstan. *Journal of Computer-Mediated Communication*, 14(3), 559–580. doi:10.1111/j.1083-6101.2009.01453.x

Stafford, T. F., Stafford, M. R., & Schkade, L. L. (2004). Determining uses and gratifications for the Internet. *Decision Sciences*, 35(2), 259–288. doi:10.1111/j.00117315.2004.02524.x

Statista. (2016). Leading countries based on number of Facebook users as of May 2016 (in millions), Retrieved from http://www.statista.com/statistics/268136/top-15-countries-based-on-number-of-facebook-users/

Stearns, P. (2006). *Consumerism in World History: The Global Transformation of Consumer Desire* (2nd ed.). London, New York: Routledge.

Steenkamp, J.-B. E. M., & de Jong, M. G. (2010). A global investigation into the constellation of consumer attitudes toward global and local products. *Journal of Marketing*, 74(4), 18–40. doi:10.1509/jmkg.74.6.18

Stein, L. (2009). Social Movement Web Use in Theory and Practice: A Content Analysis of US Movement Websites. *New Media & Society*, 11(5), 749–771. doi:10.1177/1461444809105350

Storck, M. (2011). *The Role of Social Media in Political Mobilisation: A Case Study of the January 2011 Egyptian Uprising* [Unpublished master dissertation]. University of St Andrews, Scotland.

Strizhakova, Y., Coulter, R. A., & Price, L. L. (2011). Branding in a global marketplace: The mediating effects of quality and self-identity brand signals. *International Journal of Research in Marketing*, 28(4), 342–351. doi:10.1016/j.ijresmar.2011.05.007

Sunstein, C. (2007). *Republic.com.* Princeton, NJ: Princeton University Press.

Sun, Y. (1991). The Chinese protests of 1989: The issue of corruption. *Asian Survey*, 31(8), 762–782. doi:10.2307/2645228

Suzor, N. (2006). *Transformative Use of Copyright Material* [LLM Thesis]. QUT School of Law. Retrieved from http://nic.suzor.com/articles/TransformativeUse.pdf

Tabnak. (2012, October 11). Retrieved from http://bit.ly/1ecbBo7

Tajfel, H. (1978). *Differentiation between social groups: Studies in the social psychology of intergroup relations*. London: Academic Press.

Talimciler, A. (2012). *1920'den günümüze Türkiye'de toplumsal yapı ve değişim*. İstanbul: PhoenixYayınları.

Tang, G., & Lee, F. L. F. (2013). Facebook use and political participation: The impact of exposure to shared political information, connections with public political actors, and network structural heterogeneity. *Social Science Computer Review, 31*(6), 763–773. doi:10.1177/0894439313490625

Tardini, S., & Cantoni, L. (2005). A semiotic approach to online communities: belonging, interest and identity in websites' and videogames' communities. In P. Isaías, P. Commers, & M. McPherson (Eds.), *e-Society 2005, Proceedings of the IADIS International Conference, Qawra, Malta, International association for development of the information society* (pp. 371-378).

Tarrow, S. (1998). *Power in movement: Social movement and contentious politics*. Cambridge, England: Cambridge University Press. doi:10.1017/CBO9780511813245

Tarrow, S. (2005). *The New Transnational Activism*. Cambridge: Cambridge University Press. doi:10.1017/CBO9780511791055

Taylor, A. (2011) Social Media as a Tool for Inclusion, Research Report, Canada.

Thapen, N. A., & Ghanem, M. M. (2013). Towards passive political opinion polling using twitter. Proceedings of the BCS SGAI SMA 2013 the BCS SGAI workshop on social media analysis (p. 19).

Theobald, R. (2002). Containing corruption. *New Political Economy, 7*(3), 435–449. doi:10.1080/1356346022000018775

Tian, Y. (2006). Political use and perceived effects of the Internet: A case study of the 2004 election. *Communication Research Reports, 23*(2), 129–137. doi:10.1080/08824090600669103

Tilly, C. (2004). *Social movements: 1768-2004*. Boulder, CO: Paradigm.

Tilly, C. (2003). Social Movements. Enter the Twenty-first Century. *Paper presented at the conference on Contentious Politics and the Economic Opportunity Structure*.

Tilly, C. (1984). Social Movements and National Politics. In C. Bright & S. F. Harding (Eds.), *Statemaking and social movements: essays in history and theory* (pp. 297–317). Ann Arbor: University of Michigan Press.

Tilly, C. (1995). *Popular Contention in Great Britain, 1758–1834*. Cambridge, MA: Harvard University Press.

Tilly, C. (2004). *Social Movements, 1768–2004* (p. 184). Boulder, Colorado, USA: Paradigm Publishers.

Tilly, C. (2005). *Identities*. Boundaries, and Social Ties.

Tilly, C. (2006). *Regimes and Repertoires*. University Of Chicago Press. doi:10.7208/chicago/9780226803531.001.0001

Tilly, C., & Tarrow, S. (2007). *Contentious Politics*. Colorado: Paradigm Publishers.

Toder-Alon, A., Brunel, F. F., & Schneier Siegal, W. L. (2005). Ritual behavior and community change: Exploring the social-psychological roles of net rituals in the developmental processes of online consumption communities. In *Online consumer psychology: Understanding and influencing consumer behavior in the virtual world* (pp. 7-33).

Toralieva, G. (2014). Kyrgyzstan-Challenges for Environmental Journalism. In Y. Kalyango & D. Mould (Eds.), Global Journalism Practice and New Media Performance (pp. 214-226). Palgrave Macmillan.

Totten, M. (2015). Sport activism and political praxis within the FC Sankt Pauli fan subculture. *Soccer & Society*, *16*(4), 453–468. doi:10.1080/14660970.2014.882828

Trere, E. (2008). Social Movements as Information Ecologies: Exploring the Coevolution of Multiple Internet Technologies for Activism. *International Journal of Communication*, *6*, 2359–2377.

Trilling, D. (2011). *Kyrgyzstan: Osh Blame Inquiry Censors Independent Media*. Retrieved on June 28, 2016, from www.eurasianet.org/node/63694

Tsai, H., Shillair, R., & Cotten, S. (2014) Social Support and 'Playing Around': An Examination of How Older Adults Acquire Digital Literacy with Tablet Computers. *Proceedings of the TPRC2014 Conference*.

Tufekci, Z., & Wilson, C. (2012). Social Media and the Decision to Participate in Political Protest: Observations from Tahrir Square. *Journal of Communication*, *62*(2), 363–379. doi:10.1111/j.1460-2466.2012.01629.x

TUIK. (2013). Spor istatistikleri (data). Retrieved from http://www.tuik.gov.tr/VeriBilgi.do?alt_id=1087

Tuomela, R., & Miller, K. (1985). We-Intentions and social action. *Analyse & Kritik*, *7*(1), 26–43. doi:10.1515/auk-1985-0102

Tuomela, R., & Miller, K. (1988). We-intentions. *Philosophical Studies*, *53*(3), 367–389. doi:10.1007/BF00353512

Tuomela, R. (1995). *The importance of us: A philosophical study of basic social notions*. Stanford, CA: Stanford University Press.

Turkish Statistical Institute. (2013). Demographic statistics of Turkey. Retrieved from http://www.turkstat.gov.tr

Turner, J. C., Hogg, M. A., Oakes, P. J., Reicher, S. D., & Wetherell, M. S. (1987). *Rediscovering the social group*. Oxford, England: Basil Blackwell.

Tynaeva, N. (2016). *Ограничить кыргызстанцам доступ к иностранным сайтам хотят депутаты*. Retrieved from on October 28, 2016, http://knews.kg/2016/03/ogranichit-kyrgyzstantsam-dostup-k-inostrannym-sajtam-hotyat-deputaty

United States Copyright Office. (2016). *The Making Available Right in the United States*. Retrieved from http://copyright.gov/docs/making_available/making-available-right.pdf

Valenzuela, S., Arriagada, A., & Scherman, A. (2012). The social media basis of youth protest behavior: The case of Chile. *Journal of Communication, 62*(2), 299–314. doi:10.1111/j.1460-2466.2012.01635.x

Vallina-Rodriguez, N., Scellato, S., Haddadi, H., Forsell, C., Crowcroft, J., & Mascolo, C. (2012). *Los Twindignados: The Rise of the Indignados Movement on Twitter. Proceedings of the 2012 ASE/IEEE International Conference on Social Computing and 2012 ASE/IEEE International Conference on Privacy, Security, Risk and Trust*. Washington, DC. doi:10.1109/SocialCom-PASSAT.2012.120

Van de Donk, W., Loader, B. D., Nixon, P. G., & Rucht, D. (2004). *Cyberprotest: New Media, Citizens, and Social Movements*. Routledge.

Van Laer, J., & Van Aelst, P. (2010). Cyber-protest and civil society: The Internet and action repertoires in social movements. In Y. Jewkes and Yar, Majid (Eds.), Handbook of Internet Crime (pp. 230-254). Abingdon, UK: Willan Publishing.

Van Stekelenburg, J., & Klandermans, B. (2013). The social psychology of protest. *Current Sociology, 61*(5-6), 886–905. doi:10.1177/0011392113479314

van Stekelenburg, J., & Klandermans, P. G. (2007). Individuals in movements: A social psychology of contention. In P. G. Klandermans & C. M. Roggeband (Eds.), *The Handbook of Social Movements Across Disciplines* (pp. 157–204). New York: Springer.

Vargas, R. (2014). Peña Nieto promulga la Ley Federal de Telecomunicaciones y Radiodifusión. Diario La Jornada. Retrieved from http://www.jornada.unam.mx/ultimas/2014/07/14/pena-nieto-promulgara-hoy-la-ley-federal-de-telecomunicaciones-y-radiodifusion-5219.html

Varnali, K., & Gorgulu, V. (2015). A social influence perspective on expressive political participation in Twitter: The case of #OccupyGezi. *Information Communication and Society, 18*(1), 1–16. doi:10.1080/1369118X.2014.923480

Veloutsou, C., & Moutinho, L. (2009). Brand relationships through brand reputation and brand tribalism. *Journal of Business Research, 62*(3), 314–322. doi:10.1016/j.jbusres.2008.05.010

Verba, S., & Nie, N. H. (1987). *Participation in America: political democracy and social equality*. Chicago: University of Chicago Press.

Vitak, J., Zube, P., Smock, A., Carr, C. T., Ellison, N., & Lampe, C. (2011). Its complicated: Facebook users political participation in the 2008 election. *Cyberpsychology, Behavior, and Social Networking, 14*(3), 107–114. doi:10.1089/cyber.2009.0226 PMID:20649449

Voorwald, H. (2015). A reorganização paulista e o novo modelo de escola. Retrieved from http://www.educacao.sp.gov.br/noticias/a-reorganizacao-paulista-e-o-novo-modelo-de-escola

Wang, K. Y. (2008). Online Forums as an Arena for Political Discussions: What Politicians and Activists can Learn from Teachers. *American Communication Journal, 10*(3).

Wann, D. L., Grieve, F. G., End, C., Zapalac, R. K., Lanter, J., Pease, D. G., & Wallace, A. et al. (2013). Examining the superstitions of sport fans: Types of superstitions, perceptions of impact, and relationship with team identification. *Athletic Insight, 5*, 21–44.

Wann, D. L., Hunter, J. L., Ryan, J. A., & Wright, L. A. (2001). The relationship between team identification and willingness of sport fans to consider illegally assisting their team. *Social Behavior and Personality, 29*(6), 531–536. doi:10.2224/sbp.2001.29.6.531

Warf, B. (2013). The Central Asian Digital Divide. In R. Massimo & G. Muschert (Eds.), The Digital Divide: The Internet and social inequality in international perspective (pp. 270-271). Academic Press.

Warf, B. (2012). *Global Geographies of the Internet*. New York, NY: Springer.

We are Social. (2016). 2016 Digital Yearbook. Retrieved from http://wearesocial.com/uk/special-reports/digital-in-2016

Webster, S. (2011, February 16). Has social media revolutionized revolutions? *World News, 87*(15). Retrieved from http://www.jcunews.com/2011/02/16/has-social-media-revolutionized-revolutions/

Weikum, G., Ntarmos, N., Spaniol, M., Triantafillou, P., Benczur, A. A., Kirkpatrick, S., & Williamson, M. (2011). Longitudinal analytics on web archive data: it's about time! Proceedings of CIDR (pp. 199-202).

Wells, Y., & Herd, A. (2013, November). Congregate Housing: Impacts on quality of life and social participation. *Proceedings of the Grey Expectations Ageing in the 21ˢᵗ Century AAG Conference*, Sydney.

Wenger, E., & Snyder, W. (2000). Communities of practice: The organizational frontier. *Harvard Business Review, 78*(1), 139–144. PMID:11184968

Wenger, E. (1998). *Communities of practice. Learning, meaning and identity*. Cambridge: Cambridge University Press. doi:10.1017/CBO9780511803932

Wenger, E., McDermott, R. A., & Snyder, W. (2002). Cultivating communities of practice. Boston, MA: Harvard Business School Press.

Weng, L., Flammini, A., Vespignani, A., & Menczer, F. (2012). Competition among memes in a world with limited attention. *Scientific Reports*, 2. PMID:22461971

Werra, J. (2001). Le régime juridique des mesures techniques de protection des oeuvres selon les Traités de l'OMPI, le Digital Millennium Copyright Act, les Directives Européennes et d'autres legislations (Japon, Australie). *Revue Internationale du Droit d'Auteur*, *189*, 66–213.

Wertsch, J. V. (2002). *Voices of collective remembering*. Cambridge, UK: Cambridge University. doi:10.1017/CBO9780511613715

White, H., McConnell, E., Clipp, E., Branch, L. G., Sloane, R., Pieper, C., & Box, T. L. (2002). A randomized controlled trial of the psychosocial impact of providing internet training and access to older adults. *Aging & Mental Health*, *6*(3), 213–221. doi:10.1080/13607860220142422 PMID:12217089

Whiting, A., & Williams, D. (2013). Why people use social media: A uses and gratifications approach. *Qualitative Market Research: An International Journal*, *16*(4), 362–369. doi:10.1108/QMR-06-2013-0041

WHO. (2001a). *Health and ageing: A discussion paper*. Geneva: World Health Organization.

WHO. (2001b). *Active ageing: From evidence to action*. Geneva: World Health Organization.

Wikipedia. (2016a). *About*. Retrieved from https://en.wikipedia.org/wiki/Wikipedia:About

Wikipedia. (2016b). *Five pillars*. Retrieved from https://en.wikipedia.org/wiki/Wikipedia:Five_pillars

Wikipedia. (n. d.). Gezi Park Protests. Retrieved from https://en.wikipedia.org/wiki/Gezi_Park_protests

Wilhelm, A. G. (1998). Virtual sounding boards: How deliberative is on-line political discussion. *Information Communication and Society*, *1*(3), 313–338. doi:10.1080/13691189809358972

Wilkinson, C., & Jetpyspayeva, Y. (2012). From Blogging Central Asia to Citizen Media: A Practitioners' Perspective on the Evolution of the *neweurasia* Blog Project. *Europe-Asia*, *64*(8), 1395–1414. doi:10.1080/09668136.2012.712267

Williams, W. N. (2015). Observing protest: Media use and student involvement on 7 April 2010 in Bishkek, Kyrgyzstan. *Central Asian Survey*, *34*(3), 373–389. doi:10.1080/02634937.2015.1007663

Wojcieszak, M., Smith, B., & Enayat, M. (2012). *Finding a way: How Iranians reach for news and information*. Iran Media Program.

Wojcieszak, M. (2009). Carrying online participation offline: Mobilization by radical online groups and politically dissimilar offline ties. *Journal of Communication*, *59*(3), 564–586. doi:10.1111/j.1460-2466.2009.01436.x

Wojcieszak, M., & Smith, B. (2014). Will politics be tweeted? New media use by Iranian youth in 2011. *New Media & Society*, *16*(1), 91–109. doi:10.1177/1461444813479594

Wright, S. C. (2001). Strategic collective action: Social psychology and social change. In R. Brown & S. Gaertner (Eds.), Blackwell handbook of social psychology (Vol. 4, pp. 409–430). Oxford, England: Blackwell Press.

Xenos, M. (2008). New mediated deliberation: Blog and press coverage of the Alito nomination. *Journal of Computer-Mediated Communication, 13*(2), 485–503. doi:10.1111/j.1083-6101.2008.00406.x

Xie, B., & Jaeger, P. (2008). Computer training programs for older adults at the Public Library. *Public Libraries*, (Sept/Oct), 52–59.

Yang, G. (2009). Online activism. *Journal of Democracy, 20*(3), 33–36. doi:10.1353/jod.0.0094

York, J. (2011, January 14). Not Twitter, Not WikiLeaks: A human revolution [blog post]. Retrieved from http://jilliancyork.com/2011/01/14/not-twitter-not-wikileaks-a-human-revolution/

YoSoy132. (2012). Primer comunicado de la Coordinadora del Movimiento YoSoy132 (Manifiesto). Retrieved from https://es.wikisource.org/wiki/Primer_comunicado_de_la_Coordinadora_del_Movimiento_YoSoy132_(Manifiesto)

Yu, R. P. (2016). The relationship between passive and active non-political social media use and political expression on Facebook and Twitter. *Computers in Human Behavior, 58*, 413–420. doi:10.1016/j.chb.2016.01.019

Yüksel, Ü., & Mirza, M. (2010). Consumers of the postmodern world: Theories of Anti-consumption and impression management. *Marmara Üniversitesi İİBF Dergisi, 29*(2), 495–512.

Zanoza.kg. (2015). *МВД просит помочь граждан "патрулировать" социальные сети.* Retrieved on February 21, 2016, from http://zanoza.kg/doc/330299_mvd_prosit_pomoch_grajdan_patrylirovat_socialnye_seti.html

Zavestoski, S. (2002). The Social–Psychological Bases of Anticonsumption Attitudes. *Psychology and Marketing, 19*(2), 149–165. doi:10.1002/mar.10007

Zheng, R., Spears, J., Luptak, M., & Wilby, F. (2015). Understanding Older Adults Perceptions of Internet Use: An Exploratory Factor Analysis. *Educational Gerontology, 41*(7), 504–518. doi:10.1080/03601277.2014.1003495

Zhou, T. (2011). Understanding online community user participation: A social influence perspective. *Internet Research, 21*(1), 67–81. doi:10.1108/10662241111104884

Zuckerman, E. (2014). New media, new civics? *Policy and Internet, 6*(2), 151–168. doi:10.1002/1944-2866.POI360

About the Contributors

Steven Gordon is a Professor at Babson College in the Technology Information and Operations Management Division. He has been published widely in the academic press and is the editor of three text books and two research anthologies. He serves on the Advisory Board of the International Journal of e-Politics and the Journal of Information Technology Case and Application Research, where he was previously Editor-in-Chief. Before arriving at Babson, Dr. Gordon founded and served as president of Beta Principles, Inc., a developer and marketer of accounting software and reseller of computer hardware. He has also consulted to the airline industry at Simat, Helliesen & Eichner, Inc (now SH&E). He holds a Ph.D. in Transportation Systems from the Massachusetts Institute of Technology.

***

Norah Abokhodair is a Fulbright scholar and a Ph.D. candidate at the University of Washington Information School (PhD anticipated in June 2017). She is a member of the UW Value Sensitive Design Lab and a co-founder of the UW Political Bots. org project. She researches cross-cultural information system design through social computing and human-computer interaction. Within these fields, she conducts research to examine the information practices of Arab technology users to inform product design and policy. Her research reflects her strong passion for designing and evaluating collaborative, social, and inclusive technologies. Abokhodair creatively combines her experience conducting and designing research projects, her expert knowledge of qualitative, quantitative, and visual methods, and her multilingual and cross-cultural background to turn complex ideas and results to actionable insights. She frequently works across industry research and academia, publishing my research in venues like ACM CSCW(Conference on Computer-Supported Cooperative Work and Social Computing) ACM SIGCHI(Special Interest Group on Computer-Human Interaction) and ACM DIS (Designing Interactive Systems). Numerous outlets have also featured her research, such as the CNN and the University of Washington news blog.

Julio Amador is a research associate at Imperial Business Analytics at Imperial College London. Julio is also CTO at pollstr.io. Julio received his degree in Economics from the University of Essex. Julio has previously held positions at CIDE and EGADE Business School at Tec de Monterrey.

Yonca Aslanbay is professor of marketing and the chair at the Communication PhD, Istanbul Bilgi University. She received her Ph.D. degree in 1992 and has been lecturing in different universities since then. Her current teaching agenda and prior publications are in the domains of marketing and consumer behavior. Her recent research focuses on the new types of online collectivities and sustainability.

Cynthia H. W. Corrêa (Brazil) is an Assistant Professor of Information and Communication Technologies at the School of Arts, Sciences and Humanities, University of São Paulo (USP). The leader of the Humanitas Digitalis Research Group, linked to the National Council for Scientific and Technological Development (CNPq-Brazil), and a member of the International Federation for Information Technology and Travel and Tourism (IFITT) and of the Athens Institute for Education and Research (ATINER). Dr. Cynthia has coordinated research projects with the financial support of USP and CNPq-Brazil with emphasis on digital culture, online marketing, and technological innovation, involving students in undergraduate and graduate levels. Also, research results have been published in peer-reviewed journals and books, both nationally and internationally.

İrem Erdoğmuş She was born in 1976 in Istanbul, and completed her bachelor degree on Political Science and International Relations at Boğaziçi University, Faculty of Economics and Administrative Sciences in 1998. She started her academic career as a research assistant at Marmara University, Department of Business Administration in 1999. She completed her Ph.D in Marketing at Boğaziçi University, Social Sciences Institute in 2005. Currently, she teaches at Marmara University, Department of Business Administration as an associate professor. Her research and teaching areas include brand management, services marketing, international marketing, emerging markets, and social media marketing. She has book chapters in national and international books, and articles in national and international journals, some of which include European Journal of Marketing, International Marketing Review, and Journal of Fashion Marketing Management.

Sinem Ergun Born in 1976. She studied Beyoğlu Anatolian High School. She graduated from Marmara University, Faculty of Economics and Administrative Sciences, department of Business Administration. She received Master's Degree from Middlesex University. She completed her Ph.D in Management and Organization (in English) at Marmara University, Social Sciences Institute in 2006. Since 2001, she has been member of Marmara University, Faculty of Business Administration, Business Administration (in English) department. Her research and teaching areas include entrepreneurship, strategic management, small business management and research methods in social sciences.

Itır Erhart studied philosophy and Western Languages & Literatures at Boğaziçi University. She completed her M.A. in Philosophy at the same university and her M.Phil. at the University of Cambridge. In 2001 she started teaching at Istanbul Bilgi University, Department of Media and Communication Systems. In 2006 she earned her PhD from Boğaziçi University in philosophy. She is the author of the book "What Am I?" and several articles on gender, sports, human rights and media including "United in Protest: From 'Living and Dying with Our Colors' to 'Let All the Colors of the World Unite" and "Ladies of Beşiktaş: A dismantling of male hegemony at İnönü Stadium" Erhart is also the co-founder of Adim Adim, Turkey's first charity running group. In 2009 she was featured on CNN Turk's "Turkey's Changemakers". She was awarded Ten Outstanding Persons (TOYP) award in 2010. In 2014 she became an Ashoka Fellow.

Martha García-Murillo is a Professor at the School of Information Studies at Syracuse University. She has an M.S. in Economics and a Ph.D. in Political Economy and Public Policy. She has been involved in research and consulting projects for the UN-ITU, US State Department, The World Bank and other national, regional and international organizations. Her research focuses on the impact on technology on development, the impact of regulation on business behavior, the impact of technology on regulation. In these areas she has explored the impact of ICTS on corruption, informal economies, new businesses and employment among others.

María Garrido is a Research Assistant Professor at the University of Washington's Information School. Her research explores how people, in communities facing social and economic challenges, use information and communication technologies to promote social change. Much of her work focuses on technology appropriation in the context of social movements, international migration, and youth employability. Maria holds a Ph.D. in Communications from the University of Washington and a master's degree in International Relations from the University of Chicago.

Vehbi Gorgulu (PhD) is a research assistant at Istanbul Bilgi University. His research areas include political communication, online communities and digital cultures. His most recent research has been published by SSCI-indexed journal Information, Communication & Society and AHCI-indexed journal Third Text.

Helen Hasan is an academic in the disciplines of Information Systems, Knowledge Management and Human Computer Interaction. She has extensive experience as a leader of multi-disciplinary research teams investigating a variety of phenomena, with global recognition and extensive publications. 'Grey' and 'Green' Themes dominate her current interests. The 'grey' projects include the development of the Dementia Illawarra website and an investigation into the use of IT by the elderly for their social wellbeing. Her 'green' theme takes a holistic approach to IS support for sustainable development. At the University of Wollongong Helen manages a Usability Laboratory.

Ali Honari is a PhD candidate in Sociology at the Faculty of Social Sciences at VU Amsterdam, the Netherlands. His research interests include Social movements, repression, protest participation, data mining and online social networks in particular the Iranian online social networks.

Bahtiyar Kurambayev has recently completed his doctorate in mass communication from The University of Southern Mississippi (USA). He has a master's degree in communication from the University of Wyoming (USA) and a bachelor's degree in journalism and mass communication from the American University of Central Asia (Bishkek, Kyrgyzstan). He also attended Georgetown University for summer program.

Tonatiuh Lay PhD in social sciences from the University of Guadalajara, Professor-Researcher at the Institute of Knowledge Management and Learning in Virtual Environments. Lines of research: Media legislation, civil society, de facto powers, virtual social networks and educational inclusion. Author of the book "Media Legislation and de facto powers in Mexico 2000-2012" (UDGVirtual, 2012), Coordinator of the books "Walking together, stories of families that have children with autism" (Ave editorial, 2015) Intervention and technology. Multidisciplinary approaches to the attention of the Autistic Spectrum" (University of Guadalajara, 2016). Member of the National System of researchers, Level I. Member of the Mexican Association of Right to Information (Amedi) Chapter Jalisco.

Henry Linger is Associate Professor in the Faculty of Information Technology, Monash University. He is a research-active academic conducting research at the intersection of three disciplinary areas; Information Systems Development (ISD), Knowledge Management (KM) and Project Management (PM) and has contributed to Monash University's national and international reputation in these fields. He is a Lead Researcher in Centre of Organisational and Social Informatics (COSI) and Co-Director of the Knowledge Management Research Program (KMRP) in the Faculty of Information Technology. He is also the Chair of the International Steering Committee, the governing body of the International Conference on Information Systems Development. A/Prof. Linger's research engages with, and is supported by industry, including funded projects and invitations to participate in collaborative projects. Since 1998 he has been a Research Associate with the Defence Science and Technology Group (DST-G) where he conducts projects, workshops and seminars around social and organisational learning in the Australian Defence Forces, and data, information and knowledge management within DST-G. Since 2014 he has been an international member of the Project Management Institute's (PMI) Academic Members Advisory Group (AMAG) that oversees PMI's global engagement with academics on research and teaching of project management. He is currently Associate co-Chair of the Monash University Human Research Ethics Committee and sits on the Academic Board, which is the governing body of Monash University.

Marwa Maziad is an International Relations and Middle East Media and Politics Expert. She is a columnist for Egypt's Almasry Alyoum Newspaper and a political commentator on several international media including Aljazeera English, CNN International and BBC. Maziad's BA (American University in Cairo) and MA (University of Washington) were in journalism and international and intercultural communication. She is a former faculty member of Qatar University's Social Sciences Department and Northwestern University in Qatar's Journalism Program. This experience set her research agenda in Gulf Studies with a number of publications. Her PhD research at University of Washington was on state-society relations; social movements; comparative civil-military relations in the Middle East with cases of Egypt, Turkey and Israel.

Pedro Pina is a lawyer and a law teacher in the Oliveira do Hospital School of Technology and Management at the Polytechnic Institute of Coimbra. He holds a law degree from the University of Coimbra Law School and a post-graduation in Territorial Development, Urbanism and Environmental Law from the Territorial

Development, Urbanism and Environmental Law Studies Center (CEDOUA) at the University of Coimbra Law School. He holds a master degree in Procedural Law Studies from the University of Coimbra Law School and is currently a PhD student in the Doctoral Programme "Law, Justice, and Citizenship in the Twenty First Century" from the University of Coimbra Law School and Economics School.

Carlos Piña-Garcia is a Post-Doctoral research fellow at the Computer Sciences Department of the Instituto de Investigaciones en Matemáticas Aplicadas y en Sistemas (IIMAS) of the Universidad Nacional Autónoma de México (UNAM). His research involves gathering social media information and the quantitative analysis of data in social networks. He holds a Ph.D. in Computer Science from University of Essex at the School of Computer Science and Electronic Engineering. His Thesis: "Sampling Online Social Networks through Random Walks" was supervised by Professor Dongbing Gu. During his Ph.D. studies he was an exchange student at the Beijing Institute of Technology.

Juliana Rodrigues PhD in Education from the Faculty of Education, University of São Paulo. A master's degree at the State University of Campinas - Unicamp, in the area of concentration Leisure Studies. She is a professor at the School of Arts, Sciences and Humanities of the University of São Paulo (EACH / USP) of the Bachelor of Leisure and Tourism and Postgraduate in Sciences of Physical activity, in line of research: Leisure Promotion. Currently, holds the vice presidency of the International Ibero-American Network of Sociocultural Animation - RIA and the Presidency of Brazil Node of RIA. Areas of interest: formal education, informal and non-formal practices; Social Education; sociocultural animation and Leisure.

Anıl Sayan is a research assistant at Faculty of Communication, Istanbul Bilgi University and a PhD student at Faculty of Communication, Istanbul University. His research interests are in the areas of sports sociology and new media cultures.

Marcio Wholers de Almeida graduated in Electrical Engineering from the University of São Paulo (1972), Master in Economic Science from the State University of Campinas (1975), PhD in Economic Science from the State University of Campinas (1990) and Habilitation at the State University of Campinas (2015). He is currently Professor MS 5.1 of the State University of Campinas. It has experience in economics, with an emphasis on Industrial Economics, working mainly on the following theme: Economics of telecommunications and the Internet

Moinul Zaber is an Assistant Professor at University of Dhaka, Bangladesh. He is also a Research Fellow of LIRNEasia, a Sri Lanka based regional ICT policy and regulation think tank. At LIRNEasia, Dr. Zaber conducts research related to spectrum management and policy. His past affiliation as a Post-Doctoral Research Scientist was with the Chalmers University, Sweden where he has conducted an extensive data centric research on impact of Broadband speed variability on quality of life. He has received his doctorate in Engineering and Public policy from Carnegie Mellon University, Pittsburgh, PA, USA and from Instituto Superior Técnico, Lisbon, Portugal. His dissertation was on The Influence of Institutional Structure on Regulatory Choices and the Impact of these Choices on the Telecommunication Marketplace. He has an MS in Engineering and Public policy and BS and MS in Computer Science and Engineering. Dr. Zaber is a Data scientist and Man Machine Interconnection Specialist, whose research focus is on the use of data analytics and design thinking for public policy.

Index

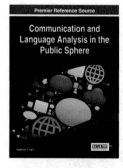

Stay Current on the Latest Emerging Research Developments

Become an IGI Global Reviewer for Authored Book Projects

Premier Reference Source

Solutions for High-Touch Communications in a High-Tech World

Premier Reference Source

Advanced Research on Biologically Inspired Cognitive Architectures

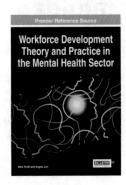

Premier Reference Source

Workforce Development Theory and Practice in the Mental Health Sector

Premier Reference Source

Resource Management and Efficiency in Cloud Computing Environments

The overall success of an authored book project is dependent on quality and timely reviews.

In this competitive age of scholarly publishing, constructive and timely feedback significantly decreases the turnaround time of manuscripts from submission to acceptance, allowing the publication and discovery of progressive research at a much more expeditious rate. Several IGI Global authored book projects are currently seeking highly qualified experts in the field to fill vacancies on their respective editorial review boards:

Applications may be sent to:
development@igi-global.com

Applicants must have a doctorate (or an equivalent degree) as well as publishing and reviewing experience. Reviewers are asked to write reviews in a timely, collegial, and constructive manner. All reviewers will begin their role on an ad-hoc basis for a period of one year, and upon successful completion of this term can be considered for full editorial review board status, with the potential for a subsequent promotion to Associate Editor.

If you have a colleague that may be interested in this opportunity, we encourage you to share this information with them.

Information Resources Management Association

Become an IRMA Member

Members of the **Information Resources Management Association (IRMA)** understand the importance of community within their field of study. The Information Resources Management Association is an ideal venue through which professionals, students, and academicians can convene and share the latest industry innovations and scholarly research that is changing the field of information science and technology. Become a member today and enjoy the benefits of membership as well as the opportunity to collaborate and network with fellow experts in the field.

IRMA Membership Benefits:

- **One FREE Journal Subscription**
- **30% Off Additional Journal Subscriptions**
- **20% Off Book Purchases**
- Updates on the latest events and research on Information Resources Management through the IRMA-L listserv.
- Updates on new open access and downloadable content added to Research IRM.
- A copy of the Information Technology Management Newsletter twice a year.
- A certificate of membership.

IRMA Membership $195

Scan code or visit **irma-international.org** and begin by selecting your free journal subscription.

Membership is good for one full year.